Nutrition

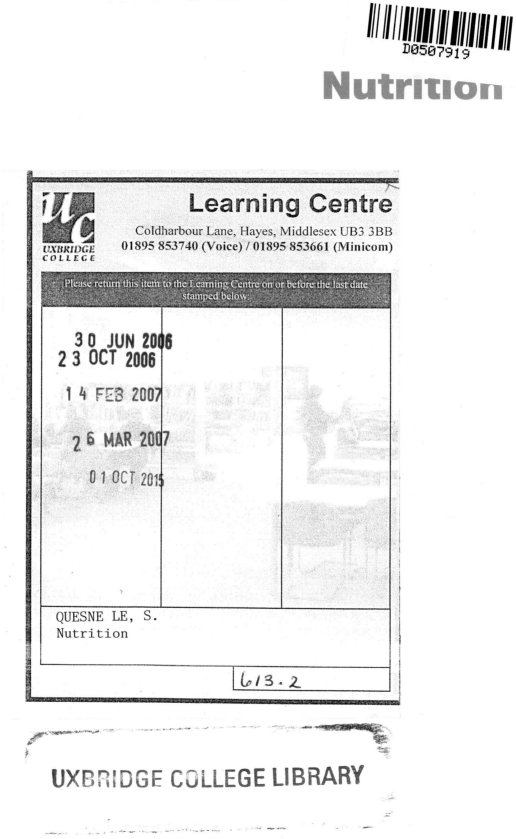

Nutrition

A Practical Approach

Suzanne Le Quesne

HABIA
Hairdressing And Beauty Industry Authority

THOMSON ™

Australia • Canada • Mexico • Singapore • Spain • United Kingdom • United States

THOMSON

Nutrition: A Practical Approach

Copyright © 2003 Suzanne Le Quesne

The Thomson logo is a registered trademark used herein under licence.

For more information, contact Thomson Learning, High Holborn House, 50–51 Bedford Row, London WC1R 4LR or visit us on the World Wide Web at: www.thomsonlearning.co.uk

British Library Cataloguing-in-Publication-Data
A catalogue for this book is available from the British Library

ISBN 1–86152–908–2

Typeset by Saxon Graphics Ltd, Derby

Printed by TJ International, Padstow, Cornwall

Contents

Foreword ix
About the author x
Acknowledgements xii
Introduction xiii
How to use this book xv
Author's note xvi

I The basics 1

1 Nutrients, anti-nutrients, enzymes and water 3

Nutrients 4
Anti-nutrients 5
Enzymes 5

2 The macronutrients – carbohydrates, proteins and fats 15

Carbohydrates 15
The sugar family 19
Fibre 20
Vegetables and fruit – at least five portions a day 21
Proteins 21
The essential amino acids 25
How much protein do you actually need? 27
Fats 28

3 Micronutrients – vitamins, minerals and trace minerals 38

Vitamins 38
The fat-soluble vitamins 41
The water-soluble vitamins 46
The unofficial B vitamins – biotin, choline, PABA and inositol 53
The macrominerals 60
The trace elements 68

4 Herbal remedies 78

What do herbs do? 78

5 Superfoods 90

6 The balanced diet, food energy values, contraindications and food myths 107

7 Food labels and conversion tables 114

Legal requirements and food labelling 115

8 Supplements 124

9 Nutrition for pregnancy and babies, athletes, the menopause and the elderly 131

Pregnancy 131
Babies 133
Athletes 135
The menopause years 136
The elderly 140

II Dietary influences affecting body systems 143

10 The cardiovascular system 145

What is the cardiovascular system? 145

11   The digestive system 162

What is the digestive system? 163

12   The endocrine system 183

What is the endocrine system? 184

13   The lymphatic system and immunity 195

What is the lymphatic system? 196

14   The muscular system 217

What is the muscular system? 218

15   The nervous system 224

What is the nervous system? 225

16   The reproductive system 233

What is the reproductive system? 234

17   The respiratory system 246

What is the respiratory system? 247

18   The skeletal system 257

What is the skeletal system? 257

19   The urinary and detoxification systems 265

What are the urinary and detoxification systems? 265

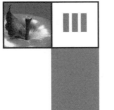

III   Putting it all together 277

20   The practical application of nutrition therapy 279

Diet planning principles 279
The Weakest Link Questionnaire 284
A suggested action plan for a nutrition consultation 291
Weakest Link questions explained 294

Glossary 309
UK web links for further study 317
Useful addresses 318
Further reading 319
Index 321

Foreword

I've been fascinated by nutrition since I bought my son a book on the subject some years ago. At the time I felt that I had a fairly balanced diet but I soon learnt otherwise.

I've been keen for the Thomson Learning/Habia series to have on a book on nutrition for ages because I feel strongly that in the world of hair and beauty there should be an emphasis on personal well-being and not just outward grooming. There is after all a lot of truth in the old cliché that beauty comes from within.

Nutrition is a fascinating book – it is written in a wonderfully accessible style and packed with useful information. Suzanne Le Quesne's enormous enthusiasm for the subject of nutrition is evident on every page. If you want to take charge of your body, or support your clients in taking charge of theirs, then you should start with this book. You will not be disappointed.

Alan Goldsbro

Chief Executive Officer
Hairdressing And Beauty Industry Authority

About the author

With sixteen years' experience in the health business, Suzanne Le Quesne has become a leading authority on nutrition and holistic therapies and has established holistic training schools in Shropshire and the Channel Islands.

Suzanne's primary role is that of clinical nutritionist and she works in this area with her husband Barry at their private clinic in Shropshire. She graduated from the Institute of Optimum Nutrition, London, in 1993 under the guidance of Patrick Holford, the founder of the Institute. Suzanne is currently a facilitator of Continued Professional Development (CPD) courses in both nutrition and holistic therapies, representing industry awarding bodies. Her work takes her all over the UK, Europe and Canada.

Suzanne is the author of the very popular Home Study Diploma course in Nutrition, accredited by Vocational Training Charitable Trust (VTCT) in 1998. It has been successfully completed by students all over the world.

Suzanne is a member of the British Association of Nutritional Therapists, the Association of Therapy Lecturers, a member of the Guild of Health Writers and founder member of the Jersey Association of Complementary Therapists; she was also a tutor at the Institute for Optimum Nutrition in London during 1995 and 1996.

In addition to her role as a clinical nutritionist, she is a leading authority on nutrition, and is an established speaker and broadcaster.

This book is dedicated to my father, who would have been very proud.

Acknowledgements

I would like to express my deepest love and gratitude to my wonderful husband Barry for all his help in the preparation of this book. His patience is second to none, and his assistance as a helpful listener and proofreader is greatly appreciated. Without his continued support, encouragement and motivation, this book would never have been started, let alone completed.

Very special thanks also to many friends, colleagues and students both past and present for their continual support and invaluable feedback.

Introduction

This book has been written out of true need. Much of my time is spent teaching postgraduate courses in advanced holistic therapies and it never ceases to amaze me how little knowledge therapists have regarding good nutrition and the little, if any, knowledge they have of the symptoms their clients present.

The general public are becoming more and more responsible for their own health. Unfortunately, they are often bombarded with so much conflicting information that they do not know which way to turn. More and more are turning to us, holistic and health practitioners, for guidance. It is our professional duty to keep learning beyond our initial basic training by way of Continued Professional Development courses in order to keep up to date with new developments.

As holistic therapists you should always undertake a thorough client consultation before giving any treatment and while many of you do, many do not, and others only record the barest minimum details due to the restricted time allocated for treatments. The consultation is the essence of a successful treatment and is where we have an advantage over General Practitioners who simply do not have the time to talk with and listen to their patients. Those of you in a salon situation should encourage your employers to allow additional consultation time for your clients.

Additionally, as holistic therapists you should always offer relevant and specific aftercare advice to each client. Again, while most of you do, others do not and with tight appointment schedules many therapists do not have time. It is of paramount importance that each individual receives aftercare advice that will ensure the treatment is special and tailor-made for each client.

With the help of this book you will now be able to expand the consultation process by learning what important questions to ask clients regarding their nutritional status and any nutritional deficiencies/excesses that may be responsible for the symptoms they present. You will have a clearer understanding of those symptoms and as such you will be able to use this book as an instant reference guide for tailor-made responsible aftercare advice. The aftercare recommendations listed use the latest and safest supernutrients, vitamin and mineral supplements, herbal remedies, superfoods, lifestyle changes and, of course, dietary advice.

I am a firm believer in the holistic approach which treats mind, body and spirit as one. I also believe that by establishing the weakest link – that is the weakest body system – and then supporting that system by way of holistic treatments, dietary supplements and diet, the result will be a domino effect on the other body systems that will eventually make the body whole and strong again.

Long-term effects of poor diet and nutrition are given for each body system. The digestive and excretory systems are the largest and most detailed chapters and are covered in greater detail to cover the underpinning knowledge required by many awarding bodies offering nutritional qualifications.

Our aim as holistic therapists is to educate, enlighten, encourage and help our clients help themselves on the way to good health.

The Weakest Link Questionnaire is a quick and easy way to establish your clients weakest body system, for which you can then offer support. You can then build on this initial questionnaire to establish your client's current diet and integrate the whole into your own client consultation form.

It would have been an impossible task to record every symptom a client will ever present to you. I have included therefore the most frequently encountered symptoms I come across in my role as clinical nutritionist, presented system by system. There are over 100 of the most common ailments listed and recommendations for each of them, as well as recommendations for the system in general.

All our food ultimately comes from plants and second hand from animals who eat the plants, and our daily intake of food should supply us with all the nutrients needed to sustain health and vitality.

Unfortunately, with the ever increasing use of ready-made and fast foods many people are not receiving all the nutrients they need from food and can be said to be overfed but undernourished. Even fresh organic food may be nutrient deficient. It may be free of pesticides but it could still have been grown in nutrient-deficient soil. As a nation we are consuming fewer calories in an effort to reduce weight, but getting fatter. The cravings many experience are not cravings for more food but for more nutrients.

Unfortunately the result of years of being undernourished but overfed are numerous diseases which can be directly linked to diet – 90 per cent of the world's cancers are diet related and as such are preventable.

The time has come to take action. We must help ourselves and our clients find the weakest link in our health by studying each body system in turn and then do everything we can to support that system. A domino effect may then begin, strengthening each body system in turn and bringing the body back to a healthy whole.

There are 42 nutrients known to be of importance to man, the most abundant being the macronutrients – carbohydrates, fats and proteins – and the micronutrients – vitamins, minerals, trace minerals, fresh clean water and fresh clean air. We need all of them daily for maximum health.

How to use this book

This book may appear long and complex. However, it is very easy to use.

The Weakest Link Questionnaire given in Part III will only take a few minutes of your client's time, but when it is completed you will be able to see at a glance the client's weakest link – that is, the system of the body which needs the most support at the time of the consultation and treatment for that day. By adding the results of the Weakest Link Questionnaire to your usual client consultation you will know what system of the body is in need of most dietary, supplement or other support.

Once you have established the client's weakest body system using the questionnaire, refer to the relevant chapter and read the general recommendations given for that system. If your client's particular symptom is listed, then refer directly to that symptom, as well as the general recommendations. Discuss the recommendations with the client and choose one or two that they can commit to. These may be changes in diet to either include or avoid a particular food or drink, or it may be to take a herbal or vitamin supplement, to start eating a superfood or to adopt a lifestyle change. By discussing the recommendations and getting the client's approval of what they feel they can take on board, you are far more likely to get good results with that client.

Key Term boxes are repeated in the Glossary at the end of the book, which also gives definitions of terms and phrases that you are likely to encounter in your work.

The aftercare advice you give your client will then truly become tailor-made for every treatment you undertake. Whilst 'drink more water, rest and eat a light diet' will of course always be essential and excellent aftercare advice, as holistic therapists you need to expand on your aftercare and recommend specific support to each client.

If you enjoy using the Weakest Link Questionnaire you can take it further by creating a more detailed Nutritional Questionnaire to accompany your own consultation. This will give you even more information and you can then expand your treatments to always include some nutritional recommendations. Alternatively you may wish to give separate consultations for nutrition alone, in which case taking a formal qualification is highly recommended.

Don't forget to visit the accompanying website to this book on http://www.thomsonlearning.co.uk/hairandbeauty/

Author's note

In my role as clinical nutritionist I see and speak to many hundreds of clients and students a year and nothing gives me more pleasure than seeing their health improve.

There may be times when you want to recommend more than one supplement or remedy in an attempt to achieve the most beneficial result for your client. However, unless you are qualified to do so, please do not be tempted to do this. Whilst nutritional supplements are generally safe, offering a cocktail of individual supplements requires specialised training. Excesses of some nutrients may result in deficiencies of others. Multivitamin and mineral formulas are therefore always a safe choice as experienced nutritionists have correctly formulated their content.

Only offer one recommendation as a food or herbal supplement and ask the client to use this for three to four months. If there is no improvement then you can go on to try another one. Always emphasise to the client the importance of following the manufacturer's instructions on the label when recommending any supplement.

It is perfectly safe to offer dietary advice in conjunction with a nutritional supplement – in fact the two go hand in hand. However, supplements alone should not be relied upon to treat or prevent disease and should never replace medication without consulting your GP.

Never treat outside your own knowledge and never be ashamed or embarrassed to refer a client to someone more experienced than yourself in a particular field. It is responsible and professional to do so.

Do not expect all foods and supplements to work the same way on all people: we are all biochemically different and, therefore, results will differ.

No single food or food type should ever be eaten to the exclusion of others for the purposes of preventing or addressing a specific disease or maintaining health, except on the advice of a GP.

Suzanne Le Quesne

June 2002

Part I
The basics

1   Nutrients, anti-nutrients, enzymes and water 3

2   The macronutrients – carobhydrates, proteins and fats 15

3   Micronutrients 38

4   Herbal remedies 78

5   Superfoods 90

6   The balanced diet, food energy values, contraindications and food myths 107

7   Food labels and conversion tables 114

8   Supplements 124

9   Nutrition for pregnancy and babies, athletes, the menopause and the elderly 131

Nutrients, anti-nutrients, enzymes and water

1

Learning objectives

This chapter covers the following:

- **identifying nutrients and anti-nutrients**

- **identifying macronutrients and micronutrients**

- **enzymes – their role in the body**

- **water – its role in the body**

Nutrition is the study of nutrients from both plants and animals, and the body's subsequent handling of them. It is a fascinating subject and can be described as a young science. The first vitamin, vitamin A, was only discovered in 1913 and there have been many exciting developments and discoveries since then, with still more to come. Nutrition can determine our quality of life. It can largely determine how we look, feel and work; whether we will be nervous, tired and pessimistic, or joyful, comfortable and happily active. Nutrition can also determine whether we will age prematurely or enjoy our lives to the full. By studying this book, not only will you learn about food and its effects on the body, but you will also learn about yourself. As you work through the many practical activities, you will learn about your own chemical make-up. It is only by experiencing different foods, drinks, supplements, herbal remedies and lifestyle changes ourselves that we make good nutritional therapists. You cannot advise someone to do something you have not experienced yourself!

A competent nutritional therapist needs to understand the role of nutrients, anti-nutrients, enzymes and water in the human body in order to give accurate dietary and supplement advice to clients.

Nutrients

Nutrients are absorbable components of food. The six important nutrients are:

- Carbohydrates
- Proteins
- Lipids (fats)
- Minerals
- Vitamins
- Water

In the body, three of the above nutrients can be described as energy-yielding. These energy-yielding nutrients are carbohydrates, proteins and fats: they are described as macronutrients, because we need large quantities of them on a daily basis. These three macronutrients can also be described as organic. Organic nutrients contain hydrogen, oxygen and carbon. Vitamins, minerals and water do not yield energy in the human body. Vitamins are also classed as organic nutrients whereas minerals and water are inorganic – they do not contain carbon. The vitamins and minerals are known as micronutrients; although they are no less important for good health we need only tiny amounts of them compared to the macronutrients.

The body can make some nutrients; vitamin K for example can be synthesised from beneficial gut flora, but it cannot make all the nutrients it needs to sustain life and must obtain the remainder from food.

The nutrients that food must supply are known as essential nutrients. When used with reference to nutrients, the word *essential* means more than just necessary, it means 'must be obtained from outside the body'. Later in the book you will be introduced to the essential amino acids, essential fatty acids and essential water.

Main functions

Necessary for good health, energy, organ function, food utilisation and cell growth.

What do nutrients do?

Nutrients maintain life. The macronutrients, the carbohydrates, proteins and fats provide energy and the micronutrients, the vitamins, minerals and trace minerals are the substances required to release the energy. The amounts of macronutrients and micronutrients needed daily to maintain life varies enormously, but each is of vital importance.

Organic or inorganic? Macronutrient or micronutrient?

	Carbon	Hydrogen	Oxygen	Nitrogen	Minerals and trace minerals	Macronutrient	Micronutrient
Organic nutrients							
Carbohydrates	✓	✓	✓			✓	
Lipids (fats)	✓	✓	✓			✓	
Proteins*	✓	✓	✓	✓		✓	
Vitamins**	✓	✓	✓				✓
Inorganic nutrients							
Minerals					✓		✓
Water		✓	✓			✓	

  * Some proteins also contain the mineral sulphur. These are referred to as the sulphur containing amino acids
** Some vitamins contain nitrogen; some contain minerals

Anti-nutrients

Although we are concerned more with nutrients than anti-nutrients, no book on nutrition would be complete without the mention of anti-nutrients. Just as nutrients maintain life, the anti-nutrients are harmful to life. In studying nutrition you learn not only what to eat and drink for good health but also what not to eat and drink, which is equally important.

What exactly is an anti-nutrient?

An anti-nutrient is any substance that stops the beneficial nutrients being absorbed and used by the body, or any substance that promotes the excretion of a beneficial nutrient.

Alcohol, cigarettes, man-made chemicals, pesticides, antibiotics and synthetic hormone residues can all be described as anti-nutrients. Even tap water in some areas may be described as an anti-nutrient. Tap water may contain nitrates, lead or aluminium, all of which are anti-nutrients in their own right. Fried food, foods cooked on a barbecue and burnt food can all be classed as anti-nutrients because they cause free radical damage to our cells. Many common medicines can also be described as anti-nutrients; aspirin, for example, irritates the gut wall, making it more permeable.

Key Term

Free radicals

Unstable and highly reactive atoms or molecules that have one or more unpaired electrons in the outer orbital.

Enzymes

Life on our planet began to evolve principally through the action of enzymes in water and gases that covered the earth's surface. Enzyme reactions started fermentation, which formed plants which in turn converted the carbon dioxide-rich atmosphere into an oxygen-rich one suitable for the evolution of animal life.

Key Term

Catalyst

A compound that facilitates chemical reactions without itself being changed in the process.

Key Term

Hydrolysis

A chemical reaction in which a major reactant is split into two products, with the addition of a hydrogen atom (H) to one and a hydroxyl group (OH) to the other (from water, H_2O).

Key Term

Intrinsic factor

A glycoprotein (a protein with short polysaccharide chains attached) manufactured in the stomach that aids in the absorption of vitamin B12.

The human digestive system is a reflection of those first processes of evolution. The digestive tract supplies the water and the food which are then metabolised through enzyme intermediaries.

What are enzymes?

Enzymes are a delicate life-like substance found in all living cells – whether animal or vegetable – complex protein molecules that perform specific biochemical reactions vital for life. They can be described as protein catalysts. Enzymes do more than just break down the foods we eat ready for absorption; they also build substances (such as bone) and transform one substance into another (amino acids into glucose for example).

Main functions

There are three classes of enzymes: digestive, metabolic and food. The main function of digestive enzymes is to break down food into particles that are chemically simple enough and physically small enough to be absorbed. Every day the liver, pancreas, stomach and intestinal wall produce an average of ten litres of digestive juices containing various enzymes to break down the food we eat.

What do enzymes do?

Enzymes change one substance to another, without actually changing themselves and carry out millions of chemical activities in our bodies every second to keep us alive. There are three types of digestive enzyme. Amylolytic enzymes (amylases) which break down carbohydrates, proteolytic enzymes (proteases) which break down proteins and lipolytic enzymes (lipases) which break down fats. Enzymatic break down of foods (hydrolysis) begins in the mouth. Saliva contains an amylase, a carbohydrate-reducing enzyme which acts on carbohydrate as food is chewed. The stomach then secretes pepsin, which gets to work on proteins, provided it is in an acid environment. The intestines, which are an alkaline environment, contain various enzymes which dismantle all the remaining nutrients, converting them to simpler substances which the body can then absorb – proteins into amino acids, fats into fatty acids, and carbohydrates into glucose. Since each specific enzyme acts only on one specific substance (substrate) and brings about only one specific chemical reaction, you can begin to appreciate that the mechanism of metabolism is very complex and delicate. The liver alone produces over 1,000 different enzymes. The lack of even one enzyme can break the chain of biochemical reactions causing imbalances, which manifest themselves as allergies, nutritional deficiencies and illness. For example, the lack of a stomach enzyme known as 'intrinsic factor' can lead to pernicious anaemia unless the diet has sufficient vitamin B12 intake. This may be a problem for vegans and vegetarians as the best source of B12 comes from animal foods.

All the organs and tissue in our bodies are maintained by metabolic enzymes. These enzymes take amino acids, fatty acids and glucose, the end products of digestion, and structure them into healthy bodies, keeping everything working properly. Every organ and tissue has its own particular enzyme systems that have specialised tasks.

Key Term

Metabolism

The process of transforming and utilising substances within the body. Through this process energy is produced and body tissues are broken down and rebuilt continuously.

Natural enzymes, the main functions of which are to start food digestion, are found abundantly in fresh, unprocessed, natural foods. However, these natural food enzymes are destroyed by heating to temperatures over 120°F (49°C) and are also sensitive to other food processing procedures. Peeling, pasteurising, refining, preserving, smoking, grilling, frying and baking largely destroy enzymes. When raw food enters the mouth, and the food is chewed well, the natural enzymes start to breakdown the food as a natural digestive process. These natural enzymes are not destroyed by stomach acid but are active throughout the digestive tract, right through to the large colon where they create good conditions for beneficial bacteria to grow.

Each enzyme facilitates a specific chemical reaction. In this diagram an enzyme enables two compounds to make a more complex structure – but the enzyme itself remains unchanged.

Building a new compound

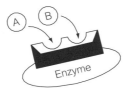 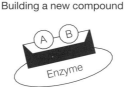 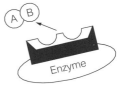

Two separated compounds, A and B, are attracted to the enzyme's activity site making a reaction likely

The enzyme forms a complex with A & B

The enzyme is unchanged, but A & B have formed a new compound, AB

Breaking down into chemically more simple and physically smaller units.

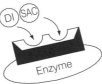  

Sucrose – a double sugar – is attracted to the enzyme amylase

The disaccharide locks in position and the enzyme can now start its work of breaking down

We now have two separate, smaller untis of monosaccharide

Enzyme action

The majority of digestive and metabolic enzymes are dependent upon vitamins and minerals to activate them. Enzymes are made up of two parts, a protein molecule and a coenzyme. The coenzyme is often a vitamin, particularly a B vitamin, a mineral, or both. So if you are nutrient deficient, you will not make the enzymes necessary to carry out their important work. For example, zinc is needed to make hydrochloric acid (stomach acid), which converts pepsin, an inactive protein-splitting enzyme into pepsinogen, the active protein-splitting enzyme in the stomach. If you become deficient in zinc, production of stomach acid will decline, you will have difficulty converting pepsin to pepsinogen and, therefore, difficulty in breaking down protein. This may initially cause indigestion, but can develop into other problems further down the digestive tract.

Our bodies produce 25 per cent of the enzymes we need for digestion; the other 75 per cent is expected to come from our diet in the form of natural, raw, unprocessed sources in fruit, vegetables grains, nuts and seeds. Many people have difficulty in eating five portions of fruit and vegetables every day and the body quickly becomes deficient, which overtaxes its ability to break down food ready for absorption.

Key Term

Digestion

The process by which food is converted in the intestinal tract into chemical substances that can be absorbed by the body.

This often results in indigestion, heartburn and fatigue. By eating raw, or lightly cooked vegetables and fruit you are providing natural enzymes to assist in breaking down all the food eaten at one meal, at the same time providing essential nutrients (coenzymes) to activate other metabolic enzymes to keep the body working efficiently. These natural enzymes cannot be stored in the body, so fresh vegetables and fruit should be eaten with every meal, every day.

Examples of foods that contain significant amounts of enzymes:

- Apples and mangos contain peroxidase and catalase whose job it is to disarm free radicals;
- Pineapple, wheat and kidney beans contain amylase, which digests sugars and protease, which digests protein;
- Mushrooms contain amylase, protease, peroxidase and catalase;
- Bananas and cabbage contain amylase;
- Raw eggs contain the four enzymes already mentioned and lipase.

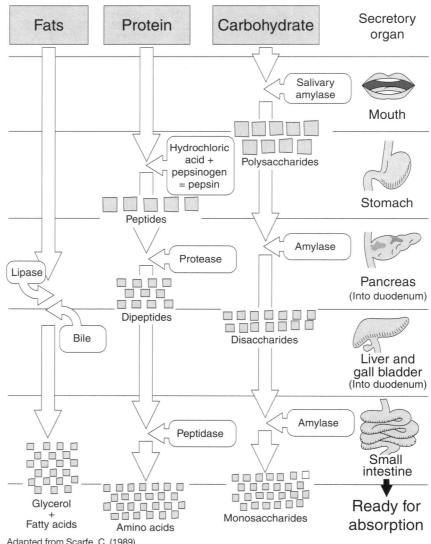

The action of digestive enzymes

Adapted from Scarfe, C. (1989)

Tip

Words ending in *ase* usually denote an enzyme – for example lact*ase* is the enzyme that splits lactose – a sugar.

Digestive enzymes

Organ	Digestive juice	Enzyme	Function
Mouth	Saliva	Ptyalin Mucin	Breaks down starch; acts as a lubricant
Stomach	Gastric juice	Rennin Lipase HCl	Clots milk (infants) Splits fat (infants) Protein hydrolysis
		Pepsinogen (activated by HCl) to become pepsin	Protein digestion
Pancreas	Pancreatic juice	Bicarbonate ions Rennin	Neutralises HC Clots milk
		Lipase	Splits fats
		Amylase	Starch to maltose
		Maltase	Maltose to glucose
		Trypsinogen – activated by enterokinase to become tripsin	Proteins to peptones
		Chymotrypsinogen – activated by trypsin to become chymotrypsin	Peptones to peptides
		Carboxypeptidase	Peptides to amino acids
		Nuclease	Nucleic acid to nucleotide
Liver	Bile (gall bladder)	Lecithin Cholesterol Bile salts	Fat emulsifier Fat emulsifier Activates pancreatic lipase
Small intestine		Peptidase Amylase Maltase Sucrase	Peptides to amino acids Starch to maltose Maltose to glucose Sucrose to monosaccharides
		Lactase	Lactose to monosaccharides
		Lipase	Glycerides to fatty acids and glycerol
		Enterokinase	Activates trypsinogen

Remember

Fruits and vegetables contain vitamins and minerals and are vital for 'enzyme action' – five portions a day, every day, are highly recommended.

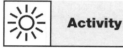

Activity

Monitor your own diet for the next week. Are you eating five portions of fruit and vegetables every day? If not, write down ideas for obtaining more in your diet. As a nutritional therapist it is important to practise what you preach!

Nutritionists often recommend a supplement of digestive enzymes for a short time to aid digestion and nutrient absorption. Many nutritional therapists consider insufficient digestive enzymes, a condition in which stress plays a big part, to be the cause of many digestive system complaints. There are several companies who manufacture vegetarian and vegan digestive enzymes but vegetarians and vegans should read labels carefully as some digestive enzymes contain ox bile extract. Digestive enzymes are often used as a temporary measure, but the long-term answer is to eat fresh, natural fruits and vegetables on a daily basis.

As the body ages, enzymes become less plentiful and shortage of enzymes is the main cause of digestive disorders, which are so widespread that they are often accepted as normal. As nutritional therapists it is imperative that we emphasise enzyme-rich foods – plenty of fresh raw vegetables, fruits and grains in our diets to aim for optimum health and well-being.

Water

Water is essential to life. A fit healthy adult can survive many weeks without food but only a few days without water. Water contains no carbon and is inorganic; while it is not a nutrient as such, this book will describe it as an essential nutrient as it is necessary in large amounts on a daily basis. Water makes up about two-thirds of our body weight. How much water do we really need? It depends upon age, weight and activity levels. Children need more water than adults as they have faster, harder working metabolisms, are very active and have a small stomach capacity, so they need to drink water more frequently than adults.

The main source of water for the body is food and drink, although some is produced when nutrients are oxidised to produce energy. For example, when glucose is oxidised it breaks down to form carbon dioxide and water – a kilogram of glucose produces just over half a litre of water on oxidation. The balance between input and output of water must be maintained at all times.

Water is unlike the other essential nutrients in that most of it passes through the body unchanged, whereas proteins, for example, are broken down to amino acids during digestion.

There is no such thing as pure natural water. Rainwater, which is the purest form of natural water, contains small amounts of dissolved gases such as oxygen and carbon dioxide. Due to industrial pollution it may also contain dissolved oxides of sulphur and nitrogen (when it is known as acid rain). Our main water supplies come from reservoirs, which receive their water from moorland catchments. This water has to be treated in a number of ways before reaching the consumer. Water is normally sterilised by adding 0.5ppm of chlorine – enough to kill bacteria but not enough to leave a taste. Hard water – water that does not lather up easily – is best for drinking water as it contains beneficial amounts of calcium and magnesium. Soft water contains low levels of calcium carbonate and is more acidic and thus capable of corroding metal pipes and cooking utensils. Evidence suggests there is more cardiovascular disease in soft water areas.

A general guide to water requirements

Age	mls of water per kg of body weight
1 – 3 years	95mls/kg
4–6 years	85mls/kg
7 – 10 years	75mls/kg
Adults	35mls/kg

As a rule of thumb a healthy adult should drink at least 2 litres of water every day – as water, not an accumulation of coffee, tea, soft drinks and alcohol! However, fruits and vegetables have a high water content so if five servings are being taken every day, water consumption can be reduced.

Activity

Starting with yourself, select a range of friends and family of different ages and weights and complete the table opposite following the example shown. Are you drinking enough water?

Name	Age	Weight	mls/kg needed daily	Estimated daily water requirement
John	42	80kg	35mls/kg	35 × 80 = 2,800 mls

Water participates in many metabolic reactions and supplies the medium for transporting vital materials to cells and waste products away from them. Other vital functions of water include:

- Enabling the formation of cells and tissues
- Regulating body temperature
- Protecting the central nervous system
- Forming a lubricant for joints and membranes
- Carrying enzymes and support for the digestive system
- Transporting nutrients around the body
- Carrying oxygen and carbon dioxide around the body.

The body cannot store water and so it needs to be replenished regularly throughout the day. The body loses water through sweat, urine, faeces and moist exhalent breath. Where should you obtain your water?

Tap water

Tap water is the most convenient and the cheapest way to obtain water; on the whole it is safe to drink in Britain. However, there have been studies in the past fifteen years where samples taken from our drinking water were found to have contaminates above the international safety limit. These contaminates include:

- Aluminium – which can occur naturally in water, but is also added during the purification process of water to remove particles which colour the water brown. Aluminium is classed as an anti-nutrient.

- Lead – lead is a poison. Lead piping was only banned in the mid-1970s and there are still many old houses with lead piping. Lead seeps into the water supply and can make children, in particular, very vulnerable to lead poisoning. Lead poisoning affects the brain and nervous system and can also be described as an anti-nutrient.

- Nitrates – only half of the nitrogen put on fields as fertiliser is taken up by plants, the rest drifts down into our water supplies. High levels of nitrate can cause methaemoglobinaemia, or 'blue baby syndrome' in bottle-fed babies. In all age groups, the body converts nitrates into nitrites, which have been shown to cause cancer in animals. Many water supplies exceed the EC safety limits for nitrates and nitrates can also be described as anti-nutrients.

- Trihalomethanes – chlorine added to water to kill bacteria unfortunately reacts with peat and other organic material found in the water to form a group of chemicals called THMs – trihalomethanes. The most common of these is chloroform and studies in the US have found a significant relationship between chloroform and cancers. THMs are often found in British tap water at levels that breach the EC safety limit.

Bottled water

Mineral waters come from natural springs and contain mineral salts such as sodium chloride, sodium carbonate and sodium bicarbonate as well as similar salts of calcium and magnesium. Bottled mineral water has a clean sharp taste and has not been treated either by chlorine, which can be detected by some people in tap water, or fluoride, which is often added to our water supply. Bottled mineral water is highly recommended when travelling abroad where the water supply may not be as clean as in the UK. However, the downside to bottled water is that it is expensive and its production involves considerable waste of resources such as packaging and transport.

Jug filters

Jug filter cartridges contain up to three different components; activated carbon, silver and ion exchange resins. Activated carbon has a large surface area, which attracts impurities like chlorine from the water. Most activated carbon has some silver added to it to inhibit bacterial growth. Ion exchange resins are synthetic materials that attract electrically charged particles like lead out of the water. However, they also remove beneficial elements from the water like calcium (softening the water) and zinc. Some jug filters now tell you when the filter needs changing.

Activity

Find out exactly what is in your water from the water supplier in your area. Ask for a free detailed list of what is in the water and for information about how your water compares with the Water Supply (Water Quality) Regulations.

Activity

Collect labels from different mineral waters and compare the differences, looking in particular for calcium, magnesium and sodium content.

Plumbed-in filters

These filters fit under the sink and connect to a separate tap which gives you filtered water. There are two types of plumbed-in filter; activated carbon or reverse osmosis.

- Activated carbon removes lead, aluminium and chlorine. Improves the taste, colour, appearance and smell of water. Filtered water is always available on tap.

- Reverse osmosis is an under the sink filter which uses a fine membrane to filter water under pressure. It is expensive and is a slow and wasteful process, but it does remove nitrates, lead, aluminium, chlorine and bacteria. The disadvantages are that it also removes beneficial elements like calcium and magnesium.

Distillers

Distillation units can be fitted under a sink, or put on a worktop. Water is boiled and then cooled, leaving behind any contaminants whose boiling point is above that of water – which is almost everything else. They are easy to install and they remove nitrates, lead, aluminium and chlorine. But distilled water also removes beneficial elements like calcium and magnesium. It is also very slow, uses a lot of electricity and produces warm, insipid-tasting water. It needs regular cleaning and takes up a lot of space.

If you decide on any of the filtering systems, you need to make sure that your diet includes plenty of green vegetables, nuts and seeds and take a good multi-mineral and vitamin supplement.

Health & Safety

Water fluid requirements increase greatly when a fever is present and when the external temperature is high.

Percentage of water in selected foods

100	Water
90 – 99	Non-fat milk, strawberries, watermelon, lettuce, cabbage, celery, spinach, broccoli
80 – 89	Fruit juice, yoghurt, apples, grapes, oranges, carrots
70 – 79	Prawns, bananas, corn, potatoes, avocados, cottage cheese, ricotta cheese
60 – 69	Pasta, legumes, salmon, ice cream, chicken breast
50 – 59	Ground beef, hot dogs, feta cheese
40 – 49	Pizza
30 – 39	Cheddar cheese, bagels, bread
20 – 29	Pepperoni sausage, cake, biscuits
10 – 19	Butter, margarine, raisins
1 – 9	Crackers, cereals, pretzels, taco shells, peanut butter, nuts
0	Oils

Knowledge review

Nutrients, anti-nutrients, enzymes and water

1   What nutrients are known as the macronutrients?

2   What nutrients are known as the micronutrients?

3   What are the main functions of nutrients?

4   What chemical compound makes a nutrient organic?

5   Can the body make its own nutrients?

6   What is meant by 'essential' nutrients? – give examples .

7   Define an anti-nutrient and give five examples.

8   Define an enzyme.

9   What foods contain natural enzymes? – give examples.

10 What mineral is needed in the stomach to activate the non-active protein-splitting enzyme pepsin into the active enzyme pepsinogen?

11 How is water lost from the body?

12 How much water should the average adult drink daily?

13 State two advantages and disadvantages of tap, filtered and bottled water.

14 What is the percentage of water in prawns, bananas, corn, potatoes, avocados and cottage cheese?

15 What is the function of intrinsic factor?

The macronutrients – carbohydrates, proteins and fats

Macronutrients, as the name implies, occur in bulk quantities in the body. Carbohydrates, proteins and fats are generously provided by the foods we eat. All foods contain varying amounts of different macronutrients. We have all heard about high-protein foods, low fat and high fat foods and simple or complex carbohydrate foods and all the various 'diets' that go with them. Macronutrients never occur alone in nature; each is accompanied by other macronutrients and micronutrients (vitamins and minerals). Every macronutrient has its own specific duties and deficiency symptoms although in many instances, the roles of macronutrients overlap. Proteins, for example, usually utilised for building and repairing the cells of the body, can be converted to carbohydrates for energy when required, while sugars usually used for energy can be converted to fat for insulation and protection when required. They are mutually dependent, not only in their natural state but in our systems as well. Each one of us needs the same basic macronutrients, although not in the same proportions. Our needs vary according to our individual metabolic requirements: age, sex, occupation, activity and hereditary factors.

A competent nutritional therapist needs to understand the role macronutrients play in the human body in order to give accurate dietary and supplement advice to clients.

Carbohydrates

As you sit and read this book, billions of glucose molecules are splitting every second to provide the energy that your brain needs to function. Glucose and its stored form, glycogen, provide about half of all the energy muscles and other body tissue use; the other half of the body's energy comes mostly from fat. When you exercise it is glycogen that is enabling your muscles to work for you. We do not eat glucose and glycogen directly – we eat foods rich in carbohydrates, which our bodies then convert into glucose for immediate energy and into glycogen for reserve energy.

What do carbohydrates do?

Carbohydrates are compounds composed of oxygen (O), hydrogen (H) and carbon (C) and are the main source of energy for all body functions and muscular exertion. The term carbohydrate includes a variety of dietary compounds varying from simple sugars to complex structures. The complex structures are composed of many simple sugar molecules interlinked. Simple carbohydrates are referred to as sugars and a single sugar is known as a monosaccharide. When two sugar molecules are joined together making a pair, they become a disaccharide; when many disaccharides are joined together they become chains and are called polysaccharides or non-starch polysaccharides. A polysaccharide is therefore composed of several chains of single sugars, or pairs of sugars, interlinked with one another. Polysaccharides are referred to as complex carbohydrates.

Simple sugars such as those in fruit and honey are very easily digested. Double sugars such as sucrose (table sugar), require some digestive action, but the polysaccharides require prolonged enzymatic action in order to be broken down into simple sugars ready for absorption.

The main difference between simple and double sugars is that monosaccharides and disaccharides are water-soluble. This means they are readily absorbed into the body through the stomach, giving a

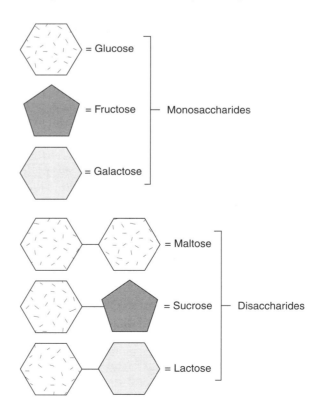

Carbohydrate molecules

burst of energy. The complex varieties – the polysaccharides – need to be digested through the small intestine and therefore provide a more steady energy source for a longer period of time. Complex carbohydrates or polysaccharides are needed for sustained energy and to keep blood glucose levels steady.

Blood sugar levels

One of the most important carbohydrates is glucose, a monosaccharide that circulates in our blood to supply energy to cells throughout the body. It is used as an energy source by all other living things. The body's metabolism and energy systems have a high demand for glucose. For example, it is the only source of energy usable by the brain, and a low level of glucose in the blood results in disturbance in brain function such as loss of concentration, even to the point of coma. When a doctor measures your blood sugar level he is only measuring your blood glucose level at that particular time. To have a better indication of your blood sugar status you would require a six-hour glucose test, which would measure the body's response to glucose over that time. Most nutritional laboratories offer glucose tolerance tests. Type II diabetes is accelerating at an alarming rate and the main factor is the large amounts of simple sugars in the modern diet.

In our modern diet, polysaccharides should comprise about 50 per cent of carbohydrate intake. However, it is estimated that sucrose (glucose and fructose combined to make ordinary table sugar) comprises about 30 per cent of carbohydrate intake, lactose (milk sugar) comprises about 10 per cent, and other less important sugars form the remaining 10 per cent. Historically, our ancestors consumed considerably more complex carbohydrate. It is only since the middle of the nineteenth century that our intake of refined carbohydrates, particularly sucrose, has been significant. This has resulted in increases in diseases like heart disease, obesity, high blood pressure, cancer, and type II diabetes – all of which can be greatly assisted or even prevented with proper dietary control.

Digestion and absorption of carbohydrates

The metabolism of carbohydrates is geared to the digestion of complex carbohydrates in the gastrointestinal tract. The digestive enzyme amylase starts the chemical work of breaking down carbohydrates in the mouth. This is produced in saliva and known as salivary amylase (ptyalin). Our teeth supply the mechanical means to make the food we eat physically small enough to swallow. In the stomach the swallowed food, known as the bolus, mixes with the stomach's acid (hydrochloric acid) and the protein-digesting enzyme (pepsin) inactivates the salivary amylase. Once the bolus leaves the stomach in a semi-liquid state and called chyme, it enters the duodenum, the first part of the small intestine. Pancreatic amylase continues the chemical work of breaking down complex polysaccharides into more simple disaccharides and monosaccharides. Enzymes present in the lining of the small intestine further break down the disaccharides into monosaccharides. In this way, all sugars are eventually broken down to monosaccharides, which are then

ready and easily absorbed into the bloodstream by diffusion.

The monosaccharides, the end products of carbohydrate digestion, then enter the bloodstream via the capillaries of the intestinal villi for absorption and travel to the liver via the portal vein.

Glucose, the simplest of sugars, is unique in that it can be absorbed to some extent through the lining of the mouth, but for the most part nutrient absorption takes place in the small intestine.

Within one to four hours after a meal, all the sugars and most of the starches have been digested. Only a small fraction of the starches and the indigestible fibres remain in the digestive tract, which moves down into the large colon and will eventually be excreted by the body.

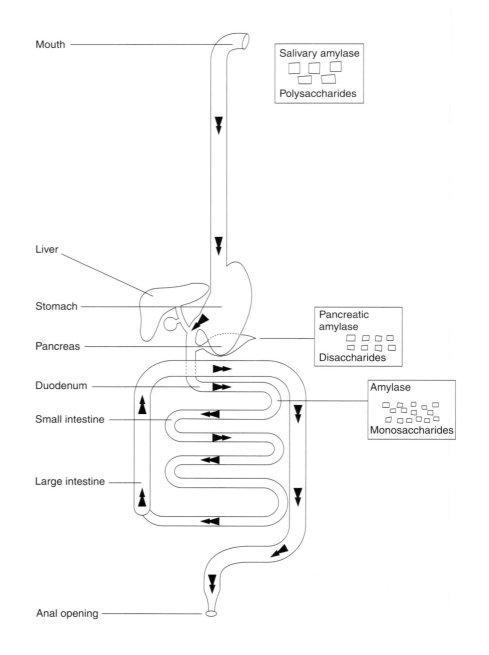

Digestion of carbohydrates

The sugar family

In general, a word ending *-ase* identifies an enzyme (*maltase*), and the stem word identifies the molecule that the enzyme works on (*maltose*). Stem words ending with *-ose* are usually sugars – sucrose, lactose, maltose

At the top of the tree are the quickly digested monosaccharide sugars like glucose and fructose – fruit and corn – then the disaccharide sugars, sucrose, dextrose, maltose and lactose coming in foods like white and brown sugar, overcooked grains, honey and milk products. Lastly we have the polysaccharides, the slow releasing carbohydrates, like grains, lentils, beans, potatoes and vegetables – also known as non-starch polysaccharides (NSP).

We can also add the indigestible polysaccharides to the bottom of this family tree otherwise known as fibre, which can also be found in grains, lentils, beans, carbohydrates and vegetables.

Lactose intolerance

Normally, the enzyme lactase ensures that the disaccharide lactose found in milk is both digested and absorbed efficiently. Lactase activity is highest immediately after birth, as befits an infant whose first and only food for a while will be breast milk or infant formula. In the great majority of the world's populations, lactase activity declines dramatically during childhood and adolescence to about 5 or 10 per cent of the activity at birth. Only a relatively small percentage (about 30 per cent) of the people in the world retain enough lactase to digest and absorb lactose efficiently throughout adult life.

Which forms of sugar are best?

Any food containing complex carbohydrate or naturally rich in fructose and vitamins or minerals is far better than refined sugar, honey or malt. Beans, lentils, brown rice, other grains and fruits and vegetables (provided they're not overcooked), are all good 'complex' sources of sugar.

Provided you avoid all forms of refined sugar, and don't have too much concentrated natural sugar in pure juice, which should always be diluted with water, or dried fruit, there is no reason to be concerned about how much sugar your diet provides. In moderate amounts, sugars add pleasure to meals without harming health. In excess, however, they can be detrimental in two ways. First, sugars can contribute to nutrient deficiencies by supplying energy (kcalories) without providing nutrients; second they contribute to tooth decay.

If you cook complex carbohydrates too long they change their molecular structure and become a 'simple' carbohydrate – don't overcook food

Simple sugars

Monosaccharides	Glucose (blood sugar)	Fruits, corn
	Fructose (fruit sugar)	Berries and grapes
	Galactose (milk sugar)	Milk
Disaccharides	Sucrose (table sugar)	White and brown sugar
	Dextrose	Overcooked grains
	Maltose	Honey
	Lactose (milk sugar)	Milk products

Complex carbohydrates

Polysaccharides (or starches)	Grains, lentils, beans, potatoes and vegetables
Indigestible polysaccharides	The fibre in grains, lentils, vegetables, (cellulose or fibre) beans

Fibre

Fibre can be classified as soluble or insoluble; both forms are largely indigestible by human beings, but important in our diets for different reasons. They are only found in plant foods.

Soluble fibre is soluble in water and includes pectins found in apples and gums found in beans, some fruits, vegetables, oats, and barley. Soluble fibre takes up bile acids, cholesterol and toxins and carries them out of the body. They therefore lower harmful cholesterol levels and reduce the risk of cardiovascular disease. Soluble fibre absorbs many times its volume of water, soothes the intestinal tract, eases bowel movements by making stools slippery and also provides food for beneficial bacteria in the intestines.

Insoluble fibre is not soluble in water. It helps prevent weight gain, colon cancer and gallstones; however, an excess of insoluble fibre can irritate the delicate lining of the intestinal tract. Insoluble fibre such as wheat bran is a harsher type of fibre and adds bulk to our stools. By bulking the waste, it can move more rapidly through the system thus preventing constipation. It also helps relieve irritable bowel syndrome, haemorrhoids, diverticulosis, varicose veins and assists in the prevention of cancer of the colon. Cellulose and hemicellulose are harsher insoluble fibre and can be found in foods such as wholewheat flour, bran, cabbage, green beans and broccoli.

How much fibre do you need?

The average adult needs to eat around 18 grams of fibre per day. The best way is to eat fibre is where it occurs naturally – for instance, in starchy foods, vegetables and fruits.

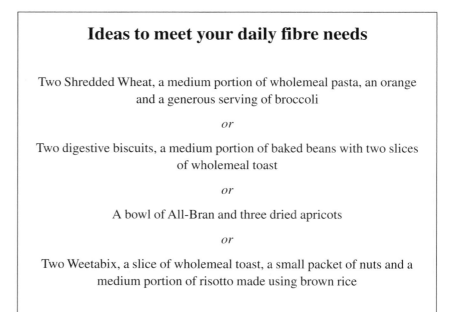

Ideas to meet your daily fibre needs

Two Shredded Wheat, a medium portion of wholemeal pasta, an orange and a generous serving of broccoli

or

Two digestive biscuits, a medium portion of baked beans with two slices of wholemeal toast

or

A bowl of All-Bran and three dried apricots

or

Two Weetabix, a slice of wholemeal toast, a small packet of nuts and a medium portion of risotto made using brown rice

Eating enough fibre may also help guard against breast cancer, either directly or indirectly. Women who eat more vegetables and fruit and starchy wholegrain cereals have a lower incidence of breast cancer, whereas a high intake of red meat and fried or browned food may increase the risk.

Carbohydrate loading before and after sport

Athletes are big fans of starchy food. Most elite athletes eat a high carbohydrate diet for a few days before an endurance event. This is called carbohydrate loading. They also eat a starchy pre-event meal, to boost their energy and endurance. The body turns the starches into glucose and glycogen, to provide both instant and stored energy for the brain and muscles. Starches are a better source of energy than sugar because they contain more nutrients and fibre.

Most of us don't need to eat the massive quantities of carbohydrates consumed by top athletes but we can all benefit from a little carbohydrate loading after exercise when a starchy snack (as opposed to sugary confectionery, fizzy drinks or fatty food) is a better way of replenishing depleted energy. A banana and some water is a lot less expensive than a fashionable sports drink – and does the job of rehydrating and boosting energy very efficiently.

Vegetables and fruit – at lease five portions a day

Fruit is the ultimate convenience food, requiring little or no preparation. It is easy to carry and enjoyable to eat any time, anywhere, making it a versatile snack. Vegetables are an integral part of all healthy meals. For optimum nutrition, five portions of vegetables and fruit per day are highly recommended – and there is additional benefit in consuming more, if you want to. Because most fruit can be eaten raw, and many vegetables can be eaten raw in salads, or lightly cooked, they retain most of their vitamins and minerals, which in other foods are depleted or destroyed by cooking. Vegetables and fruit include all fresh, frozen, chilled and canned varieties (with the exception of potatoes, which are a starchy food). Also included are dried fruits and fruit juices, but not fruit flavoured drinks which contain very little, if any, fruit juice and a lot of added sugars or sweeteners and other non-nutritious ingredients.

Proteins

The human body contains an estimated 10,000 to 50,000 different kinds of proteins. Of these, about 1,000 have been studied, although with the recent surge in knowledge gained from sequencing the human genome, this number is sure to grow rapidly. Only the essential amino acids are described in this chapter, but this should be enough to illustrate their importance for optimal health.

Key Term

Sulphur

Sulphur is an essential element in living organisms occurring in the amino acids cysteine and methionine, and therefore in many proteins.

Proteins are composed of oxygen (O), hydrogen (H), carbon (C), nitrogen (N), sulphur and iron. The key factor is nitrogen, the crucial ingredient in the formation of amino and nucleic acids (nitrogen-containing compounds).

Main function

Proteins have two main functions, structural for the growth and repair of body tissues, and metabolic for the production of enzymes, hormones, antibodies, neurotransmitters and energy.

What do proteins do?

The Greek meaning of protein is 'of prime importance', and after water, it is the most plentiful substance in the body. Proteins are also the most complex of all food compounds. Without protein we would be unable to rebuild body cells, tissue, muscles and organs and synthesise many important enzymes, neurotransmitters used in the nervous system, for example serotonin, the important structural proteins that make hair and nails, and the all-important hormones of the endocrine system. Proteins inactivate foreign invaders in the form of antibodies, thus protecting the body against disease. Protein also helps to maintain the volume and composition of body fluids. However, many people have put too much importance on protein and as a result we tend to eat it in excess, which may be an important factor or precursor in many modern diseases including osteoporosis, water retention and acidity.

Proteins are macronutrients that are supplied in the diet, digested to amino acids and absorbed in the gastrointestinal tract to be rebuilt by the body into its own proteins. They fall into three main groups.

Non-essential amino acids

More than half of the amino acids are non-essential, that is, the body can synthesise them for itself. Proteins in foods usually deliver these amino acids, but it is not essential that they do so. Given nitrogen to form the amino group and fragments from carbohydrates and fat to form the rest of the structure, the body can make any non-essential amino acid. This process is called transamination and it takes place in the liver.

Key Term

Neurotransmitter

A molecule capable of stimulating a neuron. Neurotransmitters are therefore the nervous system's chemicals of communication and are usually made out of amino acids.

Essential amino acids

There are eight amino acids that the human body either cannot make at all or cannot make in sufficient quantity to meet its needs. These eight amino acids must be supplied by the diet; they are essential for life itself. As the body is unable to synthesise these amino acids, we must actually ingest them on a daily basis. It is thought that we used to be able to synthesise these essential amino acids but somehow lost the ability to do so along the path of evolution.

Neurons

Nerve cells; the structural and functional units of the nervous system. Neurons intitiate and conduct nerve transmissions.

Key Term

Antibodies

Large proteins of the blood and body fluids, produced by the immune system in response to the invasion of the body by foreign molecules (usually proteins called antigens). Antibodies combine with and inactivate the foreign invaders, thus protecting the body.

Conditionally essential amino acids

Sometimes a non-essential amino acid becomes essential under special circumstances. For example, the body normally uses the essential amino acid phenylalanine to make tyrosine (a non-essential amino acid). But if the diet fails to supply enough phenylalanine, or if the body cannot make the conversion for some reason, as happens in the inherited disease phenylketonuria, then tyrosine becomes conditionally essential.

When we think of protein foods, we tend to focus on meat, poultry, fish, eggs and cheese. Some 30 years ago these protein foods were called 'first class protein' because they contain all the essential amino acids needed for human growth and health. Nuts, peas, beans and lentils were called 'second class proteins'; although they contain all the essential amino acids, they appear in smaller quantities and some of these more vegetarian types of proteins may be low in one particular amino acid.

These labels have been replaced by the terms 'complete' protein foods and 'incomplete' protein foods that have a 'limiting' amino acid.

A limiting amino acid is an amino acid that is present in relatively small amounts but below the recommended essential amino acid requirements. Examples would be quinoa and wheat, both of which are short in the amino acid lysine – lysine would therefore be called the limiting amino acid. A vegetarian would therefore have to top up with lysine by taking a supplement or by eating foods high in lysine, which would include soy beans, pinto beans and other legumes. These foods would then be called complementary foods.

A complete protein is therefore any food substance that contains all eight essential amino acids in the correct proportions. Eggs are an excellent example of a complete protein, with all its essential amino acids in the correct proportions. They are a valuable part of the diet because they are inexpensive, useful in cooking and a source of high-quality protein. The British Heart Foundation approves an intake of up to four eggs a week and some research suggests that eating up to one egg a day is not detrimental for healthy people. However many eggs you decide to eat, they must be boiled, poached or baked for full benefit. Eggs contain a substance called lecithin, which is also a component of bile. The function of lecithin is to break down or dismantle fat i.e. the cholesterol which is found in the yolk of the egg. If we fry eggs the high temperature destroys the lecithin and fried eggs become a high source of dietary cholesterol. However, when boiled, poached or baked, the lecithin remains intact and the cholesterol is used as nature intended.

Digestion and absorption of proteins

Protein foods are initially made smaller by the mechanical action of teeth in the mouth and the saliva which moistens the protein, but protein digestion really starts in the stomach. Hydrochloric acid denatures (uncoils) each protein's tangled strands so that digestive enzymes can attack the peptide bonds. Another function of hydrochloric acid is that it converts the inactive form of the enzyme pepsinogen to its active form, pepsin – the first of the protein-splitting enzymes.

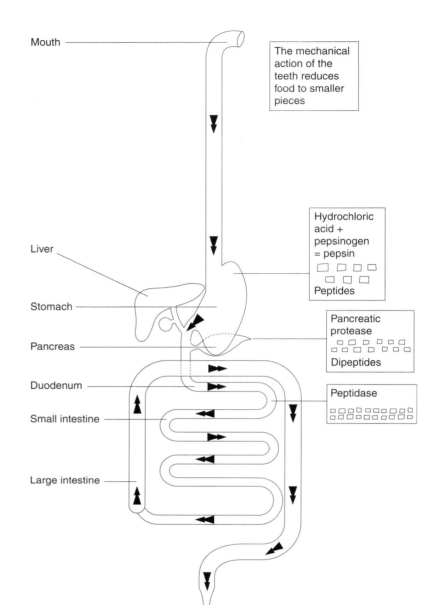

Mouth

The mechanical action of the teeth reduces food to smaller pieces

Hydrochloric acid + pepsinogen = pepsin

Peptides

Liver

Stomach

Pancreas

Pancreatic protease

Dipeptides

Duodenum

Small intestine

Peptidase

Large intestine

Anal opening

Digestion of proteins

From the stomach partially digested proteins enter the duodenum, the first part of the small intestine, where the pancreatic enzymes take over. The pancreatic enzymes include proteases that continue to break down protein, in addition to amylases and lipases – carbohydrate and fat-splitting enzymes.

Lastly, peptidase enzymes on the membrane surfaces of the intestinal cells split most of the now dipeptides and tripeptides into single amino acids. Then carriers in the membranes of intestinal cells transport the amino acids into the cells where they are released into the bloodstream and taken to the liver for processing.

Which forms of protein are best?

As already stated, one of the most complete and digestible protein foods is egg protein. Egg protein is often used as a standard for

The protein in an egg is found in the white; the yolk contains the harmful saturated fat

measuring protein quality – it is assigned a value of 100 and the quality of other food proteins is determined based on how they compared with the egg. Such a standard is called a reference protein.

The best type of protein foods are those that are low in saturated fat. Choose organic eggs, poultry, fish, cottage cheese, nuts, seeds, brown rice and pulses.

Vegetarians

Protein is not the problem it was once thought to be for vegetarian diets. Lacto-ovo-vegetarians who use animal-derived foods such as milk and eggs receive high-quality proteins and are unlikely to develop protein deficiencies. Even those who adopt only plant-based diets are unlikely to develop protein deficiencies provided that food intakes are adequate and varied. One advantage of many vegetarian protein foods is that they are generally lower in saturated fat than meats and are often higher in fibre and richer in some vitamins and minerals.

Vegetarians do need to be careful in selecting their food intake in order to consume complete protein meals. Protein is found in all foods and is especially high in complex carbohydrate foods such as quinoa (a grain) peas, beans, lentils and rice.

By eating a combination of various foods (not necessarily at one meal – the body has an 'amino acid pool' that can provide a 48-hour supply) the vegetarian can be sure of ingesting enough of all the eight essential amino acids for their needs.

In general, legumes provides plenty of isoleucine and lysine but fall short in methionine and tryptophan. Grains, on the other hand, have the opposite strengths and weaknesses, making them a perfect match for legumes. A lunch of baked beans (legumes) on toast (grain) would contain all the protein requirements for that meal. As a further example, 30gms of rice contains 21gms of complete protein; 30gms of broad beans provides 14gms of complete protein – by eating both you will get 28gms of complete protein in the right proportions (almost the equivalent of one egg that provides 30gms of complete protein).

Vegetarians do not need more protein than non-vegetarians, and do not have difficulty in obtaining enough protein. There are many studies to suggest vegetarians are healthier than meat/poultry eaters, with less risk of cardiovascular disease, cancer and diabetes.

The essential amino acids

There are 26 known amino acids, eight of which are known as essential to adults; a further two are essential to children.

Arginine (in children) and histidine (in children)

Isoleucine, leucine, lysine, methionine

Phenylalanine, threonine, tryptophan, valine

From the eight essential amino acids non-essential amino acids can be synthesised by a process called transamination; this takes place in the liver. Synthesis by the body requires Vitamin A and high protein intakes require concomitant vitamin A intake. Vitamin B6 (pyridoxine) is also required for protein synthesis as are Vitamin K and B12.

Important functions and facts about the eight essential amino acids

Arginine (an essential amino acid in children)

- accelerates wound healing
- stimulates human growth hormone (HGH) which stimulates immune function
- necessary for normal sperm count
- enhances fat metabolism
- involved in insulin production

Histidine (an essential amino acid in children)

- helps to remove toxic metals from the body
- effective in treating ulcers in the digestive tract
- has been successfully used in the treatment of rheumatoid arthritis
- helps maintain the myelin sheaths which insulate the nerves and is required by the auditory nerve for good function
- stimulates the production of red and white blood cells

Leucine and isoleucine

- two of the amino acids known as the branched chain amino acids
- both are commonly deficient in amino acid profiles of chronically sick individuals
- isoleucine is useful in the formation of haemoglobin

Lysine

- often low in vegetarian diets
- important in children's growth and development
- helps in the formation of antibodies to fight disease
- effective in treatment of herpes simplex virus, especially when combined with Vitamin C
- enhances concentration

Methionine

- an essential amino acid containing sulphur
- a powerful antioxidant preventing free radical damage to body tissues
- acts to detoxify heavy metals from the body
- strengthens hair follicles
- assists gallbladder function through synthesis of bile salts

Phenylalanine

- required by the thyroid for normal function

- needs Vitamin C to be metabolised
- acts as an anti-depressant
- may improve memory, concentration and mental alertness

Threonine

- prevents accumulation of fat in the liver
- required for digestive and intestinal tract function
- deficient in grains, but abundant in pulses, making a combination of grains and pulses a complete source of protein for vegetarians (beans on toast for example)
- suggested being essential for mental health

Tryptophan

- needed for the synthesis of Vitamin B3 in the body and the precursor of the neurotransmitter serotonin, which is a calming, sedating substance essential for normal mood and sleep patterns
- has powerful painkilling effects
- useful in weight control
- acts as a mood adaptogen – calms agitation, stimulates depressed individuals

Valine

- needed for normalising the nitrogen balance in the body
- vital for mental function, muscle coordination and neural function
- helpful in cases of inflammation
- a branched-chain amino acid

Branched-chain amino acids

The branched-chain amino acids – valine, leucine and isoleucine – protect all muscles, including the heart, and actually make exercise seem more enjoyable by reducing the feeling of fatigue.

How much protein do you actually need?

Children need more protein than adults. Most nutritionists agree that after the age of 19 protein requirements stop increasing and remain at approximately 2ozs per day (55g) for a medium-sized man and 1½ozs (45g) per day for a medium-sized woman. While it is vitally important to our diet, we do not need very much of it – approximately 15 per cent of our total daily calorie intake. If you were consuming 2000 calories per day, your protein requirement would be approximately 300 calories. Choose low fat protein sources like turkey, chicken, cottage cheese, fish and tofu.

It is difficult to become protein deficient in the Western world, but there are instances, particularly in the case of inexperienced vegetarians, vegans, or people on calorie restricting diets. Protein deficiency can be a cause of fluid retention in the body and abnormalities of growth and tissue development. In particular, the hair, nails and skin will be affected, and muscle tone will be poor. Perhaps a more accurate way of evaluating how much protein you actually need is to make a calculation by body weight.

How to calculate protein requirements

1 Find out the client's body weight in kilograms, or calculate weight in pounds and convert to kilograms (pounds divided by 2.2 equals kilograms)

2 Multiply kilograms by 0.8 to get your RDA in grams per day

Age adjustments:

Males 11 to 14 multiply by 1; males 15 – 18 years multiply by 0.9
Females 11 to 14 multiply by 1; females 15 – 18 multiply by 0.8

Example: Weight 150lbs

150lb divided by 2.2 lb/kg = 68kg (rounded off)
68kg × 0.8g/kg = 54g protein (rounded off)
54g of protein at 4kcals per gram = 216 kcals of protein

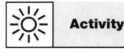

Activity

Now calculate your own protein requirements. Are you getting enough?

Fats

Many people are surprised to learn that fats have many virtues. It is only when there is either too much or too little fat in the diet that health problems may arise. The correct classification for fats is in fact lipids, but the term fats is often used to refer to all fats. The lipids important in nutrition can be divided into three classes – triglycerides, phospholipids and sterols – and we shall be looking at all these groups in the following section.

Fats are composed of oxygen (O), hydrogen (H) and carbon (C). Fatty acids may be 4 to 24 carbons long, the 18-carbon ones being the most common in foods and especially noteworthy in nutrition. Carbons and hydrogen atoms link together to form saturated and unsaturated fats.

Simple chemistry of fats

Imagine a line of carbon atoms with four 'arms' branching out from it. One arm is always holding on to another carbon atom leaving two or three arms free. If each free arm is attached to a hydrogen atom, the fatty acid is saturated. If one of the arms is brought across to connect to another carbon atom in a chain there is one place for a hydrogen atom to become attached. Therefore it is not 'saturated' (three arms) with hydrogen; a double bond to another carbon atom has been created. If there is one double bond in a chain the fat is monounsaturated. If there is more than one of these double bonds in a chain, the fat is polyunsaturated.

Hydrogenated oils are oils to which hydrogen has been artificially added at extremely high temperatures to solidify them and give them

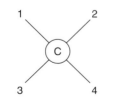

Four arms on a carbon

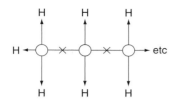

Carbons and hydrogen chain

longer shelf lives. Margarine is probably the most well known partially hydrogenated product. Although it was created to be a healthier alternative to the saturated fat found in butter, margarine unfortunately turned out to be an unhealthy alternative. The process of hydrogenating the fat cause it to change its molecular structure into what is called a trans-fatty acid, and trans-fatty acids have a harmful effect on cholesterol levels.

Main functions

Fats provide a highly concentrated source of energy, which can be stored and used instead of carbohydrates when necessary. Fats provide us with insulation and protect delicate body organs. They also produce highly active biological substances – prostaglandins – that are vital for the normal working of the body.

What do fats do?

Of all the macronutrients, fats are often the most misunderstood. It is necessary to take a brief look at the chemistry of the fats for a better understanding. Let's start with the fatty acids – the triglycerides.

Fatty acids may be saturated or unsaturated. Unsaturated fatty acids may have one or more points of unsaturation (that is, they may be monounsaturated or polyunsaturated). Of special importance in nutrition are the polyunsaturated fatty acids whose first point of unsaturation is next to the third carbon – omega 3 fatty acids – or next to the sixth carbon – omega 6 fatty acids. The 18-carbon fatty acids that fit this description are linolenic acid (omega 3) and linoleic acid (omega 6). Each is the primary member of a family of longer-chain fatty acids that regulate blood pressure, clotting, and other body functions important to health.

Triglycerides

Triglycerides are the main class of food fats. They make up about 95 per cent of all the fats we eat as well as most of the stored fat we carry around in our bodies. They are a major way of storing energy for future use. Every tryglyceride contains one molecule of glycerol and three fatty acids (basically, chains of carbon atoms).

What do triglycerides do?

We store triglycerides as adipose tissue and this is used as a reserve of energy to be called upon between meals, while asleep, during increased exertion, in pregnancy or during famine.

Adipose tissue (stored triglycerides) also acts as a shock absorber to protect the body's delicate organs while we are carrying out our daily activities – walking, jumping, running or bumping into things. Triglycerides form a layer of insulation around the body, which conserves heat to keep the body temperature constant.

The triglycerides also serve as the body's reserve of the valuable essential fatty acids, LA (linoleic acid) and ALA (alpha linolenic acid) which are required for the structure and functions of the membranes and are precursors of prostaglandins.

An important function of triglycerides is to convert excess sugar to fat, should this be necessary. The brain needs glucose to function, but sugars in excess are toxic and are converted to triglycerides, which are less harmful in large quantities. Triglycerides provide a safety net for the body by converting a potentially toxic substance (excess sugar) into a neutral one (triglycerides).

Excess triglycerides (TG) cause problems, and are associated with disease. High TG levels in the blood are associated with heart disease and are produced by over eating any type of food, but especially high intakes of refined sugars in the diet. Numerous studies have shown that overweight people tend to have higher levels of triglycerides and cholesterol in their blood compared with those of normal weight. These elevated levels contribute to cardiovascular problems, high blood pressure and heart and kidney failure. High blood triglyceride levels also increase the tendency of blood cells to clump together, decreasing the amount of oxygen the blood can carry and increasing the risk of degenerative disease, including cancer.

Saturated fats

Saturated fats are the most damaging to health. They clog up the arteries and are one of the main causes of obesity, which itself brings a host of other health problems, and are recognised to be a factor in hypertension and heart disease. Saturated fats are hard at room temperature like butter, margarine and lard. Saturated fats are responsible for inflammatory actions in the body. There are many 'hidden' fats in foods like biscuits, cakes and all confectionery.

Monounsaturated fats

Monounsaturated fats are the fats that should be used in cooking. As a result of their chemical make-up they remain stable at high temperatures. The best oil for this purpose is cold pressed virgin olive oil. As it is unrefined it is more beneficial than any refined vegetable oil.

In general, nuts have a higher polyunsaturated:saturated fatty acid ratio and a higher amount of monounsaturated fats. Pistachio nuts are 67 per cent monounsaturated and one of the nuts highest in monounsaturated fat content. Studies with walnuts and almonds have shown benefit in lowering total cholesterol and other cardiovascular risk factors. Many people have steered away from consuming nuts because their high fat and calorie content led to concerns about increased cardiovascular risk. This has not proved to be the case. As long as one is not sensitive to a particular nut, consumption is encouraged because they contain essential fatty acids, fibre and vitamin E. Nut butters make good alternatives to margarine or butter, for this reason.

Remember

Saturated fats are hard at room temperature. If a 'healthy' margarine is advertised as polyunsaturated but is hard at room temperature then It is a saturated fat. It was polyunsaturated at one time but food processing (hydrogenation) has made it saturated.

Hydrogenation

A chemical process by which hydrogens are added to monounsaturated or polyunsaturated fats to reduce the number of double bonds, making fats more saturated (solid) and more resistant to oxidation (protecting against rancidity). Hydrogenation produces trans-fatty acids.

Polyunsaturated fats

These fats are liquid at room temperature. Any oils that come in bottles – for example walnut, corn and sesame – are classed as polyunsaturated. These oils should not be used for cooking but for salad dressings, or to put directly on vegetables instead of a saturated fat like butter. Polyunsaturated fats are responsible for anti-inflammatory actions in the body and are essential in the maintenance of eczema, allergies, asthma, arthritis and many other inflammatory responses.

The polyunsaturated fats can also be described as essential fatty acids (EFAs). As with the essential amino acids, the word 'essential' here means that human beings cannot synthesise fatty acids in the body and these substances must therefore be ingested every day as food.

Unfortunately, because of the mass production of food and the ever-increasing consumption of convenience foods, many people are deficient in essential fatty acids. Foods that are high in essential fatty acids are usually high in calories and as such have been doomed by the weight-loss industry. Avocados, for example, are a highly nutritious food high in essential fatty acids, vitamins and minerals but because of their high calorie value many people on calorie restricted diets will not eat them. Nuts too have received the same fate – high in essential fatty acids but also high in calories – but are an excellent health food source of protein.

The polyunsaturated fatty acids can be divided into two groups: omega 6 fatty acids and omega 3 fatty acids.

The omega 6 group of fatty acids

We obtain the omega 6 group of essential fatty acids from the food we eat by way of linoleic acid which is found exclusively in seeds and their oils. We then convert this linoleic acid to GLA – gamma linolenic acid, which you are probably familiar with if you take evening primrose oil. This in turn is converted to DGLA – di-homo gamma linolenic acid – and from there to substances called prostaglandins. Prostaglandins are hormone-like substances which are very short-lived and have important functions in the body. They help keep the blood thin, have anti-inflammatory influences on the joints, prevent fluid retention, help lower blood pressure and help insulin work efficiently.

Many people are deficient in the omega 6 group of fatty acids. Many, women in particular, shy away from any type of oil or fat because of the calorie content, in the mistaken belief that all fats are bad.

Even if we consumed enough seeds and their oils, there are many obstacles hindering the conversion from the original LA (linoleic acid) to GLA (gamma linolenic acid). These include smoking, drinking alcohol, stress in its many forms – chemical, emotional, physical, mental – and vitamin and mineral deficiency. We need the enzyme delta-6-desaturase which is dependent on vitamin B6, biotin, zinc and magnesium, to be able to make the conversion. Without the GLA we cannot go on to make the DGLA or the all-important prostaglandins. Omega 6 deficiency signs are high blood pressure,

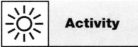

Activity

Prepare a client information sheet explaining about the different types of fats. Keep it simple but informative. Do the same for carbohydrates and proteins. Keep to 1 × A4 sheet. Use colour, illustration and no jargon.

inflammatory problems like arthritis, difficulty in losing weight and dry eyes and skin, including eczema. Good sources of the omega 6 essential fatty acids are hemp, pumpkin, sunflower, safflower, sesame, corn, walnut, soya bean and wheatgerm oil where as much as 50 per cent of the fats in these oils comes from the omega 6 family.

An excellent way of including these vital nutrients in your diet is by grinding the seeds in a coffee grinder. Two tablespoons per day sprinkled onto either cereal or over salads is considered an optimal intake. Alternatively two tablespoons of oil, sprinkled over lightly cooked vegetables or a salad, would be just as effective.

The omega 3 group of fatty acids

We obtain the omega 3 group of essential fatty acids from the food we eat by way of linolenic acid found in oily fish. We convert this linolenic acid to two substances known as EPA (eicosaopentonic acid) and DHA (docosahexaenoic acid) and then to substances called prostaglandins.

With the omega 6 group of fats the prostaglandins are known as Series 1, with the omega 3 group they are known as Series 3 prostaglandins.

Omega 3 deficiency signs are dry skin, poor coordination and impaired vision, high blood pressure, inflammatory health problems, prone to infections and fluid retention.

Still short-lived hormone-like substances but with different functions in the body, the Series 3 prostaglandins are essential for proper brain function, coordination and mood, reducing the stickiness of the blood, controlling blood cholesterol and fat levels, improving immune function and metabolism, reducing inflammation and maintaining water balance.

An excellent way of including these vital nutrients in your diet is by eating oily fish like herring, salmon, sardines, and tuna at least 3–5 times each week. By eating oily fish you are bypassing the first conversion stage and taking the EPA and DHA into your diet directly. The best seed oils for the omega 3 group of fats are flax (also known as linseed), hemp and pumpkin.

As part of a balanced diet, the maximum you should be consuming in fats is 30 per cent; 25 per cent would be even more beneficial, the 5 per cent being deducted from the saturated fats column. This can be broken down as shown in the following table. The example is for somebody consuming 2000 calories per day.

Maximum recommendations for fat intake (based on a daily intake of 2,000 kcalories from all food groups)

10% Saturated fats Non-essential	Butter, lard, margarine Any fat hard at room temperature	200 calories
10% Monounsaturated fats Non-essential	Olive oil for cooking or for making salad dressings	200 calories
10% Polyunsaturated fats Essential	Seeds, seed oils, oily fish	200 calories

Note: Of the lipids in foods 95 per cent are fats and oils (triglycerides) and 5 per cent are other lipids (phospholipids and sterols). Of the lipids stored in the body, 99 per cent are triglycerides.

Phospholipids – lecithin

Phospholipids are compounds with a unique chemical structure that allows them to be soluble in both water and fat. The fatty acids make phospholipids soluble in fat, the phosphate group allows them to dissolve in water. This versatility enables the food industry to use phospholipids as emulsifiers to mix fats with water in such products as mayonnaise and sauces.

Lecithin is the best known of the phospholipids. Whereas tryglycerides have a backbone of glycerol with three attachments of fatty acids, phospholipids have a backbone of glycerol but with only two attachments of fatty acids, the third site being occupied by a phosphate group and a molecule of choline.

What does lecithin do?

Phospholipids are important constitutes of cell membranes. Because phospholipids can dissolve in both water and fat, they can help lipids move back and forth across the cell membranes into the watery fluids on both sides. They thus allow fat-soluble substances, including vitamins A, D, E and K and hormones, to pass easily in and out of a cell. Phospholipids also act as emulsifiers in the body, helping to keep fats suspended in the blood and body fluids.

Sterols – cholesterol

Sterols are compounds with yet another different chemical structure. The most famous sterol is cholesterol, which over the years has received a bad press. However, like the tryglyceride family of fats, cholesterol has many virtues.

Cholesterol has four essential functions in the body:

- it is a constituent of cell membranes
- it is a precursor of bile acids
- it is a precursor of steroid hormones
- vitamin D is synthesised from cholesterol

What does cholesterol do?

What is it?

Cholesterol is a hard, waxy fatty substance that is essential for physical health, even though it is not required in our food supply, since our bodies can manufacture it.

As a constituent of cell membranes, cholesterol has the function of compensating for changes in membrane fluidity, keeping it within very narrow limits. This is such an important function that nature has equipped each cell with the means to synthesise its own membrane cholesterol. If cell membranes have too little cholesterol, they become too fluid and fall apart, if there is too much cholesterol they become stiff and break. The content of fatty acids in the diet varies from day to day and these fatty acids are used to build the basic structure of cell membranes. The more highly unsaturated fatty acids make membranes more fluid and the more saturated ones make the membranes harder. The function of keeping the membranes within these tight limits is a vital one.

The body makes 80 per cent of the cholesterol it needs, so there is no need to add cholesterol in the form of saturated animal fats from the diet.

Cholesterol is a precursor of bile acids and a main constituent of bile. Bile, produced in the liver and stored by the gall bladder, emulsifies (breaks down) fats into smaller globules ready for absorption. The efficient absorption of fats, oils and fat-soluble vitamins cannot take place without bile.

Cholesterol is a precursor of steroid hormones. The female hormones oestrogen and progesterone and the male hormone testosterone are made from cholesterol. Vitamin D, the sunshine vitamin required for the metabolism of calcium and phosphorus, is also synthesised from cholesterol.

As cholesterol (and other fats) do not dissolve in blood, they are carried around by proteins. The combination of a fat and a protein becomes a lipoprotein. There are two types of cholesterol, harmful cholesterol known as LDLs – low-density lipoproteins – and beneficial cholesterol known as HDLs – high-density lipoproteins. A high ratio of HDL to LDL is desirable to protect against atherosclerosis, arteriosclerosis and cardiovascular disease. Increasing the intake of polyunsaturated EFAs in favour of the harmful saturated animal fats can increase the beneficial HDL levels.

We have a total of approximately 150g of cholesterol in our bodies and of this 7g is carried in our blood. Your total cholesterol should not be above 5.2mmol/litre with the HDLs greater than 1.0mmol/litre and the LDLs 3.2mmol/litre or less. As a rule of thumb a total cholesterol of 4.8 equals an LDL of 3.2. Research has shown that lowering cholesterol to these levels in normal people, as well as those with coronary artery disease, helps prevent heart disease in the future.

Cholesterol tests now report not only your total cholesterol, but the breakdown of HDLs to LDLs. This is usually reported as the ratio of total cholesterol to HDL cholesterol. If it is five parts cholesterol to one part HDL your have an average risk; if it is 8:1 you have a high risk and if it is 3:1 you have a low risk.

Low, medium and high risk cholesterol levels

	Low risk	Medium risk	High risk
Total cholesterol	<5.18	6.2	>6.7
HDLs	<1.55	1.16	>0.9
Ratio	3:1	5:1	8:1

< Less than; > More than

Exercise is vital in reducing high levels of the harmful LDL cholesterol and increasing the HDLs. It is important for you to explain to your clients the benefits of exercise and that just one 30-minute walk, three times a week, could make all the difference in reducing high cholesterol levels.

Many foods can assist in reducing high harmful cholesterol levels and preventing them becoming high in the first place. Regular daily fibre in the diet, like fruit and vegetables and complex carbohydrates, will help remove the harmful LDL cholesterol. Apples, and other foods high in the soluble fibre pectin, can also reduce high cholesterol levels. In one French study a group of middle-aged healthy men and women added two or three apples daily for a month to their diet. LDLs, the harmful cholesterol, fell in 80 per cent of the group and by more than 10 per cent in half of them, and beneficial HDLs increased. The study also showed better results on the women with one women's cholesterol being lowered by 30 per cent.

Vitamin C, Vitamin E and other antioxidants can be described as anti-cholesterol supernutrients. They earn this title by the fact they destroy harmful free radicals that would otherwise turn the harmful LDL cholesterol toxic, making it even more dangerous. The antioxidants block free radicals and make LDL unable to infiltrate artery walls. Strawberries, guava, and yellow peppers are excellent examples of foods high in Vitamin C. Sunflower seeds, walnuts, almonds, wheat germ, and soy beans are excellent examples of foods high in Vitamin E. Alternatively, an antioxidant supplement may be taken which will give you protection.

Digestion and absorption of fats

The goal of fat digestion is to dismantle triglycerides into small molecules that the body can absorb and use – namely monoglycerides, fatty acids and glycerol.

Very little digestion of fats starts in the mouth. However the mouth does produce a fat-splitting enzyme called a lingual lipase, but this only plays an extremely small part in fat digestion in adults. In infants, however, this enzyme is much more active and efficiently digests the short and medium chain fatty acids found in milk.

In the stomach, as the mouth, little fat digestion takes place. Fats are mixed efficiently with other food and there is a gastric lipase enzyme which works primarily on short-chain fatty acids. Most of the action occurs in the small intestine. Fat in the small intestine triggers the release of the hormone CCK – cholecystokinin – which signals the gallbladder to release its stores of bile. The bile acts as an emulsifier,

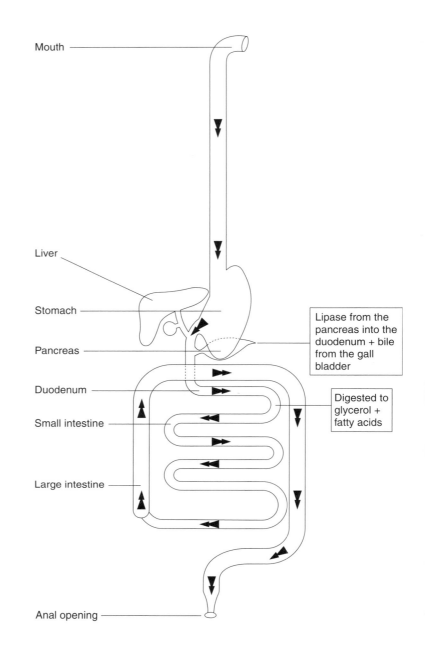

Mouth

Liver

Stomach

Pancreas

Duodenum

Small intestine

Large intestine

Anal opening

Lipase from the pancreas into the duodenum + bile from the gall bladder

Digested to glycerol + fatty acids

Digestion of fats

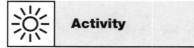

Activity

Visit your local supermarket and collect information leaflets to assist you with your course work. These could include leaflets on food labels, food safety, and additives and preservatives in foods. Read the leaflets before filing them in your portfolio! You will need this information for other activities.

drawing fat molecules into the surrounding watery fluids. Once separated, the pancreatic lipase can then start its work in digesting the fats.

The body makes special arrangements to digest and absorb lipids. It provides the emulsifier bile to make them accessible to the fat-splitting lipases that dismantle triglycerides, mostly to monoglycerides and fatty acids for absorption by the intestinal cells. The intestinal cells assemble freshly absorbed lipids into chylomicros, lipid packages with protein escorts, for transport so that cells all over the body may select needed lipids from them.

'Fat free' diet foods

This is probably a good place to mention the 'fat free' and 99 per cent fat free products that have bombarded our supermarket shelves over the last few years. Many people, those trying to lose weight in particular, pay exorbitant prices for these ready-made meals, biscuits, cakes and other products in the belief that they won't make them fat because they don't contain fat. These foods may be low in fat, but they are usually high in sugars and as you now know, the body will convert excess sugar, which could be harmful, to fat, which is also harmful but a safer alternative.

You should discourage clients from using these products and encourage going back to what nature intended; that is, to eat plenty of vegetables, fruit and wholegrains.

Knowledge review

The macronutrients: carbohydrates, proteins and fats

1   What is the main function of carbohydrate foods?

2   What is the main difference between monosaccharides and polysaccharides?

3   Give five reasons why fibre is important in the diet.

4   What is the function of lactase?

5   How long does it take for all the sugars and starches to be digested?

6   How many essential amino acids are there? Name them.

7   What are the main functions of protein?

8   What is a 'limiting' amino acid?

9   What four particular nutrients are needed by the liver to convert the essential amino acids to other amino acids?

10 Which particular essential amino acid is often low in vegetarian diets and what foods can it be found in?

11 What are the three main divisions of triglycerides?

12 What are the four main functions of cholesterol?

13 What are prostaglandins? Explain their function and give examples.

14 How can fibre help lower cholesterol levels? Name three cholesterol-lowering foods.

15 Give an example and state the function of the phospholipids.

3

The micronutrients – vitamins, minerals and trace minerals

Learning objectives

This chapter covers the following:

- **the role of vitamins, minerals and trace minerals in the diet**
- **why you need vitamins and minerals**
- **how much you need – Recommended Daily Allowances (RDA) and SONAs**
- **how vitamins and minerals protect you from damaging free radicals**
- **deficiencies**

Unlike the macronutrients, micronutrients are not energy producing nutrients, but are needed to release energy from food. Although they are required in much smaller amounts than the macronutrients they are no less important. The organic vitamins and inorganic minerals have vital roles to play in the health of a human being. Hundreds of metabolic activities in the body rely on enzymes, of which many are vitamin and mineral dependent.

Vitamins

Vitamins are organic substances obtained from food or dietary supplements. There are 13 vitamins known to date, and we need every one of them for good health. They are required in tiny amounts to perform specific functions that promote growth, reproduction, or the maintenance of health and life. The first vitamins were discovered in the early 1900s when researchers first recognised that there were substances in foods that were vital to life – vita = life. Vitamin A was the first vitamin to be discovered in 1913.

What do vitamins do?

Vitamins are components of our enzyme systems which, acting like the spark plugs in your car, energise and regulate our metabolism, keeping us tuned up and running at high performance. Although taken in minute amounts compared to the macronutrients, a deficiency in even one vitamin can endanger the whole human body.

Vitamins need not be digested but need to be liberated from food. Vitamins give us vitality and are needed not only to support all our body systems, but also to be used as coenzymes to allow other chemical reactions to take place in the body. In metabolism for example, we need good supplies of the B vitamins, or our metabolism will be unable to efficiently turn our food into energy. For carbohydrate metabolism vitamins B1, B2, B3 and B5 are needed, biotin is needed in fat metabolism and B6, B12 and folic acid are needed for protein metabolism. Vitamin B6 and the mineral zinc are needed to make the enzymes that digest food.

Deficiencies

Deficiencies in vitamins give us many minor symptoms, but if we have the symptoms long enough they may result in more serious deficiencies followed by a deficiency disease. It can be many years before a disease due to deficiency is diagnosed, so it is important to make sure you are not deficient in the first place. We all know the story of how British sailors became sick on the long sea crossings because of lack of fresh fruit and vegetables. When they were given fresh limes they recovered quickly. They didn't know it at the time, but it was of course the vitamin C content of the limes that ensured their recovery. Scientists did not identify vitamin C until 1936. Since then many more vitamins have been isolated and identified, and there are still many more to be discovered.

However, long before a deficiency disease is diagnosed, you could have a marginal or a subclinical deficiency in any of the vitamins or minerals. Good examples are vegetarians and the elderly, who may be marginally deficient in cobalamin (vitamin B12). The main symptom of classic vitamin B12 deficiency is anaemia, which a doctor can easily diagnose by a simple blood test, but there may have been marginal or subclinical deficiency symptoms for months or even years before. Pale skin, irritability, depression and confusion are all signs of vitamin B12 subclinical deficiency.

How much do you need? Figures are always being updated for vitamin and mineral requirements and it is sometimes hard to keep up to date with all the new information. The Department of Health asked the Committee on Medical Aspects of Food Policy (COMA) to set up a panel of experts to look the various figures and give a new set of updated figures. These are collectively known as Dietary Reference Values – DRVs. But with so much of our food being imported from all over the world, you may also come across measurements used in the US. Here is a list for your information.

AI   Adequate Intakes

DRI   Dietary Reference Intake was established in 1997 and is based on an average of four other measurements: AI, EAR, RDA and TUI

EAR   Estimated Average Requirement – a dietary reference value published by the UK Government

LNI   Lowest Nutrient Intake

OL   Optimum Levels (5 to 10 times higher than RDAs)

RDA   Recommended Daily Allowances

RNI   Recommended Nutrient Intake

SI   Safe Intake

SONA   Suggested Optimum Nutritional Allowances

TUI   Tolerable Upper Intake

The publication of these new dietary guidelines reflects the fact that at long last the health authorities in both the UK and USA have accepted the necessity for giving advice on minimal amounts as a guide to the general public. The majority of recommended amounts are the minimum you need to keep disease at bay – not amounts for optimum nutrition. However, there is still one big problem. In the opinion of many health professionals, the recommended amounts for vitamins and minerals are still far too low. Everyone's needs are different and many people need more of one nutrient than others do. More and more research tells us that larger doses of some vitamins and minerals not only keep you healthier now, but they can also help diseases from getting started and can control them once they do.

SONAs – suggested optimal nutritional allowances

Dr Emanuel Cheraskin and colleagues from the University of Alabama worked for fifteen years studying 13,500 people living in six regions of America. Each participant completed an in-depth questionnaire and was given physical, dental, eye and other examinations as well as numerous clinical tests for dietary analysis. The object was to find which nutrient intake levels were associated with the highest health ratings. The results consistently revealed that the healthiest individuals, meaning those with the fewest clinical signs and symptoms of disease, were taking supplements and eating a diet rich in nutrients relative to calories. The researchers found that the intake of nutrients associated with optimal health was often ten or more times higher than the RDA levels. On the basis of this evidence the SONAs were developed. These levels are more likely to be the kind of intake you need to maintain optimum health. Not all vitamins and minerals have SONAs but those that have, have been identified throughout this book for your information, together with the RDAs. All essential nutrients have established RDA figures.

Vitamins can be put into two groups: the water-soluble vitamins of the B complex group and vitamin C and the fat-soluble vitamins A, D, E and K. The main difference between the two groups is that the water-soluble vitamins cannot be stored by the body and need to be ingested every day; fat-soluble vitamins are stored in the body. The storage of these fat-soluble vitamins is one of the many functions of the liver.

Water-soluble vitamins	*Fat-soluble vitamins*
The B complex group and Vitamin C	A, D, E and K

The fat-soluble vitamins

The four fat-soluble vitamins – those that dissolve in fat but not in water – are A, D, E and K. They play many specific roles in the growth and maintenance of the body. Their presence affects the health and function of the eyes, skin, gastrointestinal tract, lungs, bones, teeth, nervous system, and blood; their deficiencies become apparent in these same areas. Because we do store these vitamins toxicity is possible, especially when supplements are being taken.

Vitamin A

Vitamin A is an antioxidant and is available to us in two forms: pre-formed vitamin A, known as retinol, which is only found in foods of animal origin, and pro-vitamin A, which is obtained from fruits and vegetables, and also known as beta-carotene.

Three different forms of vitamin A are active in the body; retinol, retinal and retinoic acid. Collectively, these compounds are known as retinoids. They each have a specific task in the body. Retinol supports reproduction and is the major transport and storage form of the vitamin. Retinal is active in vision and is also an intermediate in the conversion of retinol to retinoic acid. Retinoic acid acts like a hormone, regulating cell differentiation, growth, and embryonic development.

Main deficiency symptoms

Poor night vision, dry flaky skin, acne, frequent colds or infections and mouth ulcers.

Main food sources

The richest sources of the retinoids are foods derived from animals; fish liver oil, liver, eggs and dairy produce – especially margarine that is usually fortified. As vitamin A is fat-soluble, it is lost when milk is skimmed. Other good sources are all yellow fruits and vegetables, which contain beta-carotene that the body converts to vitamin A as needed.

Main functions

An essential vitamin for promoting vision, supporting reproduction and growth, for the maintenance of the skin and for supporting the immune system.

Liver is an excellent source of vitamin A but remember that the liver is an organ of detoxification for animals too. When we eat liver, we are ingesting the stored medications, antibiotics, and hormones that the animal may have been given throughout its life. It is suggested that eating animal liver should be restricted to once a fortnight. On the other hand, by eating carrots, red peppers, aubergines, tomatoes and other fruits and vegetables, we are taking in good amounts of beta-carotene which the body can synthesise into vitamin A when

Key Term

Pre-formed

A substance that is pre-formed, vitamin A for example, can be used immediately by the body.

Key Term

Carotenoids

A large family of red, orange and yellow plant substances found mainly in fruits and vegetables.

Key Term

Carotene

Natural pigments in red, orange and yellow plant foods (carrots, tomatoes and peppers).

! Health & Safety

Excess vitamin A during pregnancy can cause birth defects. Check vitamin A content in supplements and restrict your intake of liver to once a fortnight. There is no need to restrict beta-carotene (fruit and vegetables).

required. This is a much safer way to get adequate amounts of vitamin A into the body, as beta-carotene is water soluble and non-toxic.

Because the body can derive vitamin A from various retinoids and carotenoids, its contents in foods and its recommendations are expressed as retinol equivalent (RE). About 40 per cent of the carotenes you eat are converted to vitamin A in your liver as you need it. Some supplements report their vitamin A contents using international units (IUs), an old measure of vitamin activity used before direct chemical analysis was possible.

To convert from IUs to mcgRE, divide by 5, in other words:

4,000 IUs is equal to 800 mcgRE

1 microgram (mcg) of retinol is equivalent to 1mcgRE

12 micrograms (mcg) of beta-carotene is equivalent to 1mcgRE

Vitamin A (as retinol)	Adults	Children
RDA	600mcgRE	350–500mcgRE
SONA	2,000mcgRE	800–1,000mcgRE
Therapeutic	2,250–6,000mcgRE	1,250mcgRE
Cautions	3,000mcgRE maximum if pregnant or trying to conceive	Toxicity may occur if doses exceed 4,000mcgRE daily

Vitamin D

Vitamin D (calciferol) is different from all other nutrients in that the body can synthesise it, with the help of sunlight, from a precursor that the body makes from cholesterol. Therefore, vitamin D is not classed as an essential nutrient; given enough time in the sun, you need no vitamin D from foods. All you need is 10 minutes a day in the sun, exposing just your arms and legs while walking around – there is no need to actually sunbathe. After the 10 minutes you will then need to apply your usual sunscreen to protect yourself against sunburn, sun-damaged skin and skin cancer.

Vitamin D comes in many forms, the two most important being a plant version called vitamin D_2 or ergocalciferol and an animal version called vitamin D_3 or cholecalciferol.

Main deficiency symptoms

Joint pain or stiffness, lack of energy, rheumatism or arthritis, hair loss, osteoporosis, rickets in children and osteomalacia in adults.

Main food sources

Fish liver oils, sardines, herring, salmon, tuna, fortified milk, meat and eggs.

Main functions

Known as the sunshine vitamin, vitamin D is an antioxidant and promotes absorption of calcium and phosphate from food. It is also necessary for strong bones and teeth, for the correct function of thyroid and parathyroid glands, promoting release of calcium from bones and ensuring proper distribution in the body as well as increased uptake of mineral by bone. As a fat-soluble vitamin, we do not need to ingest it every day, as it is stored in our liver.

Causes of deficiency are a lack of meat, fish and dairy products in the diet, and lack of exposure to sunlight. In vitamin D deficiency, production of the protein that binds calcium in the intestinal cells slows. Thus, even when calcium in the diet is adequate, it passes through the gastrointestinal tract unabsorbed, leaving the bones under-supplied. Consequently, a vitamin D deficiency creates a calcium deficiency.

Vitamin D deficiency is especially likely in older adults for several reasons. First, the skin, liver and kidneys lose their capacity to make and activate vitamin D with advancing age. Second, older adults typically drink little or no milk – the main dietary source of vitamin D. Finally, older adults typically spend much of the day indoors, and when they do venture outside, many of them cautiously apply sunscreen to all sun-exposed areas of their skin. All of these factors increase the likelihood of vitamin D deficiency and its consequences – including loss of bone density and fractures.

Vitamin D is the most toxic of all the vitamins but also the most stable. It is synthesised naturally from sunlight and your body will stop making vitamin D when you have enough stored. Calcium and phosphorus are needed for the utilisation of vitamin D, and vitamins A, C and E, protect vitamin D. You may see vitamin D given in either IUs or mcg; one mcg is equivalent to 40 IU. Large doses (over 1,000 IUs) from supplements can cause a build up of calcium in your blood.

Vitamin D	Adults	Children
RDA	10mcg	10mcg
SONA	10–20mcg	10–20mcg
Therapeutic	10–25mcg	10–20mcg
Cautions	1,250mcg potentially toxic	

Vitamin E

Vitamin E was originally called tocopherol from the Greek words *tokos* – meaning 'offspring' and *pheros* meaning 'to bear' – after researchers found vitamin E improved fertility in rats. Four different tocopherol compounds have been identified and are designated by the first four letters of the Greek alphabet, alpha, beta, gamma, and delta. Alpha-tocopherol is the only one with vitamin E activity in the human body.

Main deficiency symptoms

Easy bruising, exhaustion after light exercise, slow wound healing, lack of sex drive, varicose veins and loss of muscle tone.

Main food sources

Soya beans, unrefined corn oils, broccoli, Brussel sprouts, green leafy vegetables, sunflower seeds, sesame seeds, peanuts, whole grain cereals, wheat germ, tuna and sardines. Vitamin E is readily destroyed by heat processing (such as deep-fat frying) and oxidation, so fresh or lightly processed foods are preferable sources.

Main functions

Vitamin E is a fat-soluble antioxidant, and one of the body's primary defenders against the adverse effects of free radicals. Its main action is to stop the chain reaction of free radicals producing more free radicals. Vitamin E prevents oxidation of fat compounds as well as vitamins A, C and D, the mineral selenium, and two sulphur amino acids. It protects the cardiovascular system, prevents thrombosis, arteriosclerosis, thrombophlebitis, increases HDLs, maintains healthy blood vessels, reduces the oxygen needs of muscles, and promotes white cell resistance to infection. Vitamin E enhances the activity of vitamin A and selenium and is important as a vasodilator and an anticoagulant.

Causes of deficiency are fat malabsorption (for example a very low fat diet or gallbladder removal); high intake of refined oils; alcoholism; intestinal surgery; cirrohosis of the liver and coeliac disease.

Taking vitamin E may initially raise blood pressure as it reduces blood clotting, so a gradual increase in dosage is recommended with cardiovascular problems. Vitamin E supplementation has risen in recent years as its protective actions against chronic diseases have been recognised. Still, toxicity is rare, and its effects are not as detrimental as with vitamin A and D. The upper level for vitamin E (1,000 mgs) is more than 65 times greater than the recommended intake for adults (15 milligrams).

Vitamin E	Adults	Children
RDA	3–4mg	0.3mg
SONA	100–1,000mg	70mg
Therapeutic	100–1,000mg	70–100mg
Cautions	Toxicity – none reported below 2,000mg long-term use and 35,000mg short-term use	

Vitamin K

Like vitamin D, vitamin K (phylloquinone) can be obtained from a non-food source. Bacteria in the gastrointestinal tract synthesise vitamin K that the body can absorb. Vitamin K acts primarily in blood clotting, where its presence can make the difference between life and death.

Main deficiency symptoms

Excess bleeding (nose bleeds), abnormal blood clotting, fall in the prothrombin content of blood.

Main food sources

Cabbage family, lettuce, beans, peas, watercress, potatoes, tomatoes, asparagus and corn oil provide the best sources. Milk, meats, eggs, cereals, fruits, and vegetables provide smaller but still significant amounts.

Also synthesised by gut flora, vitamin K can be made in the gastrointestinal tract by the billions of bacteria that normally reside there. Once synthesised, vitamin K is absorbed and stored in the liver. This source provides only about half of a person's needs.

Main functions

The main function of vitamin K is that of blood clotting, the formation of prothrombin (a blood clotting chemical) and normal liver function. It helps in preventing internal bleeding and haemorrhages and aids in reducing excessive menstrual flow.

Vitamin K also participates in the synthesis of bone proteins. Without vitamin K, the bones produce an abnormal protein that cannot bind to the minerals that normally form bones. An adequate intake of vitamin K may help protect against hip fractures.

Causes of deficiency are birth – all new-born babies lack vitamin K because they do not have sufficient intestinal flora present to produce any. Other causes are anticoagulant therapy, liver cirrhosis and viral hepatitis.

Supplementing vitamin K is usually unnecessary, as there is generally an abundance of natural vitamin K in the diet. However, antibiotics destroy the vitamin K-producing bacteria in the intestine and foods containing vitamin K should be increased after taking antibiotics. If taking the Pill or HRT supplementing vitamin K should be avoided as vitamin K is involved in blood clotting and the risk of blood clots are increased by synthetic hormones. There is never any need to restrict dietary forms of vitamin K from cauliflower and other vegetables.

Tip

One cup of green tea, made from leaves, provides approximately 16 mcg of vitamin K. As well as being an effective antioxidant green tea is a healthy alternative to coffee or tea.

Health & Safety

Vitamins A, D, E and K – are fat-soluble vitamins that are stored in the liver. As supplements they need to be taken with meals containing fats and minerals to be properly dissolved and digested before they can be absorbed.

Vitamin K	Adults	Children
RDA	Not established	Not established
SONA	55–80mcg	45mcg
Therapeutic	300mcg (after antibiotics)	45mcg (after antibiotics)
Cautions	The synthetic form of Vitamin K – menadone – is best avoided	The synthetic form of Vitamin K – menadone – is best avoided

The water-soluble vitamins

The water-soluble vitamins do not provide the body with fuel for energy. The energy-yielding nutrients – carbohydrates, proteins and fats – are used for fuel. However, the B vitamins, help the body to use that fuel. Several of the B vitamins – thiamin, riboflavin, niacin, pantothenic acid and biotin – form part of the coenzymes that assist certain enzymes in the release of energy from carbohydrates, fats, and proteins. Other B vitamins play equally indispensable roles in metabolism. Vitamin B6 assists enzymes that metabolise amino acids; folate and vitamin B12 help cells to multiply. Among these cells are the red blood cells and the cells lining the gastrointestinal tract – cells that deliver energy to all the others.

The B complex group of vitamins works as a family and work together synergistically. An excess of one could produce a deficiency in another, so if supplementing always choose a B complex rather than individual B vitamins. A shortage of any one of the B complex group of vitamins can hinder many metabolic processes, which is another good reason to take a B complex supplement containing all of the vitamins rather than individual ones.

B1 – (Thiamin)

Main functions

Essential for energy metabolism, brain function and digestion. Acts as a coenzyme in converting glucose into energy, involved in the production of acetylcholine, involved in protein metabolism.

A coenzyme is a small organic molecule that associates closely with certain enzymes; many B vitamins form an integral part of coenzymes.

Main food sources

Pork, dried brewer's yeast, yeast extract, brown rice, wheatgerm, nuts, wheat bran, soya flour, whole grains, especially germinating grains and liver.

Key Term

Acetylcholine

A stimulating neurotransmitter, associated with memory, mental alertness, learning ability and concentration. Acetylcholine deficiency can lead to memory loss, depression, mood disorders and possibly even Alzheimer's disease. It is also the neurotransmitter at all nerve–muscle cell junctions that allows skeletal muscles to contract, controlling movement, coordination and muscle tone.

Key Term

Antacids

Medications used to relieve indigestion by neutralising acid in the stomach. Common brands include Alka Seltzer, Tums and Rennies.

Main deficiency symptoms

Tender muscles, fatigue, stomach pains, burning or numbness in legs/toes/soles of feet, eye pains, insomnia, confusion, irritability, poor concentration, poor memory and constipation.

Causes of deficiency

A diet high in refined carbohydrates, pregnancy, breast-feeding, fever, surgery, physical and mental stress and overuse of antacid drugs. Severe thiamin deficiency is often related to heavy alcohol consumption, as alcohol blocks your ability to absorb B vitamins and also makes you excrete them faster. The elderly are also at risk as many do not eat properly.

Therapeutic uses

Beriberi (a deficiency disease of the nervous system caused by a diet of refined rice), improvement of mental ability, indigestion, improving heart function, alcoholism, lumbago, sciatica, neuralgia and facial paralysis.

Prolonged cooking can destroy thiamin, which leaches into water when foods are boiled. Steaming food, that requires little or no water, conserves the thiamin content. Smoking, drinking, stress, and antacid tablets deplete vitamin B1 in the body.

Most beneficial as part of a B complex formula.

B1 (Thiamin)	Adults	Children
RDA	0.8–1mg	0.4–1.1mg
SONA	3.5–9.2mg	3.1–3.3mg
Therapeutic	25–100mg	12.5–50mg
Cautions	No known toxicity	No known toxicity

B2 riboflavin

Main functions

Acts as a coenzyme concerned with conversion of fats, sugars and protein into energy; needed to maintain body tissues and mucous membranes; acts in conversion of tryptophan to nicotinic acid, helps to regulate body acidity.

Main food sources

Milk and milk products, yeast extract, brewer's yeast, cheese, organ meats (especially liver), wheatgerm, eggs, legumes, mushrooms, watercress, cabbage and asparagus.

Main deficiency symptoms

Cracks and sores in the corners of mouth and eyes, bloodshot, tired eyes, feeling of grit under eyelids, conjunctivitis, cataracts, photophobia, inflamed tongue and lips, scaling of skin around face, duly oily hair and hair loss, trembling, sluggishness, dizziness, insomnia, slow learning.

Causes of deficiency

The causes of deficiency are alcohol, the contraceptive pill, smoking and poor dietary habits.

Therapeutic uses

Therapeutic uses are for mouth ulcers, gastric and duodenal ulcers, eye ulceration and cataracts, eczema, hypothyroidism, certain cancers, nervous disorders, vaginitis, fevers, stress from injury or surgery, malabsorption. Heat, ultraviolet light, the birth control pill and alkaline agents (baking powder) deplete B2 in the body. Most beneficial as part of a B complex formula.

B2 (Riboflavin)	Adults	Children
RDA	1.1–1.3mg	0.4–1.1mg
SONA	1.8mg–2.5mg	1.8–2.0mg
Therapeutic	25–100mg	12.5–50mg
Cautions	No known toxicity	No known toxicity

B3 niacin

Main functions

Acts as a coenzyme responsible for cell respiration. Produces energy from sugars, fats and proteins. Crucial for brain function (involved with the production of serotonin). Component of glucose tolerance factor (GTF) – helps maintain normal blood sugar levels. Maintains healthy skin, nerves, brain, tongue, digestive system and is involved in the synthesis of sex hormones.

Main food sources

Yeast extract, brewer's yeast, wheat bran, turkey, chicken, fish, whole grains (especially sprouting grains) peanuts, mushrooms and milk products.

Main deficiency symptoms

Dementia, depression, anxiety, irritability, digestive disturbances, insomnia, dermatitis, rashes, acne, rough inflamed skin, inflamed mouth, tremors, allergies. Pellagra is a major deficiency disease affecting the skin, digestive and nervous systems.

Causes of deficiency

Alcohol; anti-leukemia drugs. Pellagra develops in areas where maize (corn) is the staple diet.

Therapeutic uses

Schizophrenia, alcoholism, tobacco addiction, acne, arthritis, reducing blood cholesterol, digestive problems, diarrhoea, migraine and insomnia. Very stable but losses occur during cooking and food processing. Destroyed by alcohol. Antibiotics, coffee, tea and the birth control pill deplete B3 in the body. Most beneficial as part of a B complex formula and additional chromium (to make GTF). B3 is available in two forms; niacin which may cause flushing and niacinamine.

B3 (Niacin)	*Adults*	*Children*
RDA	13–17mg	5–10gm
SONA	25–30mg	25mg
Therapeutic	50–150mg	25–50mg
Cautions	No known toxicity below 3000mg	

B5 pantothenic acid

Main functions

Involved in energy production, production of anti-stress hormones, controlling fat metabolism, formation of antibodies, maintaining healthy nerves and the health of skin and hair.

Main food sources

All animal and plant tissue (named from *panthos,* meaning everywhere), mushrooms, avocados, whole wheat, lentils and eggs.

Main deficiency symptoms

Burning feet, poor concentration, apathy, fatigue, restlessness, vomiting, asthma, allergies, muscle cramps, loss of appetite and indigestion.

Causes of deficiency

Stress and antibiotics.

Therapeutic uses

Rheumatoid arthritis, allergic reactions, stress, nerve disorders and epilepsy and for detoxifying drugs, especially antibiotics. Destroyed by heat, food processing extremes of acidity and alkalinity (vinegar and baking powder). Biotin and folic acid aid absorption. Most beneficial as part of a B complex formula.

B5 (Pantothenic acid)	Adults	Children
RDA	3–7mg	3–7mg
SONA	25mg	10mg
Therapeutic	50–300mg	25–150mg
Cautions	None known below 100 times RDA level	

B6 pyridoxine

Main functions

Acts as a coenzyme in protein metabolism. Needed for synthesis of certain brain chemicals and conversion of tryptophan to B3. Crucial to blood formation, energy production and EFA metabolism. Also has anti-depressant and anti-allergy functions.

Main food sources

Brewer's yeast, wheat bran, yeast extract, animal and dairy produce, bananas, broccoli, red kidney beans, watercress, cauliflower and cabbage.

Main deficiency symptoms

Irritability, depression, bloatedness, fluid retention, hair loss, cracks around mouth, numbness, muscle cramps, slow learning, pregnancy sickness, allergies, tingling hands, poor dream recall and memory, flaky skin.

Causes of deficiency

Contraceptive pill, many drugs (penicillamine), alcohol, smoking, fasting and reducing diets.

Therapeutic uses

PMT, depression, disorders caused by the contraceptive pill, morning sickness, travel sickness, radiation sickness, fluid retention, facial dermatitis, anaemia, bronchial asthma, skin allergies, diabetes, kidney stones. Works synergistically with zinc. Most beneficial as part of a B complex formula to balance. Alcohol, smoking, the birth control pill, processed foods and a high protein diet will all deplete this vitamin in the body. If taken without other B vitamins a tolerance to B6 may be built up and deficiency of other B vitamins arises.

B6 (Pyridoxine)	Adults	Children
RDA	1.2–1.4 mg	0.5–1mg
SONA	10–25mg	2–5mg
Therapeutic	50–250mg	25–125mg
Cautions	Toxicity reported in doses over 1,000mg taken alone	

Key Term

Vegan

A person who eats only plant products.

Key Term

Helicobactor Pylori

H. pylori. This is a bacteria that survives in the acidic environment of the stomach. It can cause ulcers and can lead to serious disease. Although this bacteria is known to be the most common cause of ulcers, many people with *H. pylori* do not develop ulcers.

B12 cyanocobalamin

Main functions

Essential for production of red blood cells which carry oxygen to all other cells in the body, protects our nerves, needed for making use of protein, needed for synthesis of DNA, detoxifies tobacco smoke and other toxins in food.

Main food sources

Oysters, pig's liver and kidney, sardines, pork, beef, lamb, white fish, eggs, cheese. Best sources found in foods of animal origin. Spirulina algae contains twice as much B12 as liver, and would be a good source for vegans and vegetarians.

Main deficiency symptoms

Both B12 and folic acid deficiencies have been shown to cause psychiatric illness such as dementia. Smooth sore tongue, nerve degeneration (tremors, numbness, psychosis, mental deterioration), anaemia, lassitude and weakness, menstrual disorders.

Many people, especially those over 60, develop atrophic gastritis, a condition that damages the cells of the stomach. Atrophic gastritis may also develop in response to iron deficiency or infection with *Helicobacter pylori*, the bacterium implicated in ulcer formation. Without healthy stomach cells, production of hydrochloric acid and intrinsic factor diminishes. Even with an adequate intake from foods, vitamin B12 status suffers. The vitamin B12 deficiency caused by atrophic gastritis and a lack of intrinsic factor is known as pernicious anaemia.

Intrinsic factor is a glycoprotein (a protein with short polysaccharide chains attached) manufactured in the stomach that aids in the absorption of vitamin B12. (Intrinsic = on the inside.)

Causes of deficiency

Intestinal parasites, veganism, pregnancy, ageing, alcohol, and heavy smoking. Non-absorption due to lack of intrinsic factor in gastric mucosa (and/or HCl) produces pernicious anaemia.

Therapeutic uses

Pernicious anaemia (by injection from GP), moodiness, poor memory, paranoia, mental confusion, tiredness, poor appetite.

There have been no reported problems with B12 supplementation in the oral form, although rarely an allergic reaction may arise with an injected dose. B12 is not readily absorbed and as such can be bought in a nugget form, which is placed under the tongue for more efficient absorption.

Key Term

RNA – Ribonucleic acids

RNAs are acids which are found in certain portions of cells and which play key roles in chemical reactions within cells.

B12 (Cyanocobalamin)	Adults	Children
RDA	1.5mcg	0.3–1.2mcg
SONA	2–3mcg	2mcg
Therapeutic	5–100mcg	2.5–25mcg
Cautions	None reported	

Folic acid – folate, folacin

Main functions

Helps regulate histamine levels, critical during pregnancy for the child's development, involved in the function of RNA and DNA in protein synthesis and red cell blood formation.

Main food sources

Chicken livers, bulgar wheat, spinach, red kidney beans, wheatgerm, orange juice, avocado, chickpeas, broccoli, beetroot, raspberries, peanuts, asparagus, cashew nuts.

Main deficiency symptoms

Anaemia (linked with B12), weakness, fatigue, breathlessness, irritability, insomnia, forgetfulness, cracked lips, prematurely greying hair and depression. In pregnancy, can result in miscarriage, premature birth, toxemia, and possibly spina bifida. Folic acid deficiency impairs cell division and protein synthesis – processes critical to growing tissues. In a folic acid deficiency the replacement of red blood cells and gastrointestinal tract cells falters. The first two symptoms of a folic acid deficiency are therefore anaemia and gastrointestinal tract deterioration.

Causes of deficiency

Pregnancy, the contraceptive pill, old age; 50–90 per cent is lost in cooking.

Therapeutic uses

When planning a pregnancy, pregnancy problems, mental deterioration, psychosis, malabsorption problems. There are many studies showing that if women take folic acid before conceiving and in the early days of pregnancy neural tube defects may be prevented. Neural tube defects are malformations of the brain, spinal cord, or both during embryonic development. The two main types are spina bifida (literally 'split spine') and anencephaly ('no brain').

Works best with B12 and as part of a B complex formula. High temperature and light and food processing also cause losses of folic acid. Supplementation of folic acid can mask a B12 deficiency anaemia, therefore it should not be taken without a basic intake of B12.

Of all the vitamins folic acid appears to be most vulnerable to interactions with drugs, which can lead to a secondary deficiency. Anticancer drugs in particular, that have a similar chemical structure to folic acid, can displace the vitamin from enzymes and interfere with normal metabolism. Cancer cells, like all cells, need the real vitamin to multiply; without it, they die. Unfortunately, these drugs create a deficiency for the other cells in the body that also need folic acid. Aspirin and antacids also interfere with the body's handling of folic acid. Oral contraceptives and smoking may also impair folic acid status.

Folic acid	Adults	Children
RDA	200mcg	50–150mcg
SONA	400–1,000mcg	300mcg
Therapeutic	400–1,000mcg	300mcg
Cautions	Seldom reported, but in some cases more than 15mg daily can lead to loss of appetite, nausea, flatulence, abdominal distention and sleep disturbances	

The unofficial B vitamins – biotin, choline, PABA and inositol

Vitamins are classified as essential nutrients because the body cannot make them and they must be taken in the diet every day. Biotin and choline can be synthesised by the body, which is why they are not officially vitamins. Large quantities are produced by healthy beneficial intestinal bacteria. However, sometimes the body cannot make all the biotin and choline it needs and supplements may need to be taken.

Biotin – vitamin H, coenzyme R
Main functions

A coenzyme in many body actions including metabolism of proteins, fats and carbohydrates, maintaining healthy skin, hair, sweat glands, nerves and bone marrow.

Main food sources

Found in all animal and plant tissues, especially yeasts, liver and kidney and milk produce, watermelon, cauliflower, sweet corn, almonds, eggs and tomatoes.

Main deficiency symptoms

Fatigue, depression, nausea, sleepiness, smooth pale tongue, loss of appetite, muscular pains, loss of reflexes and hair loss. In babies; dermatitis, scaly skin, anaemia and diarrhoea.

Causes of deficiency

Stress, feeding a newborn child with unfortified dried milk, excessive intake of raw egg and very low calorie diets. Biotin deficiency is rare but people who have taken large amounts of antibiotics such as tetracycline for a long time might become deficient because antibiotics kill all bacteria, including the beneficial ones that make biotin.

Therapeutic uses

Seborrheic dermatitis, Leiner's disease, alopecia, scalp disease, skin complaints, candidiasis. Most beneficial as part of a B complex formula with magnesium and manganese. Fried food destroys biotin. Biotin is also known as vitamin H, and coenzyme R. All cells contain some biotin, with large quantities in the liver and kidneys.

Biotin	Adults	Children
RDA	10–200mcg	10–200mcg
SONA	50–200mcg	50–200mcg
Therapeutic	50–200mcg	25–100mcg
Cautions	None reported	None reported

Choline
Main functions

Choline is vital for making the neurotransmitter acetylcholine, which you need to send messages about your emotions and behaviour from one brain cell to another. It is a fat stabilising agent – as a component of lecithin it helps to break down accumulating fats in the liver and facilitates the movement of fats into cells. Choline is a precursor of betaine, needed in metabolism, is essential for the health of myelin sheaths, and protects the lungs. Choline is present in all living cells. Recent evidence shows that choline is extremely important for proper cognitive development in newborns. All pregnant and nursing women need to be especially certain to get plenty of choline.

Main food sources

The best sources are lecithin granules, desiccated liver, eggs, fish, liver, wheatgerm and brewer's yeast.

Main deficiency symptoms

No specific symptoms, but lack can lead to fatty liver, nerve degeneration, high blood pressure, atherosclerosis, thrombosis, high blood cholesterol, senile dementia and reduced resistance to infection.

Causes of deficiency

Alcohol and birth control pills.

Therapeutic uses

Cardiovascular problems, alcoholism, diabetes, liver and kidney diseases. Alcohol and the birth control pill will deplete choline in the body. As choline is synthesised in the body it is not a true vitamin and is therefore known as a semi-essential nutrient; it is also known as lipotropic factor. Choline works well with B5 and lithium. Because choline is not officially a vitamin there is no RDA for it. However, a therapeutic dose would be 25–150mg for adults.

PABA – para-aminobenzoic acid

PABA is not a B vitamin but it does make up part of the folic acid molecule and can therefore be classed as an unofficial B vitamin.

Main functions

PABA blocks ultraviolet radiation from sunlight; that is why it is an ingredient in sunscreens and shampoos. Restores hair to its natural colour and relieves arthritis.

Main food sources

Liver, wheat germ, brown rice and whole grains.

Causes of deficiency

It is very difficult to become deficient in PABA.

Therapeutic uses

Arthritis, grey hair and infertility problems. Although a powerful antioxidant, there is no RDA for PABA. However, nausea, diarrheoa, fever or skin rash can occur in doses of over 1g.

Inositol

Main functions

Inositol and choline work together closely to make neurotransmitters and the fatty substances in your cell membranes; they also combine to move fats out of your liver.

Main food sources

Most people get about 1,000 mg a day from their food. Phytic acid, a substance found in the fibre of plant foods, gets turned into inositol when bacteria in your intestines digest it – another good reason to ensure you have enough fibre every day. Other good sources include organ meats, citrus fruits, nuts, beans and whole grains.

Key Term

Carcinogens

Substances or agents that are capable of causing cancer.

Causes of deficiency

Deficiency is unlikely

Therapeutic uses

Said to help liver problems, depression and panic attacks, but scientific evidence is scarce. There has been no RDA set for inositol but doses as high as 50g a day have no side effects.

Vitamin C – ascorbic acid

Main functions

An antioxidant that protects other nutrients, prevents cellular damage, detoxifies heavy metals and carcinogens, makes collagen, and keeps skin, bones, joints and arteries healthy. (An antioxidant is a substance in foods that significantly decreases the adverse effects of free radicals on normal physiological functions in the human body.) Vital for supporting the immune system and antibody production, it is a natural antihistamine, reduces cholesterol levels, aids absorption of iron, produces anti-stress hormones and activates folic acid.

Main food sources

All fruits and vegetables, especially guava fruit, yellow peppers, cantaloupe melon, pimentos, papaya, strawberries, Brussels sprouts, grapefruit juice and sprouted seeds and beans.

Main deficiency symptoms

Frequent colds and infections, lack of energy, allergies, bleeding gums, easy bruising, nose bleeds, slow wound healing, anaemia, premature ageing. Deficiency disease is scurvy.

Causes of deficiency

Diet high in refined foods, low in fruit and vegetables, poor absorption, stress, alcohol, infections, ageing, drugs (aspirin and barbiturates) contraceptive pill and antibiotics.

Therapeutic uses

Iron deficiency anaemia, viral infections, exposure to pollutants, wound healing, recovery from surgery/fractures, dental/gum disease, respiratory problems, alcoholism, arthritis, antihistamine, cancer, gastrointestinal problems.

Vitamin C is available in various forms. The most popular is as ascorbic acid, which is mildly acidic. This can be bought in tablets or in powder form; I prefer the latter, which can then be added to bottled water and drunk throughout the day giving you the benefit of the vitamin and the water.

Calcium ascorbic and magnesium ascorbic are probably more easily tolerated, but in amounts excess of 5g could neutralise stomach acid which is necessary for protein breakdown. If you want to take in excess of 5g of this type of Vitamin C, it should not be taken with food.

Vitamin C also affects oestrogen: 1g turns a low-dose contraceptive pill into a high dose, so no more than 500mg of vitamin C should be taken if you are on the pill.

High doses can lead to loose bowels. This is not a sign of toxicity but a sign of bowel tolerance, which is different in everyone. Can be used as a natural laxative in this way.

Lead, copper, aluminium, cadmium (exhaled cigarette smoke), mercury, smoking, alcohol, drugs, barbecued food, sunbed use, pesticides and many other pollutants will deplete Vitamin C in the body.

Vitamin C (Ascorbic acid)	Adults	Children
RDA	40mg	25–35mg
SONA	400–1,000mg	150mg
Therapeutic	1,000–10,000mg	150–1,000mg
Cautions	If you wish to take high doses of Vitamin C up to bowel tolerance is a good indicator	

Antioxidants, vitamins A, C, E and the mineral selenium

Main functions

To protect body cells against free radical damage, collagen binding and stabilising, anti-inflammatory, anti-allergic, enhances vitamin C, protects capillaries. Antioxidants are substances that can protect another substances from oxidation, and are added to foods to keep oxygen from changing that food's colour. Antioxidants include the vitamins A, C, E and the mineral selenium. There are also substances referred to as OPCs – (oligomeric proanthocyanidins) pine bark extract and grape seed extract – which are super-antioxidants and are even more potent than the antioxidants.

Main food sources

Fresh fruits and vegetables – preferably organic.

Main deficiency symptoms

Signs of premature ageing, cataracts, high blood pressure, frequent infections, easy bruising, slow wound healing, varicose veins, loss of muscle tone, infertility.

Causes of deficiency

Lack of dietary intake, stress, smoking, alcohol, coffee, tea, other stimulants.

Therapeutic uses

Protection against heart disease, prevention and treatment of vascular disorders such as varicose veins, phlebitis and haemorrhoids, improved circulation, prevention and treatment of arthritis, preventing allergic reactions such as hay fever and food allergies, protecting the skin from wrinkles and lack of elasticity, promotes healing, protection against eye disorders like cataracts, macular degeneration, diabetic retinopathy and prevention and treatment of oedema.

Free radicals

Antioxidants protect the body against free radical damage, but what exactly are free radicals? Free radicals are described as any molecule that has an unpaired electron in its outer sheath. Each of the molecules in our bodies has electrons spinning around them in pairs. These paired electrons keep the molecules in balance. If, for any reason, a molecule loses or gains one of these electrons, it becomes out of balance. Free radicals are those molecules which have become unstable due to their having an unpaired electron.

Cells are made up of many complex molecules and have very specific functions. Free radicals damage cell tissue by stealing electrons from balanced molecules in the cell. They do this in an attempt to bring themselves back into balance. When a molecule loses an electron, it weakens the host cell severely. With excess free radical activity in our bodies, we are destroying more cells than we can create. With cell death we have tissue death which becomes organ death with eventual body death. It all begins with free radicals. Excess free radicals are the direct result of the chemical, emotional, physical and infectious stresses we encounter. Poor diet, smoking, alcohol, exercise, pesticides, emotional upset and infections all produce free radicals.

There are many types of free radicals. One type results from the cellular energy production system in our body. During normal aerobic cellular metabolism, oxygen and food nutrients are utilised to create adenosine triphosphate (ATP), the basic energy molecule. Some free radicals are formed as by-products of this process. These particular free radicals are oxygen molecules with unpaired electrons and are called superoxides. Under normal conditions, these free radicals are kept in check by the antioxidant enzyme, superoxide dismutase. When exposed to stress, the production of these superoxides increases. Excess superoxides are extremely dangerous to cell integrity and work not only to break up cell walls, but also to react with other molecules to form even more toxic free radicals.

To fight free radical damage in our bodies, we need antioxidants, which protect cells against free radical attack. In addition to the well-known antioxidants, Vitamins A, C E and the mineral selenium, we also have super-antioxidants.

OPCs

Powerful antioxidant free radical scavengers. They are as much as 50 times more potent than Vitamin E and 20 times more than Vitamin C.

Common supplemental sources of OPCs are Pycnogenol a patented form of pine bark extract more commonly known as pine bark extract and grape seed extract.

In addition to their very effective antioxidant effect, pinebark extract and grape seed extract may also reduce allergic reactions, in part by inhibiting histamine, the compound most associated with allergic reactions. The ability of OPCs to strengthen collagen may reduce the susceptibility of tissues to allergic processes.

Whilst pine bark and grape seed extracts are excellent sources of OPCs, it is important to understand that OPCs are not the only beneficial compounds found in these two products. They both contain OPCs, but the quantity and quality of the OPCs differ and there are compounds, such as organic acids and catechins in pine bark and gallates in grape seed, that further differentiate these two important materials. Grape seed extract is not better than pine bark extract and vice versa; both supplements are important and may be taken together in a complementary way. Looking at the differences between these two products is like comparing oranges to carrots. Both have similar properties, however, in that both are very different and supportive in different ways. There have been no Recommended Daily Allowances set for these two nutrients.

Minerals and trace elements

Minerals and trace elements are inorganic substances mined from the earth. They perform functions necessary to life, for example regulating metabolic processes and building tissue.

What do minerals do?

Our bodies are made up of two fundamentally different groups of substances; organic and inorganic. Organic substances are produced by the chemical reactions of life. They are created, broken down, and recreated in our bodies from the constituents of the food we eat and the air we breathe, forming the dazzling array of molecular structures we need in order to live – nerves, skin, organs and muscles.

Organic structures by their very nature exist in a state of flux, participating in a continual series of chemical transformations, with one succeeding another like the generations of a family. Organic structures are proteins, vitamins, carbohydrates and fats and thanks to them we can grow and multiply, adapt and evolve.

On the other hand, there is no known way in which our bodies can create or break down inorganic substances. These unchanging chemicals are called minerals and trace minerals. They existed long before organic life first appeared on Earth and the role they play in sustaining the dynamic, ever-changing processes of life is invaluable. Until recently the way that minerals affected our bodies was poorly understood and as such they tended to be ignored in favour of other nutrients. It is now clear that without them there would be no life at all.

About 60 different minerals have been identified in the body, of which 21 are considered to be 'essential'. Essential minerals, as with essential amino acids and essential fatty acids, are minerals that must be supplied in the food daily, as they cannot be manufactured in the body. Some minerals are required in substantial amounts, often referred to as the gross minerals or the macro-minerals; calcium, magnesium, sodium, potassium and phosphorus. Others are needed in minute or trace amounts but equally important to health. These are the trace minerals: boron, chromium, copper, iron, manganese, molybdenum, selenium, sulphur and zinc. Four minerals tend to be particularly low among Western people: calcium, magnesium, zinc and iron.

Macro minerals	*Trace minerals*
Calcium	Boron
Magnesium	Chromium
Potassium	Copper
Sodium	Iron
Phosphorus	Manganese
	Molybdenum
	Selenium
	Sulphur
	Zinc

The macrominerals

Calcium – Ca

Calcium is an essential element for living organisms, being required for normal growth and development.

Main functions

Builds and maintains healthy bones and teeth, controls nerve and muscle excitability, controls conduction of nerve impulses, controls muscle contraction, aids blood clotting, controls cholesterol levels, aids B12 absorption and reduces menstrual cramps.

Main food sources

Ricotta cheese, Parmesan cheese, milk, mackerel, salmon and sardines, dried figs, tofu, low fat yogurt, sesame seeds, oats, millet, almonds, kelp, green leafy vegetables, parsley and pumpkin seeds.

Main deficiency symptoms

Rickets in children, osteomalacia in adults, bone pain, muscle weakness and cramps, delayed healing of fractures, tetany (twitches and spasms), tooth decay, brittle nails, insomnia or nervousness, joint pain or arthritis, tooth decay, high blood pressure, fragile bones, menstrual cramps, eczema and rheumatoid arthritis.

Causes of deficiency

Low dietary intake, lack of vitamin D, high intake of wheat bran, phosphates, animal fats, oxalic acid (from spinach and rhubarb – reduces absorption), the contraceptive pill, corticosteroid drugs, malabsorption due to low stomach acid, coeliac disease, lactose intolerance, diuretic drugs, pregnancy, breast feeding and oestrogen loss after menopause.

Therapeutic uses

Rickets, osteomalacia, osteoporosis, tetany, coeliac disease, allergy complains, detoxifies heavy metals, depression, anxiety, panic attacks, insomnia, arthritis, muscle and joint pains, pregnancy, and breast feeding. Calcium is the most abundant mineral in the body and of this 99 per cent is in the bones and teeth. The remaining 1 per cent is found in the blood and is needed for balanced nerve function, blood clotting, the heart muscles and for enzyme reactions.

Many people think of bone as a hard substance that stops growing when we reach adulthood, and are therefore surprised when they discover that the whole skeleton is in a constant state of flux. The calcium phosphate that gives the bone its hardness is continually forming, dissolving and being reformed. New calcium phosphate deposits are usually built into the protein matrix along the bone shaft while older material is flushed away in the blood to be used for other purposes or excreted by the kidneys in the urine. This constant bone refurbishment allows for growth in the young and ensures that adult bones remain strong and resilient. In this way, an average of 700mg of calcium moves into and out of the bones every day.

The distinction must be made clear regarding weight-bearing exercise. Swimming, whilst a beneficial overall exercise, is not a weight-bearing exercise as the water is offering protection to the bones. Cycling, another excellent aerobic exercise, is again not weight-bearing. Weight bearing exercises include walking, jogging, running, climbing stairs and skipping rope.

A number of factors may prevent sufficient calcium from reaching your nerve cells. Excess dietary fibre is one, as it bonds with calcium in the small intestine and prevents it from being absorbed as well as it might. Phytic acid – a substance found in grains – as well as too much fat in your diet have the same effect. Alcohol too prevents your body from utilising calcium by causing the kidneys to excrete it in the urine. The result will be too few calcium ions in the nerve cells, which then become over-susceptible to stimuli. In time this could cause the person to become tense, irritable, bad-tempered and highly sensitive.

The adequate intake of sufficient calcium for children, girls in particular, during puberty and early adulthood cannot be stressed enough. Sufficient calcium taken as milk, cheese and green leafy vegetables during the puberty years builds strong bones and will present fewer problems later in life, especially in the menopause

Activity

Estimate your calcium intake. An easy way to calculate your calcium intake is by using a points system. Your aim is for 3–4 points daily

Daily adult average – 1,000mgs of calcium = 4 points

250mls milk = 250mgs calcium = 1 point (it is slightly more than this but you need to keep calculations simple). Using this quick and easy method it is easy to see at a glance if your requirements are being met. Investigate good sources of calcium. 100g sardines for example would provide over 400mg of calcium, Swiss cheese and yoghurt are excellent sources. Green leafy vegetables are also good sources, and are well absorbed but only score half a point for every serving. Cottage cheese and ice cream, also good sources, only scores half a point. Are you getting enough?

If you therefore look at your own or someone else's diet summary for a few days and milk, cheese, yoghurt, green leafy vegetables and fish are not evident, then the daily calcium requirements will be inadequate. If however, these foods are evident, the chances are RDAs are being met.

Health & Safety

Children should be given full-fat milk and not skimmed or semi-skimmed, as these are slightly lower in nutritional content.

years for women. With milk being an unfashionable drink, high numbers of young adults who do not have their Recommended Daily Allowance of calcium will be more prone to osteoporosis later in life. Osteoporosis is also known as the silent disease as it goes undetected for many years. Often it is only detected by a fall or a stumble, with a fracture as the result.

Low fat or skimmed milk contains as much calcium as full-fat milk, as only the fat is removed from the whole milk. All other nutrients such as calcium remain. However, the general rule of thumb to choose low-fat over full-fat products needs to be considered carefully when giving milk to young children. Vitamins such as A and D are fat soluble. The removal of milk fats consequently diminishes the amount of these vitamins in the milk. For most adults this presents no problems but children, with their high nutritional needs, should be given full-fat milk.

Calcium	*Adults*	*Children*
RDA	800mg; 1,200 for teenagers	600mg
SONA	800–1200mg	600–800mg
Therapeutic	800–1200mg	600–800mg
Cautions	None reported from calcium itself but may arise from other factors. Excess Vitamin D in amounts over 25,000ius daily	

Magnesium – Mn

Main functions

Strengthens bones and teeth, promotes healthy muscles so helping them to relax, beneficial for PMS, heart muscles and nervous system. Involved as coenzymes for many functions in the body and essential for energy production.

Main food sources

Wheatgerm, almonds and cashew nuts, soybeans, whole grains, green leafy vegetables and sesame seeds, potato skins and crab meat.

Main deficiency symptoms

Depression, muscle tremors or spasms, muscle weakness, insomnia or nervousness, high blood pressure, irregular heart beat, constipation, fits or convulsions, hyperactivity, poor memory, irritability, calcium deposits in soft tissue, e.g. kidney stones.

Causes of deficiency

Low dietary intake due to eating refined foods whose magnesium has been lost in the refining process, and a lack of green leafy vegetables.

Therapeutic uses

Depression, cardiovascular disease, PMS, muscle twitches and spasms.

Large amounts of calcium in milk products, proteins, fats, oxalates (spinach, rhubarb) and phytate (wheat bran and bread) all deplete magnesium from the body. Works well with B1 and B6. Usually taken in conjunction with calcium giving a good balance. There are many forms of magnesium in supplements but the best absorbed is magnesium citrate. Works well combined with calcium as a 3:2 calcium:magnesium ratio.

Magnesium	Adults	Children
RDA	300mg	170mg
SONA	375–500mg	200–375mg
Therapeutic	400–800mg	400–800mg
Cautions	None below 1,000mg	

Sodium – Na

Main functions

Maintaining intra- and extracellular water balance, in nerve impulse transmission (with potassium), in all muscle contraction, especially heart muscle, involved in control of acid/alkaline balance in the body, active transport of amino acids and glucose into cells.

Main food sources

Table salt, sea salt, yeast extract, bacon, smoked fish, salami, sauces, cornflakes, processed cheese and cheese spread, olives, pickles, many meats, especially the smoked variety, and ready-made meals most other refined and processed foods, which should be kept to a minimum.

Main deficiency symptoms

Low blood pressure, rapid pulse, dry mouth, mental apathy, loss of appetite, muscle cramps and twitches, dehydration, giving 'sunken' features and sagging skin.

Causes of deficiency

Dehydration due to high temperatures, hard exercise or work, water intoxication – after heavy sweating when thirst is quenched with water containing no sodium. Low blood sodium causes kidney and liver disease, hormone imbalance, lung cancer or lung infections, meningitis, myxoedema, toxaemia of pregnancy, hyperglycaemia. In babies – diarrhoea.

Key Term

Hypertension

The correct term for higher than normal blood pressure. Hypertension that develops without an identifiable cause is known as essential or primary hypertension. Hypertension that is caused by a specific disorder such as kidney disease is known as secondary hypertension.

Therapeutic uses

Salt replacement corrects the above conditions. Your body contains approximately 100 grams of sodium in the body, a third of which is packed into the bone. A small fraction of the remainder combines with other minerals in the blood to prevent it from clogging. The rest is found in the fluid surrounding the cells, helping to regulate the passage of nutrients, transmissions of nerve impulses, muscle tone and fluid volume. Whilst sodium is a very important mineral, the majority of people consume too much of it. Salt is in abundance in prepared and processed foods and many people also add salt to their cooking and to prepared food. Clients need to be reminded of this and encouraged to cut back salt intake. Potassium supplements also help to restore the balance, as do saunas and regular exercise.

Over-consumption leads to fluid retention, loss of potassium, high blood pressure, stomach ulcers, arteriosclerosis, oedema, weight gain, renal failure, and bronchial asthma.

Is salt the same as sodium?

Confusingly, nutrition panels on food labels give only sodium content. Salt is actually sodium chloride. Sodium, as a mineral, is essential for a variety of body functions but eating too much, especially in combination with a low potassium intake and being overweight, can lead to high blood pressure in older people. High blood pressure increases the risk of strokes and heart disease; hence the importance of cutting down on salt.

Some foods claim to be 'reduced salt' or 'low salt', but this is meaningless when the nutrition panel only lists the sodium content. As a consumer, you might think this is a plot to keep you ignorant of the true amount of salt you are eating. Amazingly enough it is actually illegal to give the amount of salt in a particular food on the nutrition panel!

Whatever the motives of the government and the food industry, you can work out how much salt is in your food by a simple sum: multiply the sodium content by 2.5. Or you can memorise the daily maximum amount of sodium or salt recommended in the example below.

Deficiency is rare, problems arising from the body's tendency to retain sodium leading to high blood pressure, heart disease, oedema and kidney disease.

How much salt and sodium should you eat?

Daily salt	*Daily sodium*
Men – less than 7g per day	Men – less than 2.5g per day
Women – less than 5g per day	Women – less than 2g per day

Salt substitutes

Most salt substitutes mix ordinary salt (i.e. sodium chloride) with potassium chloride and/or magnesium sulphate (and other ingredients, such as anti-caking agents), so do not be fooled into thinking you are avoiding salt altogether. Products vary widely in the amount of sodium they contain. Reduced sodium 'salts' can contain 50 per cent salt, but very low sodium products may contain only 0.9g per 100g sodium, compared with 38.9g in ordinary salt. Some people detect an aftertaste with potassium products in particular.

The sodium/potassium ratio

Food processing removes the potassium found naturally in foods. Our bodies need potassium to keep sodium in balance. The best sources of potassium are vegetables, fruit, fish and lean meat. These fresh foods also leave less room for salty, processed foods in your diet. As much as 80 per cent of our salt intake can come from processed and ready-made foods.

How much salt is in common foods?

High salt foods	*Moderate to low salt foods*
Table/cooking salt	Fresh fruit and vegetables
Cured/smoked meat	Eggs
Smoked fish	Meat
Canned meat	Game
Cottage cheese	Poultry
Salted butter/margarine/spreads	Fresh fish
Savoury crackers/crisps	Milk
Salted nuts/savoury snacks	Oatmeal and oats
Some sweet biscuits	Pulses
Baked beans	Dried fruit
Canned vegetables	Nuts
Olives	Unsalted butter and low-salt spreads
Sauces – ketchup, Worcestershire, brown and soya sauce	Breakfast cereals without added salt – puffed wheat, Shredded Wheat, porridge oats
	Brown rice
	Wholemeal flour and pasta

Recommendations for controlling salt intake:

- Replace canned, pre-packaged, convenience, take-away and ready-made meals with freshly cooked meals made from fresh/frozen vegetables, fish poultry and meat.
- Eat more fruit, vegetable and low-salt starchy foods such as rice, pasta, potatoes and bread as part of a balanced diet.

Key Term

Peristalsis

Wavelike muscular contraction of the GI (gastro intestinal) tract which pushes its contents along.

- Gradually cut down on the salt you add during cooking and at the table.

Taste buds respond rapidly to salt – the more you have, the more you want. Gradually cutting down results in what you once found tasty becoming unpleasantly salty. It sounds simple, and it is – if you cut down very gradually you won't even notice it. Think of the health benefits.

Potassium – K

Main functions

Essential for healthy nerves and muscles, maintains fluid balance in the body, relaxes muscles, helps secretion of insulin for blood sugar control, enables nutrients and waste products to enter and leave cells, maintains heart functioning and stimulates peristalsis to encourage proper movement of food through the digestive tract.

Main food sources

Kelp, brewer's yeast, raisins, peanuts, dates, vegetables and fruits, wheatgerm, bananas, avocado, dandelion coffee, prunes, grapes, whole grains and nuts, blackstrap molasses, baked potatoes, cantaloupe melon, dried peaches, tomato juice, low-fat yoghurt, salmon, apricots, herring.

Main deficiency symptoms

Muscle weakness and loss of muscle tone, fatigue, constipation, mental apathy, poor reflexes, nervous disorders, arthritis, irregular heartbeat and low blood sugar.

Causes of deficiency

An excess of sodium may lead to an increased intake of potassium to maintain the correct water balance in the body. Potassium is easily absorbed and excreted, unless there is some kidney malfunction. Therefore dietary excess is not usually a problem. However, diets high in fat, refined sugars and over-salted foods may lead quickly to a state of potassium deficiency. As we age our potassium levels drop substantially and this is one of the main reasons for the weakness and decline in strength of the elderly.

Potassium	Adults	Children
RDA	2,000mg	1,600mg
SONA	2,000mg	1,600mg
Therapeutic	200–3,500mg	200–1,600mg
Cautions	Over 18,000mg cardiac arrest may occur	

Key Term

pH

A measure of the concentration of H+ ions that expresses a substance's acidity or alkalinity. The lower the pH, the higher the H+ ion concentration and the stronger the acid. A pH above 7 is alkaline or base (a solution in which OH– ions predominate).

Therapeutic uses

Muscle weakness, pins and needles, irritability, nausea, vomiting, diarrhoea, swollen abdomen, cellulite, confusion, mental apathy. Magnesium helps to hold potassium in cells.

Phosphorus – P

Main functions

Forms and maintains bone and teeth, needed for milk secretion, builds muscle tissue and is a component of DNA and RNA, helps maintain pH of the body and aids metabolism and energy production.

Main food sources

Carbonated soft and diet drinks, red meat and junk food are loaded with phosphorus additives, brewers' yeast, wheat bran, cheddar cheese, brown rice, nuts and eggs.

Main deficiency symptoms

Calcification causing spurs and imbalance such as osteoporosis, loss of muscle control and strength, trembling, convulsion, high blood pressure, arteriosclerosis and heart disease.

Causes of deficiency

Unlikely to be deficient in phosphorus.

Therapeutic uses

For correct balance of calcium: magnesium: phosphorous. Phosphorus plays a crucial role in determining how well calcium is absorbed, extracted and distributed in the body. Eighty per cent of all the phosphorus in the body is contained in the bones and whenever we speak of calcium's role in bone manufacture we should always include phosphorus in the same breath. This is because the two are stored together in the bone as a compound called calcium phosphate.

Phosphorus	*Adults*	*Children*
RDA	800mg	800mg
SONA	None established	None established
Therapeutic	Not usually necessary	Not usually necessary
Cautions	None established	

The trace elements

Boron, chromium, copper, iron, manganese, selenium, sulphur and zinc are the trace elements.

Boron

Boron helps absorb calcium into your bones and keeps it there. There has been no RDA set for this trace element but many nutritional therapists suggest 3mg per day. There is usually no problem getting this amount from food and most people would absorb 2–5mg daily.

Main food sources

Good food sources are fruits, especially apples, pears, peaches, grapes, dates and raisins. Nuts and beans are also high in boron.

Chromium – Cr

A hard silvery trace element.

Main functions

Forms part of glucose tolerance factor (GTF) to balance blood sugar, helps to normalise hunger and reduce cravings. Essential for heart function and protects DNA and RNA.

Main food sources

Brewers yeast, whole grains especially rye, oysters, green peppers, eggs, liver, beef, mushrooms and molasses.

Main deficiency symptoms

Excessive or cold sweats, dizziness or irritability after six hours without food, need for frequent meals, cold hands, need for excessive sleep or drowsiness during the day, excessive thirst and addicted to sweet foods, arteriosclerosis, improper glucose metabolism, hypoglycemia, diabetes, heart disease, decreased growth and improper fat metabolisms.

Causes of deficiency

High intakes of refined/processed foods.

Chromium	Adults	Children
RDA	None established	None established
SONA	100mcg	35–50mcg
Therapeutic	20–200mcg	35–50mcg
Cautions	None reported	None reported

Therapeutic uses

Imbalances in blood sugar levels, heart disease. Widespread deficiencies of chromium have been reported in developed countries. It is believed to be partly due to the use of refined sugar and wheat products, which have between 50 per cent and 94 percent of their chromium removed. Exercise will improve chromium status. Works well with B3 and best bought as a chromium+B3 together to enhance each other.

Copper – Cu

A red-brown trace element.

Main functions

Essential for life in small amounts, with only 2g daily required. It is involved in many enzyme systems including one which protects us from free radicals and is needed to help iron carry out its functions of oxygen transfer to the cells. It helps manufacture a thyroid-stimulating hormone, assists protein manufacture, helps iron to form red cells and assists in the formation of the pigment melanin. Copper helps relieve rheumatism and assists in the metabolism of cholesterol. It is also used for the formation of insulation of the myelin sheath around the nerves.

Main food sources

Shellfish especially oysters, organ meats, cereals, dried fruit, almonds, beans and green leafy vegetables. We also take it in by absorbing excess copper from water pipes, water softeners, fungicides and metal utensils. Oestrogen-containing birth control pills and HRT may also elevate blood copper levels.

Main deficiency symptoms

General weakness, anaemia, osteoporosis, arthritis, atherosclerosis, heart damage, skin sores, hair loss, digestive problems and diarrhoea. Excess symptoms include hardening of the arteries, high blood pressure, kidney disease, psychosis, early senility and other signs of early ageing. Said to be linked to postnatal depression.

Causes of deficiency

High doses of zinc may induce copper deficiency; excess more likely to be a problem.

Therapeutic uses

Rheumatoid arthritis. Copper deficiency is uncommon because of its abundant availability in our drinking water via copper pipes. In large amounts it is considered toxic. Copper and zinc are strongly antagonistic so a deficiency in zinc can increase the absorption of copper, as can an over-acidic diet. An excess of copper causes zinc loss. There has been no RDA established for copper.

 Key Term

Antagonist

A competing factor that counteracts the action of another factor. When a drug displaces a vitamin from its site of action, the drug renders the vitamin ineffective and thus acts as a vitamin antagonist.

Key Term

Haemoglobin

The globular protein of the red blood cells that carries oxygen from the lungs to the cells throughout the body.

Iron – Fe

Main functions

Iron is an essential nutrient, vital to many of the cells' activities, but it can pose a problem for many people who simply do not get enough iron from the food they are eating. There are between 3 and 4 grams of iron in the body, and more than half of this is used in the blood as a substance called haemoglobin. Iron transports oxygen and carbon dioxide to and from cells, is a component of enzymes, and vital for energy production.

Main food sources

Meats, fish, pumpkin seeds, parsley, almonds, brazil and cashew nuts, dates and prunes.

Main deficiency symptoms

Anaemia, poor vision, insomnia, pale skin, sore tongue, fatigue or listlessness, loss of appetite or nausea, heavy periods or blood loss, breathlessness, difficulty in swallowing, general itching, nail deformities, cramping, depression, palpitations and an underactive thyroid gland.

Causes of deficiency

Low dietary intake, heavy bleeding, menorrhagia and malabsorption due to lack of stomach acid.

Therapeutic uses

Iron-deficient anaemia, generalised itching, impaired mental performance in the young and insomnia.

Heme and nonheme iron

Iron absorption depends in part on its source. Iron occurs in two forms in foods; as heme iron, which is found only in foods derived from the flesh of animals, such as meats, poultry and fish and as non-heme iron, which is found in both plant-derived and animal derived foods. On average, about 10 per cent of the iron a person consumes in a day comes from heme iron. Iron from animal sources is easily absorbed and about 25 per cent of heme comes from these foods. On the other hand only 10 per cent of nonheme iron is absorbed, depending on other dietary factors and the body's iron stores. People with severe iron deficiencies absorb both heme and nonheme iron more efficiently and are more sensitive to absorption-enhancing factors than people with adequate iron status.

Most of the body's iron is found in two proteins; haemoglobin in the red blood cells and myoglobin in the muscle cells. Haemoglobin is the oxygen-carrying protein of the red blood cells; it transports oxygen from the lungs to tissues throughout the body and accounts for 80 per

Key Term

Myoglobin

The oxygen-holding protein of the muscle cells.

Activity

Are you getting enough iron? Keep a food diary for one week. Highlight all the iron-rich foods – meat, poultry and fish. Highlight in a different colour all the iron-rich foods coming from non-animal sources. Are you eating fruit (vitamin C) with the meal (this will assist absorption). Make a table and estimate how many milligrams of iron you are ingesting in one week. Remember you will only absorb approximately 25 per cent from animal sources and 10 per cent from non-animal sources. Discuss your findings with a colleague or in a group discussion.

Key Term

Electron transport chain (ETC)

The final pathway in energy metabolism where the electrons from hydrogen are passed to oxygen and the energy released is trapped in the bonds of ATP (adenosine triphosphate).

cent of the body's iron. Heme is the iron-holding part of both haemoglobin and myoglobin proteins. About 40 per cent of the iron in meat, fish and poultry is bound into heme; the other 60 per cent is nonheme iron.

Iron has two ionic states in the body: the reduced state known as ferrous iron which has lost two electrons and therefore has a net positive charge of two, and the oxidised state known as ferric iron where iron has lost a third electron and has a net positive charge of three. Because it can exist in these different ionic states, iron can serve as a cofactor to enzymes involved in oxidation-reduction reactions. The iron-containing electron carriers of the electron transport chain are known as cytochromes. Cytochromes enable the cells to use oxygen in their metabolic pathways. Iron therefore helps the body make full use of its oxygen, both transporting it to where it is needed and then ensuring that it is utilised properly. Every organ in the body is dependent upon oxygen; therefore if we are iron-deficient every organ in the body will suffer. Amino acid chelated iron is three times more absorbable than iron sulphate or oxide. Some companies offer a gentle iron that is non-constipating.

Iron	Adults	Children
RDA	10–14mg; Women aged 19–50 18mg	7–10mg
SONA	15mg	7–10mg
Therapeutic	15–25mg	7–10mg
Cautions	None below 1000mg	None below 1000mg

The average male tends not to have difficulty in maintaining his iron requirements, as many eat meat, poultry, and fish on a regular basis. However, because the iron requirements for women are much higher, because of menstruation, and because the requirement for energy (kcals) is less, and more women than men tend to be vegetarian, then many women find it difficult obtaining enough iron. On average women receive only 12–13 milligrams of iron per day, not enough until after the menopause. Pre-menopausal women therefore need to choose iron-rich foods ideally at every meal, but at least every day. It is estimated that 18 per cent of ingested iron is absorbed. In general the bioavailability of iron in meats, fish and poultry is high, in grains and legumes, intermediate and in most vegetables, especially those high in oxalates such as spinach, low. Foods that contain vitamin C assist in the absorption of iron. A glass of orange juice will therefore aid the absorption of iron from a boiled egg. Meat, poultry and fish also aid the absorption of iron from other foods. For example, iron from baked beans will be improved if eaten with some ham, and the iron from bread would be enhanced by vitamin C in a slice of tomato on a sandwich.

Manganese – Mn

Main functions

Cofactor in over 20 enzyme systems involving growth, the health of the nervous system, energy production and health of joints, female sex hormones, production of thyroxin, cofactor for vitamins B, C and E, maintenance of healthy bones, stimulates glycogen storage in the liver.

Main food sources

Seeds, nuts and grains, green leafy vegetables, beetroot, pineapple, bran, wheat, egg yolk, kelp, nuts, tropical fruit and black tea.

Main deficiency symptoms

Muscle twitches, childhood 'growing pains', dizziness or poor sense of balance, fits or convulsions, sore knees and joints.

Causes of deficiency

High intakes of refined/processed foods, long-term zinc deficiency, rarely due to excess copper intake, alcohol, malabsorption, and certain antibiotics.

Therapeutic uses

Schizophrenia, anaemia, zinc and other deficiency conditions, blood sugar problems, cartilage problems, allergies and fatigue. Like a number of vitamins and minerals complete deficiency of manganese is virtually impossible, because of its presence in so many foods. However, there are widespread deficiencies in the Western world. Depleted by antibiotics, alcohol, refined foods and excesses of calcium and phosphorus. Manganese citrate is a good source.

Manganese	Adults	Children
RDA	3.5mg	2.5mg
SONA	5mg	2.5mg
Therapeutic	2.5–15mg	2.5–5mg
Cautions	None reported	None reported

SELENIUM – Se

Main functions

Protects the body against toxic metabolites and cancer as an antioxidant and cofactor of glutathione peroxidase. Protects against toxic minerals, maintenance of normal liver function, production of

Key Term

Co-enzyme-Q-10

A co-enzyme is a substance that enhances the action of other enzymes. An enzyme is a protein that catalyses chemical changes in other substances, remaining unchanged by the process. First discovered in 1957, Co-Q-10 works everywhere in the body to increase energy and fend off disease.

prostaglandins, supports male reproduction, maintains the health of eyes, hair and skin, anti-inflammatory agent, maintains the health of the heart, potentiates action of vitamin E and helps produce coenzyme Q.

Main food sources

Organ meats, fish and shellfish, muscle meats, wholegrains, cereals, dairy produce, fruit and vegetables, brazil nuts, puffed wheat, sunflower seeds, brewers yeast and garlic.

Main deficiency symptoms

No specific symptoms yet established but appear to be related to liver disease, cancer, cataracts, heart disease, ageing, growth and fertility problems.

Causes of deficiency

High intake of refined/processed foods and/or high intake of foods grown on selenium-deficient soil.

Therapeutic uses

Arthritis, high blood pressure, angina, hair, nail and skin problems, detoxification of cadmium, arsenic and mercury, cataracts, nutritional muscular dystrophy, liver disease, male infertility and cancer. Since the discovery that cancer rates are low in areas with selenium-rich soil, scientists have focused their attention on this trace mineral. As an antioxidant, it works well with vitamins A, C and E.

Selenium	Adults	Children
RDA	70mcg	30mcg
SONA	100mcg	50mcg
Therapeutic	25–100mcg	30–50mcg
Cautions	None below 750mcg	

Sulphur – S

Sulphur is an essential element in living organisms, occurring in the amino acids cysteine and methionine, and therefore in many proteins. It is also a constituent of various cell metabolists, e.g. coenzyme A. Sulphur is absorbed by plants from soil.

Main functions

Joint protection and repair, antioxidant/free radical scavenger, protection and strengthening of skin, hair and nail tissue, detoxification, heavy metal removal and general connective tissue

Key Term

Heavy metals

Any of a number of mineral ions such as mercury and lead, so-called because they are of relatively high atomic weight. Many heavy metals are poisonous.

repair. Helps maintain the oxygen balance necessary for proper brain function.

Main food sources

Eggs, onions, garlic, seafood, milk, cabbage, lean beef, dried beans.

Main deficiency symptoms

Joint aches and pains, frequent infections, poor nails, hair and skin, back pain.

Causes of deficiency

Insufficient intake in the diet, stress, excessive exercise.

Therapeutic uses

Rheumatoid arthritis, after strain or injury, back pain, joint pain, reducing inflammation caused by damage or overuse, improves circulation. MSM (methyl sulfonyl methane) is a major source of organic sulphur. Preliminary research suggests that MSM may provide significant relief from arthritis and other types of joint injury. Sulphur acts as a very powerful antioxidant. Heavy metals such as lead, mercury and cadmium are very destructive to the body in many ways. Sulphur-containing compounds generally are effective chelators of heavy metals and latch on to them assisting their removal from the body. Works well with B-complex group of vitamins and forms part of the tissue-building amino acids, known as the sulphur-containing amino acids.

 **Key Term**

Chelate

A substance that can grasp the positive ions of a metal.

Sulphur	Adults	Children
RDA	None reported	None reported
SONA	None	None
Therapeutic	Sufficient protein in diet	Sufficient protein in diet
Cautions	No known toxicity	

Zinc – Zn

Main functions

Essential for bone growth, sexual development, energy production and maintenance of blood sugar levels (as it is needed for insulin production). It is needed to use B6 and vitamin A efficiently, and carries carbon dioxide from the cells to lungs. It maintains acid-alkaline balance in the body and is an essential in maintaining the health of the prostate, ovaries and testes.

Main food sources

Oysters, beef, lamb, sardines, crabmeat, calf's liver, dark turkey meat, brazil nuts, egg yolk, yeast and pumpkin seeds.

Main deficiency symptoms

Poor sense of taste or smell, white marks on more than two finger nails, frequent infections, stretch marks, acne or greasy skin, low fertility, pale skin, tendency to depression and poor appetite.

Causes of deficiency

Kidney disease, alcoholism, oestrogen also affects zinc levels, the contraceptive pill causes a drop in zinc, as does the high level of natural oestrogen in the body before a period, frequent sexual intercourse in men, high intake of refined/processed foods.

Therapeutic uses

Frequent infections, stretch marks, acne or greasy skin, poor appetite, tendency to depression, low fertility, loss of menstruation.

Many zinc supplements are on the market. Zinc citrate, or an amino acid chelate are effective supplements. Zinc can also be obtained in liquid form whereby a few drops are added to bottled water and taken throughout the day. Phytates (wheat) and oxalates (rhubarb and spinach) prevent zinc being absorbed. Care must be taken as zinc and copper are highly antagonistic – a high intake of zinc may induce a copper deficiency.

Zinc	Adults	Children
RDA	15mg	7mg
SONA	15–20mg	7mg
Therapeutic	15–50mg	5–10mg
Cautions	Toxicity – 2g or more can cause problems, vomiting and stomach irritation	

Activity

Now you have studied all the vitamins and minerals compare the nutrition information, including the vitamins and minerals, of two different types of breakfast cereals. Complete the table opposite and discuss your findings with a colleague or as part of a class discussion. Make sure you use the same serving size to make your comparisons. You are looking for a breakfast cereal that is high in vitamins, minerals and complex carbohydrate but low in fats, artificial sweeteners, sugars (including honey) and sodium.

	Product 1	Product 2	Product 3
	Weetabix Crunch		
Energy per 40g serving size	144 kcal		
Protein	3.5g		
Carbohydrate Of which are sugars	30.4g (11.6g)		
Fat of which are saturates	0.9g (0.2g)		
Fibre (Soluble) (Insoluble)	3.0g (0.7g) (2.3g)		
Sodium	0.2g		
Vitamins B1 – Thiamin B2 – Riboflavin B3 – Niacin Folic acid Iron	0.5mg 0.5mg 6.1mg 68.0ug 4.8mg		
Price for 500g	£		

Knowledge review

The micronutrients – vitamins, minerals and trace minerals

1   Vitamins are divided into two main divisions. What are they?

2   What do the initials SONA stand for and when should we use them?

3   What vitamin is needed to prevent rickets in children?

4   What Health & Safety precaution should be taken with vitamin E?

5   What are the four main antioxidants, and what is their main function?

6   List four functions of vitamin B12 and list the main food sources of this vitamin.

7   Why do we recommend folic acid before and during pregnancy?

8   What are the main functions of calcium?

9   What is the RDA for calcium in adults and children?

10   Why is it important for the vitamins A,D,E and K to be taken with meals?

11 How would a vegan obtain adequate levels of vitamin B12?

12 What are OPCs – give one example.

13 List four symptoms of magnesium deficiency.

14 What is the RDA for iron in adults? List the main food sources for iron.

15 What mineral deficiency symptoms are the following related to: poor sense of taste or smell, white marks on more than two finger nails, frequent infections, stretch marks, acne or greasy skin, low fertility, pale skin, tendency to depression and poor appetite?

16 What are the main functions of the trace mineral manganese?

17 Give three recommendations for reducing salt intake.

18 What is MSM?

19 An excess of copper in the body may result in a deficiency of which mineral?

20 Which foods are good sources of chromium?

4

Herbal remedies

Learning objectives

This chapter covers the following:

- **herbs and their functions**

- **popular herbal remedies and their functions**

- **advice on suitable herbal remedies that support specific body systems**

Herbs are plants the stem of which is not woody or persistent and which dies down to the ground after flowering. The main functions of herbs are their use as food, medicine, scent, and flavour.

What do herbs do?

Herbs have been used for many thousands of years and have numerous uses. They are one of the oldest forms of therapy practised by humans. They can be used as preventative preparations like echinacea to support the immune system, as diuretics like agrimony, or to support systems of the body, like black cohosh and vixex both of which support the endocrine system, and rhodiola, that supports the nervous system.

They are also used to aid recovery of many everyday ailments – for example burns, insect bites, scalds, catarrh, diarrhoea and indigestion. They can be used as suppositories (bolus), which either help draw out toxic poisons or act as a carrier for healing agents. They can be taken as capsules, extracts, tinctures or applied externally as creams, compresses, ointments or oils. They can be used in conjunction with hydrotherapy or taken into the body by infusions or syrups for treating coughs, mucus congestion, and sore throats.

We add herbs to our foods for flavour, but they also have a significant role to play in digestive health, working in several ways on symptoms of digestive disorders. Some herbs play vital roles in good digestion.

Activity

Experiment – try a different herbal drink every day for the next seven days and note your comments for class discussion. Individual teabags can now be bought for approximately 10p each, or buy a mixed box and share the cost with your colleagues. Try peppermint, camomile, nettle, elderflower and also try dandelion coffee. Note that fruit teas can be very acidic, so stick with the herbal varieties for the most benefit.

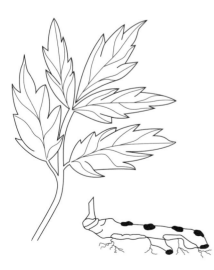

Black cohosh

Sage contains beneficial properties for the liver and kidneys; it has anti-putrefactive and anti-scorbutic properties, especially when cooking meat dishes. It is also said to prevent tooth decay. It is necessary to add herbs whilst foods are cooking to extract the full potential of their essential oil properties. When meat is cooked it produces a poison called cadaverine. When sage is added, whilst cooking, it prevents the putrefaction of the meat and combats the cadeverine. Our liver will produce anti-toxins to prevent us from being poisoned, but if we continually put pressure on our liver by what we eat, we will eventually have problems with this organ. If you enjoy meat, then adding sage to any dish will support your liver.

Thyme will ease stomach cramp and has antispasmodic properties, especially for the stomach. The laxative herbs, senna, cascara and tamarind speed up the bowel. However they should only be used for short period since the bowels may become unable to work independently. Peppermint relaxes the gut – helpful for dealing with colic, bloating or wind. Camomile and ginger are said to improve the motility of food through the intestinal tract and to help reduce muscle spasms in the gut. Many herbs, like camomile, blue mallow and peppermint stimulate the liver, aiding bile production and thus absorption.

Aloe vera is a bitter herb said to have benefits for ulcers, irritable bowel syndrome (IBS), Crohn's disease and acid indigestion. The herbs slippery elm and mallow, as well as linseed and psyllium (which we're more used to think of as fibres) contain mucilage, which gives the gut a protective lining, helpful for treating inflammation or ulcerative conditions. These are now used more than bran which has gone out of fashion since studies showed that it can be irritating to the gut – not the result we are looking for.

Black cohosh – Cimicifuga racemosa

Black cohosh is a hardy perennial growing up to 9 feet tall. It is native to eastern North America and Native Americans have used black cohosh for centuries to treat snakebites, as a mild relaxant and for 'women's concerns' – hence the common names snakeroot and squawroot.

Main functions

A female hormonal tonic, lowers blood pressure, and nerve calming.

What does black cohosh do?

The herb's major active compound, 27-deoxyactein, possesses oestrogen-like activity, and the ability of black cohosh to selectively reduce serum concentrations of luteinising hormone (LH) even further enhance its oestrogenic effect. Black cohosh is a phytoestrogen and causes LH to be suppressed, resulting in oestrogen levels remaining higher.

Health & Safety

Do not use black cohosh when pregnant. Do not confuse with blue cohosh – an entirely different plant with different properties.

A female hormonal tonic

The phytoestrogenic action and suppression of LH are primarily responsible for the dramatic, and clinically proven, ability of black cohosh to relieve common menopausal symptoms, such as hot flushes, depression and vaginal dryness. Comparison studies have shown black cohosh to be far superior to HRT in reducing menopausal complaints. Although research into the effect of black cohosh on bone density is currently lacking, there is justification for its use in combination with bone-building nutrients in prevention of osteoporosis. This herb may also benefit certain symptoms of premenstrual tension (primarily oestrogen-deficient forms).

Blood pressure lowering

Evidence shows that black cohosh exerts a significant hypotensive effect.

Nerve calming

Anti-anxiety and general calming effects on the nervous system have been observed. This action of black cohosh is independent of the herb's reproductive hormone effects and would further enhance any reduction in nervous tension and anxiety reported in menopausal or PMT research.

Echinacea – Echinacea augustifolia

Echinacea is a perennial growing up to 2–5 feet tall. It is native to North America and Plains Americans are said to have used echinacea for more medicinal purposes than any other plant group. It is a member of the sunflower family and its common names are Sacred Plant (by Native Americans), Black Sampson, and Sampson root.

Main functions

Support for the immune system and relief of prostate problems.

What does echinacea do?

Echinacea can stimulate the immune system by stimulating the immune response, increasing the production of white blood cells and thus improving the body's ability to resist infections by helping to quickly eliminate infections of all kinds. Studies have shown that echinacea even enhances the immune system in healthy people. In essence it is a natural antibiotic

Support for the immune system

Echinacea stimulates the body's immune system against all infectious and inflammatory conditions, specifically pathogenic infection by stimulating phagocytosis, T-cell formation, and by inhibiting the hyalurinadase enzyme secreted by bacteria to effect

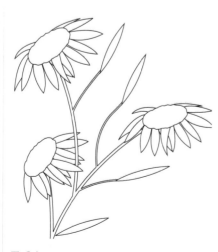

Echinacea

Garlic

the breakdown of cell walls and the formation of pus. It is one of the most powerful and effective remedies against all kinds of bacterial and viral infections.

Prostate problems

Echinacea is said to be good for enlarged or weak prostate glands.

Garlic – Allium sativun

Garlic is an onion, with the bulb made up of cloves instead of layers. Its strong-smelling pungent-tasting root is used as a flavouring in cooking and for medicinal purposes. Garlic usage dates back to the Ancient Egyptian periods and civilisations have been using it for various ailments ever since.

Main functions

Garlic keeps heart and blood vessels healthy and lowers harmful cholesterol in the body.

What does garlic do?

It is believed that the sulphur compounds and allin/allicin cause the beneficial actions. It is effective against bacteria that may be resistant to other antibiotics, and it stimulates the lymphatic system to throw off wasted materials. Unlike other antibiotics, however, garlic does not destroy the body's beneficial flora. Instead, it has the ability to stimulate cell growth and activity, thus rejuvenating all body functions. It also fends off respiratory infections like bronchitis, pneumonia, colds and flu and infections of the urinary and digestive tract. Raw garlic crushed into salad will undoubtedly give the most benefit but can be a little anti-social.

Keeps heart and blood vessels healthy

Garlic opens up blood vessels, reduces hypertension and keeps blood pressure in the normal range, whatever the stressful situation may be.

Lowers harmful cholesterol in the body

Its benefits also include lowering the harmful type of cholesterol in the body – the LDLs.

Bear paw garlic (Allium ursimum) – also known as alpine wild garlic – is said to have more active substances than (Allium sativun) and is therefore a potent supplement.

Ginger – Zingiber officinale

Ginger is a perennial plant that grows in India, China, Mexico and several other countries. The rhizome (underground stem) is used, which contains approximately 1–4 per cent volatile oils. Traditional Chinese medicine has recommended ginger for over 2,500 years.

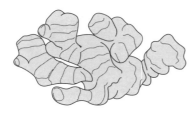

Ginger

Key Term

Rhizome

The root of a plant or herb that can be used for its beneficial properties.

Activity

Now you have experimented with drinking herbal teas from teabags, try making some ginger tea from the fresh rhizome. Cut several slices of the fresh rhizome for every cup of water; simmer gently for 15 minutes, strain and drink, preferably around mealtimes.

Health & Safety

Be patient – it may be two weeks before you start noticing the benefits. Do not exceed stated dose to get quick results. This refers to all herbal remedies, not just ginkgo biloba.

Main functions

Digestive system stimulant and alleviates nausea and vomiting.

What does ginger do?

The rich oils within the ginger-root warm and stimulate stomach and intestinal juices, encouraging complete digestion. Ginger will also benefit a congested liver with notable protective and stimulating properties. For any kind of upset stomach ginger tea, with a little lemon and honey if required, should do the trick. A cup of ginger tea after meals will assist in more complete digestion, assimilation and elimination.

Digestive system stimulant

Ginger is a classic tonic for the digestive tract. Classified as an aromatic bitter, it stimulates digestion. It also keeps the intestinal muscles toned. This action eases the transport of substances through the digestive tract, lessening irritation to the intestinal walls. Ginger may protect the stomach from the damaging effect of alcohol and non-steroidal anti-inflammatory drugs (such as ibuprofen) and may help prevent ulcers.

Nausea and vomiting

Research is inconclusive as to how ginger acts to alleviate nausea. Ginger may act directly on the gastrointestinal system, it may affect the part of the central nervous system that causes nausea, or it may exert a dual effect in reducing nausea and vomiting. Double-blind research has shown that ginger reduces nausea after surgery. Other studies have found ginger helpful for preventing motion sickness, chemotherapy-induced nausea, and nausea of pregnancy.

Gingko biloba

According to fossil records the gingko tree has existed for some 150 million years. The tree is definitely a survivor – when the atom bomb destroyed Hiroshima, the first green shoot to emerge from the blackened ashes was gingko. Gingko's history goes back over 5,000 years in Chinese herbal medicine and it is probably the planet's longest living tree.

Main functions

Increases circulation and protects nerves.

What does gingko biloba do?

Gingko is an adaptogen and an antioxidant. It can increase circulation to the brain, the hands and the feet, improve memory and alertness and protect the heart. Recent studies in Europe have found that ginkgo helps prevent strokes by preventing the formation of blood clots. Its ability to inhibit the clumping of blood platelets is beneficial because clumps and clots contribute to heart problems, strokes and artery disease. The herb strengthens arteries in the legs and relieves pain, cramping and weakness. By increasing circulation it prevents muscular degeneration.

Increases circulation

Gingko regulates the tone and elasticity of blood vessels, making the circulation more efficient. This improvement extends to both large vessels (arteries) and smaller vessels (capillaries) in the circulatory system.

Nerve protection

One of the primary protective effects of the active ingredients within the plant are their ability to inhibit a substance known as platelet-activating factor (PAF) which, when released from cells, causes platelets to clump together. High amounts of PAF have a negative effect on the nervous system. Much like free radicals, higher PAF levels are also associated with ageing. The active ingredients protect nerve cells in the central nervous system from damage.

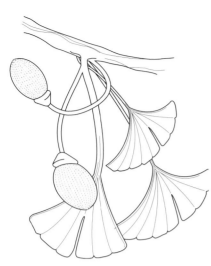

Gingko biloba

Ginseng

Known as 'the king of the herbs' in the Orient ginseng is native to China. There are several varieties: *Panax schin-seng*, Korean ginseng; *Eleutherococcus*, Siberian ginseng and *Panax quinquefolium*, wild American ginseng. Used for over 5,000 years ginseng is known for its rejuvenating qualities. It takes six years to mature and there are 700 species of herbs, trees and shrubs. It grows in tropical and temperate regions especially in the American tropics and the Indo-Malaysian region. Ginseng is extracted from the roots.

Main functions

Anti-stress herb and rejuvenation remedy.

What does ginseng do?

Ginseng stimulates the entire body to overcome stress, fatigue and weakness. There are several types of ginseng. People over 40 should only use Red Ginseng which is sold as Korean or Chinese ginseng. It warms up and regulates hormones; supports energy and sex drive and is also excellent for the digestive tract. American ginseng soothes jangled nerves and regulates hormones, is good for rejuvenation and promotes a good night's sleep. It is fine for any age and can be used continuously for up to nine months for full effect. It is best taken with food mornings and evenings.

Siberian ginseng comes from a different botanical plant group and is known as eleuthero. It is used to help you adapt to stress of any kind and maintain 'balance' in your life. This herb will help you go the distance whether a sportsman or businessman and is great for travellers for reducing the unpleasant side effects of jet lag. Its effects get better as time goes on and it can be taken continually.

Ginseng

Anti-stress herb

In stressful situations, the adrenal glands release corticosteroids and adrenaline, which prepare the organism for the fight or flight reaction. When these hormones are depleted, the organism reaches an exhaustive phase. Siberian ginseng delays the exhaustive phase and allows a more economical and efficient release of these hormones.

Quercetin

Quercetin belongs to a class of water-soluble plant pigments called flavonoids. It can be found in onions, apples, and black tea with smaller amounts found in leafy green vegetables and beans.

Main functions

Antihistamine, antioxidant and anti-inflammatory. Quercetin also protects the stomach from ulcer disease and gastric distress and strengthens capillary walls.

What does quercetin do?

Antihistamine medication bought from a pharmacy works by preventing the binding of IgE and antigens to mast cells. *(See pp 197–8 on the immune system for fuller details)*. Quercetin blocks histamines at the site of release by stabilising mast cells and basophils and inhibiting inflammatory enzymes and decreasing the number of leukotrienes coursing through the body. It is also said to inhibit enzymes like lipo-oxygenase, which are found in the inflammatory pathways that cause allergy symptoms. Quercetin has no known side effects and works quickly. When taken with other natural antihistamines and anti-inflammatories, there are even more remarkable results.

Quercetin works in two ways. First by its anti-inflammatory properties, keeping lungs, nasal passages and eyes from swelling as they normally do when allergens like pollen come into contact with the body. Second, it is a potent antihistamine that prevents the release of chemicals that make our nose run and our eyes water. This is achieved without the usual side effects of antihistamine drugs. It is extremely rare for quercetin to cause side effects.

The antioxidant activities of quercetin protects LDL cholesterol (the harmful cholesterol) from becoming damaged. Cardiologists believe that damage to LDL cholesterol is an underlying cause of heart disease.

Since flavonoids help protect and potentiate vitamin C, quercetin is often taken with vitamin C. Quercetin is perfectly safe for children to use and a much better choice than an over the counter antihistamine.

Rhodiola

Rhodiola is an adaptogenic herb that acts predominantly on the hypothalamus in a way that normalises the manner in which the body responds to stress triggers.

Key Term

Histamine

A substance produced by cells of the immune system as part of a local immune reaction to an antigen; participates in causing inflammation.

Key Term

Antigens

Substances that elicit the formation of antibodies or an inflammation reaction from the immune system. A bacterium, a virus, a toxin or a protein in food that causes allergy are all examples of antigens.

Key Term

Hypothalamus

The brain centre that controls activities such as maintenance of water balance, regulation of body temperature and control of appetite.

Main functions

Antioxidant, anti-depressant, mental enhancer, male sexual tonic and immune supportive.

What does rhodiola do?

This herb's active components are shown to be powerful antioxidants.

Anti-depressant

Rhodiola also aids depression, and this is due to various factors. Active compounds in this herb enhance the transport of serotonin precursors (tryptophan and 5-HTP) into the brain. The serotonin amino acid precursor of tryptophan is found in protein-containing foods such as fish, turkey, chicken, cottage cheese, avocados, bananas and wheatgerm. The tryptophan in these foods needs folic acid and vitamin C for it to become 5-HTP, which is one step closer to turning into serotonin. Tryptophan cannot be bought as a supplement, but 5-HTP (5-hydroxytryptophan) can be bought and has been shown to produce mood-enhancing results. Through an MAO inhibiting effect these compounds also reduce the degradation of mood-elevating neurotransmitters. MAOI – monoamine oxidase inhibitor – is a type of anti-depressant drug that inhibits the enzyme, monoamine oxidase, that breaks down neurotransmitters, thereby having the effect of keeping more neurotransmitters in action thus promoting a feeling of well-being. With respect to serotonin, the studies show a 30 per cent increase of levels in the brain. As stress accelerates the destruction of mood-boosting neurotransmitters, the adaptogenic effects of rhodiola would be additionally valuable.

Mental enhancer

Rhodiola intake may also boost learning and memory skills. Improvements have been shown even after 10 days treatment with rhodiola extract.

Male sexual tonic

Rhodiola has traditionally been used as a tonic to enhance male sexual function. Subsequent research in the field has confirmed its therapeutic effect in certain sexual dysfunction. For example, in one study involving men suffering from a weak erection and/or premature ejaculation, treatment with rhodiola extract led to substantial improvement in sexual function.

Immune supportive

Research suggests that rhodiola's benefits extend to the immune system – a factor that combines especially well with its adaptogenic activity. Not surprisingly, it has been reported that rhodiola is particularly effective in aiding recovery after viral infection.

St John's Wort

St John's Wort – (Hypericum perforatum)

The herb St John's Wort is found throughout North and South America, Europe and the Canary Islands, North Africa, large parts of Asia, China, Australia and New Zealand and is often described as the many sided healing plant. If you hold the leaves up to the light they look perforated, hence the Latin name *Perforatum*. These perforations are actually glands which contain volatile oil. When the flowers are squeezed between the fingers, a blood red juice emerges. Its colour comes from the main active component of St John's Wort – hypericin.

Main functions

Anti-depressant, anti-bacterial, nerve relaxant and mild sedative, anti-microbial, inhibits infections, pain reducing, reduces bleeding, protects capillaries, and helps insomnia (especially when linked to depression).

What does St John's Wort do?

For a long time St John's Wort was only known as 'red oil' for external use in the treatment of wounds. Its effect as a nerve medication and anti-depressant when applied internally has only recently been rediscovered. Prescribed by doctors throughout Europe this is a safe, natural way to ease depression and anxiety. German medical researchers have shown the herb to be just as effective as pharmaceutical anti-depressants like Prozac but without the side effects.

It is scientifically proven that depressed people have a disturbed biochemical equilibrium, which prevents the brain from operating optimally. This can lead to mental, spiritual and emotional disturbances as well as physical disturbances which fall under the heading of 'depression'. St John's Wort affects the messenger compound dopamine, which regulates the hormone adrenaline and neurotransmitter noradrenaline. It inhibits nerve signals so that the psychic equilibrium is re-established. St John's Wort stabilises dopamine so that the noradrenaline is not released.

Latest research also shows that St John's Wort also has an effect on the pineal gland which, among other things, regulates the release of the hormone melatonin. When there is not enough light, for example in winter, too much melatonin may be released during the day so that the disturbed rhythm leads to sleepiness, irritability and depressive symptoms. This is the case in the typical winter depression.

St John's Wort also influences the enzyme monoamine oxydase (MAO) (which degrades mood-elevating neurotransmitters in the brain). St John's Wort inhibits MAO, which itself inhibits the activity of the neurotransmitter serotonin in the brain. This is an activity which should be as free and uninhibited as possible because serotonin is a type of happy hormone-releasing substance that reduces pain, makes one feel relaxed and allows sleep.

As opposed to anti-depressants, which require a prescription and often produce side effects, St John's Wort can easily be bought from health food stores in capsules, juice to drink or massage oil, and side

Key Term

Serotonin

A neurotransmitter associated with mood, sleep patterns, dreaming and visions. It influences many physiological functions, including blood pressure, digestion, body temperature and pain sensation. Serotonin also affects our circadian rhythm, the body's response to the cycles of day and night.

Health & Safety

Patience – patience is needed when taking St John's Wort for depression. It may take 3–4 weeks before any improvement is apparent.

Key Term

MAO inhibiting factor

A type of antidepressant drug that inhibits the enzyme monoamine oxidase, that breaks down neurotransmitters, thereby having the effect of keeping more neurotransmitters in action.

Saw palmetto

effects very seldom occur. If they do they disappear immediately after the herb is discontinued. Excessive intake may cause photosensitivity. St John's Wort is compatible with all other medications with the possible exception of MAO inhibitors. Avoid using the herb with MAO inhibiting or selective serotonin re-uptake inhibiting (SSRI) drugs, unless directed by a qualified medical practitioner.

Saw palmetto – Serenoa repens

Saw palmetto is a dwarf palm tree native to the Atlantic coast of the United States. The active ingredient in saw palmetto is from a specific fat-soluble extract found in the tree's berries.

Main functions

Prostate support, and general healing purposes.

What does saw palmetto do?

The prostate is a walnut-shaped male genital gland that sits at the base of the penis, right below the bladder. It surrounds the first inch of the urethra, the thin tube that carries urine to the bladder. Benign prostatic hypertrophy (BPH) occurs when the prostate grows enlarged or swollen. Common symptoms include frequent urination, urinary urgency, burning while urinating and 'dribbling', all of which stem from the blockage of the bladder and urethra due to the enlarged prostate. As the bladder gets squeezed smaller and smaller, it thickens, leaving less room to store urine and causing the urgent and persistent need to urinate. Many men, usually over 40, may begin to experience problems in urinating, which can be painful and embarrassing. As men reach this age, the prostrate gland starts to grow. As it gets bigger the tube that conducts the urine out of the body gets smaller and urine flow slows or emerges in little spurts, resulting in having to go to the toilet more frequently, especially at night. A series of controlled trials showed saw palmetto to reduce nocturia by up to 74 per cent.

After the age of 50 men should consider using saw palmetto as a routine precaution, and especially if they notice any symptoms. Choose brands that are familiar to you and are solvent free and hexane free. Again patience is necessary – it may take 3–5 weeks before you notice the benefits, which include less pain, more frequency, less irritation, more control and comfort – so the wait is worth it.

Valerian – valeriana officinalis

Valerian is a herb grown all over Europe although most of the valerian used for medicinal extracts is cultivated. The root is used.

Main functions

To treat insomnia and anxiety.

What does valerian do?

Known as the relaxing and sleep-promoting herb, it works on the brain and spinal cord and, unlike pharmaceutical drugs like Valium, has no side effects. Valerian root contains many different constituents, including essential oils that appear to contribute to the sedating properties of the herb. Central nervous system sedation is regulated by receptors in the brain known as GABA-A receptors. Valerian weakly binds to these receptors to exert a sedating action and helps people deal with stress more effectively.

Double-blind studies have repeatedly found that valerian is more effective than a placebo and as effective as standard sleep medications for people with insomnia. Generally valerian makes sleep more restful as well as making the transition to sleep easier, but it does not tend to increase total time spent sleeping according to these studies. Combining lemon balm and honey with valerian did not make it any more effective in another double-blind study of people having difficulty sleeping.

Valerian is a very safe herb. It does not impair ability to drive or operate machinery, and does not lead to addiction or dependence, is not contraindicated during pregnancy or lactation, and is safe for children at half the adult dose. A cup of valerian tea before bedtime works wonders.

Vitex – Agnus Castus

The chaste tree is a member of the Verbena family, native to the Mediterranean and Central Asia. It is a shrub with finger-shaped leaves and slender violet flowers. It blooms in the summer and develops a dark brown or black berry the size of a peppercorn. The fruit has a spicy pepper-like aroma and taste. The dried ripe fruits are used medicinally.

Main functions

PMS, breast tenderness, infertility due to anovulation, menstrual problems including hypermenorrhea, poor lactation, may be helpful for hot flushes, uterine fibroids, ovarian cysts and endometriosis.

What does vitex do?

Vitex or *Agnus Castus* as it is often called, modulates progesterone levels by increasing luteinizing hormone (LH) and decreasing follicle stimulating hormone (FSH) in the pituitary gland. It also modulates prolactic secretion from the pituitary gland. Also known as chaste-berry, vitex is one of the best-known herbs for PMS and menopausal symptoms. The liquid tincture gives good results, and taken in a little warm water in the mornings can help such symptoms as mood swings, cravings, acne, excessive menstrual bleeding and irregular cycles.

A large study in Europe of 153 gynecologists working with 551 patients with premenstrual syndrome and menstrual disorders found it to be quite effective. Improvement in symptoms were found in 31.9 per cent of patients within the first four weeks and 83.5 per cent

Key Term

Placebo

An inert, harmless medication given to provide comfort and hope; a sham treatment used in controlled research studies.

Health & Safety

TAKE CARE – vitex and black cohosh have *opposite* actions. Use black cohosh for low oestrogen levels (30 per cent of clients) and vitex for high oestrogen (70 per cent of clients) the herb *Don Quai* is an adaptogen and can safety be used for either high or low oestrogen levels.

Health & Safety

Always read the label and follow the manufacturer's instructions.

within 12 weeks, with 29 per cent becoming symptom free by the end of the study. Only 11 per cent showed no response to the treatment. About 5 per cent reported side effects, all of them mild, with the exception of one individual who experienced heavy headaches and did not complete the treatment. Vitex has few side effects: 1–2 per cent of patients in studies reported nausea, increased menstrual flow, acne and skin rash. It is contraindicated in pregnancy due to hormonal effects, but is used in lactation to increase milk production.

Knowledge review

Herbal remedies

1   What is the main function of herbs?

2   Which herb has antihistamine, antioxidant and anti-inflammatory properties and is usually recommended for allergies?

3   Which herb has anti-depressant, anti-bacterial, and sedative properties and is usually recommended for mild depression?

4   What important difference must you remember between the herbs vitex (*Agnus Castus*) and black cohosh?

5   If a client had poor circulation, especially to their hands and feet, what herb might you consider?

6   What are the health and safety aspects when considering herbal remedies for clients?

7   Which herb is considered beneficial for all men over the age of 50 and why?

8   Which herb can easily be simmered and made into a beneficial tea to aid the digestive system?

9   There are many forms of the herb ginseng. Which one should only be used by people over 40? Why do you think this is?

10   Which herb is reputed to boost learning and memory skills?

11   What is a placebo?

12   Which herb may cause photosensitivity?

13   Do herbal remedies work immediately?

14   What active ingredient in garlic is said to cause the beneficial actions?

15   Name one effect the herb rhodiola has in aiding depression.

5 Superfoods

Let food be your medicine and let medicine be your food.

Hippocrates 470BC–410BC
The father of medicine

Learning objectives

This chapter covers the following:

- **dietary influences affecting the digestive system**

- **common disorders associated with the digestive system**

- **recommendations of foods to increase/decrease**

- **supplements and herbal remedies**

- **superfoods and lifestyle changes relating to disorders of the digestive system**

Superfoods is the term used to describe some of the most nutritionally concentrated foods known to man. Low on the food chain and bursting with vitality and energy they include microscopic algae, humble grasses and exotic mushrooms, some of which have been around for thousands if not millions of years. They include sprouted grains we may pass by in the supermarket like alfalfa, and ordinary foods such as mushrooms and cabbage. These foods are known as superfoods because they are packed with powerful nutritional and medicinal properties, including enzymes, pigments, vitamins, minerals and other nutrients essential for health vitality and well-being.

There is no doubt that early physicians used food as the mainstay prescription against disease. Among these medicinal foods, cabbage was considered a 'cure all' and ancient Egyptians declared that consumption of cabbage would cure as many as 87 diseases and that consumption of onions would cure 28. Garlic was considered a holy plant. Cruciferous vegetables (cabbage and broccoli) were cultivated primarily for medicinal purposes and were used therapeutically against headache, deafness, diarrhoea, gout, and stomach disorders. The ancient Romans believed that lentils were a cure for diarrhoea and conducive to an even temper. Raisins and grapes had many medicinal uses and were incorporated into oral preparations, enemas, inhalations and topical applications.

There follows a brief description of eleven superfoods. Experiment with these and other new foods for yourself, before recommending them to your clients. A recommendation is much more convincing if you have experienced the benefits for yourself.

Alfalfa – Medicago sativa

The Chinese have used alfalfa since the sixth century to treat kidney stones, and to relieve fluid retention and swelling. It is a perennial herb that grows throughout the world in a variety of climates. Alfalfa grows to about three feet and has blue-violet flowers that bloom from July to September.

First discovered by the Arabs, they dubbed this valuable plant the 'father of all foods'. They fed alfalfa to their horses claiming it made the animals swift and strong. The leaves of the alfalfa plant are rich in minerals and nutrients, including calcium, magnesium, potassium and carotene (useful against both heart disease and cancer). Leaf tablets are also rich in protein, vitamins E and K. Alfalfa extract is used by food makers as a source of chlorophyll and carotene.

The leaves of this remarkable legume contain the eight essential amino acids.

Alfalfa

Main functions

Alfalfa is a good laxative and a natural diuretic. It is useful in the treatment of urinary tract infections and kidney, bladder and prostrate disorders. Alfalfa also alkalises and detoxifies the body, especially the liver, promotes pituitary gland function and contains an anti-fungus agent.

Alfalfa can be bought in many different ways all of which are beneficial, but the best all-round use of it is to sprout it yourself. In this way you can have fresh alfalfa sprouts every day and benefit from its many medicinal effects. Alfalfa sprouts are delicious – pack them into sandwiches and pitta breads instead of or as well as lettuce.

Algae

With the advent of intensive farming in the West and the progression of nutrient-depleted soils, there has been much interest in the benefits of blue-green micro-algae as a truly complete food form which comes from many unspoiled lakes around the world. The three main varieties that are now sold commercially as food supplements in their dried state are spirulina, chlorella and blue-green algae.

Main functions

Antioxidant, assists weight control, stimulates red blood cell formation, natural liver cleanser, aids colon irregularities, boosts the immune system, counteracts inflammatory conditions such as sore throats, ulcers, arthritis and gingivitis (gum disease), iron deficiency anaemia, depression and has uplifting qualities.

Spirulina, chlorella and blue-green algae all contain a broad spectrum of vitamins, minerals and other nutrients. Their protein content is highly absorbable; they possess more chlorophyll and nucleic acids than any other plant and are abundant in enzymes. Much of the healing properties of blue-green algae are put down to their chlorophyll content. Chlorophyll is the green pigment in plants that functions to collect and store energy from the sun. Because the chlorophyll molecule is almost identical to the haemoglobin molecule in red blood cells, it has become known as 'nature's blood'. Like haemoglobin, chlorophyll consists of a linked series of four carbon and nitrogen-containing rings (pyrrole rings). In haemoglobin the centre of the ring contains iron and in chlorophyll it is magnesium.

It has been shown that chlorophyll can stimulate the production of red cell formation in the blood. Foods rich in this substance have been used to treat iron deficiency anaemia with exceptional results. Chlorophyll has the added bonus of being rich in organic iron and promotes the growth of beneficial bacteria. Other benefits of chlorophyll include its ability to cleanse the body and aid colon disorders. It also helps to speed up wound healing.

Spirulina is rich in vitamin B12, containing more than twice the amount found in liver. It also has 58 times more iron than raw spinach and is particularly high in beta-carotene and many other antioxidant nutrients. Spirulina also provides one of the highest sources of gamma-linolenic acid (GLA) and contains all eight of the essential amino acids, making it a favourite supplement for athletes wanting to maintain lean muscle mass and a healthy muscle to fat ratio.

Spirulina is beneficial for weight control, not only because it nourishes the body so completely that it thwarts the craving for excessive food intake, but because it contains high levels of phenylalanine, an amino acid that curbs the appetite. Russian scientists have discovered that spirulina contains thyroxin factors which may nourish the thyroid, normalise the metabolism and promote weight loss.

Chlorella can protect the liver from toxic damage by way of a substance called ethionine. Chlorella contains slightly less protein than spirulina, but it contains four times as much chlorophyll, which contributes to its powerful detoxifying properties. Its cell walls can bind to toxic substances in the body and carry them out of the system. These toxic substances not only include uranium, lead, cadmium and mercury but insecticides and pesticides. The substance ethionine is a compound that prevents the build up of fatty tissue in the liver. Chlorella possesses a greater quantity of essential fatty acids than other forms of micro-algae and about 20 per cent of these are the omega 3 variety. Being a good source of vitamin B12, iron and zinc, vegans and vegetarians, the elderly and those recovering from illness can benefit from supplementation.

Blue-green algae is grown wild in the mineral rich waters of Klamath Lake in Oregon, USA. The algae contains a range of all the essential amino acids, almost identical to the balance required for human health. It is valued for its potent antioxidant properties, high levels of B12, trace minerals, and substances called sulpholipids, which have the ability to inhibit the spread of viruses.

Blue-green algae can be used to alleviate depression and mental or physical sluggishness. It contains low molecular weight peptides, which are precursors of neurotransmitters, responsible for firing and calming the brain. Because of its effect on the mind, small daily dosages are recommended at first, which can then be built on over a period of several weeks. The elderly have reported a return of mental alertness after taking blue-green algae, and it has been known to arrest the degenerative process of Alzheimer's disease.

Blue-green algae has also been shown to be useful in the treatment of certain neurostimulant addictions, such as cocaine and amphetamines. This is because it stimulates the opening of neural pathways and provides a healthy, natural energising effect. Because of its uplifting qualities, wild blue-green algae should be used with caution in those with a frail or sensitive constitution. Spirulina or chlorella in these instances would be more appropriate. However, it can be excellent for those with a sluggish metabolism, those who are overweight or where there are signs of dietary excess.

A comparison between some of the nutrients in spirulina, chlorella and blue-green algae

100 gram samples (dry weight)	Spirulina	Chlorella	Blue-green algae
Protein	68%	55%	60%
Beta-carotene	250,000 ius	55,000 ius	70,000 ius
Iron	58mg	133mg	130mg
Chlorophyll	0.7–1.1%	7%	3–6%
RNA/DNA	4.5%	13%	N/A

Barley grass – Hordeum vulgare

Main functions

Respiratory infections, lowers cholesterol levels, immune stimulant, natural cleanser, and stimulates blood circulation – particularly to the peripherals.

Young cereal grasses have long been recommended as a part of a cleansing and detoxifying diet but in addition they are extremely rich in vitamins, minerals, proteins and enzymes as well as containing high levels of chlorophyll, the pigment which gives all plants their green colour.

Wheat and barley, common cereal grains, start as short grasses. The plants grow slowly throughout the winter, accumulating and storing vitamins and minerals in their leaves. This grass stage lasts for about 200 days and as the plants reach their nutritional peak in the spring, they begin to form a joint which will go on to produce the stalk of grain. Once jointing occurs, the nutrient levels drop dramatically. These stored nutrients are not needed for the production of the grain so the grass is usually harvested just before jointing, using only the top three inches of the plant which is the most nutritious part. The leaves are then spray dried at low temperature and turned into tablets and powders.

Barley grass is said to be the only vegetation on the earth that can supply sole nutritional support from birth to old age. Barley has served as a food staple in most cultures. The use of barley for food and medicinal purposes dates to antiquity. Agronomists place this ancient cereal grass as being cultivated as early as 7000 BC. Roman gladiators ate barley for strength and stamina. In the West, it was first known for the barley grain it produces.

Barley grass is one of the richest natural sources of the enzyme superoxide dismutase (SOD). This is an antioxidant, which occurs naturally in the body and protects against free radical damage. Known as the anti-ageing enzyme, it is found in every single cell of the body and studies have shown that it can help repair damaged DNA which may help to slow down the ageing process.

Astounding amounts of vitamins and minerals are found in green barley leaves. The leaves have an ability to absorb nutrients from the soil. When barley leaves are 12–14 inches high, they contain many vitamins, minerals and proteins necessary for the human diet, plus chlorophyll. These are easily assimilated throughout the digestive tract, giving our bodies instant access to vital nutrients. These include potassium, calcium, magnesium, iron, copper, phosphorus, manganese, zinc, beta carotene, B1, B2, B6, vitamin C, folic acid, and pantothenic acid. Indeed, green barley juice contains 11 times the calcium in cows' milk, nearly five times the iron in spinach, seven times the vitamin C in oranges and 80mg of vitamin B12 per hundred grams.

Barley also contains a glucan, a fibre also found in oat bran and reported to reduce cholesterol levels. The root contains the alkaloid hordenine, which stimulates peripheral blood circulation and has been used as a bronchodilator for bronchitis. Barley bran, like wheat bran, may be effective in protecting against the risk of cancer.

Many health food stores sell dried barley powder to make up into a drink or as tablets, which is also an excellent way of obtaining this wonderful health food, but nothing compares to the real thing. The next time you visit London go to Planet Organic where they will prepare a shot of fresh green barley grass for you to drink on the spot. Make it your first call before your shopping trip, and you will still be going strong at the end of the day!

Bee pollen

Main functions

Enhances fertility, antioxidant, enhances vitality, natural tonic, strengthens the immune system, natural antihistamine, regulates blood pressure and assists weight loss, colitis and constipation.

Honey bees produce not only bee pollen, but also propolis, honey, royal jelly, beeswax and venom. The Bible, the Koran and ancient writings from Greece, Rome and Russia all mention and praise bee pollen as a superfood, possessing many health giving and medicinal qualities.

Bee pollen contains the male gametes of plants found as small dust pellets in the stamen of flowers. It is gathered from pollen-laden bees by a special device placed at the entrance of the hive designed to brush the material from their hind legs. Bee pollen has been called nature's perfect food. It is very rich in vitamins and contains almost all known minerals, trace elements, enzymes and amino acids. It contains the essence of every plant from which bees collect pollen, in combination with digestive enzymes from the bees.

Bee pollen contains a broad spectrum of nutrients, including all of those required by the human body. It is made up of approximately 25 per cent complete protein, consisting of at least 18 amino acids. This makes it a better class of protein than beef. Pollen also provides more than a dozen vitamins, 28 minerals, 11 enzymes, 14 beneficial fatty acids and 11 carbohydrates.

These combinations of elements make bee pollen an excellent source of antioxidants. Research studies and clinical tests have demonstrated that bee pollen not only has an immunising effect but enhances vitality, and can counteract the effects of radiation and chemical toxins.

Used as an immune system builder, bee pollen is thought to have the ability to correct body chemistry and eliminate unhealthy conditions. It is considered to have the ability to throw off poisons and toxic materials from the body. Radiation and chemical pollutants are known as the most severe stressors to your immune system. Side effects of radiation treatment decrease the body's production of blood cells and nutrients in the blood.

Bee pollen is rapidly absorbed into the blood stream and stimulates immunological responses. It has proved beneficial for nausea, sleep disorders, and urinary and rectal disorders following radiation treatment.

Athletes often use this supplement to help increase their strength, endurance energy and speed. Bee pollen aids the body in recovering from exercise, returning breathing and heart rate to normal, and improves endurance for repeat exertion. It provides energy, stamina and strength as well as improving mental and physical reactions.

Those who do taxing mental work also can see benefits from this natural energy food. Bee pollen can relieve brain fatigue and improve alertness. This can increase your capacity for intense concentration and enable longer periods of work without becoming tired. Stress can use up vitamins quickly and bee pollen can relieve stress and anxiety by replacing essential nutrient reserves in the body.

Many people with allergies have found relief by ingesting bee pollen. It reduces the production of histamine which can cause allergic responses such as hay fever. It can strengthen the respiratory system and provide protein that can help the body build a natural defence shield against allergic responses.

Bee pollen has an effect on blood pressure and sexual function. People who suffer from low blood pressure can be subject to deficiencies in the sex glands. Pollen increases blood pressure especially when taken with kelp and may increase hormone levels and sexual strength.

Weight loss may also occur as lecithin, an ingredient in bee pollen, increases the speed calories are burned and stabilises poor metabolism. It aids in the digestive process and the assimilation of nutrients. Bee pollen may also relieve anaemia, cerebral haemorrage, colitis and constipation.

Cabbage

Main functions

Anti-bacterial, anti-viral, heals stomach ulcers, manages oestrogen, prevents colon cancer and fights against stomach and other cancers.

The indoles in cabbage, and the other cruciferous vegetables, accelerate a process in which the body deactivates or disposes of the type of oestrogen that can promote breast cancer. Cabbage is rich in vitamins A, B, C, K and E, potassium, sulphur and copper plus a variety of antioxidants.

Oestrogen is a known promoter of breast cancer, thus all women, but especially women with breast cancer and pre-menopausal women, should try to reduce the oestrogen circulating in their bodies, the oestrogens that may promote cancers. Cabbage and other cruciferous vegetables, such as broccoli, as well as wheat bran, have accelerated the metabolism of such oestrogen in human studies. Both foods tended to deplete body oestrogen supplies that could otherwise feed cancer. It is recommended that all women may want to try to lower circulating oestrogen by eating raw cruciferous vegetables, cabbage, broccoli, cauliflower, kale and turnips as well as wheat bran foods.

In addition cabbage contains natural anti-ulcer drugs. In the 1950s Garnett Cheney MD, a professor of medicine at Stanford University School of Medicine, showed that cabbage could help heal ulcers. He demonstrated that just over 1½ pints (850ml) of fresh cabbage juice every day relieved pain and healed both gastric and duodenal ulcers better and faster than standard treatments did. In a test of 55 patients who drank cabbage juice, 95 per cent felt better within two to five days. X-rays and gastroscopy revealed a rapid healing of gastric ulcers in only one-quarter of the average time. The duodenal ulcers of patients fed cabbage also healed in one-third the usual time.

In a double-blind study of 45 inmates at San Quentin Prison in California, 93 per cent of the ulcers in prisoners taking cabbage juice concentrate in capsules – the equivalent of just over 1½ pints (850ml) of fresh cabbage juice every day – were healed after three weeks. Only 32 per cent of the ulcers healed in those taking a placebo. It works by seemingly strengthening the stomach lining's resistance to acid attacks. Cabbage contains gefarnate, a compound used as an anti-ulcer drug, as well as a chemical that resembles carbenoxolone, another infrequently used anti-ulcer drug. Essentially, the drugs incite cells to spin out a thin mucus barrier as a shield against acid attacks. G. B. Singh, of India's Central Drug Research Institute in Lucknow, induced ulcers in guinea pigs and cured them with cabbage juice. During the healing he took extensive microscopic photos of the cell changes, documenting that cabbage juice generated increased mucus activity that rejuvenated ulcerated cells leading to healing.

Another possibility is that cabbage is an antibiotic. It can destroy a variety of bacteria in test tubes, perhaps including *H.Pylori* bacteria, now implicated as a cause of ulcers. In studies, eating cabbage more than once a week cut men's colon cancer odds by 66 per cent. As little as two daily tablespoons of cooked cabbage protected against stomach cancer.

Remember what your mothers and grandmothers told you about throwing away the cabbage water? So now you know – never throw away the water but make the gravy with it or better still drink it. For best results raw cabbage, as in a coleslaw, is the most beneficial, or very lightly steamed. Chinese cabbage is said to have even more beneficial properties.

Honey

Main functions

Anti-microbial and anti-bacterial – stimulates the immune system, used to treat stomach ulcers, varicose and skin ulcers, wounds, burns, sore throats, acne, eczema and boils.

Honey is manufactured in one of the world's most efficient factories, the beehive. Bees may travel as far as 55,000 miles and visit more than two million flowers to gather enough nectar to make just a pound of honey. It is the most popular of the bee products.

Honey is primarily composed of fructose, glucose, maltose, and water. It also contains other sugars as well as small amounts of trace enzymes, minerals, vitamins and amino acids. Honey can both destroy harmful bacteria that could be causing digestive upset and promote beneficial bacteria in the gut.

There is no doubt that honey has healing properties. Its use can be traced back to Egyptian times. However, the therapeutic activity of honey differs according to which types of flowers the nectar has been gathered from. Honey can be made from clover, eucalyptus, and lavender to name just three. There are certain honeys that are particularly high in anti-bacterial properties, the most notably active being Manuka (or tea tree) honey from New Zealand.

Manuka honey can be effective against the *H.pylori* bacteria that is implicated in peptic ulcers. Active Manuka honey is also effective in treating bacterial gastroenteritis in infants and there is evidence that some strains of honey are prebiotic (stimulates the activity of the body's own existing good bacteria). Honey is not the only superfood that has these gut flora boosting properties – other foods include chicory, artichoke, garlic, onion, leek, asparagus, peaches and bananas.

Used topically, honey can be applied to burns, varicose and skin ulcers, wounds, acne, eczema and boils. Excellent results were found in recent clinical trials held in New Zealand when active Manuka honey was used on previously unresponsive skin ulcers and wounds.

Other research in its early stages has found that New Zealand honeys have useful levels of antioxidants, with active Manuka honey having the highest of all. This is why it was chosen as a superfood; it is used to stimulate the immune system, helping the body deal with infections. For sore throats or at the onset of a cold, honey can be taken neat or mixed with a little warm water and swallowed. A little lemon juice added to the honey will make it even more effective.

The quality of honey can vary in its potency, depending on production. It is advisable to purchase products that have not been subjected to heat treatment as part of their processing. Heating honey above hive temperature of 36°C destroys many of its active ingredients and alters the nature of the sugars in the raw material. Raw, cold-pressed honey is the best to buy.

Liquorice – Glycyrrhiza glabra

Licorice is a perennial herb native to southern Europe, Asia and the Mediterranean. It is extensively cultivated in Russia, Spain, Iran and India. It is one of the most popular and widely consumed herbs in the world.

Main functions

Anti-viral, benefits respiratory tract infections – coughs, hoarseness, sore throat, bronchitis and anti-ulcer properties.

Liquorice

Although mainly known for its flavouring in sweets, liquorice also contains many health benefits. Ancient cultures on every continent have used liquorice, the first recorded use by the Egyptians was in the third century BC. The Egyptians and the Greeks recognised the herb's benefits in treating coughs and lung disease. Liquorice is the second most prescribed herb in China followed by ginseng, it is suggested for treatment of the spleen, liver and kidney. The Japanese use a liquorice preparation to treat hepatitis.

The most common medical use for liquorice is for treating upper respiratory ailments including coughs, hoarseness, sore throat and bronchitis. The main constituent found in the root is glycyrrhizin. The plant also contains various sugars (14 per cent), starches (30 per cent), flavonoids, saponoids, sterols, amino acids, gums, and essential oil. Glycyrrhizin stimulates the secretion of the adrenal cortex hormone aldosterone.

It can be as effective as codeine, and safer, when used as a cough suppressant. Rhizomes in liquorice have a high mucilage content which, when mixed with water or used in cough drops, soothes irritated mucous membranes. The herb also has an expectorant effect, which increases the secretion of the bronchial glands. Liquorice is an effective remedy for throat irritations, lung congestion and bronchitis.

Homeopathic use of liquorice for gastric irritation dates back to the first century. Today, herbal preparations are used to treat stomach and intestinal ulcers, lower acid levels and coat the stomach wall with a protective gel. Rarely used alone, it is a common component of many herbal teas, as a mild laxative, a diuretic and for flatulence. It has also been known to relieve rheumatism and arthritis, regulate low blood sugar and is effective for Addison's disease. The root extract produces mild oestrogenetic effects and it has proven useful in treating symptoms of menopause regulating menstruation and relieving menstrual cramps.

The main ingredient, glycyrrhizin, has also been studied for its anti-viral properties in the treatment of AIDS. In clinical trials in Japan it prevented progression of the HIV virus by inhibiting cell infection and inducing interferon activity. Glycyrrhizin also encourages the production of hormones such as hydrocortisone, which give it anti-inflammatory properties. Like cortisone, it can relieve arthritic and allergy symptoms without side effects.

The constituent glycyrrhizin is 50 times sweeter than sugar, making it a widely used ingredient in the food industry. The distinctive flavour of liquorice makes it a popular additive to baked confectionery, liqueurs, ice cream and sweets. It is also widely used in other medicines to mask bitter tastes and also to prevent pills from sticking together. Take care as some liquorice sweets are not the real thing – they may be flavoured with anise, which does not have liquorice's therapeutic effects.

Medicinal mushrooms

Main functions

Immune enhancement, combats viruses and bacteria, protects the body from cancer, increase energy, wards off hunger, extends longevity and promotes overall vitality and virility, lowers blood cholesterol levels, balances blood pressure and inhibits platelet aggregation (thus reducing the likelihood of heart disease).

Another line of research has indicated that shiitake extracts may assist in the treatment of AIDS, herpes, and other viral conditions. Shiitake may also help to prevent or treat hepatitis and other liver conditions, chronic fatigue syndrome, influenza, tuberculosis, environmental allergies, bronchial inflammation, Hodgkin's disease and stomach ulcers.

Some species of mushrooms seem to possess certain immune-enhancing properties which, although scientists do not yet fully understand them, may hold potential for the treatment of cancer and other diseases. The medicinal mushrooms include shiitake (*Lentinus edodes*), maitake (*Grifola frondosa*) and reishi (*Ganoderma Lucidum*).

Unlike blue-green algae, spirulina and chlorella, mushrooms lack chlorophyll, which means they cannot make food from sunlight like other plants but must absorb nutrients from the surrounding medium such as soil, decaying wood and other forest waste material.

Many of our forests would not exist without mushrooms growing amongst the roots of trees. They help their hosts to obtain mineral nutrients, resist disease and survive in conditions of drought. Fungi also have an important role to play in the role of nutrient recycling. By decaying wood and other forest wastes, they release minerals and nutrients for use by a great variety of other organisms.

Shiitake mushrooms

Studies indicate that shiitake extracts can boost the immune system and combat viruses and bacteria. Shiitake protects the body from cancer and may even shrink existing tumours, and extracts have been successfully tested in recent years in Japan as an adjunct to chemotherapy. Researchers have found that cancer patients administered shiitake have increased survival times and more positive outcomes.

Shiitake mushroom

Shiitake is a rich source of various vitamins and minerals, amino acids, enzymes, fibre and nucleic acid derivatives. It contains the solid plant alcohol ergosterol, which can be converted by sunlight into Vitamin D. Much of the research into shiitake has focused on its polysaccharides, especially lentinan, which are found in both the fruiting body and the mycelium. Lentinan is thought to be crucial to the mushroom's ability to inhibit cancer, primarily by stimulating certain types of white blood cells prominent in immune function rather than by directly attacking cancer cells. Shiitake's anti-viral effects may be due to its ability to induce the production of interferon in the body. The amino acid compound eritadenine may be responsible for helping to reduce blood levels of cholesterol and fats by promoting their excretion.

Maitake mushrooms

The maitake mushroom is native to north-east Japan and has been prized in Japanese herbology for hundreds of years to strengthen the body and improve overall health. Recent research indicates that it is the most potent immunostimulant of all mushrooms. The compounds contained in maitake have the capacity not only to stimulate immune function but also to inhibit tumour growth. These compounds include polysaccharides (such as beta-glucan) and high-molecular weight sugar polymers. Polysaccharides are complex natural sugars of plant origin that typically boost the immune system. Popular herbal immune stimulants like echinacea and astralagus also contain polysaccharides. A fraction obtained from maitake – D-fraction – has been found very effective as an anti-tumour agent when administered orally.

Reishi mushrooms

Traditional Chinese medicine (TCM) values reishi as the highest ranked medicine. Among 365 species in Seng Nong's Herbal Classic, regarded as the cornerstone of TCM, the reishi mushroom is ranked as number one. Reishi is an ancient and revered herb, effective for calming the nervous system, strengthening the blood and cardiovascular system, and supporting the immune system, especially for people who have cancer and are undergoing western treatments like chemotherapy and radiation therapy.

In China it is called Ling Chi – the Mushroom of Immortality. Recent medical research has indicated that reishi mushrooms are useful for treating a host of diseases including hepatitis, bronchitis, bronchial asthma, coronary disease, gastric ulcers, stomach ache and migraine.

With their ancient heritage, these simple, basic superfoods appear to have immense potential for human health and may even hold the key to some of the world's most serious diseases.

Reishi mushroom

Nuts
Main functions

Nuts reduce LDL cholesterol levels, can help maintain strong teeth and bones, reduce the risk of coronary artery disease, boost levels of omega 3 fatty acids, reduce the effects of free radicals, boost brain power and concentration and supports the immune system.

Nuts are one of the food groups we tend to avoid because of their high fat and calorie content; however, they are a very nutrient-dense food and quantity of nutrients should also take priority over quantity of calories. Nuts make an easy, highly nutritious snack food, but they can also be ground into milk that relieves intestinal spasm and inflammation in cases of irritable bowel syndrome. They are ideal for sprinkling over breakfast cereal to make breakfast into a more balanced meal.

Almonds

Of all the different variety of nuts, almonds have the highest calcium content. They also contain essential fatty acids, the vitamins A and B and the minerals magnesium, phosphorus and potassium. Almonds help maintain strong bones and teeth because of its calcium and phosphorus content, but research has shown above all that almonds lower LDL cholesterol. One study found a 12 per cent decrease in LDL levels in people consuming 100mg of almonds a day for just nine weeks. Although all nuts have the ability to lower cholesterol levels, almonds have the most dramatic effect.

Brazil nuts

Brazil nuts have the highest concentration of selenium, containing as much as 250 times that of most foods, making them a high anti-oxidant food. They also contain vitamin E, which assists in supporting your immune system, and the essential fatty acids that assist in lowering LDL cholesterol levels and reducing the effects of free radical damage.

Chestnuts

Chestnuts contain Vitamins B, C and the minerals iron, magnesium, potassium and zinc; they are particularly beneficial for the blood and circulatory system and relieve dyspepsia. Chestnuts are a good nut to choose for the elderly and for convalescents, as when cooked, they become soft and easy to eat. They benefit those prone to varicose veins and hemorrhoids.

Hazelnuts

Hazelnuts are high in calcium, phosphorus, copper, iron, magnesium, potassium, sulphur and essential fatty acids. Hazelnuts also contain good levels of folic acid, making them a good snack in pregnancy. They also contain high boron levels, which not only assists the absorption of calcium but is an exceptional brain food, stimulating electrical activity in the brain. The essential fatty acids and fibre make it another good snack or something to add to breakfast cereals which would add balance and extra energy. Hazelnuts are recommended for people who are prone to kidney or gall bladder stones. They may also help to dispose of intestinal worms by taking 1 tablespoon of cold-pressed hazelnut oil every morning on an empty stomach for 15 days!

Peanuts

Fresh peanuts taken fresh from the shell (not salted peanuts) contain vitamins B and E, trace elements, amylase and the antioxidant resveratrol. Peanuts contain the enzyme amylase which is especially beneficial for the digestive system, in particular for those suffering with dyspepsia. Peanuts are believed to be particularly helpful at lowering your risk of suffering a heart attack or stroke. The powerful antioxidant resveratrol, also found in red wine, prevents the oxidation of LDL cholesterol, a process that results in the deposit of cholesterol causing arteries to fur up. Peanuts are also effective insulin and blood sugar regulators, making them a good choice for anyone suffering from glucose intolerance or diabetes. Salted or dry roasted peanuts do not have the same beneficial effects as fresh peanuts taken from the shell.

Walnuts

Walnuts contain vitamins A, B and C, and the minerals copper, iron, magnesium, potassium, selenium, and zinc. They have the highest amounts of omega 3 fatty acids, which assists with the prevention of conditions such as psoriasis, eczema, arthritis and mental illness. They are also reported to be good for the elimination of intestinal parasites and for alleviating heart and circulatory problems.

Super sprouts

Main functions

Cleansing, anti-inflammatory, rejuvenating and immune boosting.

Sprouts are a rich source of vitamins, and a clean, cheap, uncontaminated food source. Bean sprouts, mung in particular, have been grown in the Far East for thousands of years, and are mentioned in Chinese writings dated around 2939 BC. At the end of the eighteenth century, their benefits in keeping illness at bay delighted Captain Cook when not a single man died of scurvy on the three-year voyage of the *Endeavour*. However, limes replaced this role and the sprout was soon forgotten in Europe.

Sprouting your own seeds is a quick, easy and incredibly cheap way of providing organic, fresh food bursting with vitality. Sprouted seeds are an almost perfect food. Grown easily at home they are the richest source of naturally occurring vitamins known. A mere tablespoon of alfalfa seeds will produce about 1kg of sprouts.

Sprouted seeds are incredibly versatile and are best eaten raw in salads, sandwiches or on their own. They can also be added to hot dishes such as soups or casseroles, but this should be done at the last minute to maintain their freshness and nutrient value. The larger legumes such as chickpeas and soya beans can be lightly steamed, which aids their digestibility, or added to curries and stews.

Upon germination, a seed rapidly absorbs water and swells to at least twice its original size. At the same time its nutrient content changes dramatically. The husk of the seed contains the embryo, which grows into both the root and the shoot, while the endosperm and cotyledons (the two halves which you can see inside a pea, seed or bean) become the food supply for the growing plant. During sprouting the content and activity of enzymes increase converting starch into simple sugars, protein into amino acids and fats into fatty acids. These processes in effect pre-digest the seed, making it much easier for us to break down and absorb. This is the reason why many sprouted grains and legumes are less likely to cause the allergic reactions that their non-sprouted counterparts can trigger.

The vitamin content of a sprout is particularly significant. Sprouted mung beans contain as much as 120mg of vitamin C per 100g compared with oranges, which have around 53mg. It has also been shown that the amount of B vitamins rise as a seed sprouts. The vitamin B2 content in an oat grain multiplies by 1300 per cent as soon as the seed germinates, although some Bs do not increase until the small plant grows leaves and starts to photosynthesise. Whether sprouts contain vitamin B12 appears to be a moot point, although most sprouted cereals are said to possess trace amounts. The fat-soluble vitamins A D and E are also present. Minerals, which are in abundant supply, combine with amino acids to form chelates. These significantly increase their uptake and use in the body. While the protein content in vegetables is not significant, sprouts are an exception. A bean or seed's protein value actually diminishes as it germinates, but a sprout is still a valid source as it builds new protein from stored nutrients within the seed.

Soya sprouts are the only ones to contain all eight essential amino acids. For people who follow a diet of food combining, i.e. not mixing protein foods with starch, sprouts bring an added bonus of being a 'neutral' so that they can be eaten with either.

Because they contain an excellent balance of amino acids, fatty acids and natural sugars, plus a high content of minerals, sprouts are capable of sustaining life on their own, provided several kinds are eaten together. They are also the cheapest form of foods around. In an age when most vegetables and fruits are grown on artificially fertilised soils and treated with hormones, DDT, fungicides, insecticides, preservatives and all manner of other chemicals, home-grown sprouts emerge as unadulterated, fresh, unpolluted and marvellous-tasting food grown in just a few days.

Common seeds for sprouting are alfalfa, mung beans, aduki beans, wheat, barley, fenugreek, lentils, mustard, oats, pumpkin seeds, sesame seeds, sunflower seeds and soya beans. Most supermarkets now sell ready sprouted seeds. Try a few different ones in salads and as additions to your sandwiches and then experiment and try sprouting your own.

How to sprout

Small commercial sprouters are available in health food stores and usually comprise four small trays stacked upon each other with a selection of seeds and beans and a set of instructions – they make ideal unusual presents. Alternatively, you can use a standard seed tray, a colander or sieve.

1   Place a handful of your selected seeds or beans in a bowl, cover with cold water and leave them to soak overnight. Most seeds will expand up to eight times their size so be generous with the water and totally submerge them.

☼ **Activity**

Have a go! Plan your sprouting to coincide with one of your lessons, and bring your sprouted seeds along for the class to try. If you are in a group, all choose a different seed and have a sprout-swapping party

2   The following morning, drain off the water, rinse well and lay the seeds in the base of the sprouter.

3   Either leave on the window sill (this is what I do) or place in an airing cupboard. The seeds need to be rinsed thoroughly at least once a day, preferably twice.

4   Continue to rinse the seeds daily until ready to harvest. After about three to five days you should have a crop of sprouts. Once they are the right size for eating, give them one final rinse and store them in the fridge to stop them from growing any further.

Sprout harvesting times

Seed/sprout	Harvest time in days
Alfalfa	5–7
Aduki beans	4–6
Barley	3–4
Chickpeas	4
Fenugreek	4–5
Flageolet beans	3–5
Green lentils	3–5
Green peas	3–5
Mung beans	2–3
Radish	4–5
Rye	3–5
Soya beans	3–6
Sunflower seeds	4–6
Wheat	2–4

Yoghurt – probiotics and prebiotics

Main functions

Maintains a healthy digestive tract restoring total health to the ecology of our gastointestinal systems, supports the immune system, guards against cancer, combats yeast overgrowth and fungal infections such as *Candida Albicans*, prevents constipation, diarrhoea, flatulence and bloating, protects against osteoporosis and rheumatoid arthritis, overcomes skin problems, lowers cholesterol levels and enhances nutritional status.

No book on nutrition or indeed a chapter on superfoods could be complete without mention of probiotics. Probiotics means 'for life', the opposite of antibiotics which means 'against life'. When we take even one course of antibiotics, the harmful bacteria in our intestines are destroyed together with the beneficial bacteria resulting in a suppressed immune system. Of all the superfoods mentioned thus far, the probiotics must I feel take priority place. The roles they play in our bodies are quite amazing.

At the turn of the century a scientist named Elie Metchnikoff proposed that yoghurt was the elixir of life because it contained a strain of bacteria known as *Lactobacillus* that purportedly cleared the large intestine of toxins. We now know that two particular species of probiotics, *Lactobacillus bulgaricus* and *Streptococcus thermophilus,* are the primary cultures in yoghurt, and make it a supremely healthy food by combating certain bad bacteria and improving lactose tolerance. These two strains work together and combine their unique powers to defend the gut from potentially harmful bacteria.

Yoghurt is an ancient wonder food, strongly anti-bacterial and anti-cancer. Eight ounces (225g) taken on a daily basis can boost the immune function by stimulating production of gamma interferon. As well as the vitally important beneficial culture yoghurt contains, it is also a good source of absorbable calcium. There have now been thousands of studies confirming that probiotics are indispensable in keeping us healthy by cleansing our intestines of excess pathogens, thus preventing allergies, yeast infections, diarrhoea, gas, bloating and digestive problems.

The good flora also manufacture B-vitamins, such as biotin, B3, B6 and folic acid and by providing the enzyme lactase they enhance, and indeed allow, the digestion of milk-based foods and the vital calcium which they contain, for people who cannot otherwise digest milk. They help considerably to enhance bowel function. Where bowel bacteria are absent, the function of peristalsis is impaired, and the amount of time it takes for food to pass completely through the system is much increased. The beneficial bacterial also act as anti-carcinogenic (anti-cancer) factors with powerful anti-tumour potentials.

Problems usually begin after a course of antibiotics when beneficial bacteria is killed and not replaced. This good flora needs to be replaced after every course of antibiotics we take. Probiotics is all about the use of specially cultured friendly bacteria and yoghurt is one way of getting some of this good flora back into your system. Unfortunately it is impossible to know exactly how many live cultures are in the yoghurt you are eating and they may only provide a couple of hundred bacteria per pot. This is fine if you are just keeping topped-up with friendly bacteria, but if you have been on a course of antibiotics, and especially if you have had concurrent courses of antibiotics, you need to replace the billions of destroyed bacteria as soon as possible. These need to come in the form of a good supplement. Always choose probiotics from human origin – and follow storage instructions carefully. Once opened the probiotics need to be refrigerated.

Many babies and children are given multiple courses of antibiotics, some even before they are one year old, suppressing an immature immune system. Antibiotics can be life saving but whenever they are used, you should always follow up with a course of probiotics. Children's formulas are available from all good health food stores.

Activity

How many of these superfoods have you tried?

Introduce one new food every week and make notes for discussion on the nutritional value of the foods you have chosen, how you prepared the food, and how much you enjoyed it. Try all the foods in this chapter, plus others like pumpkin seeds, sunflower seeds, any new fruit or vegetable, dried apricots, game, or absolutely anything you have never tried before – be adventurous!!

Prebiotics

Probiotics and prebiotics work in different ways to achieve the same end – keeping numbers of good bacteria up so that they outweigh pathogenic bacteria. Probiotics deliver ready made good bacteria to the body whereas prebiotics stimulate the activity of the body's own existing good bacteria. Each of us carries 1kg of bacteria in our body of which 95 per cent are beneficial. If the balance of these flora changes gut dysbiosis results and digestive disorders, stomach upsets, food poisoning and worse can arise. Numerous clinical trails show the benefits of probiotics and prebiotics in aiding digestion, stimulating gastrointestinal immunity, and relieving IBS symptoms.

Knowledge review

Superfoods

1 What superfood would you consider for a vegan or strict vegetarian?

2 Honey can be described as a prebiotic. What are prebiotics and what other foods come into this category?

3 Which superfood is anti-bacterial, anti-viral, and heals stomach ulcers?

4 Which of the superfoods has anti-viral properties, and benefits respiratory tract infections?

5 What are the main functions of bee pollen?

6 Unlike blue-green algae, spirulina and chorella, mushrooms lack chlorophyll. Where do these medicinal mushrooms obtain their healing properties?

7 Which of the superfoods is one of the richest sources of the enzyme SOD?

8 In addition to bee pollen, what other products come from bees?

9 Which nuts have the highest calcium content?

10 List six common seeds suitable for sprouting.

The balanced diet, food energy values, contraindications and food myths

6

Learning objectives

This chapter covers the following:

- **the definition of health**
- **what is meant by a healthy, balanced diet**
- **contraindications to nutritional therapy**
- **food energy values**
- **some common food myths**

Having studied the main nutrients, herbal remedies and super foods you can start thinking about how to combine them to give a healthy, well balanced diet.

The foods you choose to eat and the combinations in which you eat them have a huge impact on your overall health. Your role as a nutritional therapist is to offer advice to develop and educate healthy eating habits for your clients, and in so doing improving their health status.

Being healthy is much more than the opposite of being ill. The World Health Organisation's definition of health is: 'A state of complete social, mental and physical well-being and not merely the absence of disease or infirmity.'

What is a balanced diet?

A balanced diet is one that contains the nutrients needed, in their correct proportions, to provide an adequate provision of energy taking into account, age, sex, occupation, activity levels and current health, to gain and maintain health.

However, although we all have our different likes and dislikes and are all biochemically very different, we have to have an average base point upon which to work. The example of a balanced diet below is for an average person. There are classes of people who do not fall into average. They usually need more specialised advice, and are unlikely to be included in the syllabus you are working to. Check with your awarding body and your insurance. Here is the example of a balanced diet for 'average' people.

- 55 per cent from carbohydrates foods
- 15 per cent from protein foods
- 30 per cent from fats which can be broken down into 3 × 10 per cent groups:
  - 10 per cent polyunsaturated fats (most beneficial for health)
  - 10 per cent monounsaturated (fats that should be used in cooking) – olive oil
  - 10 per cent saturated fats (those solid at room temperature and the least important – if fats are to be reduced, they should be reduced from this section).

What is meant by a healthy, well balanced diet.

55 per cent carbohydrates – 55 per cent of the total number of daily calories should come from this category of food. Working to a daily intake of 2,000 kcals this would give you a total of 1100 kcals coming from carbohydrate foods. Ideally, these calories should be spread throughout the day over breakfast, lunch and your evening meal.

15 per cent protein – 15 per cent of the total number of daily calories should come from this category of food. Working to a daily intake of 2,000 kcals, this would give you a total of 300kcals coming from protein foods. Ideally, these calories should be spread throughout the day, over breakfast, lunch and evening meal.

30 per cent fats – 30 per cent of the total number of daily calories should come from this category of food. Working to a daily intake of 2,000 kcals, this would give you a total of 600 kcals coming from fat sources. Ideally, these calories should be spread throughout the day, over breakfast, lunch and evening meal.

Guidelines for healthy eating

The Department of Health has issued eight guidelines for ensuring a healthy diet.

1   If you do drink alcohol stay within sensible limits. Adults should be careful about alcohol. Moderate drinking, such as a daily glass or two of red wine, may even be beneficial, but heavy drinking can cause irreversible damage and excessive drinking can be lethal.

2   Do not eat sugary foods too often. Sugar-rich foods and drinks are fine as a very small part of your diet but they provide few nutrients and are classed as 'empty calories'. Eating too many fills you up and so replaces foods which are nutritious and needed by the body.

3   Do not eat too much fat. Keep fat intake to a maximum of 30 per cent of your daily calories, preferably 25 per cent, with saturates being the lowest. Essential fatty acids are beneficial and should not be avoided.

Key Term

Anorexia nervosa

Psychological disturbance resulting in a refusal to eat; sensations of hunger are usually not felt and there may be a restriction of the diet to particular foods; the result is considerable weight loss, atrophy of tissue and a fall in the basal metabolic rate.

The balanced diet

Key Term

Bulimia nervosa

A psychiatric illness characterised by powerful and intractable urges to overeat, followed by self-induced vomiting and excessive use of purgatives. Mostly affects women between 15 and 30 – considered to be a variant of anorexia nervosa.

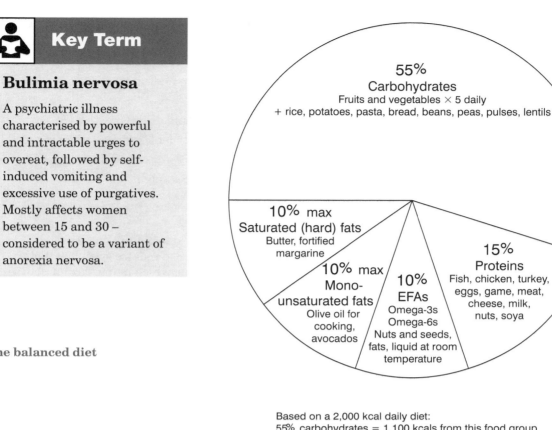

Based on a 2,000 kcal daily diet:
55% carbohydrates = 1,100 kcals from this food group
15% proteins = 300 kcals from this food group
30% fats = 300 kcals in total from 3 sub-groups
    10% = 100 kcals from saturated fats
    10% = 100 kcals from monounsaturated fats
    10% = 100 kcals from polyunsaturated fats (EFAs)

Key Term

Obesity

A body mass index (BMI) of over 30 is considered to be obese. A BMI of 40 or greater or 100 lbs or more overweight for an average adult is termed clinically severe obesity.

4   Eat fresh foods rich in vitamins and minerals. Nutritional therapists recommend everyone has a minimum of five servings of fruit and vegetables every day, preferably six.

5   Eat plenty of foods rich in fibre and starch. Foods rich in fibre and in starch contain important nutrients and also help to fill you up without having a high number of calories. Eating a high fibre diet will reduce your chances of getting colon cancer.

6   Eat the right amount to be healthy. Eating the right amount helps you to keep to a healthy weight, and provides optimum nutrition. Do not eat more than you need as obesity is a major contributor to ill health. Remember, we eat to live, not live to eat!

7   Eat a variety of different foods. This will help to ensure you have a wide range of all the necessary vitamins and minerals and guards against dietary imbalances and deficiencies.

8   Enjoy your food, it is one of life's pleasures! Enjoy the fact that it is giving you energy and making you healthy.

Contraindications to nutritional therapy

There are few contraindications to nutritional therapy, however, qualifications vary and you will need to check with your particular awarding body who exactly you may offer nutritional therapy to.

Activity

Consider as honestly as you can some of your own attitudes to eating food.

- Do you regularly try to lose weight?
- Are you happy with your eating and your attitudes to food?
- Do you eat regular meals?
- Do you eat breakfast?
- Do you usually eat with other people or alone?
- Do you ever eat out of boredom, or because you are upset or annoyed?
- Do you eat and then wish you had not!

Write down your thoughts and then discuss with a colleague or with your teacher.

Here is a list of contraindications that may apply to the qualification you are taking.

- Clients under 18 or over 70 years of age
- Clients currently undergoing medical treatment
- Clients with severe obesity
- Clients suffering with an eating disorder
- Clients who have a medically identified food intolerance
- Clients already on a medically prescribed diet
- Clients who are severely underweight
- Clients who are pregnant

Whilst the majority of the above would benefit from general recommendations in their diet, they also require specialist dietary and supplementary recommendations, which many shorter courses do not cover. To include the above list of clients, a three-year degree course may be required.

As a professional who is going to be working with the public and their diets, it is important to consider your own attitudes to food and to eating. Although we may develop different tastes and preferences as we grow older, our fundamental attitudes to food and to eating are formed in childhood. Before considering helping clients, it may be useful to consider your own eating habits and present views on food, dieting and eating.

Perhaps you feel you would like some professional help yourself before embarking on a course whereby you will be helping other people? We must be able to practise what we preach! Taking your health, through nutrition and exercise, into your own hands, will make you a more thorough nutritional therapist.

Food energy values (kcals/kJs)(food groups)

Remember

Choosing foods only by their calorific values is not nutritionally sound practice. The nutritional value of food must be considered in addition to the calorific value

A competent nutrition adviser must be able to calculate the energy available from any given food or group of foods.

A calorie is the amount of energy that is released as heat when food is metabolised. Scientists determine the number of calories in foods by burning them in a laboratory device called a calorimeter and measuring the amount of heat produced. The calorie is the amount of heat necessary to raise the temperature of one liter of water one degree celsius – 1 kilocalorie (kcal) = 4.2 kilojoules (kJ)

The process by which nutrients are broken down to yield energy or rearranged into body structures is known as metabolism. The amount of energy a food provides depends on how much carbohydrate, fat and protein it contains. When completely broken down in the body, a gram of carbohydrate yields 4 kcals of energy; a gram of protein; 4 kcals; a gram of fat; 9 kcals and alcohol yields 7 kcals per gram.

Although alcohol contributes 7 kcals per gram that can be used for energy, it is not considered a nutrient; a more accurate title would be an anti-nutrient, because it interferes with the body's growth, maintenance and repair. Alcohol can be regarded as 'empty calories' – calories without nutrients.

The nutrient content of different foods as compared to their caloric content is the basis of what nutritional therapists call nutrient density. Some foods are naturally healthy to consume, with a high nutrient value in relation to their calorie (energy) content. A fundamental rule of diet planning to promote health is to choose foods with a high nutrient density. Problems arise when needed nutrients are missing from a diet, as well as when too many calories are consumed for daily energy needs. Whole grains and beans provide enough B vitamins to help process the energy they contain, and are therefore of proper nutrient density. A white flour high-fat food may contain more calories than its nutrient value can handle and this robs health.

Activity

Staying with the example below, one slice of bread with 1 tablespoon of peanut butter, calculate the percentage of carbohydrate and protein in this snack.

How to calculate the kcals/energy from food

To calculate the energy available from a food, multiply the number of grams of carbohydrate, protein, and fat by 4, 4, and 9 respectively. Then add the results together. For example: 1 slice of bread with 1 tablespoon of peanut butter on it contains 16 grams of carbohydrate, 7 grams protein and 9 grams fat:

16 g carbohydrate × 4 kcal/g	= 64 kcals	(16 × 4)
7 g protein × 4 kcal/g	= 28 kcals	(7 × 4)
9 g fat × 9 kcal/g	= 81 kcals	(9 × 9)
	Total = 173 kcals	

Activity

A cup of fried rice contains 5 grams protein, 30 grams carbohydrate and 11 grams fat. Calculate the kcals/energy provided by the rice as kcals.

5 × 4 = 20 kcals protein

= kcals carbohydrate

= kcals fat

Total = kcals

How to calculate the percentage of individual macronutrients

From this information, you can calculate the percentage of kcals each of the energy nutrients contributes to the total. To determine the percentage of kcals from fat, for example, divide the 81 fat kcals by the total 173 kcals:

81 kcals fat divided by 173 total kcals = 0.468 (rounded to 0.47)

Then multiply by 100 to get the percentage: 0.47 × 100 = 47 per cent

Our slice of bread with a tablespoon of peanut butter therefore represents a 47 per cent fat content!

Our total daily intake from fats should not exceed 30 per cent of kcals and these kcals should be spread throughout the day. Knowing that this snack provides 47 per cent of its kcals from fat should alert you to recommend the client needs to make lower-fat selections throughout the rest of the day.

Food myths

We have all heard sayings referring to food and drink. Some are new

Activity

What percentage of the energy in the fried rice comes from each of the energy-yielding nutrients?

	=	% kcals from protein
	=	% kcals from carbohydrate
	=	% kcals from fat
Total	=	%

Note: the total should add up to 100 per cent; 99 per cent or 101 per cent due to rounding is also acceptable.

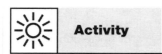

Activity

Calculate how many of the 146 kcals. provided by a 12-ounce can of beer comes from alcohol, if the beer contains 1 gram protein and 13 grams carbohydrate. (Hint: the remaining kcals derive from alcohol).

1 g protein	=	kcal protein
13g carbohydrate	=	kcal carbohydrate
	=	kcal alcohol

How many grams of alcohol does this represent?

g of alcohol

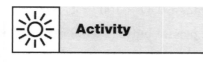

Activity

How many other food myths can you think of? Note down as many sayings about food, drink and eating as you can recall. Discuss them in class. Discuss if there is any element of truth in the sayings. How many new sayings have you learnt as a result of this exercise?

and some have been passed down through the generations; some are true but many can be misleading. Let's identify some of these myths and examine their accuracy.

Brown eggs are better for you than white – the nutrient content of an egg is totally unaffected by the colour of its shell.

Eating fat makes you fat – we all need some fat in the diet, and consuming essential fatty acids actually assists in weight loss. Eating too much of any food will make you fat.

Carrots help you see in the dark – carrots are high in beta-carotene, which is necessary for good night vision.

An apple a day keeps the doctor away – apples provide good dietary fibre – so there is a little truth in this old saying. However, a diet containing a variety of as many foods as possible is more likely to keep the doctor away.

Potatoes, pasta and bread are fattening – no, they are excellent sources of complex carbohydrate. It is the toppings we add to these foods that are usually fattening.

Moderation in all things – the recommendation of many expert committees on nutrition. Don't eat too much, or too little of anything and don't follow one of the extreme unorthodox regimes.

Variety is the spice of life – well, it's a good idea in relation to diet. Eating a wide variety of different foods help ensure you have a wide range of all the necessary nutrients.

One man's meat is another man's poison – referring to food sensitivity. Foods we love may make other people ill.

Enough is as good as a feast – more leads to obesity. People's energy requirements differ. 'Enough' is an individual amount.

Old habits die hard – food habits must be respected. Dietary recommendations are more likely to be followed if they can be fitted easily into the current diet. You will be more successful as a nutritional therapist if you recommend slow, gradual but permanent changes, rather than recommending too many changes all at once.

A little of what you fancy does you good – don't make your dietary recommendations more rigid than they need be. Moderation, flexibility and balance in all things, including diet, usually works well.

Knowledge review

The balanced diet, food energy values, contraindications and food myths

1. What is the WHO definition of health?

2. What is a balanced diet for the average adult?

3. White a short paragraph to explain the term 'balanced diet'.

4. Explain the term nutrient density.

5. The Department of Health has issued guidelines for ensuring a healthy diet. How many guidelines are there?

6. What are the Government's guidelines on drinking alcohol?

7. How many kcals per gram of alcohol can be used as energy? How can calories from this source be described?

8. List six classes of people who may fall outside the 'average' adult category and who may be considered contraindicated to nutritional therapy.

9. What is the recommended number of servings of fruits and vegetables that should be consumed each day?

10. What does 'moderation in all things' mean to you?

7 Food labels and conversion tables

Learning objectives

This chapter covers the following:

- **how to read food and product label information to make informed choices to promote healthy, balanced, and safe eating**

- **legal requirements of food labels**

Would you expect to find cream in cream crackers? Probably not, but you *would* expect fish to be in fish fingers; yet in many cases fish makes up less than half of the ingredients. As a nutritional therapist you must be able to read a food label accurately, and what the label doesn't tell you can be as important as what it does. The ability to understand and decipher food labels correctly can be the difference between making good or poor food choices. Food labelling is a huge subject and covering the topic comprehensively would fill a book on its own. This chapter covers the minimum you need to know.

It would be wonderful as a nutritional therapist to recommend that everyone eat fresh, organic, unadulterated foods, go shopping daily and prepare all meals from fresh raw ingredients. Unfortunately life is not like this, and we all succumb to buying processed foods, mostly because of price and convenience. But we still have a choice as to which processed foods we buy and how processed they actually are.

The laws on food labelling are under review all the time, and there are many consumer groups working endlessly to improve our food labels making them less complicated and giving us the information we need, not just what the manufacturer wants us to know. All consumers want is honest labelling and easy to read labels. Too much of the information given on products is misleading, inaccurate and incomplete. Examples of poor labelling include products such as 'mince and onions' whose main ingredient is actually mechanically recovered chicken and 'haddock fillets' made from several fish rather than single fillets. Meaningless adjectives such as 'premium', 'wholesome' or 'traditional' have also been criticised.

Key Term

MRM

Mechanically recovered meat (MRM) is the carcass scrapings removed from bones once the best meat has been removed.

There are two main areas to read on food labels:

- the list of ingredients
- nutrition information.

Ingredients' lists have always been a problem, but the nutritional information can also be misleading. Labels which advertise the merits of products that are 90 per cent fat free, disguise the fact that the product contains 10 per cent fat.

Legal requirements and food labelling

The law states a food label must:

- Give product information: what it is – the product's name is the main guide to what you're buying. The law states that the name of a food must not be misleading; however, it often is. Don't assume that a product name is a full guide to what it contains. For example, prawn crackers may contain no prawns and raspberry flavour milkshake probably won't contain raspberries. If a product states raspberry 'flavour' the chances are very high that they will be artificial flavours from the laboratory. However, raspberry flavour*ed* milkshake must be made from real raspberries – although there is no minimum to the percentage of raspberries!
- Country of origin.
- Address of the distributor or manufacturer.
- Net weight or volume of contents.
- List the ingredients the product contain: all ingredients are listed in descending order of content quantity, that means the heaviest first – so if water is the main ingredient, water will be first on the list. If you are buying a chicken pie, the only way to see how much chicken is actually in the pie is to look at the ingredients list. Quite often the chicken will be well down the list offering only 30 per cent of chicken in the product – not a good buy.
- Ensure the relevance of any pictures: illustrations and product description must reflect actual ingredient content. Many manufacturers give a picture of a 'suggested serving idea' showing the product alongside a healthy salad. This is often misleading.
- Give information for safe usage: storage and cooking instructions must be clear and a sell by, best before or use by date must be shown.

Fruit *flavour*
More than likely to be artificial flavours from the laboratory – raspberry flavour.

Fruit *flavou**red***
Must be made from the stated main ingredient – raspberry flavou**red**.

Alcohol

There is no law stating that alcohol must give an ingredients list, so we are denied the right to know what we are drinking.

Let's start looking at the nutrition information on labels and extracting what is needed to make the decision to buy the product or not.

Weight

Most labels will give you one or two sets of figures. One will almost definitely be figures relating to 100g of the food and the second may be a serving size of the product (which often is 100g or 3½ ozs) or may give the listing for the whole product. The first thing you need to do is to check the weight of the actual food portion you are going to consume. For example you may be reading a nutrition information list for 100g of food but the packet may be 400g – you would then need to multiply by four to get accurate figures for the whole product and then maybe divide by two if you were going to eat half the packet. A common mistake is to look at the calories, assume it for the whole product, eat the product, and then realise that the figures related to 'a suggested serving' of one quarter of what you have just consumed!

We often think of quiche as a healthy food with cheese and eggs as the main ingredients. Let us look at an example of a salmon and broccoli quiche and see just how healthy it is.

The first information you will see after the total kcals per 100g are figures for carbohydrates, protein and fat. The carbohydrates should also state 'of which are sugars' and the fats should state 'of which are saturates'. You should be able to calculate quickly the percentage of these foods compared to the total energy/kcals the product is offering. Labels can be very misleading, as we shall see.

Nutritional information

Typical composition	A 100g (3½ oz) serving provides:
Energy	1111kJ/267kcal
Protein	8.8g
Carbohydrate of which are sugars	17g 2.6g
Fat of which saturates Monounsaturates Polyunsaturates	18.2g 9.6g 6.8g 1.8g
Fibre	1.8g
Sodium	0.3g

Grams of food are difficult to visualise and percentages are often clearer for us to understand. Our daily requirement for a balanced diet, as detailed in Chapter 6, is approximately 55 per cent of our foods from carbohydrates, 15 per cent from proteins and 30 per cent from fats (10 per cent saturated, 10 per cent monounsaturated and 10 per cent polyunsaturated). Let's see the percentages this quiche offers us:

	Grams	Calculation	Total calories	% of total
Calories per serving			267	100
Total fat	18.2	18.2 × 9	163.8	62 (rounded)
Total protein	8.8g	8.8 × 4	32	12 (rounded)
Carbohydrate	17g	17 × 4	68	26 (rounded)
Total				**100**

This food is not a healthy choice is because of its high fat content. At a glance we can now see that there are almost 164 fat calories from the total 267 kcals for one small serving of quiche. Whilst total fat content of 18.2 per cent may sound acceptable, bearing in mind that 30 per cent of our daily calories may come from fats, once we have made the simple calculation we now see that the total fat is in fact 62 per cent of the product. As a product to be eaten on its own, it would be a very unbalanced food (55 per cent Carbohydrates, 15 per cent protein and 30 per cent total fats). We could, by adding carbohydrate in the form of salad or vegetables, make a more balanced meal, but the fact remains that it is a high saturated fat product.

Using the same calculation, we can also work out the percentages of the different types of fat:

	Grams	Calculation	Total calories	% of total
Calories per serving from fats			163.8	100
Saturated fats	9.6g	9.6 × 9	86.4	53 (rounded)
Monounsaturated fats	6.8g	6.8 × 9	61.2	37
Polyunsaturated fats	1.8g	1.8 × 9	16.2	10
Total				**100**

We now can see that the total figure for saturated fat is more than 50 per cent!

The next items on our list relate to fibre and sodium. The total fibre required by most adults per day is 35g – so this product with its meagre 1.8g per serving falls far short.

You need to note the sodium content as many people are on low salt diets. On the label for the salmon and broccoli quiche, the sodium is listed as 0.3g. The actual 'salt' content of one serving of this food is actually 0.8g. This was stated on the box, although in small lettering.

However, many products do not make this calculation for you and many people may confuse a 'sodium' figure, which will be low to a 'salt' figure which will be two and a half times higher.

The nutrition information table may then give you figures for vitamins and minerals usually stated as a percentage of the Daily Recommended Allowance, but remember that this falls far short of what we need for optimum health.

You may then need to refer to the ingredients list of the product to see if it contains any artificial sweeteners, colours, preservatives and flavours. Not all E numbers are bad and you need to learn which are good and which not so good. Ascorbic acid (vitamin C), for example, is a good antioxidant and takes the number E300, whereas tartrazine, E102, is an artificial colour which may cause hyperactivity in children.

Are artificial sweeteners safe?

Take a close look at many food labels and you will see the inclusion of artificial sweeteners in all kinds of foods. You will find them in soft drinks and desserts but also in savoury foods such as baked beans, pasta sauces and soups. There are two main types of artificial sweetener: the intense ones such as saccharin, aspartame, acefulfame-K and cyclamate, which are many times sweeter than sucrose and are used in very small concentrations. The second type are the bulk sweeteners which include sorbitol, isomalt and mannitol, which are the usual choice for diabetic and 'tooth friendly' foods. These bulk sweeteners are about as sweet as sucrose and hence are used in roughly the same proportions.

Despite their approval for use there are doubts over the safety of several artificial sweeteners. Why use them at all? Well, they are a fraction of the cost of sugar so, as often happens, profitability takes priority over the safety of the consumer.

- Acesulfame-K (trade name Sunett) is facing demands in the US for safety reassessment over fears that it might cause cancer.

- Aspartame (trade name NutraSweet) produces phenylalanine (a problem for suffers of phenylketonuria), though products now carry warning labels. Aspartame has been linked anecdotally to neurological problems and migraines, though this has not been proven and is disputed by the manufacturers.

- Saccharin is linked to bladder cancer in test animals. In the US products containing saccharin must carry the warning 'Use of this product may be hazardous to your health. This product contains saccharin, which has been determined to cause cancer in laboratory animals'. Some people, especially young children, may exceed 'safe' levels of consumption. People with diabetes and others who use tabletop sweeteners are also at risk of exceeding safe limits.

- Cyclamates were banned in 1968 because of cancer fears. They are now back despite research which shows they can shrivel the testicles of laboratory animals! They are now

Remember

All carbohydrates are broken down into simple sugars ready for absorption. If blood sugar levels become too high because of any high carbohydrate food, the body will turn this excess sugar into triglycerides (stored fat) – even though the meal may be 99 per cent fat free!

Health & Safety

Eggs are date stamped and should *not* be eaten after 'best before' date.

Health & Safety

Always read food labels on products for children. Often these foods and drinks contain very high quantities of sugars, fats and artificial sweeteners.

permitted at levels which independent scientists say could put men and boys at risk. It's frighteningly easy for young children to exceed 'safe' levels. Just a third of a litre of soft drink (the size of a regular can) containing cyclamates could put a four-year-old over the limit.

Foods for babies and young children are not permitted to contain a range of additives, including artificial sweeteners, but a loophole in the law means that other foods including soft drinks, crisps and other snacks and ice lollies often contain artificial sweeteners, some as a double sweet dose along side sugar. Safe levels are said to be 5mg/kg body weight/day.

Explaining dates on labels

Most packaged food will carry a date mark as a health and safety precaution.

- Use By dates are for highly perishable foods such as some meat products or ready-prepared foods. Eating food after its 'use by' date could cause a serious health risk.

- Best Before dates are usually put on foods which can safely be kept for longer periods than perishable goods – tinned or packet foods for example. The food will be 'best before' the stated date, but will not be dangerous and can still be eaten after the date – however, the food will not be at it best.

- The Sell By date is the last date a shop can legally sell an item.

The five categories and purposes of food additives

Colours

Do not provide any nutrients and are not necessary to keep food safe. Legally many foods cannot have colour added, including baby foods, tea, coffee and fresh fruit and vegetables. Colour additives are mainly used either to restore natural food colours lost during processing or to enhance foods to make them look brighter and more appealing, such as making strawberry yoghurt a better pink. There are about 20 permitted artificial colours and many from natural sources. E102 tartrazine and E133 brilliant blue, both artificial colours, are said to cause hyperactivity in children and should be avoided where possible. E100 turmeric and E162 beetroot red are both natural colours. Brown FK (E154) is used to colour kippers and other smoked fish – the FK means 'for kippers'. Caramel (E150) is the most common food colouring and accounts for about 98 per cent of all colours used; it is added to a huge range of foods from colas and chocolate to bread and beer. E150 is also used as flavouring. Not all caramel is burnt sugar, most is made chemically and it's relatively easy to exceed safe limits for some types. Choose foods with as few added colours, artificial or natural, as possible.

Activity

Make yourself aware of unfamiliar words. A food list may not state sugar but words ending in 'ose' often denote a sugar as in fructose, glucose, dextrose and maltose. Honey too is a sugar. A food list may not state salt content, but will often give figures for sodium. Whey, lactose, and curd are all unfamiliar words indicating that they come from milk.

Preservatives

Used to give food a longer shelf life. Without food preservatives food would deteriorate too quickly and become unsafe for consumption. Preservatives also keep harmful bacteria at bay.

Antioxidants

Just as you would sprinkle lemon juice on to an avocado to stop it going brown (lemon juice being an antioxidant), antioxidants are added to food to stop fat becoming rancid and fruit going brown through oxidation. The most common antioxidant used is E300 ascorbic acid (vitamin C). It is also used to help bread to rise and to increase the shelf life of beers.

Emulsifiers

Emulsifiers, stabilisers and gelling agents act as thickeners, setting or binding agents to improve the consistency and texture of food and to keep it stable. Emulsifiers help foods combine well and prevent separation of oils and water. Lecithin, found in eggs, is a natural emulsifier (E322) and is used in making mayonnaise.

Flavourings

As their name implies, these are used to enhance flavour that has been lost during processing. They have no E numbers but can be identified on foods which usually use the words fruit *flavoured,* or vegetable *flavoured.* The flavour will certainly be chemical.

Sweeteners

Costing only a fraction of sugar, artificial sweeteners mimic the taste of natural sugar and usually have fewer calories. They are widely used in slimming products, soft drinks and confectionery. Artificial sweeteners are banned from baby foods.

A guide to E numbers – categories and additives

Category	*Usually found E number band*
Colours	E100s
Preservatives	E200s
Antioxidants	E300s
Emulsifiers and stabilisers	E400s
Flavourings	Not yet classified, referred to as flavourings
Processing aids	E500s
Flavour enhancers	E620 – E635
Sweeteners	E420 (sorbitol) and E421 (aspartame) are the main ones
Glazing agents	E900 – E914
Miscellaneous additives!	E999 – 1518

Confused? Fat free, low fat, less fat, saturated fat free, cholesterol free, low cholesterol – all claims made by manufacturers to possibly mislead us. Here are some explanations:

Description	Actual content
Fat free	Less than 0.5 grams of fat per serving with no added oil
Low fat	3 grams or less of fat per serving
Less fat	25% or less fat than the comparison food
Saturated fat free	Less than 0.5g of saturated fat and 0.5 grams of fatty acids per serving
Cholesterol free	Less than 2mg cholesterol per serving, and 2 grams of saturated fat per serving
Low cholesterol	20mg or less cholesterol per serving and 2 grams of saturated fat per serving
Reduced calorie	At least 25% fewer calories per serving than the comparison food
Low calorie	40 calories or less per serving
Extra lean	Less than 5 grams of fat, 2 grams of saturated fat, and 2 grams of cholesterol per (100g) serving of meat, poultry or seafood.
Lean	Less than 10 grams of fat, 4.5g of saturated fat and 3g of cholesterol per (100g) serving of meat, poultry or seafood
Light (fat)	50% or less of the fat than in the comparison food
Light (calories)	One-third fewer calories than the comparison food
High fibre	5 grams or more fibre per serving
Sugar-free	Less than 0.5g of sugar per serving
Sodium or salt-free	Less than 5mg of sodium per serving
Low sodium	140mg or less per serving
Very low sodium	35mg or less per serving
Healthy	A food low in fat, saturated fat, cholesterol and sodium and contains at least 10% of the RDAs for vitamin C, iron, calcium protein or fibre
High, Rich in, or Excellent source	20% or more of the RDA for a given nutrient per serving
Less, Fewer, or Reduced	At least 25% less of a given nutrient or calories than the comparison food
Low, Little, Few or Low source of	An amount that would allow frequent consumption of a product without exceeding the RDA for the nutrient but can only make the claim as it applies to all similar foods
Good source of, or Added	The food provides 10% more of the RDA values for a given nutrient than the comparison food

 Activity

Study food labels from popular drinks, snacks and foods. Examples to work on: a packet of salted crisps, a can of fizzy drink, a pre-packed sandwich, a tin of soup, a pre-prepared meal, a breakfast cereal. Make up a table with your findings – what is the healthiest processed food you can find?

Food allergies

The number of people affected by food allergies is increasing steadily, with an estimated 8 per cent of children and 3 per cent of adults currently believed to suffer from a range of problems, from reduced quality of life to life-threatening allergic reactions. Accurate labelling of food ingredients is essential for allergy sufferers. Ingredients to watch out for are peanuts, which many people react to – they are included in the most unlikely products. Mustard can cause severe anaphylactic reactions and ingredients like yeast, gluten and lactose can also cause problems for many people.

Genetically modified (GM) foods

There have been many surveys carried out over the past couple of years on GM foods and food labelling in particular. Products that carry less than 1 per cent GM foods need not reveal this on the label, but foods with more than this amount should. However, some surveys have found that food labelled organic contained genetically modified ingredients! The amounts were small, but contained in the product nonetheless. Some labels actually stated 'contains no GM ingredients' but the product did. Currently there are no known health problems connected with GM ingredients, but this is an issue of enabling consumers to be informed *before* they make a purchase should they choose not to buy GM foods.

Conversion tables and useful measurements

Abbreviation	Word in full	Explanation
kcal	kcalories	A unit by which energy is measured
g	grams	A unit of weight equivalent to about 0.03 ounces
mg	milligrams	One-thousandth of a gram
mcg	microgram	One-millionth of a gram, also represented as ug
IU	International Unit	An old measurement of vitamin activity determined by biological methods (as opposed to new measures that are determined by direct chemical analysis). Many fortified foods and supplements still use IU on their labels. ● For Vitamin A, 1 IU = 0.3ug retinol, 3.6ug b-carotene, or 7.2ug other vitamin A carotenoids ● For Vitamin D, 1 IU = 0.025ug cholecalciferol ● For Vitamin E, 1 IU = 0.67 natural a-tocopherol (other conversion factors are used for different forms of vitamin E)

Many recipes refer to Imperial or American measurements. The table below gives conversions of Imperial and Metric equivalents.

Imperial	Metric
½oz	15g
3½ozs	100g
9ozs	250g
1lb 2ozs	500g
2lbs 4ozs	1kg

Knowledge review

Food labels and conversion tables

1   What are the legal requirements of food labelling?

2   What word on food labels gives you an indication of the salt content of a product?

3   Referring to food labels, what is the difference between the words fruit 'flavour' and fruit 'flavour*ed*'?

4   What is the difference between intense sweeteners and bulk sweeteners?

5   To what category of E numbers do E620–E635 relate?

6   How much fibre must there be in a food to claim 'high fibre' on the label?

7   How much sugar is allowed in products stating they are 'sugar free'?

8   What does 'less fat' imply?

9   What is the E number for the antioxidant ascorbic acid (vitamin C)?

10   What is the E number for tartrazine, an artificial food colouring that may cause hyperactivity in children?

8 Supplements

This chapter covers the following:

- **the arguments for and against taking supplements**
- **how to choose dietary supplements**
- **the dos and don'ts about supplements**

We are continually told by doctors, health professionals, or dietitians that if we eat a well balanced diet there is no need to take dietary supplements. If this is true why do millions of people take dietary supplements every day? Other doctors, health professionals and nutritional therapists also tell us that modern food, even fresh fruit and vegetables, do not contain sufficient of all the essential nutrients for us to remain healthy and disease free and that everybody needs a daily dietary supplement. Who is right? Opinions vary hugely on the need for supplements, but as with most things, individual circumstances always have to be taken into consideration. The majority of people taking supplements are self-prescribed. They read articles in magazines or newspapers, listen to friends and family, read books, and then decide for themselves what they feel they need. As a nutritional therapist, recommending supplements forms part of the consultation process and your clients will expect you to have knowledge in this area.

There are hundreds of different dietary supplements available and the diversity of choice is astounding. Not all vitamins are the same and not all companies are the same so always purchase on recommendation from a qualified nutritional therapist or from reputable health food shops. It is not recommended you buy from mail order companies or from supermarkets or decide by price alone. The most expensive is not always the best and the cheapest may be full of fillers and binders and not much of the nutrient you really want. Study labels carefully. Many capsules are made from gelatin and are unsuitable for vegetarians. Some weight reduction supplements may contain animal derived thyroid, which again would be unsuitable for some people. Many children's supplements contain artificial colours, flavourings and sugar! So take care when buying supplements.

It would be wonderful if we could get all the nutrients we needed for good health from the food offered to us in our stores. Unfortunately, due to intensive farming that leaves our soil nutrient deficient, and the ever-increasing desire for fast and convenient foods, that is just not possible. Combined with an increased nutrient requirement due to modern living, it is generally felt that we all need some basic form of supplementation. There have been many studies carried out recently showing that on average our fruit and vegetables have 60 per cent *less* vitamin and mineral content than they had just 50 years ago.

The argument for supplements

- If a deficiency of a particular vitamin or mineral were established, then it would be appropriate for supplementation.

- There are many types of people who may need to improve their nutritional status from dietary supplements. Vegetarians, who may omit whole food groups; elderly people who just don't eat enough food to deliver the necessary amount of nutrients; habitual dieters who are often deficient in many nutrients and those with eating disorders. All of these may need to improve their nutritional status through supplementation.

- Some people take dietary supplements to reduce disease risk. Post-menopausal women, for example, may wish to supplement calcium to deter osteoporosis, or a woman considering becoming pregnant may wish to take folic acid as a measure to guard against neural tube defects.

- Special circumstances may create a need for dietary supplements. For example, women who lose a lot of blood during menstruation each month may feel they need an iron supplement. Newborn babies often receive a supplement of vitamin K at birth to prevent abnormal bleeding. Athletes, training for a big event, may feel the need for supplementation to prevent becoming deficient when the body is working so hard.

- Appropriate supplementation may be necessary for people overcoming surgery or disease to improve the body's immune system and to build the body's defences.

The argument against supplements

- Taking individual supplements can cause other imbalances.
- Toxicity – the extent and severity of supplement toxicity remains unclear.
- There are no guarantees that supplements will be effective.
- They can be expensive – someone may spend a lot of their money on supplements, thinking they are superior to food, and not leave money enough for real food. This can lead to a false sense of security regarding nutrition and all sorts of problems involving disordered eating patterns may follow.
- Supplements cannot provide energy.
- The belief that a balanced diet can supply all the nutrients needed to maintain health.

Key Term

Supplements

A product that contains one or more dietary ingredients such as vitamins, minerals, herbs, amino acids or other ingredients used to support the diet.

The Bateman Report published in 1985 found more than 85 per cent of people who generally thought they ate a well balanced diet failed to meet RDA levels. There is little sign that the diet of the nation has improved.

How to buy a supplement

Where do you start? Do you choose a tablet, a capsule or a liquid? Do you choose by price alone? Is the most expensive always the best or will a supermarket brand be just as good? There are many aspects of buying nutritional supplements that you should be aware of. The most important thing to do when purchasing a food supplement is to check the label carefully.

The label should include:

1   Title – the label should clearly state what it represents. For example a multivitamin complex with iron, or an antioxidant formula, or a multimineral formula etc. You should then check the ingredients list to see that everything you are expecting to be in the supplement is present. A B complex supplement should contain all the B vitamins including cobalamin (vitamin B12) and B5 which is often omitted because it is expensive.

2   Check how many tablets/capsules are in the bottle. If there are 30 tablets but you need two a day, you are only purchasing two weeks' supply. However, you may find a better value supplement which may appear more expensive at first glance, but may offer 30 × one-a-day tablets – a month's supply.

3   Check to see if the ingredients list gives amounts per tablet so you are not misinformed. Look at label A. At first glance you may think that you were getting 1.5g of iron with your multivitamin, but on closer inspection you are only getting 1.5g of iron per 100g, and there is only 50g in the whole bottle! Not a good choice if you want a multivitamin with iron. One tablet of Formula A would only provide 0.015g of iron.

4   Supplement labels should always state the instructions for use, and any safety data.

5   Supplement labels should always have the manufacturer's name and address.

6   Good companies also tell you what is not in the product as well as what is. For example a product should state whether it is free from yeast, gluten, artificial sweeteners and colours. (Many children's supplements contain artificial colours!)

7   Products should always carry a guarantee of quality.

Other things to look out for:

If you are buying a mineral supplement, be sure it contains it in forms you can easily absorb. On the whole, liquid supplements tend to be better absorbed than tablets or capsules. You can also purchase powdered forms of vitamins, ascorbic acid (vitamin C) for example, which is half the price of a tablet because it has had less processing. One gm of ascorbic acid powder (or any liquid supplement or other powdered supplement) can be added to bottled water, which gives this a pleasant taste, and drunk over the day.

Calcium citrate for example is the easiest form of calcium to absorb. Also check the amount states 'elemental', or be prepared to get your calculator out. For example if a supplement label states 10mg of elemental zinc, then you will get 10mg of zinc. Many labels will say, for example, 1,000mg calcium carbonate of which 40 per cent is elemental – in other words you will be getting 400mg of elemental calcium from it. If the label states the elemental value you know exactly what you are getting. There are many calcium supplements to choose from and as with most things in life, you get what you pay for. Calcium citrate is the most expensive but is the best absorbed. Here is a list of other calcium supplements.

- Calcium carbonate – the cheapest calcium, calcium carbonate is also the highest in elemental calcium at 40 per cent. However, it dissolves very slowly in the stomach, so you will not get the full benefit of all the calcium.

- Calcium citrate – the most expensive calcium, calcium citrate is only 21 per cent elemental calcium, but dissolves very well in your stomach, even if you don't produce much acid, so you are more likely to absorb more calcium from this supplement.

- Calcium gluconate – this form is also found in many supplements but only contains 9 per cent elemental calcium. It is not a very good choice.

- Calcium lactate – also found in many supplement formulas. It only contains 13 per cent elemental calcium, but it is relatively easily dissolved. It would be a second choice to calcium citrate.

Supplement label 'A'

Multivitamin with iron	Take one a day	Per 100g
	Zinc	50mg
	Copper sulphate	5mg
50 tablets Net weight 50g	Folic acid	50mcg
	Nicotinic acid	2mg
	Riboflavin	2mg
A Vitamin Company	Thiamine	2mg
Somewhere	Ascorbic acid	40mg
	Calcium carbonate	50mg
	Iron	1.5mg

This is a very poor supplement label; 50mg of zinc is the first item on the ingredients list, but you are not told if it is in elemental or chelated form. It is unlikely to be 50mg of elemental zinc, so you must presume that it is zinc glutamate or other chelate in which case it is probably only 10 per cent of what is stated, i.e. 5mg of zinc. It is important to keep your zinc and copper levels in balance, because the two minerals compete with each other to be absorbed into your body. Good supplements will give you a ratio of 10 parts zinc to one part

Key Term

Chelated

Minerals which have been treated to alter their electrical charge, usually by binding them chemically to a harmless salt such as a gluconate, citrate, picolinate, aspartate or another 'ate' substance.

Activity

Compare these two labels and make notes for discussion. What would tempt you to buy Supplement B as opposed to Supplement A?

copper. In other words if you are taking 30mg of zinc, be sure to take 3mg of copper as well. If you have identified (and we are still only guessing) that this supplement is 5mg of zinc then the 5mg of copper is far too much and out of balance.

Supplement label 'B'

Multivitamin and mineral formula	Take one tablet daily with food	Per tablet
Guarantee of quality To ensure that you get at least 100% out of the stated ingredients, we have a strict policy of quality control. Each batch of all our supplements is independently analysed before offering them for sale. Net weight 36g 30 tablets This product is yeast free, gluten free and contains no sugars or artificial colours. We use only natural fillers and binders. A Vitamin Company Somewhere	Each protein-coated natural tablet contains: Calcium citrate Ascorbic acid (Vitamin C) Thiamin (B1) Riboflavin (Vitamin B2) Niacin (Vitamin B3) Pantothenic acid (Vitamin B5) Pyridine (Vitamin B6) Elemental zinc Manganese gluconate Magnesium sterate Vitamin B12 Biotin Folic acid Copper Protein coating	 400mg 45mg 25mg 25mg 25mg 25mg 25mg 15mg 8mg 50mg 2.5mcg 25mcg 20mcg 1.5mg 10mg

Label B is more informative. You have a guarantee of quality, instructions and a list of what it does not contain. There are good amounts of all the B vitamins. You are told that the supplement contains calcium citrate, which is the most absorbable, which is good, that the zinc is measured as elemental and 15mg is generous for a multivitamin. The supplement contains pantothenic acid (vitamin B5), which is sometimes left out of formulas because it is expensive, and there is also B12, which is often omitted from supplements. There is also the 10: 1 ratio of zinc to copper.

Evening primrose oil supplements

Many people buy EPO supplement for PMS symptoms, especially for breast tenderness. When you buy evening primrose capsules, you are actually buying GLA – gamma linolenic acid, that is the active, anti-inflammatory substance. Prices vary enormously and you need to be aware exactly what you are buying. EPO (and starflower oil which contains slightly more GLA) is usually sold as either 1,000mg or 500mg. However, not all of this is gamma linolenic acid – this comes

Health & Safety

Always follow the manufacturers instructions on any supplements you may purchase – and *never* exceed the stated dose.

☀ **Activity**

Ask friends and neighbours for empty packets of their evening primrose or starflower supplements. Compare each for the GLA content – making your calculations carefully. Discuss with a colleague or as a class activity.

as a percentage. You need to read the small print which states what per centage of GLA is contained in the supplement. This may range anywhere from 5 per cent to 24 per cent. For example, you may purchase a 1,000mg EPO supplement containing 5 per cent GLA, giving you 50mg of GLA for £5. Alternatively, you may purchase a 500mg EPO supplement containing 20 per cent GLA, giving you 100mg of GLA, for the same price. So the smaller total quantity of the supplement (500mg) gives you double of the active ingredient GLA and therefore half the price.

Amino acid supplements

If you have an adequate food intake, you will have a more than adequate protein intake. Supplementing individual amino acids may be harmful and is not recommended. Single amino acids do not occur naturally in foods and offer no benefit to the body. The body was not designed to handle the high concentrations and unusual combinations of amino acids found in supplements. An excess of one amino acid could create such a demand for a carrier that it could prevent the absorption of other amino acids, leading to a deficiency. The amino acids that are taken in excess could create the possibility of a toxicity state. Toxicity of single amino acids in animal studies raises concerns about their use in human beings. Anyone considering taking amino acid supplements should check with a registered nutrition consultant or physician first.

There is only one exception to this rule and that is the amino acid lysine which is taken to suppress herpes simplex infections. Three grams per day taken in divided doses with meals; 1 gram × 3 times per day is the usual recommendation.

Dos and don'ts about vitamin supplements

While nutrition supplements can only be toxic in extremely large doses, there are a number of situations in which supplementation is not advised. Please check these before advising any client.

- Vitamin A in doses in excess of 8,000 IUs per day should not be given to pregnant women or women trying to conceive, unless there are clear signs of deficiency.
- Vitamin C should not be given above the level which causes loose bowels. Everyone has a different bowel tolerance of vitamin C, which can be used as a natural laxative. If a client experiences loose stools, cut back 1g until the stool becomes more solid.
- Vitamin B2 in doses in excess of 25mg can cause yellow colouration of urine (and breast milk). This is fine and is not an indication to stop or reduce supplementation.
- Vitamin B3 in the form of niacin can cause vasodilation, resulting in skin blushing, slight itchiness and temperature changes. This effect can occur from 100mg and generally lasts up to 30 minutes. It is beneficial, although some people of a nervous disposition can find this uncomfortable.

Key Term

DMAE

One of the building blocks of acetylcholine (the other being choline). It is a precursor for choline which crosses readily into the brain, hence helping to make acetylcholine. Improves concentration and learning. It is a great natural mind and memory booster.

● Vitamin B12 and folic acid deficiency both result in anaemia. Since supplementing folic acid can mask B12 deficiency anaemia, folic acid in large doses should only be supplemented with B12.

● If a client has a serious illness which is currently under medical treatment, ask the client to check with their doctor whether there are any indications for not supplementing nutrients. Listed below are some drug-nutrient interactions you should know about:

  ● Warfarin – don't take vitamin E or EPA (fish oils) with it.

  ● Monoamine oxidase inhibitors – don't take large amounts of yeast with it. Common brand names are Parstein and Nardil.

  ● DMAE and GLA – has been known to make some epileptics worse.

If a client is seriously ill, make sure they have seen their doctor first. If in doubt, always refer your client to their doctor.

A safe practice is to recommend multivitamins and minerals where all the difficult calculations have already been carried out on your behalf. There are many companies who offer daily packs of vitamins; for example, a pregnancy pack for before, during and after having a baby, will ensure that there is not too much vitamin A, good levels of folic acid and the correct balance of all the other supplements, whereas a menopause pack will ensure a different range of supplement to cater for that class of client. You can get metabolic packs for clients wanting to lose weight, an osteo pack for prevention of osteoporosis and a general vitamin vitality pack for general good health. The choices are endless. Never recommend anything you are not absolutely sure about. Most of the reputable supplement companies have technical advisers who will be only too pleased to answer your questions.

Knowledge review

Supplements

1   State three reasons for not taking supplements.

2   State three reasons for taking supplements.

3   Which types of vitamins tend to have the better absorption rates?

4   Name four things a supplement label should include.

5   What ratio of zinc to copper should there be in a supplement?

6   What is the active ingredient of evening primrose oil?

7   What is bowel tolerance?

8   What might happen with a vitamin B2 supplement?

9   What is the rule concerning B12 and folic acid supplements?

10   Would you ever recommend amino acid supplements?

Nutrition for pregnancy and babies, athletes, the menopause and the elderly

9

Learning objectives

This chapter covers the following:

- **foods to avoid during and after pregnancy**

- **the order of food for weaning babies**

- **important guidelines for athletes**

- **phytoestrogens explained and guidelines for the menopause**

- **co-Q-10 and how to stay healthy in later years**

The nutrition qualification you are taking may address some of the people in this chapter as contraindicated. These are specialist areas in nutrition usually covered at degree level. By the end of this chapter you will be able to give general guidelines to the groups of people discussed here. Be sure to check with your awarding body and insurance company that you are covered to do so.

Pregnancy

Optimum nutrition is vital for mother and baby, before, during and after birth. During embryonic development (between 2–8 weeks) many of the tissues are in their critical periods. Critical periods are events that occur that will have irreversible effects on the development of those tissues. The critical period for neural tube defects, for example, is from 17–30 days gestation. Consequently, neural tube development is most vulnerable to nutrient deficiencies, nutrient excesses, or toxins at this critical time when most women do not even know they are pregnant.

Good nutrition is absolutely vital during pregnancy and an expectant mother should not only increase her intake of fresh fruits and vegetables and wholesome, nutrient-dense foods, but also be aware of avoiding the anti-nutrients – the substances that can hinder nutrients being absorbed into the body. Taking specific supplements, especially folic acid, is also recommended at this time.

Key Term

Gestation

The period from conception to birth. For human beings gestation lasts from 38–42 weeks. Pregnancy is often divided into thirds, called trimesters.

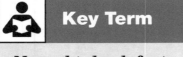

Key Term

Neural tube defects

A serious central nervous system birth defect that can often result in lifelong disability or death.

Health & Safety

Never offer nutritional advice unless you are competent to do so.

Folic acid should be taken prior to conceiving if planning a pregnancy, or as soon as pregnancy is diagnosed, and for the first trimester as it protects against neural tube defects. The RDA for women for folic acid is 0.4mg daily and 0.6mg in pregnancy. All women of childbearing age who are capable of becoming pregnant are advised to take folic acid.

Avoid soft mould ripened cheeses such as Camembert, blue-veined cheeses and any type of paté, as these foods may contain listeria. Listeria is a germ that can cause miscarriage, stillbirth or severe illness in a newborn baby. If buying ready-made meals, always cook through thoroughly until piping hot.

Avoid eating raw eggs and foods containing raw or partially cooked eggs (home-made mayonnaise for example). Only eat eggs that have been cooked long enough for both the whites and yolk to be solid. This is to avoid the risk of salmonella, which causes a type of food poisoning.

Always wash your hands thoroughly after handling raw meat and store raw and cooked foods separately. This is to avoid other types of food poisoning from meat – campylobacter and *E.Coli*. Only eat well-cooked meat and take particular care with sausages and minced meat.

Avoid eating liver and liver products such as paté and avoid taking high doses of vitamin A in supplement form. You need some vitamin A, but as it is a fat-soluble vitamin it may build up in the body to unsuitable levels for pregnancy. Vitamin A can be synthesised in the body by the water-soluble vitamin beta-carotene, obtained from red, yellow and purple fruits and vegetables.

Eating for two? Pregnant women do need extra energy from food, but not too much. During the second and third trimesters pregnant women need an extra 300 calories a day. Pregnant teenagers, underweight women and very active women may need more calories. These extra calories should come from nutrient-dense foods.

Weight gain during pregnancy

All pregnant women must gain weight, but it need not be an excuse to eat excessively.

The recommended gain for a woman who begins pregnancy at a healthy weight and is carrying a single fetus is 25 to 35 pounds. However, there are many different starting posts. Underweight young adults still growing themselves, overweight women, tall and short women, and even different cultural backgrounds, can all be factors in the final weight gain. The doctor will weigh a woman immediately pregnancy is ascertained and work out a healthy gain for that individual woman. There is no need to stop exercising during pregnancy, an active, physically fit woman experiencing a normal pregnancy can continue to exercise throughout, adjusting the duration and intensity as the pregnancy progresses.

Energy and nutrient needs are high during pregnancy. A balanced diet that includes an extra serving from each of the five food groups can usually meet these needs, with the exception of iron where supplementation is usually necessary. The nausea, constipation, and heartburn that sometimes accompany pregnancy can usually be alleviated with a few simple strategies.

Babies

Once the baby is born the mother must continue to eat sensibly, especially if breast-feeding, as the quality of her diet will affect the quality of the breast milk and subsequent nutrition for the baby. Babies need food for growth and replacement of body tissues, for regulation of their body temperature, the formation of bones, the transmission of nerve impulses and for having enough energy for the body to function and to move. During the first year of a life the baby's growth rate is at its greatest and this is especially so during the first months.

Babies' growth rates

Age in months	Weight gain per week
0–6 months	4–8 ozs
6–12 months	3–5 ozs

A thriving healthy baby will put on between 4–8 ozs a week from birth to six months old. From 6–12 months a baby should gain between 3–5 ounces a week. However, whilst weight and growth are vital to the baby's health the most important rate of growth happens within the brain.

Choosing between breast and formula feeding is a big decision for any new mother – there are many advantages and disadvantages to both methods. All new mothers will be given professional advice and information on different feeding methods, but the final decision will always rest with the mother.

Weaning is the gradual process of introducing a range of foods into the baby's diet, at first to supplement and eventually to replace milk as the sole nutritional source. The process involves moving the baby from a purely liquid diet to one which includes a range of textures and consistencies. The order of weaning is vitally important. New foods should be introduced very gradually and not before four months old or when the infant seems dissatisfied with milk alone. During these first four months, the baby will have a store of iron which supplies their needs for these first few months of life.

The first weaning foods should be simple, bland, gluten-free (no wheat-based products) and with nothing added except the baby's usual milk to improve the consistency. Healthy babies, like healthy adults, need food that is fresh, unprocessed and additive-free, sugar free, salt free and low in fat. To prevent allergies later on, specialists in this field have devised a list of foods to be introduced. The list starts with those foods least likely to cause an allergic reaction and the foods get more complex the further down the list you go. The best advice you can give a mother who is weaning an infant is to have patience. There is no rush and the later you introduce a new food, the less chance there is to there being an allergic reaction.

Do not be in too much of a rush to introduce new foods. Start at the top of the list and introduce only one new food every four or five days. It is a very good idea at this stage to keep a notebook of foods,

Health & Safety

If approached for advice on feeding a baby, stongly recommend a visit to the GP or antenatal clinic.

Health & Safety

Baby foods should *never* have salt or sugar added to them. Sugar is unnecessary, and only provides empty calories.

Key Term

Colostrum

The milk produced by mammals during the first few days after parturition; human colostrum contains more protein (2 per cent compared with 1 per cent, slightly less lactose, considerably less fat (3 per cent compared with 5 per cent) and overall slightly less energy than mature milk introduced dates and any noticeable adverse reaction.

- vegetables – pureed; nothing added but the baby's usual milk to give a familiar taste
- fruits (except oranges) – puréed
- nuts and seeds – ground and tiny amounts added to vegetables
- pulses and beans
- rice
- meat
- oats, barley and rye
- oranges (after nine months old)
- wheat (after nine months old)
- food milk products – yoghurt, milk puddings or custard, not milk as a drink (after nine months old)
- eggs (after nine months old)
- do not introduce peanuts until after three years old.

Most difficulties in weaning are caused by adults and not by the baby! Weaning is a slow process – there is no hurry and it is not a race – just be patient. Do not encourage a sweet tooth. There is nothing wrong with giving the infant puréed vegetables for breakfast. The first two years of a baby's eating habits will set the scene for the rest of his/her life!

External influences affect a young child's eating behaviours and attitudes to food. If you know you have a problem with food or eating, it is vital that the child does not pick this up through your body language. It is important to be aware of how strongly we influence young children in everything, including food.

It must be stressed again that this is a specialised area of nutrition, and you should refer to a specialist in this area if anyone asks you for dietary advice for a baby.

The early years

Whatever the age of a child, nutrition is of paramount importance. Do all you can to instil good habits from an early age. Strongly discourage junk food, fizzy drinks and empty calorie foods. There have been numerous studies showing that good nutrition improves IQ and behaviour. Moreover, it has also been shown that poor nutrition resulting in:

- sugar imbalances (too many convenience foods)
- deficiency of vitamins and minerals (too much fast/junk food)
- deficiency of essential fatty acids (not enough fish, nuts and seeds in the diet) allergies (possibly caused by weaning and introducing foods in the wrong order or too early)

may result in one or more of the major problems facing our children these days. Dyslexia, attention deficit disorder, hyperactivity and delinquency have all been linked to poor diet during the early years.

All the nutrients are important as the child is still growing. Calcium is of particular importance, as good calcium intake now, through the growing years, will lay down strong foundations and may prevent osteoporosis much later in life.

Athletes

As with the other sections in this chapter, sports nutrition, or nutrition for professional athletes, is a specialised and unique area of nutrition and it is probably not covered within the syllabus you are working to. Below you will find general guidelines for athletes, but referral to a professional in this area is strongly recommended. The success of an athlete's performance depends heavily on their intake of nutrients – where, when and what is taken into the body has to be strictly monitored. Every sportsperson has unique needs. The nutritional requirements of a runner will be very different to that of a body builder. As well as the many different types of sport, many other factors need to be taken into consideration; for example the frequency of training means that the diet will probably be adjusted several times the closer to an event an athlete gets. Other factors that need considering are climate, sleep, sex, caffeine and supplements. Even competitors in the same sport have very different needs. The nutrients levels suggested by the DRIs (dietary reference intakes) for high performance athletes may be impossible to meet with diet alone, so the value of supplementation must be considered. This means a sports nutritional adviser would need to be aware of the hundreds of bars, gels, capsules, powders and supplements formulated for sportspeople.

Athletes are not average. They test themselves against unusual environmental stressors; they work at a different rate from the general population and that can dramatically raise their macronutrient and micronutrient requirements. Athletic performance will be adversely affected if there is a deficiency of certain minerals or trace elements. The problem is a recovery issue, because athletes often suffer mineral deficiencies as a direct result of the exercise itself. Intense activity increases the metabolic need for minerals. Studies have shown that concentrations of magnesium and potassium in the urine of athletes on a workout day can be double that of a non-workout day. Minerals move out of the body with sweat, so exercising in a hot climate can make this problem considerably worse.

If you combine this mineral loss through sports with factors that cause deficiencies in the general population, the effect on athletic performance can be profound. Birth control pills, for example, can cause elevated copper levels and an excess of copper means reduced levels of zinc.

We know how important zinc is, but for athletes zinc is vital as one of its functions is to break down and utilise carbohydrates and to build muscle. Deodorant too may cause a problem as those deodorants that contain aluminium, as most do, sap the body of magnesium.

Mineral deficiencies in athletes

Deficiency	Result
Iron	Decrease in oxygen transport throughout the body
Copper	Weakened connective tissues, ligaments and tendons
Chromium	Depressed energy metabolism
Magnesium	Decrease in oxygen transport to muscle tissue
Zinc	Decrease in muscle strength and endurance

An important area for sportspeople to consider is water. Athletes need to do whatever it takes to avoid dehydration. A runner can sweat off 50 ounces of water in an hour and even mild dehydration can slow your metabolism by as much as 3 per cent and cause some degree of fatigue.

Every athlete will be unique, but here are some guidelines for a daily diet.

- Water and water-rich foods like fruits and vegetables will make up the majority of the diet
- 2 grams of protein/kg of body weight. This includes vegetable sources of protein such as nuts and legumes (soybeans, lentils, kidney beans etc.)
- Fibre-rich grains – oats, kasha, quinoa, millet, amaranth and barley
- Small amounts of olive oil, omega 3 fats in the form of cold water fish and flaxseed (linseed).

These are stringent guidelines but for the best results in competition, athletes need to be exact in their eating and drinking habits.

Nos for serious athletes

- NO white bread – void of most nutrients especially chromium
- NO alcohol – an anti-nutrient that affects sleep, metabolism and hydration
- NO caffeine – affects dehydration and risks diarrhoea. If they must 3mg/kg of body weight is acceptable but more than that will affect athletic performance
- NO processed foods – the majority of processed foods lack nutrients. Avoid cakes, biscuits and all refined foods.

A serious athlete will keep a food log. If you are approached by a client requesting nutritional help for athletic performance – get them to keep a food/performance/sleep log for 2–3 weeks and refer to a specialist in this area. When your client turns up with a completed food log this will enable the sports nutrition therapist to give more recommendations at that first appointment. He/she may then in turn send clients needing general nutritional advice to you.

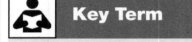

Key Term

Dehydration

The condition in which body water output exceeds input. Symptoms include thirst, dry skin and mucous membranes, rapid heartbeat, low blood pressure and weakness.

The menopause years

Menopause is not an illness but an important stage of a woman's life. One of the most fundamental ways to approach the menopause is through sound nutrition. With the increased risks of breast cancer and heart disease associated with HRT, many women are looking for a natural answer to menopausal symptoms – that answer is nutrition.

What is the menopause?

Just as the word menarche means a woman's first menstrual period, menopause means the last period she will ever have – *meno* comes from the Greek word meaning month. However, when referring to menopause, we usually mean the whole period a woman goes through from months to years before and after her last period.

What happens during the menopause?

Production of reproductive hormones, oestrogen and progesterone slow down, periods may become irregular, there may be fluctuations in temperature resulting in hot flushes and changes in sleep patterns. This total transition from child bearing to past-child bearing years is properly known as the climacteric. As has been stated many times throughout this book, because we are all so biochemically different, this change can last from a few months to as long as ten years!

The climacteric is usually divided into three parts; peri menopause, the menopause and post menopause.

The climacteric periods of change

Peri menopause	The time when hormonal shifts have already begun but a woman is still menstruating
Menopause	The time at which the last period occurs
Post menopause	All periods have ceased but contraception is still recommended for a further two years

Between puberty and menopause four related hormones, whose levels all fluctuate during the month, affect the cycle. The function of two of these, the gonadatrophins, is to stimulate the production of two other hormones, oestrogen and progesterone. In the first two weeks of the menstrual cycle, FSH (follicle stimulating hormone), helps an egg cell in the ovary to mature. When the egg is ready to break out of its follicle, the amount of FSH reduces as LH (luteinising hormone) takes over to complete the process called ovulation – the point at which the egg is released. By the time a woman has reached the menopause, few eggs remain and the hormone levels tend to fluctuate more wildly, which causes periods to be irregular.

The importance of exercise and osteoporosis

Weight-bearing exercise is by far the most beneficial step a woman can take to prevent or reverse osteoporosis. While swimming and cycling are good, they are classed as aerobic exercise. You need weight-bearing exercise, which means going to the gym and joining a class for lifting weights. The harder the muscles have to work, putting strain on the bones, the stronger the bones become. The instructor will devise a workout for you as an individual, a balanced routine between the weight-bearing anaerobic exercise, and the aerobic exercise.

If you are worried about osteoporosis try this home test. Ask a colleague/friend/husband to mark your height on a wall every couple of months. If your height drops as much as three millimetres in a year, this is an indication that you are losing height and therefore bone mass. You should go to your doctor immediately.

Hot flushes

Three-quarters of all British menopausal women experience some hot flushes. Hot flushes are not directly a sign of oestrogen deficiency, but are a result of increased activity of the hypothalamus gland in the brain to bring about the production of the hormones FSH and LH. High levels of these two hormones occur as the menopause approaches. They are working extra hard to stimulate any remaining eggs to grow and develop. Oestrogen and progesterone levels fall towards the menopause. Raising progesterone levels would increase receptors in oestrogen-sensitive cells and reduce hot flushes. Progesterone levels can be raised by using a natural progesterone cream which is applied externally to the skin for the last 14 days of a cycle. Supplementing vitamin E combined with vitamin C and bioflavonoids may also reduce hot flushes. When vitamin E levels are low there is a tendency for the hormones FSH and LH to increase. Vitamin E appears to stabilise the output of oestrogens.

Fibroids

Fibroids are the most common growths of the female reproductive system. They are benign, firm, round lumps that attach themselves to the muscular wall of the womb. There is usually more than one. They often grow to the size of a grapefruit and routinely disappear after the menopause. Fibroids give rise to irregular, heavy and painful periods. The weight of the fibroids can weaken the pelvic floor muscles, leading to stress incontinence. The usual treatment is to have them surgically removed. Fibroids are strongly linked to too much oestrogen. Yam is a rich source of natural progesterone which should help redress the balance if taken as a food, or applied as a cream, as mentioned above.

Foods to increase and food to decrease

All our lives what we do not eat and drink can be as beneficial to our health as what we do eat and drink and the menopause years are no exception. The main food groups to decrease during this time are red meat and dairy foods. These foods are high in saturated fats and synthetic hormones – the hormones are in havoc enough without introducing more to the system! Increase fruit (particularly purple, red and orange fruits) and vegetables, nuts and seeds, and choose soya milk as an alternative to cows' milk.

Phytoestrogens

Many common plant-based foods and herbs contain powerful substances known as phytoestrogens. There are hundreds of active compounds which largely fall into two main categories – isoflavones and lignans. Phytoestrogens are substances found in food that play a protective role in the body and are particularly helpful during the menopause years.

What do phytoestrogens do?

In order for oestrogen to affect the body, it must enter the cells by binding to certain receptors. Phytoestrogens have the ability to attach to oestrogen's receptor sites. By binding to these receptors, phytoestrogens can block some of the oestrogen circulating in the body from getting into cells. These excess oestrogens are either made in the body or taken in from the environment (synthetic oestrogens) by way of the air we breathe, the water we drink and in pesticides, plastics, the contraceptive pill and tampons. As phytoestrogens are described as weak oestrogens the result is much less oestrogen in the body cells. Studies have shown that this may actually help prevent hormonally linked cancers like breast, endometrial and prostrate cancer.

Genistein

Genistein is the best studied of all the isoflavones – a category of phytoestrogens. The isoflavones have three main functions:

- Oestrogen regulating
- Cardiovascular benefits
- Cell protection.

What does genistein do?

Genistein is an oestrogen regulating phytoestrogen (a weak oestrogen) and together with another phytoestrogen diadzein (also a weak oestrogen) is found in soy beans. Genistein can also be described as an adaptogen. It has the remarkable ability to adapt to the body's needs. A phytoestrogen is a plant oestrogen. They latch on to the same receptor sites as the oestrogen we make in our bodies; however, because plant oestrogens are 1/1000th or more weaker than our own oestrogen, the resulting blocking of the receptor sites would lower the total oestrogenic effect on the body. The excess circulating oestrogen would then be excreted by the body with the fibre that is taken in the diet daily. Whether you are oestrogen dominant or oestrogen deficient, genistein, being an adaptogen, may be of benefit to you. This would include anyone suffering from PMS and/or menopause symptoms.

Cardiovascular disease

Genistein and diadzein may help prevent cardiovascular disease in various ways, such as preventing free radical oxidation of cholesterol, reducing platelet aggregation, reducing plaque formation, reducing adherence of plaque to artery walls and lowering cholesterol levels.

Cell protection

Soy isoflavones such as genistein appear to possess many mechanisms that may inhibit cell damage. It may inhibit an enzyme which stimulates growth of damaged cells, and it may aid in reverting certain damaged cells back into normal cells. Genistein has antioxidant activity and may also inhibit oestrogen-dependent cell damage through blocking excessive oestrogenic activity.

Flaxseed fibre

Flaxseed is the best studied of all the ligans – a category of phytoestrogens – and it is a fibre. It reduces heart disease, blood pressure and reduces inflammation of bodily tissues; prevents constipation and reduces cholesterol levels; maintains healthy bones, prevents cancer and regulates blood sugar. It is also known as linseed.

What does flaxseed fibre do?

Heart disease, blood pressure and inflammation

Due to its high level of omega 3 fatty acids, flaxseed is extremely useful in reducing coronary heart disease, blood pressure and inflammation of bodily tissues (see omega 3 fatty acids pp. 32–3).

Constipation and cholesterol levels

There are two types of fibre available to us in food. Insoluble fibre reduces bowel transit time, is good for constipation, and allows faecal matter to be expelled from the body more rapidly. Soluble fibre helps regulate blood glucose and reduces cholesterol levels. Flaxseed is two-thirds insoluble fibre and one-third soluble fibre, so it carries both benefits. Fibre regulates our blood sugar by slowing our body's absorption of carbohydrates.

Healthy bones and prevents cancer

Flaxseed can balance the hormone oestrogen in the body due to its phytoestrogen effects. By taking up the oestrogen receptor sites, the excess oestrogens are carried out of the body. It is now widely accepted by nutritionists that people who consume a fibre rich diet have a lower incidence of hormone-related cancers like breast, endometrial and prostate cancer.

The elderly

On average adult energy needs decline an estimated 5 per cent per decade. One reason is that people usually reduce their physical activity as they age, although they need not do so. Eating recommendations for the elderly are the same as for any age group. Elderly people need carbohydrates for energy, protein for repair and renewal and fats for insulation, energy and protection just as they have all the rest of their life. The main change is that the energy/kcal requirement will be less.

One risk for older adults, however, is dehydration. There are many possible causes for this. Older adults who have lost bladder control may deliberately reduce their fluid intake to save any embarrassment with accidents. Total body water decreases as people age, so even mild stresses such as fever or hot weather can precipitate rapid dehydration in older adults. This can have a knock on effect to more frequent urinary tract infections, pneumonia, pressure ulcers, confusion and disorientation. To prevent dehydration, older adults need to drink at least six glasses of water a day. Milk and juices may replace some of this water, but beverages containing alcohol or

Key Term

Digestive enzymes

Proteins found in digestive juices that act on food substances causing them to break down into simple compounds. Available in supplement form.

Key Term

Mitrochondria

The cellular organelles responsible for producing ATP aerobically; made of membranes (lipid and protein) with enzymes mounted on them.

caffeine should be limited because of their diuretic effect. Fruit should be encouraged as many fruits, like strawberries for example, are 90–99 per cent water.

The production of stomach acid and enzymes often declines with age. As we saw in Chapter 1, stomach acid is dependent upon zinc so it is important to ensure that adequate zinc is taken in the diet; a supplement may be considered. Zinc also depresses taste and smell, leading to a liking for salt, sauces and strong-tasting food like cheese and meat. A lack of enzymes could also lead to poor absorption of nutrients from food into the body. To ensure proper assimilation of food, it may be necessary to recommend a digestive enzyme. Zinc can be obtained in liquid form and added to drinks for better absorption.

Exercise is as important for the elderly as for all age groups. Regular exercise in the form of walking will provide essential weight-bearing exercise to strengthen the bones. Fresh air and exercise also improves appetite.

Coenzyme-Q10

Coenzyme-Q10 is not described as a vitamin, because the body can make it. However, as we get older we do not make as much as we need and therefore supplementation is often necessary especially for the elderly. Co-Q-10 is often referred to as the cellular spark plug. It works in the mitochondria of your cells, shuttling tiny electrically charged particles back and forth among the three essential enzymes that are needed to generate energy. Without Co-Q-10 this process grinds to a halt. As your heart has the most mitochondria of any muscle in your body, it should also have the most concentration of Co-Q-10. People with heart problems often have low levels of Co-Q-10, which is probably why they often improve when they take it as a supplement. It has no side effects.

Main functions

To improve the cell's ability to use oxygen.

Main food sources

Fish, meat, peanuts, sesame seeds, walnuts, green beans, spinach, broccoli, soya oil.

Main deficiency symptoms

Low levels can result in high blood pressure, heart attack, angina, immune system, depression, periodontal disease, lack of energy and obesity.

Causes of deficiency

Age, lack of exercise.

 **Activity**

Whatever your age – really look at your diet. Are you getting all you require in the form of nutrients for your age? Are there any changes you could make? List some foods you could decrease and another list of foods you could increase to enhance your health. Take one food at a time to decrease and one food at a time to increase. You will benefit in the long term from gradual change now.

Therapeutic uses

Cardiovascular health, hypertension, angina, cardiomyopathy, heart arrhythmia, fatigue, weight control, gum disease, immune function, sports nutrition and antioxidant protection. It is thought that Co-Q-10 is beneficial for diabetics by helping to prevent many complications, such as heart disease. It also may help keep blood sugar levels down.

Co-Q-10 is a component of every living cell, and as body levels of Co-Q-10 drop so does the general status of health. High doses may reduce the effectiveness of the drug warfarin. If taking warfarin, do not take Co-Q-10 without the advice of a physician and also consult the physician if Co-Q-10 is being used prior to starting warfarin therapy. There has been no RDA established for Co-Q-10, although a therapeutic dose would be 10–90mg per day for adults.

Nutrition for those over 70 is another specialist area. Do not give any recommendations unless your insurance cover will allow you to do so. There is nothing wrong in referring a client to someone more experienced than you.

Knowledge review

Lifestyle changes

1 What foods should be avoided during pregnancy?

2 What is the recommended gain for a woman who begins pregnancy at a healthy weight for her height?

3 At what age approximately should weaning commence, and what are the first four foods that should be introduced?

4 What poor nutritional states could lead to dyslexia, attention deficit disorder, hyperactivity and delinquency?

5 What are the main mineral deficiencies in athletes?

6 State two important guidelines for the daily diet of an athlete.

7 What happens during the menopause?

8 What causes hot flushes?

9 What are fibroids?

10 Name two possible causes of dehydration in the elderly.

Part II
Dietary influences affecting body systems

10 The cardiovascular system 145

11 The digestive system 162

12 The endocrine system 183

13 The lymphatic system and immunity 195

14 The muscular system 216

15 The nervous system 224

16 The reproductive system 233

17 The respiratory system 246

18 The skeletal system 257

19 The urinary and detoxification systems 265

The cardiovascular system

Learning objectives

This chapter covers the following:

- **dietary influences affecting the cardiovascular system**
- **common disorders associated with the cardiovascular system**
- **recommendations of foods to increase/decrease**
- **supplements and herbal remedies**
- **superfoods and lifestyle changes relating to disorders of the cardiovascular system**

What is the cardiovascular system?

The cardiovascular (circulatory) system is the body's transport system and comprises the heart, the arteries, the veins and the capillary network of arterioles and venules. The capillary network of the human body consists of over 62,000 miles of blood vessels through which our blood travels.

What does the cardiovascular system do?

Responsible for continuously pumping the blood around the body.

Main functions

The main functions of the blood are protection, equilibrium, clotting and transport.

Protection – blood offers protection against foreign microbes and toxins which are destroyed by certain white blood cells that are phagocytic (engulfing) in their actions, or specialised proteins such as antibodies, interferon and complement. White blood cells are collectively called leucocytes and they play a major role in combating disease and fighting infection.

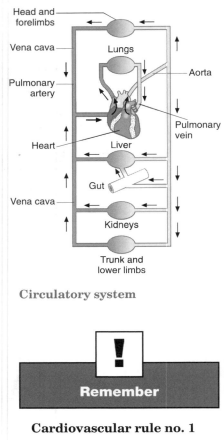

Head and forelimbs
Vena cava
Lungs
Pulmonary artery
Aorta
Heart
Liver
Pulmonary vein
Gut
Vena cava
Kidneys
Trunk and lower limbs

Circulatory system

!

Remember

Cardiovascular rule no. 1

We only have one heart.
Take care of it.

Equilibrium – blood also regulates normal body temperature. It does this by absorbing large quantities of heat produced in the liver and the muscles. This is then transported around the body to help to maintain a constant internal temperature. The blood also helps to regulate the body's pH balance. These two actions are collectively known as homeostasis.

Clotting – blood protects against blood loss through the clotting mechanism. Specialised red blood cells called platelets clot to prevent blood getting out and bacteria getting in.

Transport – the blood is responsible for transporting many substances around the body. Oxygen is carried from the lungs to the cells of the body in red blood cells. It also carries carbon dioxide from the cells to the lungs, nutrients from the gastrointestinal tract to the cells, waste products from cells, hormones from endocrine glands to the cells and heat from various cells.

Cardiovascular disease is the number one killer in the UK, and there are many risk factors associated with it, most of which can be managed, although some cannot. The ageing process and hereditary predisposition are risk factors that cannot be altered. Until the age of fifty men are at greater risk than women of developing heart disease, although once a woman enters menopause, her risk triples.

High cholesterol levels immediately spring to mind when you think of the cardiovascular system, and many people with cardiovascular disease do have elevated cholesterol levels. Although cholesterol has received some bad press over the years, it isn't all bad – there is a good side to cholesterol as well. It is a constituent of cell membranes, is a precursor of bile acids and steroid hormones and vitamin D, the sunshine vitamin, also comes from cholesterol.

Homocysteine, on the other hand, is something we should be concerned about. Often cholesterol has taken the blame for heart disease when homocysteine may have been the culprit.

Homocysteine

Having a high level of homocysteine in the blood is as great a risk factor for cardiovascular disease as smoking or having a high blood cholesterol level. Homocysteine is made from protein in the diet. The amino acid methionine is converted into homocysteine in the body and provided you have enough vitamin B6, B12 and folic acid, the body will convert it into cystanthionine. We now know that homocysteine is very toxic and can cause the initial damage to the artery wall that starts the whole process of cardiovascular disease. There has been much research confirming that homocysteine has a role to play in cardiovascular disease and that cholesterol, in its antioxidant capacity, and in an attempt to repair the initial damage caused by the homocysteine, builds up inside the scarred arteries. This can lead to fatal blockages, and the cholesterol may then take the blame for the initial damage caused by the homocysteine.

Homocysteine levels rise with age and women have, on average, 20 per cent lower levels than men until the menopause, when the levels between the sexes are more or less equal. Those most at risk of high homocysteine levels are people who consume a high protein diet with a poor dietary status of B6, B12 and folic acid. High homocysteine levels have been identified as an independent risk factor for coronary heart disease.

Clients should be advised that if they are concerned about high cholesterol levels they should also be aware of the homocysteine connection. Tests are available to evaluate homocysteine levels, which can be measured by a blood test.

Dietary influences affecting the cardiovascular system

A high meat and dairy diet accompanied by a low fibre intake are the main culprits. There is insurmountable evidence showing that people on a low animal fat and high fibre diet have less heart disease than others who restrict animal fats and dairy food in their diet. However, nothing is that simple. Fat plays a vital part in our diet, and essential fatty acids need to be ingested every day, so the type of fats we choose is important. Heart disease is not about diet alone, but the result of total lifestyle habits.

Common disorders associated with the cardiovascular system

Angina

There are three main types of angina. The first is stable angina, a type of chest pain that comes on during exercise and is both common and predictable. Stable angina is associated with atherosclerosis. A second type, variant angina, can occur at rest or during exercise. This type is primarily due to sudden coronary artery spasm, though atherosclerosis may also be a component. The third, most severe type is called unstable angina. It occurs with no predictability and can quickly lead to a heart attack. Anyone who has significant or new chest pain or a worsening of previously mild angina must seek medical assistance immediately.

Angina is caused by an insufficient supply of blood to the walls of the heart, which in turn induces oxygen starvation. The serious symptoms do not appear all at once, but increasing instances of acute heart cramps accompanied by a feeling of tightness across the chest – this is called cardiac insufficiency – is a warning that immediate action should be taken. Refer clients to their GP if they complain of any type of chest pain.

From a holistic point of view, relieving constipation, encouraging proper bowel function and ensuring the elimination of all waste materials is important for anyone with angina.

Cigarette smoking causes damage to the coronary arteries and can contribute to angina. Stopping smoking is the most important lifestyle change for anyone who has angina. Smoking has also been shown to reduce the effectiveness of treatment of angina. Secondary smoking (cadmium exhaled by smokers) should also be avoided.

Increasing physical exercise has been clearly demonstrated to reduce symptoms of angina and relieve the underlying causes. One study found that ten minutes' intense daily exercise was as effective as beta-blocker drugs in one group of patients with angina. However, anyone with a heart condition including angina or anyone over the age of forty should consult a doctor before beginning an exercise plan.

Coffee should be avoided as drinking five cups or more a day has been shown to increase the risk of angina.

Carnitine is an amino acid important for transporting fats that can be turned into energy in the heart. Several studies using one gram of carnitine two to three times per day show improvement in heart function and reduced symptoms in patients with angina.

Co-Q-10 also contributes to the energy-making mechanisms of the heart. Angina patients given 150mg of Co-Q-10 experienced greater ability to exercise without problems. This has been confirmed by independent investigations.

Low levels of antioxidant vitamins in the blood, particularly vitamin E, are associated with greater rates of angina. This is true even when smoking and other risk factors are taken into account. Early, short-term studies using 300iu per day of vitamin E could not find a beneficial action on angina. However, a later study supplementing small doses of vitamin E (50iu per day) for longer periods of time showed a minor benefit.

Fish oil, which contains the beneficial fatty acids known as EPA and DHA, has been used in the treatment of angina. In some studies, three grams or more of fish oil three times per day (providing a total of about three grams of EPA and three grams of DHA) have reduced chest pains as well as the need for nitroglycerin, a common medication used to treat angina. If fish oil is supplemented, vitamin E should be taken with it, as vitamin E may protect the fragile oil against free radical damage. Those affected by variant angina have been found to have the greatest deficiency of vitamin E compared with other angina patients.

Recommendations for angina

Diet	A high fibre, unrefined carbohydrate diet providing well balanced meals containing all of the main food groups
Increase	Cold water fish, plenty of fruits and raw or lightly steamed vegetables, onions, sunflower seeds and seed sprouts
Decrease	Coffee, salt, alcohol, sugar, refined grains, hydrogenated fats, dairy products, fried foods, red meat
Superfoods	Medicinal mushrooms, avocados, hazelnuts and almonds
Supplements	Carnitine, Co-Q-10 Anti-oxidant complex containing vitamins A, C, E and selenium.
Herbals	Garlic, preferably raw with food or a supplement.
Lifestyle changes	Stop smoking Gentle exercise – daily walking recommended, no less than 10 minutes

Key Term

Trans fatty acids

The result of polyunsaturated fats undergoing a process called hydrogenation to make them hard, and therefore 'spreadable'. Once hydrogenated the body cannot make use of these once beneficial fats.

Key Term

Double-blind research

Research in which neither the subject nor the researchers know which subjects are members of the experimental group and which are serving as control subjects, until after the research is over.

Arteriosclerosis and atherosclerosis

Arteriosclerosis is a degenerative change in the arterial walls, affecting first the middle and later the inner layers, and resulting in loss of elasticity and possible calcification. It is commonly referred to as hardening of the arteries. Atherosclerosis is a degenerative change in the arterial walls which principally affects the larger arteries such as the aorta, coronary, and cerebral vessels. It is more commonly referred to as a narrowing of the arteries.

The most important dietary changes for protecting the arteries from atherosclerosis include avoiding meat and dairy fat, increasing fibre and avoiding foods that contain trans-fatty acids (margarine, some vegetable oils, and many processed foods containing vegetable oils). The fibres most linked to the reduction of cholesterol levels are found in oats, psyllium seeds, and fruit (pectin). Leading researchers have recently begun to view the evidence linking trans-fatty acids to markers for heart disease as 'unequivocal'.

It has been shown that foods that contain high amounts of cholesterol, mostly egg yolks, can induce atherosclerosis, so it may make sense to reduce intake of egg yolks. However, eating eggs does not increase serum cholesterol as much as eating saturated fat, and eggs may not increase serum cholesterol at all if the overall diet is low in fat. A decrease in atherosclerosis resulting from a pure vegetarian diet, meaning no meat, poultry, dairy or eggs, combined with exercise and stress reduction has been proven by medical research.

Many experts agree that LDL – low-density lipoproteins – the harmful cholesterol, triggers atherosclerosis only when reactive molecules called free radicals have damaged it. There are several antioxidant supplements that protect LDL, for example, vitamin E is an antioxidant that protects LDL from oxidative damage and has been linked to prevention of heart disease in double blind research. Many nutritional therapists recommend 400–800ius of vitamin E per day to lower the risk of atherosclerosis and heart attacks.

Other studies have shown that people who consume more selenium and quercetin from their diet have a lower risk from heart disease. Quercetin, a bioflavonoid, also protects from LDL damage and can be found in apples, onions, black tea and as a supplement. In some studies dietary amounts linked to protection from heart disease are as low as 35mg per day.

Preliminary research shows that chrondroitin sulfate may prevent atherosclerosis in animals and humans and may also prevent heart attacks in people who already have atherosclerosis. However, further research is needed.

Reservatrol, found primarily red wine, is a naturally occurring antioxidant that decreases the stickiness of blood platelets and may help blood vessels remain open and flexible. As reservatrol is now available in supplement form, there is no need for that one glass of beneficial red wine any more! The supplement will give you the reservatrol without the alcohol.

Garlic has also been shown to prevent excessive platelet adhesion in humans. Allicin often considered the main active component of garlic is not alone in this action. The constituent known as ajoene has also

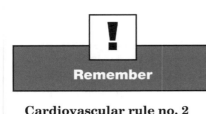

Cardiovascular rule no. 2

The heart is a muscle like any other – it needs exercise!

Remember

Branched chain amino acids

The branch chain amino acids, valine, leucine and isoleucine protect all muscles, including the heart and actually make exercise seem more enjoyable by reducing the feeling of fatigue.

shown beneficial effects on platelets. Garlic has also lowered cholesterol levels in doubl-blind research.

Several herbs have been shown in research to lower lipid levels. Of these, psyllium has the most consistent backing from multiple double-blind trials showing lower cholesterol and triglyceride levels.

Ginkgo biloba may reduce the risk of atherosclerosis by interfering with a chemical the body sometimes makes in excess – platelet activating factor (PAF). PAF stimulates platelets to stick together too much; ginkgo stops this from happening. Ginkgo also increases blood circulation both to the head and to the arms and legs.

Garlic and ginkgo together also decrease excessive blood coagulation. Both have been shown in double-blind or single-blind studies to decrease the overactive coagulation of blood that may contribute to atherosclerosis.

Recommendations for arterioslcerosis and atherosclerosis

Diet	A diet consisting of brown rice, soft white cheese (quark) and salads can have fantastic results if adhered to consistently. Rice bran influences the regeneration of the arteries. Iodine-rich foods can be taken as seasonings or salts. Low animal fat and dairy are recommended together with a high fibre diet
Increase	Oily fish – sardines, salmon, herring, tuna and mackerel with plenty of fruits and raw or lightly steamed vegetables, onions, nuts and seeds
Decrease	Salt, alcohol, coffee, sugar, refined grains, hydrogenated fats, dairy products, fried foods and red meat
Superfoods	Olive oil, strawberries, avocados, hazelnuts and almonds
Supplements	Vitamin E alone or an antioxidant complex containing vitamins A, C, E and selenium; folic acid; lecithin granules and psyllium seeds or husks
Herbals	Garlic, preferably raw in salads or as a supplement; ginkgo biloba
Lifestyle changes	Gentle daily exercise, swimming is ideal

Chilblains

Red/blue skin patches that hurt at every movement are known as chilblains – they mainly effect hands and feet and are caused by prolonged exposure to severe cold. Chilblains are a circulatory disorder and can easily be prevented.

Ginkgo biloba can help with a variety of circulatory problems from strokes to varicose veins, and is a good choice for chilblain sufferers. However it can take a few months to 'kick-in'. In the meantime you will want to do something about your chilblains. This is one condition where you can use an aromatherapy essential oil neat. For almost instant relief from chilblains, apply one drop of neat geranium oil to the affected area for two or three days, after which a massage oil can be used. Blend 10mls of sweet almond base oil into three drops of geranium, one drop of lavender and one drop of rosemary. Massaging daily, leaving the oil on the skin, will quickly alleviate chilblain symptoms. At night, massaging the oil into the affected area and wearing cotton socks or gloves to sleep in will also be of benefit.

Recommendations for chilblains

Diet	A whole food approach to food where quality is more important than quantity. Plenty of fruits and vegetables, low-fat protein, and plenty of water
Increase	All fruits and vegetables Oily fish – sardines, salmon, herring, tuna and mackerel.
Decrease	Everything refined – especially white bread and flour, confectionery, and alcohol
Superfoods	Manuka honey, which can be applied directly to chilblains and lightly bandaged for a few hours. Also to eat together with alfalfa, algae, medicinal mushrooms, and bee pollen
Supplements	Multivitamin and mineral complex
Herbals	Ginkgo biloba
Lifestyle changes	When coming in from the cold, do not stand in front of a fire, chilblains do not like sudden changes in temperature. Keep feet and legs well covered with natural fibres

Cholesterol

Although it is by no means the only major risk factor, elevated serum cholesterol – hypercholesterolemia – is clearly associated with a high risk of heart disease. There are many dietary, lifestyle and supplement changes that can be of great benefit for this condition.

Usually you hear about foods you should avoid when you're trying to not raise your cholesterol such as eggs, red meat, cheeses and fried foods. There are also, however, foods known to lower your cholesterol levels. Eating these cholesterol-lowering foods, does not mean that you can indulge in the foods that are said to increase levels. The cholesterol-lowering foods are oat bran, cooked beans, carrots, olive oil and soy.

Remember

These top five cholesterol-lowering foods will only be effective if you make them part of a diet that gets no more than 30 per cent of its total calories from fat and less than 7 per cent from saturated fatty acids.

Top five cholesterol-lowering foods

Oat bran, cooked beans, carrots, olive oil and soy

Oat bran is a rich source of soluble fibre, which has been shown to help reduce cholesterol levels. Cooked beans, such as pinto and kidney, are another great source of soluble fibre as well as being an inexpensive and versatile food source. Carrots on the other hand, are not a good source of soluble fibre, but a recent study showed that one raw carrot a day at breakfast could lower total cholesterol by as much as 11 per cent. Carrots contain insoluble fibre, which aids in normal

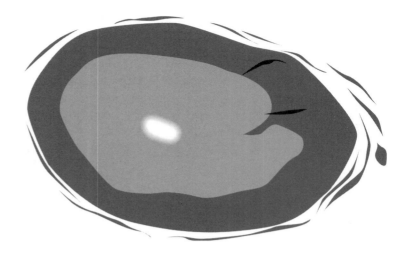

A partially blocked artery. The build-up along the inside of the artery walls is mainly composed of cholesterol.

bowel function by helping to flush dietary cholesterol more quickly from the body. Olive oil is high in monounsaturated fatty acids, which has been shown to help manage cholesterol when part of a low-fat, low-cholesterol diet. This oil should replace more saturated fats in the diet like butter and margarine whenever possible, if trying to reduce cholesterol levels. Lastly, soy – found in tofu, tempeh, soy milk, roasted soy nuts and more, can help reduce cholesterol levels in the body. The higher your cholesterol level the more soy will help bring your levels to where they should be, but if you already have a healthy cholesterol level soy will have no effect.

Eating fish has been reported to increase HDL, the beneficial cholesterol, and is linked to a reduction in heart disease in most studies undertaken. Fish contains very little saturated fat, and fish oil contains EPA and DHA, omega 3 oils that protect against heart disease.

Vegetarians have lower cholesterol and less heart disease than meat eaters, principally because they avoid animal fat. Vegans (people who eat no meat, dairy produce, or eggs) have the lowest cholesterol levels, and going on such a diet has reversed heart disease.

Like cholesterol, egg consumption still remains a controversial issue. Many nutritional therapists advise that eggs are safe to eat provided they are boiled, poached or baked, and while eggs cooked in this way are undoubtedly safer than eggs that are scrambled or fried, care must be taken over egg consumption. It is often said that eggs are safe if the rest of the diet is low in fat, but does not appear to be the case, even for people consuming a low fat diet. When cholesterol from eggs is cooked or exposed to air, it oxidises. Oxidised cholesterol is linked to increased heart disease and eating eggs also makes LDL cholesterol more susceptible to damage, another change linked to heart disease. Moreover, egg eaters are more likely to die from heart disease even when serum cholesterol levels are not elevated. Therefore the idea that egg consumption is unrelated to heart disease, a position taken by many nutritional therapists and doctors of natural medicine, is not supported by most scientific evidence. My own recommendations to clients are a maximum of two free-range eggs per week, boiled, poached or baked.

Remember

Cardiovascular rule no. 3

Supplementing vitamins E and C effectively halves the risk of ever having a heart attack!

There have been many studies showing that chromium supplementation has reduced LDL cholesterol and increased HDL cholesterol in humans. Brewer's yeast, which contains readily absorbable chromium, also lowers cholesterol levels and people with higher blood levels of chromium appear to be at a lower risk of heart disease. A reasonable and safe intake of supplemental chromium is 200mcg per day. People wishing to use brewer's yeast as a source of chromium should look for products specifically labelled 'from the brewing process' or 'brewer's yeast' because most yeast found in health food stores is not brewer's yeast and does not contain chromium. Optimally, true brewer's yeast contains up to 60mcg of chromium per tablespoon, and a reasonable intake is two tablespoons per day.

There have also been many studies showing favourable results with garlic, wild yam, and psyllium. In addition, artichoke has moderately lowered cholesterol and triglycerides in some reports.

Recommendations for high cholesterol

Diet	A whole food approach to food where quality is more important than quantity. Plenty of fruits, vegetables, nuts and seeds with adequate essential fatty acids, low-fat protein, and plenty of water.
Increase	One raw carrot daily with breakfast, olive oil, soy, oat bran and cooked beans. Oily fish – sardines salmon, herring, tuna and mackerel to be eaten at least three times a week.
Decrease	Red meat, eggs, hard cheese, fried foods and sugar
Superfoods	Alfalfa, barley grass, chlorophyll, medicinal mushrooms, super sprouts and low-fat bio-yoghurt
Supplements	A multivitamin and mineral containing at least 50mgs of the B-complex group of vitamins 600ius of Vitamin E daily 500mg Vitamin C daily Chromium in the form of brewer's yeast Flaxseed fibre
Herbals	Black cohosh and garlic
Lifestyle changes	Regular gentle exercise Giving up smoking would be of great benefit

Haemorrhoids

Haemorrhoids are enlarged raised veins in the anus or rectum and are commonly known as piles. They are often associated with chronic constipation in the dense network of blood vessels that run through the intestinal lining, but can also be linked to diarrhoea.

When the stool in the rectum becomes hard and accumulates there, the blood vessels become stretched. The resulting obstruction causes the walls of the vessels in the anal canal to become dilated, turning them into varicose veins. Sometimes, the pressure needed to force out hard stools makes the veins in the thin membranes rupture; making the haemorrhoids bleed. At the time of evacuation, light coloured blood may be noticed on the stool. If this condition is not remedied, the tissues will become inflamed and hard, resulting in piles. Hard stools can push the piles outwards so they hang outside the anus; these can sometimes enlarge to the size of a plum.

The first action to be taken is that of curing the constipation. Only when the constipation has been remedied you can concentrate on the haemorrhoids, as constipation may worsen haemorrhoid symptoms. An excellent herbal product is psyllium seeds. Two teaspoons of the seeds or one teaspoon of the husks once or twice a day with water should be of benefit. Another herb used in the treatment of haemorrhoids is witch hazel, which is topically applied to haemorrhoids three to four times daily in an ointment base.

Fibre is undoubtedly an important aspect with regard to the treatment of haemorrhoids. Countries with high fibre intakes have a very low incidence of haemorrhoids. Insoluble fibre – the kind found primarily in whole grains and vegetables – increases the bulk of the stool. Drinking water with a high-fibre meal or supplement results in softer, bulkier stools, which can move through the large colon more easily.

Recommendations for haemorrhoids

Diet	A high-fibre, whole grain approach to bread must be taken along with plenty of fresh fruit and raw vegetables
Increase	Rice bran Fruits and vegetables, prunes, figs, and dates Lots of fluids
Decrease	Alcohol, all refined foods, all stimulants like coffee and tea
Superfoods	Barley grass, spirulina
Supplements	A multivitamin and mineral containing at least 50mgs of the B-complex group of vitamins
Herbals	Cayenne, ginkgo biloba, psyllium seeds or husks, witch hazel. A tea made from stinging nettles is also beneficial
Lifestyle changes	Abdominal exercises Keep off your feet as often as possible Cold water bathing each morning to the anus is also recommended

Hypertension

Hypertension is a medical term used to describe high blood pressure – a condition with many causes but which cannot be attributed to any one single cause. Symptoms of high blood pressure are headache, dizziness, nervousness, irritability, low energy, fatigue and insomnia. In most cases of hypertension we find that increased peripheral resistance (narrowing of the blood vessels, especially the small arteries) is the primary cause. Another accepted cause of high blood pressure is narrowing of the blood vessels due to cholesterol and other fatty molecules.

It is estimated that 85 per cent of all cases of high blood pressure are both treatable and preventable without drugs. Diet remains the single most important factor in controlling high blood pressure. People with mild to moderate high blood pressure should work with a nutritional therapist or a nutritionally oriented doctor to help reduce blood pressure using diet alone. However, people with extremely high blood pressure (malignant hypertension) or rapidly worsening blood pressure (accelerated hypertension) almost always require treatment with conventional medicine.

Vegetarian diets have been reported to significantly lower blood pressure. This occurs partly because fruits and vegetables contain potassium – a known blood pressure-lowering mineral. The study *Dietary Approaches to Stop Hypertension (DASH)* increased intake of fruits and vegetables (and therefore fibre) and reduced cholesterol and dairy fat which led to large reductions in blood pressure in just eight weeks.

There are many supplements that may significantly assist in lowering high blood pressure. Vitamin C plays an important role in maintaining the health of arteries and a review of vitamin C research reported that most studies linked increased blood and dietary levels of this vitamin to reduced blood pressure. The omega 3 fatty acids found in fish oil have also been found to lower blood pressure as has Co-Q-10. There are also many studies to show that magnesium supplements help – typically 350–500mg per day to be beneficial. Magnesium appears to be particularly effective in people who are taking *potassium depleting diuretics*. Potassium-depleting diuretics also deplete magnesium, so the drop in blood pressure resulting from magnesium supplementation in people taking these drugs may result from overcoming a mild magnesium deficiency.

Smoking is particularly harmful for people with hypertension. The combination of hypertension and smoking greatly increases the chances of heart disease. People with high blood pressure should make stopping smoking a major priority.

As with conventional drugs, the use of natural substances sometimes controls blood pressure if taken consistently but does not lead to a cure for high blood pressure. Thus someone whose blood pressure is successfully reduced by weight loss, avoidance of saturated fats and increased intake of fruits and vegetables would need to maintain these changes *permanently* in order to maintain control of blood pressure.

Recommendations for hypertension

Diet	A low fat, high fibre diet with plenty of salads and fruits
Increase	Dietary fibre, fruits and all vegetables
Decrease	Animal fats, saturated fats, salt in cooking and on food, caffeine and alcohol
Superfoods	Flaxseed, super sprouts, medicinal mushrooms and bee pollen
Supplements	Flaxseed fibre. A multivitamin and mineral complex with additional 1g of vitamin C. Vitamin E. Fish Oils and Co-Q-10
Herbals	Black cohosh, garlic, ginger, Siberian ginseng
Lifestyle changes	Weight loss and an increase in regular gentle exercise. Do not add salt to your food. Give up smoking.

Hypotension

Hypotension is a medical term used to describe low blood pressure. A person with low blood pressure (hypotension) may be subject to dizziness or even occasional fainting spells at high altitudes. Every little exertion may upset the blood circulation or the normal heart activity. In 90 per cent of all cases the symptoms appear as a result of insufficiency of the gonads. In a woman, the ovaries do not function correctly and in a man it is the male sex glands that are out of order. Blood pressure can return to normal when stimulation of glandular activity is given. I am not suggesting powerful synthetic hormone preparations but natural remedies.

One renowned remedy for low blood pressure is hyssop, a plant that has been known and used since biblical times. Bee pollen too can help increase a low blood pressure due to its stimulating effects on the sex glands. Many leading naturopaths feel that bee pollen is so effective at raising blood pressure that people with hypertension should never take it as to do so may cause a stroke.

Raw carrot juice is another natural remedy for increasing blood pressure. Carrots eaten raw or in a salad they will have no effect on the blood pressure; it is only the pure juice that is curative. This also applies to beetroot juice.

Recommendations for hypotension

Diet	Small frequent meals, containing all of the major food groups, carbohydrates, essential fatty acids and low fat protein.
Increase	Carrot and beetroot juice. Good sources of complex carbohydrate. Oily fish – sardines salmon, herring, tuna and mackerel.
Decrease	Everything refined – especially white bread and flour, confectionery and alcohol.
Superfoods	Medicinal mushrooms, bee pollen, rotate spirulina, chlorella and blue-green algae. Barley grass and bio-yoghurt.
Supplements	Phytoestrogens, calcium and magnesium.
Herbals	Hyssop
Lifestyle changes	Ensure there is adequate protein in the diet at every meal. Take a bath with four drops of geranium essential oil, which is a natural hormone balancer.

Obesity

Obesity is the medical term used for people who have excess weight above a body mass index of 25. Excess body weight is implicated as a risk factor for many different diseases including heart disease and diabetes, two of the major killers of modern civilisation. Usually caused by eating too much refined carbohydrates and saturated fats in conjunction with exercising too little. However there are, of course, other causes of obesity. Hormone imbalances play a large role, particularly that of the thyroid, but also the adrenals, pancreas and pituitary can play their part. The origins of obesity often lie in early childhood. Statistically, children who are overweight by the age of two turn into fat adults more frequently than their lean friends. Heredity, too, plays its part.

Obesity is on the increase and is a huge subject in its own right. Eating less and exercising more is not always the answer for these unfortunate people. Many clinically obese clients need psychological help so do not give any specific recommendations in this area unless you are qualified and confident to do so. You can, however, refer them to a specialist in that area.

Societies in which very little fat is eaten have virtually no obesity. Reducing fat, and in particular saturated fat from the diet has to be the most important component of weight loss. Foods with a high proportion of calories from fat should be eliminated or limited in the diet, these include red meat, poultry skins, dark poultry meat, fried foods, butter, margarine, cheese, whole milk, junk foods and most processed foods.

Many people who are diagnosed as obese do not have eating disorders as such, but many experience disordered eating. The first stage of any serious weight-reducing regime is to regulate the eating pattern. Depending upon the client's lifestyle and commitments, he or she would list up to five times in a 24-hour period times which would become regular eating times. Whether hungry or not, the client would eat at these times, which eventually become a habit, resulting in a regular pattern of eating. After an initial period of a couple of weeks of regulating the pattern of when to eat, further address would be made as to what to eat. Many obese and overweight clients know exactly what to eat and have probably bought every slimming magazine ever written. They need help in breaking old habits permanently, and regulating eating times has proved an excellent way to begin this process.

Many low calorie diets are also low in nutrients, therefore a daily multivitamin is always recommended. Chromium is usually added to the supplement recommendations as it plays an essential role in the metabolism of carbohydrates and in the action of insulin. Chromium in a form called chromium picolinate has been studied for its potential role in altering body composition, and preliminary research in animals and humans suggested that supplementation with chromium picolinate promoted loss of body fat and an increase in muscle mass.

The precursor to the neurotransmitter serotonin, 5-Hydroxytryptophan (5-HTP), has been shown in two short-term controlled studies to reduce appetite and to promote weight loss. In one of these studies, a twelve-week double-blind trial, overweight women who took 600–900 mg of 5-HTP per day lost significantly more weight than did women who received the placebo.

The herb guarana contains guaranine (which is nearly identical to caffeine) and the closely related alkaloids theobromine and theophylline; these compounds may curb appetite and increase weight loss. Caffeine's effects (and hence those of guaranine) are well known and include stimulating the central nervous system thus

Remember

The first stage to any serious weight reducing regime is to regulate the eating pattern.

increasing metabolic rate, and producing a mild diuretic effect. Because of concern over potential adverse effects, many nutritional therapists do not advocate using guarana or caffeine-like substances to reduce weight.

Another herb, *Ephedra sinica*, commonly known as ma huang, is also a central nervous system stimulant. Double blind studies have shown that ephedra, particularly when combined with caffeine, promotes weight loss. Again, because of possible adverse effects, especially when combined with caffeine, ma huang is not usually recommended as an aid to weight loss.

The superfood spirulina has been the subject of one double-blind study of sixteen overweight individuals who ingested 2.8 grams of spirulina three times per day for four weeks. The results showed a small but statistically significant weight loss.

Many clients with weight problems know that reducing fat in their diet should result in a weight loss. Unfortunately, many of these clients are eating 99 per cent fat free foods (that are usually high in salt and hidden sugars) or try to eliminate fat altogether in their diets. These clients need educating in the importance of the right kind of fat in the diet – essential fatty acids should make up 10 per cent of daily calorie intake are anti-inflammatory and promote health.

Many clients lose weight on weight reducing diets only to gain it again when they resume their 'normal diet'. Encouragement and advice should be given to overweight and obese clients that the weight reducing diet will become a lifelong lifestyle change and should in time become their normal diet.

You can of course greatly assist overweight clients by encouraging them to eat more natural foods, fish and poultry, fruit and vegetables, unpolluted water and take gentle regular exercise. You should advocate the benefits of nutritious food against the immense health problems associated with fast food, adulterated and denatured food and to discourage the overfed but undernourished population we are becoming.

Recommendations for obesity

Diet	A high fibre, low saturated fat diet
Increase	Fruit, vegetables, oily fish – sardines salmon, herring, tuna and mackerel, water
Decrease	Dieter's foods, red meat, hard cheese, all ready-made meals, and all refined foods and alcohol
Superfoods	Algae, especially spirulina. super sprouts, alfalfa, bee pollen and yoghurt
Supplements	Flaxseed fibre. A good multivitamin and mineral containing 50mg of the B vitamins. Chromium.
Herbals	Ginger, ginkgo biloba, rhodiola
Lifestyle changes	Movement – regular gentle daily walking

Varicose veins

Disturbances in the venous system are much more frequent than in the arterial system and women especially suffer from stagnation of blood in the veins. The valves of the veins, whose function it is to prevent back-flow, cease to work efficiently and stagnation of blood occurs. The body has an amazing ability to repair itself given the right conditions and the veins should, like other organs of the body, be regenerated rather than removed. The first course of action for varicosed veins is sensible clothing and sensible shoes – with a maximum height of one-and-a-half inches. Clothes should be well-fitting and not excessively tight, especially lingerie, as this can constrict circulation. Avoid standing for long periods of time, especially on stone or concrete. If this is unavoidable because of work commitments then good quality insoles should be fitted inside shoes and replaced regularly. A diet rich in vitamins and fresh fruit is, as always, highly recommended. Lastly circulation must be stimulated by regular exercise. This provides the blood with regular exercise thus providing sufficient oxygen for maximum function.

Many people who have varicose veins also suffer from constipation and if this is the case then the first course of action is to establish proper bowel elimination. Although witch hazel is known primarily for combating hemorrhoids it may also be used for varicose veins. Application of witch hazel ointment three or more times per day for two or more weeks is necessary before results can be expected.

Horse chestnut can be used both internally and as an external application for disordered venous circulation, including varicose veins. Preliminary studies in humans have showed that 300mg three times per day of a standardised extract of horse chestnut can produce some benefit on one aspect of varicose veins.

General care of the legs is of paramount importance. Do not consider putting your feet up as a luxury – look at it as a necessity. Carefully empty the veins by careful stroking and gentle massage in an upward direction. A good time to do this is in the evening before going to bed and using a natural oil, like sweet almond, avocado or St John's Wort, that all have high nutritive values in their own right, will be even more beneficial. Patience and perseverance are needed when treating varicose veins the natural way. It took a long time for them to become varicose in the first place and the harm cannot be reversed overnight.

Remember

Lifestyle changes to benefit varicose veins are to avoid leg-crossing and sitting or standing for long periods of time.

Recommendations for varicose veins

Diet	A whole food approach to food where quality is more important than quantity. Plenty of fruits, vegetables, nuts and seeds with low-fat protein and adequate essential fatty acids.
Increase	Oily fish – sardines salmon, herring, tuna and mackerel Plenty of fresh fruit and vegetables – blended in a juicer as well as whole, and low-fat protein foods
Decrease	Everything refined – especially white bread and flour, confectionery, and alcohol
Superfoods	Alfalfa, barley grass, spirulina
Supplements	Multivitamin and mineral with additional 1g vitamin C daily. GLA in evening primrose oil.
Herbals	Witch hazel and horse chestnut both as an ointment
Lifestyle changes	Avoid leg crossing. Keeping legs elevated relieves pain. Avoid sitting or standing for prolonged periods of time and walk regularly.

General recommendations for the cardiovascular system

Diet	Oily fish – sardines, salmon, herring, tuna and mackerel to be eaten at least three times per week. Garlic, fruits and green leafy vegetables such as kale and broccoli. Olive oil for cooking.
Foods to avoid	Refined foods – those high in white flour and sugar. All foods high in saturated fat such as fatty bacon, fat within meat and 'hidden' fats in biscuits and confectionery. High sodium foods and all alcohol.
Superfoods	Barley grass, algae especially spirulina, super sprouts, alfalfa, bee pollen and yoghurt.
Supplements	B-Complex vitamins – commonly known as the 'heart healers' Magnesium Flaxseed fibre. Branched chain amino acids Co-Q-10, and vitamins E and C.
Herbal remedies	Garlic Ginkgo biloba Siberian ginseng
Lifestyle changes	Regular aerobic exercise is the most beneficial change you can make to support and strengthen the cardiovascular system. Always check with your GP before embarking on any exercise programme.

Knowledge review

The cardiovascular system

1　Name four main functions of the blood.

2　What is the number one killer disease of Great Britain?

3　Name four benefits of cholesterol.

4　Briefly describe homocysteine and its role in the body.

5　List two lifestyle changes you would recommend for a client with angina.

6　Arteriosclerosis and atherosclerosis are more commonly referred to as what?

7　What herb can be recommended for chilblain sufferers?

8　Name five cholesterol-lowering foods.

9　If you have a client with high cholesterol levels, what foods would you recommend they eat more of?

10　What are haemorrhoids, and what foods would you recommend a client suffering with haemorrhoids to decrease?

11　Describe hypertension and list the superfoods recommended for this condition

12　Describe hypotension and list the recommended supplements for this condition.

13　Vegetarian diets have been reported to significantly lower blood pressure – why?

14　What is the Body Mass Index (BMI) of a person described as obese?

15　What is 5-HTP and what does it do?

16　What superfoods would you recommend for an obese client?

17　What is the first stage of any serious weight-reducing regime?

18　What three lifestyle changes would you recommend for a client with varicose veins?

19　What supplement is commonly known as the 'heart healer'?

20　Name five foods that support the cardiovascular system.

11

The digestive system

Learning objectives

This chapter covers the following:

- **dietary influences affecting the digestive system**
- **common disorders associated with the digestive system**
- **recommendations of foods to increase/decrease**
- **supplements and herbal remedies**
- **superfoods and lifestyle changes relating to disorders of the digestive system**

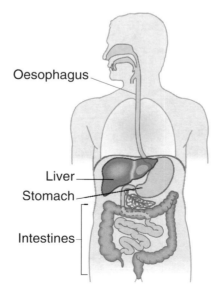

Digestive system

What is the digestive system?

The digestive system is the system of the body that prepares the food we eat ready for absorption into the body via the villi of the small intestine.

Main function

To make food physically small enough and chemically simple enough to be absorbed into the body by the villi and lacteals of the small intestine or to be eliminated out of the body. The terms used for these activities are ingestion, digestion, absorption and defecation.

What does the digestive system do?

The digestive system is a complex tube running from the mouth to the anus. It is the only body system that has contact with the outside world from the openings at the mouth and anus. Everything we put into our mouths has to be chemically changed into a substance that can be absorbed by the small intestine before being transported to the liver.

Digestion starts when we see, smell or just think of food. These senses trigger the brain to start to produce enzymes ready for breaking down food. Thus our mouths start to water. This water is actually saliva in which is found salivary amylase – the enzyme that begins carbohydrate breakdown.

Enzymes are proteins that change one substance into another and there are three types of digestive enzymes. These are amylase that break down carbohydrates, protease that break down proteins and lipase that break down fats. There are many different enzymes within each particular group.

When we eat carbohydrates (bread, pasta, fruit, peas, beans, lentils, vegetables) the process of breaking down these foods into substances that we can actually absorb begins in the mouth by the action of salivary amylase. It is of vital importance therefore that we allow the food to stay in our mouths long enough for this chemical breakdown to begin and allow the enzyme to begin its work.

At the same time mechanical breakdown begins with breaking down the food into smaller pieces by our teeth. The smaller the food can become in the mouth, the easier it is for the stomach and the remainder of the digestive system to do their job properly.

Once the food has been chewed well, it forms into a ball called a bolus at the back of the mouth, the bolus is then swallowed. It travels down the oesophagus, through a sphincter at the bottom of the oesophagus and directly into the stomach. Liquids take seconds to arrive in the stomach; well-chewed food takes several seconds and reaches the stomach by peristalsis. Peristalsis is an automatic action stimulated by the presence of food and occurs in all sections of the alimentary canal – from the oesophagus through to the large intestine.

Protein digestion does not start until it reaches the stomach, but it is still important to chew protein foods into small pieces. By chewing protein foods (meat, cheese, eggs, fish, and nuts) thoroughly, you are assisting the function of the stomach when the proteins arrive there.

There is a lipase that is produced in the mouth for fat breakdown, but the production is so small that we say that all fat breakdown begins in the duodenum. As with the carbohydrates and proteins, chewing is of vital importance to assist proper digestion and absorption later.

Unfortunately, this very simple, primitive action of putting food into our mouths and chewing thoroughly and slowly before swallowing is being lost, resulting in thousands of people suffering major digestive problems because of not doing this simple act. The consequences of not chewing your food thoroughly are many and varied and may include indigestion, heartburn, bloating, malabsorption, irritable bowel syndrome and constipation.

The main function of the stomach is one of breaking down protein foods into smaller chains, which will finally become amino acids and can then be absorbed into our bodies. By chewing our food well, the protein that arrives in the stomach should be in quite small pieces. The stomach produces hydrochloric acid, the main function of which is to straighten out the long curly protein chains into smaller molecules. The stomach also produces an enzyme called pepsinogen. This is an inactive enzyme, or it would start digesting the stomach itself, but when protein food enters the stomach the pepsinogen mixes with the hydrochloric acid and becomes an active enzyme called pepsin. This enzyme can then begin its work and start to break down proteins into dipeptides – smaller chains of proteins.

To put larger pieces of unchewed food, protein in particular, into the stomach places an immense strain on this organ, making the function of the pepsin much harder. The food has to stay in the stomach longer which makes you feel uncomfortable and the carbohydrate eaten with the same meal will also be sitting in the stomach. The salivary amylase works for a little while in the acidic environment of the stomach but then ceases.

Protein breakdown is therefore dependent on hydrochloric acid and pepsinogen mixing together to make pepsin. But what happens if there is not enough hydrochloric acid? Without adequate amounts of hydrochloric acid it is impossible for the protein to be broken down. A low level of hydrochloric acid is known as hypochloridia and an absence of hydrocloric acid is known as achlorhydria.

Stress plays an important part in the whole digestive process as stress may reduce the production of hydrochloric acid. The symptoms of having too much or too little hydrochloric acid are very similar and it is therefore very difficult to determine if you are producing too much or too little without having a clinical test. Many people are diagnosed as producing too much acid and are given antacids to combat the problem. However, if the diagnosis was incorrect and the person was not producing sufficient acid then the problem will be made worse by taking antacids.

Hydrochloric acid secretion in the stomach in an important part of the digestive process, and interference with this process can be a potential source of malnutrition. Hydrochloric acid is essential for the absorption of several trace minerals, most notably calcium and iron.

Remember

Digestive system rule no. 1

Chew your food thoroughly – always!

Key Term

Hypochloridia

Low level of hydrochloric acid.

Key Term

Antacids

Medications used to relieve indigestion by neutralising acid in the stomach. Common brands include Alka-Seltzer, Tums and Rennies.

Difficulties that start at the beginning of the digestive tract can manifest themselves as more complicated problems further down the tract.

The food eventually passes from the stomach to the duodenum, the first part of the small intestine, changing from the acid environment of the stomach to an alkaline environment. Bile from the bile duct of the liver and pancreatic enzymes enter the duodenum, helping to create an alkaline environment. The pancreas has two functions, one as an endocrine gland and one as an exocrine gland. It produces all three main digestive enzymes – pancreatic protease, amylase and lipase – all of which pass directly into the duodenum.

It is here that the fats from our food begin to be broken down. Bile and pancreatic lipase emulsifies the fat, breaking it down into molecules small enough to be absorbed through the lacteals of the villi. Fats are broken down into glycerol and fatty acids before absorption.

Eventually the food will have been broken down into units physically small enough and chemically simple enough for absorption. Absorption takes place through the villi of the small intestine, which are designed in millions of tiny folds for greater surface absorption area. The carbohydrates and proteins go straight into the bloodstream to the liver and the fats are absorbed through the lacteals and into the lymphatic system.

What is not or cannot be absorbed travels into the large colon via the ileocecal valve. Indigestible fibre makes up most of this bulk, which is needed to help carry away unwanted materials of digestion and toxins.

The large colon has four main functions; the absorption of most of the water from the faeces in order to conserve water in the body and form faeces; storage of the faeces, the production of mucous to lubricate the passage of the faeces and the expulsion of the faeces out of the body.

Dietary influences affecting the digestive system

Digestive disorders are on the increase and millions of people are suffering in silence. This is a worrying trend but there is tremendous help available by way of small but permanent lifestyle changes; changes in basic dietary habits and by regularly supplementing and supporting the system with natural products. The most important dietary influences affecting the digestive system are fibre and water. The fibre in our diets can be described as an intestinal broom as it sweeps the system clean.

The recommended daily intake of water is at least one litre a day and many people struggle to meet this quantity. Many people regard water as merely an uninteresting liquid. However, natural water can provide significant quantities of minerals and spring water in particular is a good source. Water that has been artificially carbonated on the other hand can actually rob our bodies of minerals. Tap water should be avoided as in many areas tap water contains significant levels of nitrates, lead and aluminium. Using a filter only addresses half the problem, as although the nitrates may be removed, so too are the essential minerals. It is imperative therefore that we obtain our minerals from either the foods that we eat or from a dietary supplement.

Many symptoms associated with digestive disorders can signal more serious conditions. A visit to a nutritional therapist or the client's GP for a check-up, should always be recommended.

Colonic irrigation

Colonic irrigation is a thorough cleaning of the colon, almost like a glorified enema, which is administered by an operator trained and accustomed to this work. The treatment lasts approximately 45 minutes to one hour and during that time water is inserted into the colon through the rectum, at the rate of several ounces at a time, then expelled, before the process is repeated. The therapist can see what has been removed from the colon by a 'glass viewing tube'. By seeing the colour, texture, the size and amount of air bubbles, undigested food and consistency of the faecal matter, many digestive disorders can be ascertained. It is a perfectly safe and painless treatment and can be a valuable diagnostic tool.

Common disorders associated with the digestive system

Celiac disease

Celiac disease is a hypersensitivity to gluten, which is a protein found in wheat, rye, barley and oats. Although gluten sensitivity is not a food allergy, individuals with celiac disease avoid these foods in the same way that those with food allergies avoid the foods to which they are allergic. Celiac disease can also be described as a chronic malabsorption syndrome due to gluten intolerance.

Celiac disease has many symptoms, the main ones being failure to thrive, weight loss, loss of appetite, vomiting in some cases, diarrhoea, stools bulky, pale, frothy and/or foul-smelling, floating; dermatitis, abdominal distention and pain, weakness, and anemia.

For persons with celiac disease the toxic part of the gluten molecule is the prolamin portion – gliadin in wheat, secalin in rye, horedin in barley, and evedin in oats. The gluten found in corn and rice does not contain this toxic portion.

In celiac disease, gluten ingestion results in damage and destruction of the villi. You can visualise the damage by thinking of a shag carpet changing into linoleum. The flattened surface of the small intestine reduces its capacity to digest and absorb nutrients. It changes the lining of the upper part of the intestine, making it less able to absorb nutrients from food. It affects approximately 1 in 1,000 people and is being increasingly recognised. There is no known cure. A gluten-free diet is the only treatment and there must be lifelong adherence to this diet.

Recommendations for celiac disease

Diet	Strictly no wheat, rye, barley, millet and oats
Increase	Brown rice, corn, brown rice cakes, corn tortillas
Decrease	Everything refined – especially white bread and flour, confectionery and alcohol
Superfoods	Alfalfa, medicinal mushrooms, blue-green algae
Supplements	Multivitamin/mineral liquid formula for better absorption
Herbals	Quercetin, slippery elm tea
Lifestyle changes	Read labels rigorously

Constipation

This is a common problem but a serious one. Constipation is not to do with regularity but more to do with the consistency of the stool. If the bowels move once or twice a day and the stools are hard and difficult to pass, the person is constipated – no matter how regular they are. Constipation results when food moves too slowly through the gastrointestinal tract (GI). The longer the stool is in the body the more concentrated it will become and the more difficult to pass.

A useful index is the time it takes food to pass through the body. In diets of unrefined cereals, fruits and plenty of raw vegetables the transit time is usually 12 hours or so. Faecal matter is bulkier, less dense and easier to pass along the digestive tract. The amount of time food waste spends inside the body is therefore also decreased. A tablespoon of linseeds taken with breakfast cereal can make passage of stools easier.

If our digestive systems are working efficiently, then every time we eat something, we should go to the toilet soon after. When we see, smell or taste food, then the whole of the digestive system should start working from the oesophagus to the anus. As food enters the oesophagus from the mouth then the entire tube should go into action, by way of peristaltic muscular actions. Unfortunately, due to low fibre diets and convenience foods, this does not always happen and many people often go days before eliminating. Gentle massage around the colon moving in a clockwise direction may help loosen the compacted matter inside the colon. Again, advice may be to see a nutritional therapist, as simply eating more fibre may not be the answer. Less than three bowel actions a week is considered a problem or if a person has to strain to endure a movement. Any change in bowel habit, which occurs for no obvious reason in people aged around 40 or over, should be discussed with their GP, as it could be the sign of a more serious problem.

Many nutritional therapists recommend taking 7.5 grams of psyllium seeds or 5 grams psyllium husks, mixed with water or juice, once or twice a day. Some therapists use a combination of senna (18 per cent) and psyllium (82 per cent) for the treatment of chronic constipation. This has been shown to work for people in nursing homes.

Health & Safety

Any change in bowel habit, which occurs for no apparent reason, should be reported to the GP.

One colonic irrigation treatment may be of benefit in cases of chronic constipation. In constipation, peristalsis is inhibited due to the compacted faeces, but after a colonic treatment, when much of the compacted faecal matter has been eased and removed from the colon, then peristaltic action can be restored.

Recommendations for constipation

Diet	A diet high in insoluble fibre – vegetables, beans, brown rice, whole wheat, rye, and other whole grains
Increase	Water intake. Brown bread and brown rice
Decrease	White bread, white rice and alcohol
Superfoods	Alfalfa, barley grass, chlorophyll, super sprouts
Supplements	Flaxseed oil, psyllium husks
Herbals	Ginger, aloe, cascara, senna Dong quai – naturally relaxes the bowels to speed healing
Lifestyle changes	Exercise may increase the muscular contractions of the intestine. Investigate colonic irrigation in your area

Clients are advised to see their doctor if they have the following symptoms:

- Any change in bowel habit that lasts more than a couple of days
- Blood or black matter in the stools
- Pain in the abdomen that may or may not be linked to passing stools
- Difficulty in controlling bowel movements.

Crohn's disease and ulcerative colitis

Ulcerative colitis and Crohn's disease (collectively called inflammatory bowel disease or IBD) are chronic illnesses for which at present there are no known causes or cures. Both sexes can suffer equally and IBD can strike at any age from the very young child to an older person. Onset of the symptoms will include, pain, diarrhoea, fever, loss of appetite, weight loss, abdominal fullness, incontinence, joint pain, and foul smelling and/or bloody stools.

Incidence of Crohn's disease is rising, particularly among young people. It is now thought that IBD affects over 120,000 people in the UK with 8,000 new cases each year. Diagnosis is complicated and other diseases must first be ruled out. Treatment for both conditions involves a healthy balanced diet, particularly important after a severe attack to replace lost nutrients. Crohn's disease is limited to the small intestine in 90 per cent of cases.

The cause of Crohn's disease is said to be unknown, but overeating, chemical poisoning, or bacterial invasion all seem to be possible factors or etiologic agents. Substantially greater numbers of people with the disease give a history of using more refined sugar, less dietary fibre, and considerably less raw fruit and vegetables than the

Key Term

Inflammatory bowel disease – IBD

A collective name for Crohn's disease and ulcerative colitis.

controls. This kind of diet favours the development of Crohn's disease. Some investigators point out that sugary foods tend to contain more chemical additives such as dyes, flavours, and stabilisers. These investigators also suggest that a high sugar intake itself may influence the intestinal bacteria flora to produce compounds toxic to the intestinal lining.

Exercise is important and should include daily walking whenever possible. Avoid any gas-forming foods such as cabbage, corn, certain greens, pickles and relishes of all kinds, skins of apples, potatoes, and legumes. It is as well to try an elimination diet to determine if one is sensitive to any group of the most common foods causing sensitivity. Milk and all dairy products including whey products, sodium lactate, sodium caseinate and all other milk residues should also be avoided, as an allergy to dairy produce is very common with Crohn's disease. Avoid all spices, food additives, dyes, preservatives and stimulants such as coffee, tea, cola, and alcohol.

A small percentage of patients suffer from uveitis, a painful inflammation of the eye. This complication usually improves when the IBD is brought under control. A physician should always evaluate any inflammation of the eye.

Recommendations for Crohn's disease and ulcerative colitis

Diet	A bland, low-fat diet should be instituted
Increase	Liberal quantities of complex carbohydrates – fruits (without the skins), vegetables and whole grains
Decrease	Milk and cheese should be avoided, and all refined foods. Ideally there should be no saturated fats, no fried foods, no sugar and no extremely hot or cold foods
Superfoods	Alfalfa, bee pollen, spirulina, chlorella and blue-green algae – rotate one month on each
Supplements	A complex of omega 3 and 6 fatty acids and probiotics
Herbals	Ginger – relieves gas and settles stomach, quercetin
Lifestyle changes	All foods should be chewed well, or mashed with a fork, or pureed in a blender. Two meals a day are preferable to three as proper digestion and assimilation are more vital. Consider allergy testing to identify any substances you may be sensitive to.

Diarrhoea

Any attack of frequent watery stools is called diarrhoea, and many different conditions can cause it. Diarrhoea is often a symptom of gastrointestinal distress caused by bacteria. In cases like this, probiotics may normalise bowel function by neutralising infectious micro-organisms.

Allergies and food sensitivities are common triggers for diarrhoea. For example, some infants suffer diarrhoea when fed a cow's milk-based formula but improve when switched to soy-based formula. People with chronic diarrhoea not attributable to other causes should discuss the possibility of food sensitivity with a nutritional therapist who specialises in allergies.

Drinking lots of coffee can cause diarrhoea. People with chronic diarrhoea who drink coffee should avoid all coffee for a few days to evaluate whether coffee is the cause.

The malabsorption problems that develop during diarrhoea can lead to deficiencies of vitamins and minerals. For this reason it makes sense for people with diarrhoea to try a multiple vitamin/mineral supplement. Two of the nutrients that may not absorb as a result of diarrhoea are zinc and vitamin A, both needed to fight infections. In third world countries supplementation with zinc and vitamin A has led to a reduction in or prevention of infections diarrhoea. Whether such supplementation would help people in a less deficient population remains unclear.

Some foods contain sugars that absorb slowly such as fructose in fruit juice or sorbitol in diabetic confectionery. Through a process of osmosis, these unabsorbed sugars hold on to water in the intestines, sometimes leading to diarrhoea. By reading labels, people with chronic non-infectious diarrhoea can easily avoid fruit juice, fructose, and sorbitol to see if this eliminates the problem.

People who are lactose intolerant, meaning they lack the enzyme needed to digest milk sugar, often develop diarrhoea after consuming milk or ice cream. People whose lactose intolerance is the cause of diarrhoea will rid themselves of the problem by avoiding milk and ice cream or in many cases by taking lactase, the enzyme needed to digest lactose. Lactase is available in a variety of forms from health food stores.

Large amounts of vitamin C or magnesium found in supplements can also cause diarrhoea although the amount varies considerably from person to person. Unlike infectious diarrhoea, other signs of illness do not generally accompany diarrhoea caused by high amounts of vitamin C or magnesium. The same is true when the problem comes from sorbitol or fructose.

Carob is rich in tannins that have an astringent or binding effect on the mucous membranes of the intestinal tract. It is often used for young children and infants with diarrhoea, and a double-blind study suggests it is effective. Commonly, 15 grams of carob powder is mixed with apple sauce (for flavour) when given to children. Carob can also be used for adult diarrhoea.

Camomile reduces intestinal cramping and eases the irritation and inflammation associated with diarrhoea, according to test tube studies. Camomile is typically drunk as tea, but many nutritional therapists recommend dissolving 2–3 grams of powdered chamomile or adding 3–5 ml of a chamomile liquid extract to hot water and drinking it three or more times per day, between meals. Alternatively, two to three teaspoons of the dried flowers can be steeped in a cup of hot water and covered for ten to fifteen minutes before drinking.

Diarrhoea can also be the result of food poisoning, gastroenteritis, anxiety, antibiotic treatment, excess alcohol or irritable bowel syndrome. Other more rare conditions can cause chronic diarrhoea, including some bowel cancers and hormonal changes such as diabetes, so it is important that sufferers seek medical attention if diarrhoea goes on for more than a few days.

Recommendations for diarrhoea

Diet	A whole food approach to food where quality is more important than quantity. Plenty of vegetables, nuts and seeds with adequate essential fatty acids, low-fat protein, and plenty of water.
Increase	Dietary fibre
Decrease	Fruit juice, fructose and sorbitol
Superfoods	Alfalfa, medicinal mushrooms, barley grass, yoghurt, super sprouts
Supplements	Multivitamin/mineral to protect against deficiencies Folic acid, brewer's yeast, probiotics. Lactase for lactose intolerant people
Herbals	Carob, camomile
Lifestyle changes	Control stress levels by taking up yoga. Meditation and visualisation techniques may also help.

Diverticulitis

Diverticula are sac-like pouches on the wall of the large colon in places where the muscularis has become weak. The development of diverticula is called diverticulosis. Many people who develop this condition are asymptomatic and experience no complications. About 15 per cent of people with diverticulosis will eventually develop an

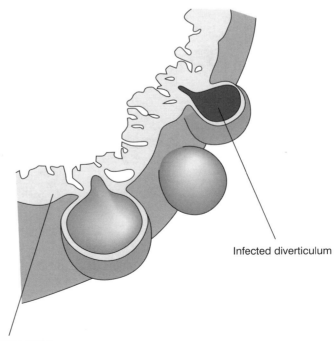

Diverticulitis

Wall of large colon

Infected diverticulum

inflammation within diverticula, a condition then known as diverticulitis. Research indicates that diverticula form because of lack of sufficient bulk in the colon. The powerful contractions, working against insufficient bulk, create a pressure so high that it causes the colonic walls to bulge.

Symptoms are usually pain above the right hip area of the abdomen, nausea, vomiting and abdominal distention, constipation and/or diarrhoea. Most common causes are fibre deficiency, refined diet, white bread and white rice, nutritional deficiency in general and muscular weakness in intestinal walls. Constipation and obesity are considerations, as are poor bowel habits. An allergy, especially to dairy products, is also indicated in some people.

Recommendations should only be given after referral from the client's GP. In the meantime, a liquid multivitamin would be recommended. It is also important to regulate eating times – little and often with quality rather than quantity being of paramount importance. The following recommendations are for clients with established diverticulitis, that is, once the condition is under control, as the initial treatment could be a low fibre diet followed by introductions to higher fibre foods.

Recommendations for diverticulitis

Diet	A whole food approach to food where quality is more important than quantity. Plenty of fruits, vegetables, nuts and seeds with adequate essential fatty acids, low-fat protein, and plenty of water.
Increase	Bran flakes (if no wheat sensitivity) Oily fish – sardines salmon, herring, tuna and mackerel Dietary fibre
Decrease	Refined foods including white bread and rice
Superfoods	Alfalfa, medicinal mushrooms, chlorophyll, bio-yoghurt
Supplements	A liquid multivitamin and mineral Vitamins E and C Probiotics – can be bought powdered to mix up into a drink
Herbals	Garlic, preferably raw in salads Slippery elm tea and marshmallow
Lifestyle changes	The daily consumption of six to eight large glasses of water *every day* is a very useful aid to proper bowel function and the most important lifestyle change you can make.

Dysbiosis

Dysbiosis describes the state of health of the internal human gastrointestinal system. Everything that enters the mouth ultimately undergoes various forms of digestion. Any imbalance within the human gastrointestinal system will not only disturb digestion but predisposes people to nutritional deficiencies and numerous related health problems.

This occurs particularly when pathogenic microorganisms take up residence in the spaces located between the villi of the small intestine. Each species of microorganism produces potentially harmful digestive by-products and toxic chemical compounds that can be absorbed into the blood stream, causing a predisposition to health problems which are often undiagnosed or misdiagnosed. Many people who have food allergies, dietary irregularities and nutritional imbalances have, unknown to them, internal gastrointestinal putrefactive dysbiosis producing generations of toxic chemicals. These chemicals not only alter digestion but also allow those toxic chemicals to enter the blood stream and cause systemic health problems.

As assessment of the gut wall can be undertaken at many nutritional laboratories throughout the country to determine the permeability of the gut. The test employs the use of an oral challenge containing a mixed molecular carbohydrate solution of various sized molecules. Depending upon the size of molecules collected in a urine sample after the challenge, the laboratory is able to assess the degree of gastrointestinal permeability in the sufferer.

Treatment is quite straightforward. The first stage is to remove the cause, followed by improving the gut function before healing the gut wall. Removing the cause may mean making significant changes to lifestyle, including the avoidance of food allergens and overuse of caffeine, alcohol and other anti-nutrients. Improving the gut function is accomplished by improving the general diet and healing the gut is usually done with various supplements.

Health problems related to dysbiosis include: Arthritis, Acne, Alcoholism, Allergies, Anaemia, Anorexia, Asthma, Attention deficit syndrome, Anxiety, Back problems, Bulimia, Candidiasis, Cancer, Constipation, Colitis, Diabetes, Diarrhoea, Drug addiction, Dysmenorrhea, Earaches, Eczema, Endometriosis, Epilepsy, Fibrocitis, Fibromyalgia, Gastritis, Headaches, Hypoglycemia, Hormone problems, Hyperactivity, Indigestion, Impotence, Infections, IBS, Cystitis, Insomnia, Joint pains, Lactose intolerance, Loss of hair, Loss of libido, Loss of memory, Meningitis, Mood swings, Nervousness, Osteoporosis, Pimples, Psoriasis, Sinusitis, Skin rashes, Septicaemia, Weakness, Incontinence, Uterine cysts, Uterine fibroids, Vaginitis, Lupus, Menstrual problems, Muscle aches, Obesity, Pains.

Recommendations for dysbiosis

Diet	A whole food approach to food where quality is more important than quantity. Plenty of fruits, vegetables, nuts and seeds with adequate essential fatty acids, low-fat protein, and plenty of water
Increase	Raw fruits and vegetables
Decrease	All refined denatured foods, salt, sugar, coffee, tea, chocolate, confectionery and alcohol
Superfoods	Rotate spirulina, chlorella and blue-green algae Yoghurt, alfalfa, medicinal mushrooms, barley grass

Supplements	Probiotics – taken in powder form mixed up into a drink L-glutamine – used for cell growth and repair
Herbals	Garlic, milk thistle, dandelion coffee and tincture
Lifestyle changes	Avoid alcohol, and all stimulants Consider a 'gut permeability' test to establish the permeability of your gut wall

Flatulence

Flatulence is abnormal amounts of gas passing upwards or downwards with or without intestinal discomfort. The symptoms are excess gas, abdominal distention and discomfort. Flatulence is usually caused by improper diet by way of excess acidity, poor food combinations, beans, hurried meals, frequent meals, allergies or too much liquid with meals. It may also be caused by digestive enzyme deficiency, inadequate mastication, poor elimination, or abnormal intestinal flora/yeast overgrowth.

Flatulence is a sign that the digestive system is not working efficiently. Food will not have been completely digested, or digested inadequately by the time it gets to the large colon, so this organ is unable to do its job properly. Digestive enzymes are essential in the digestive process to break down complex proteins, fats, and carbohydrates into small molecules for proper absorption. The result of foods that are too complex passing through the gastrointestinal tract and into the large intestine is fermentation, gas and abdominal pain.

Diet is therefore of the utmost importance in all cases of flatulence. Beans are a common problem for many people. They contain oligosaccharides, which have digestive enzyme-resistant chemical bonds between the sugar molecules causing food to be incompletely broken down and passed into the small intestine where fermentation and gas may result. Soaking the beans overnight should overcome this problem.

Recommendations for flatulence

Diet	A whole food approach to food where quality is more important than quantity. Plenty of fruits, vegetables, nuts and seeds with adequate essential fatty acids, low-fat protein, and plenty of water. Beans soaked overnight then cooked in fresh water usually lose their gas-forming characteristics. Chew foods well
Increase	Fruits and vegetables, and sufficient water
Decrease	All refined foods. Fried foods, hydrogenated fats, all junk food
Superfoods	Slippery elm tea, wild yam root tincture
Supplements	None specifically but digestive enzymes help initially Flaxseed fibre.
Herbals	None specifically although ginger assists the entire digestive system
Lifestyle changes	Never eat until full and never rush your meals. Chew all foods very well and do not drink liquids, especially milk, while eating. The liquids dilute the digestive juices and hinder proper digestion, often resulting in flatulence.

Heartburn

Heartburn is described very much as it feels – as a burning pain in the upper chest area over where the heart is – however, it is usually nothing to do with the heart at all. Heartburn is a common way to describe indigestion or 'too much acid'. If it is an excess of hydrochloric acid, the acid may well give a burning feeling. If you have clients with these symptoms advise them to see a nutritional therapist.

Heartburn can however be a symptom of too little acid. The symptoms of too much acid and too little acid are very similar and it is difficult to differentiate between the two.

With hypochlorhydria (low stomach acid) it is undigested protein foods causing the trouble. Due to a *lack of* hydrochloric acid in the stomach, the stomach is unable to function as it should by breaking down the long curly protein molecules into smaller chains. The protein food will therefore just sit in the stomach making you feel uncomfortable with the accompanying burning feeling. Many clients only get heartburn after a protein meal.

This may seem a paradox but based on the clinical experience of doctors, supplementing with betain HCl relieves the symptoms of heartburn and improves digestion.

Another cause of heartburn is a condition called hiatus hernia. With this condition a small portion of the stomach gets caught in the sphincter that separates the oesophagus from the stomach. A hiatus hernia usually does not require any specific therapy, but anyone suffering with accompanying reflux should be receiving treatment.

To relieve heartburn some people try antacids, which often provide symptom relief. However, antacids can have their own side effects, since they can interfere with the absorption of some vitamins and minerals. Many antacids also contain aluminium and there has been several conclusive trials indicating that there may be a link between aluminium and Alzheimer's disease. Of course if you take antacids to reduce acidity in the stomach, but in fact you have hypochlorhydria and are producing insufficient acid, then taking the antacids will only make the situation worse.

A potentially beneficial category of herbs for people with indigestion and/or low stomach acid are bitters. Gentian, dandelion, blessed thistle, yarrow, devil's claw, bitter orange and centaury are thought to stimulate digestive function by increasing saliva production and promoting both stomach acid and digestive enzyme production. Bitters are taken either by mixing 1–3 ml tincture into water and sipping slowly ten to fifteen minutes before eating, or by making a tea from the dried herbs, which is also sipped slowly before eating.

Remember

Digestive system rule no. 2

Never eat under stressful conditions or until you are full.

Recommendations for heartburn

Diet	No specific diet required for heartburn. Ensure that protein foods are chewed well. Stir-fry is a good choice for people suffering with heartburn as the protein is already in smaller pieces, assisting the stomach with its function.
Increase	Raw food that contains their own enzymes for better digestion. Brown rice
Decrease	Refined foods of all types, and acid forming foods like meat, cheese and milk until the problem has been rectified.
Superfoods	Cabbage. Pineapple contains the enzyme bromelain that assists in the breakdown of protein foods.
Supplements	Betain HCl, or digestive enzymes containing betain HCl. Lactase (for lactose intolerance only). Lecithin.
Herbals	Bitters, goldenseal, slippery elm tea
Lifestyle changes	Avoid high protein meals. Eat slowly, not under stressful conditions, and chew all food well. Smaller meals more frequently are more beneficial than fewer large meals.

Hypochlorhydria (low stomach acid)

As explained in the section on heartburn, hypochlorhydria is a condition where there is low stomach acid, and the symptoms of too little as opposed to too much are very difficult to differentiate. However, low stomach acid is very common because hydrochloric acid is dependent upon zinc, and many people are zinc deficient due to poor soil conditions and intensive farming. Stress, parasites and B12 deficiency may also be associated with low stomach acid.

Since the 1930s medical researchers have been concerned with the consequences of too little stomach acid. While all the health consequences are still not entirely clear, some have been well documented. Many minerals and vitamins require proper stomach acid to be absorbed optimally. Examples are iron, calcium, zinc, and B-complex vitamins, including folic acid. People with achlorhydria (no stomach acid) or hypochlorhydria (low stomach acid) may be at risk for developing certain mineral deficiencies. Since minerals are important not only for body structure (as in bones and teeth), to activate enzymes (such as superoxide dismutase) and hormones (such as insulin), deficiencies can lead to many health problems.

One of the major tasks of stomach acid is to break proteins down to the point that pancreatic proteolytic enzymes can easily work. If this does not occur, these proteins could be absorbed as more complicated chains. This has been suggested by some researchers as a major cause of immunological stress and food allergies.

In addition, partially digested protein provides a favourable environment for unfriendly bacteria that live in the colon. Some of these bacteria produce toxic substances that can be absorbed by the body. If there is doubt as to whether the problem is too much acid or too little acid, there are clinical tests that can be done very easily.

Recommendations for hypochlorhydria (low stomach acid)

Diet	No specific diet required for low stomach acid. Ensure that protein foods are chewed well. Stir-fry is a good choice for people suffering with low stomach acid as the protein is already in smaller pieces, assisting the stomach with its function.
Increase	Raw food that contains their own enzymes for better digestion
Decrease	Refined foods of all types, and acid forming foods like meat, cheese and milk until the problem has been rectified.
Superfoods	Cabbage. Pineapple contains the enzyme bromaline that assists in the breakdown of protein foods.
Supplements	Betain HCl, or digestive enzymes containing betain HCl Lactase (for lactose intolerance only)
Herbals	Bitters, peppermint, slippery elm tea
Lifestyle changes	Avoid high protein meals. Eat slowly, not under stressful conditions, and chew all food well.

Indigestion

Indigestion, often referred to as functional dyspepsia, is similar to heartburn but the symptoms are not as severe. Eating too quickly and under stressful conditions can cause indigestion. By following Digestive rule no. 2, never eat under stressful conditions, and by eating slowly and chewing food very well, indigestion can be avoided.

Extracts of artichoke have been repeatedly shown in double-blind research to be beneficial for people with indigestion. Artichoke is a mildly bitter plant and healthy food and is particularly useful when the problem is a lack of bile production by the liver. Extracts providing 500–1,000mg per day of cynarin, the main active constituent of artichoke, are recommended by many nutritional therapists.

Turmeric, the bright yellow herb we use for colouring rice and other food, has also been used in trials in Thailand. The results from a double-blind study showed that it relieved indigestion problems.

Recommendations for indigestion

Diet	No specific diet required for indigestion. Good well-balanced meals covering all the major food groups.
Increase	Raw food that contains their own enzymes for better digestion
Decrease	Refined foods of all types, and acid forming foods like meat, cheese and milk until the problem has been rectified
Superfoods	Cabbage. Pineapple contains the enzyme bromaline that assists in the breakdown of protein foods
Supplements	Digestive enzymes containing all three types of enzyme. Lactase (for lactose intolerance only)
Herbals	Bitters, peppermint, slippery elm tea
Lifestyle changes	Avoid high protein meals. Eat slowly, not under stressful conditions, and chew all food well.

Irritable bowel syndrome (IBS)

This is a disease of the entire gastrointestinal tract, and probably the most common gastrointestinal disorder. The main symptoms of IBS are constipation and diarrhoea, and/or uncomfortable bloating. Excessive amounts of mucus may appear in the stools, and other symptoms include flatulence, nausea and loss of appetite. How the client actually got IBS will often be a mystery. There may be a connection with allergies or food sensitivities and anxiety, depression and stress can also be related to IBS. Yeasts and bacteria in the gut emit carbon dioxide and methane gas as natural by-products of respiration and this is often a cause for bloating.

Although increased fibre intake can be helpful in IBS, many sufferers are sensitive to wheat in any form, including wheat bran. Rye, brown rice, oatmeal, and barley are high in hypoallergenic fibre, as are vegetables and psyllium husk.

Some young women with IBS experience worsening symptoms before and during their menstrual periods. Taking evening primrose oil capsules or tables containing 350–400mg of gamma linolenic acid (GLA), the active ingredient, may help such women.

Enteric-coated peppermint oil capsules, providing 0.2ml of peppermint oil, have been shown in some, but not all, studies to be an effective symptomatic treatment for IBS. Many people take one to two capsules three times per day, between meals. The enteric coating protects the peppermint oil while it passes through the acid environment of the stomach. In the intestinal tract, peppermint oil acts as a carminative, eases intestinal cramping and soothes irritation. Peppermint may also be taken as a tincture in the amount of 2–3ml three times a day.

Camomile acts as a carminative as well as soothing and toning the digestive tract. Camomile's essential oils also ease intestinal cramping and irritation. It is often used for those with IBS experiencing alternative bouts of diarrhoea and constipation. Camomile is typically taken in a tea form by dissolving 2–3 grams of powdered camomile or by adding 3–5ml of herb extract tincture to hot water, three times per day, between meals. Supplements that combine an assortment of carminative herbs are often useful for IBS. A combination of peppermint leaves, fennel seeds, caraway seeds, and wormwood may be an effective treatment for upper abdominal complaints, including IBS. Some people with IBS benefit from bulk-forming laxatives. Psyllium, mentioned above, helps regulate normal bowel activity and reduces the alternating constipation and diarrhoea suffered by some people with IBS.

Recommendations for IBS

Diet	A good well balanced diet covering all food groups but taking care to avoid foods you know are liable to disagree with you
Increase	Brown rice, rye, oatmeal and barley
Decrease	White bread and rice, all refined foods. Spicy foods.
Superfoods	Alfalfa, rotate – spirulina, chlorella and blue-green algae
Supplements	Probiotics, evening primrose or starflower oil
Herbals	Camomile, ginger, peppermint
Lifestyle changes	Identify food intolerances from an experienced practitioner. Practicing stress management skills can be beneficial. Hypnosis for relaxation may also be helpful for those with IBS.

Malabsorption/underweight

Malabsorption can be quite difficult to identify and to help. It is often found in people who tend to eat continually but never seem to put on any weight. Whilst many people like this are in good health, there are many others who have very inefficient digestive systems and are absorbing very little of the food, and therefore nutrients, that they are consuming. Digestive enzyme deficiency is often one factor in malabsorption and often is connected to food allergies or sensitivities. This is one condition I immediately investigate when clients who come to see me are eating a really good balanced diet, but are quite obviously not at all well in themselves. Malabsorption syndromes due to allergy or food insensitivity are also very common.

Endocrine imbalances are sometimes responsible for clients not putting on weight and also hypoglycemic and diabetic clients have a particularly difficult time maintaining proper weight. Zinc deficiency has been known to reduce the appetite and stress and/or emotionally based weight loss may require psychological help.

Recommend zinc 15mg taken in the evenings and a B-Complex of up to 50mg taken in the mornings.

Recommendations for malabsorption/underweight

Diet	A whole food approach to food where quality is more important than quantity. Plenty of fruits, vegetables, nuts and seeds with adequate essential fatty acids, low-fat protein, and plenty of water.
Increase	Adequate and complete proteins are essential
Decrease	Everything refined – especially white bread and flour, confectionery and alcohol
Superfoods	Alfalfa, algae, barley grass, medicinal mushrooms, super sprouts, bio-yoghurt
Supplements	Digestive enzymes and probiotics
Herbals	Ginger, quercetin.
Lifestyle changes	Rule out food sensitivities or food allergies. Colonic irrigation can be a useful treatment and diagnostic aid to check for undigested foods in the stool.

Ulcers

An ulcer is a crater-like lesion in a membrane and the common symptoms are a burning pain, heartburn, or local tenderness. Ulcers that develop in areas of the gastrointestinal tract exposed to acid gastric juice are called peptic ulcers. Peptic ulcers occasionally develop at the lower end of the oesophagus, but most occur on the lesser curvature of the stomach, where they are called gastric ulcers, or in the first part of the duodenum, where they are called duodenal ulcers – these are the most common. Peptic ulcers therefore result when the stomach's digestive juices break the normal defence mechanisms and eat away at the lining of the stomach or duodenum. These ulcers often bleed and may cause sharp burning pain in the area of stomach or just below it. Peptic ulcers should never be treated without proper diagnosis.

About 1 in 10 men and 1 in 15 women have an ulcer at some stage in their life. Too much stomach acid is not always the cause. Another prime culprit is thought to be the bacteria called *Helicobacter pyori*. People with peptic ulcers due to infection should discuss conventional treatment directed toward eradicating the infection with a medical doctor.

Ulcers can be caused or exacerbated by stress, alcohol, smoking and dietary factors. Aspirin and related drugs, alcohol, coffee (including decaf) and tea are known to increase stomach acidity, which can interfere with the healing of an ulcer. Smoking is known to slow ulcer healing. Whether or not an ulcer is caused by infection, people with a peptic ulcer should avoid use of these substances.

Many years ago researchers reported that cabbage juice accelerated healing of peptic ulcers. Drinking up to 5 × 6oz glasses of cabbage juice per day was necessary for symptom relief. Although only preliminary modern research supports this aproach, nutritionally oriented doctors and nutritional therapists claim considerable success using this quantity of cabbage juice every day for fourteen days with ulcer symptoms frequently decreasing in only a few days. Carrot juice may be added to improve the flavour. Cabbage juice contains metioninic acid which helps to normalise the mucous membrane in both stomach and duodenum. Drink as much as you can – up to 5 × 6oz glasses daily which can be mixed half-and-half with either carrot juice or celery juice. This is a very soothing drink.

Food allergies have also been linked to peptic ulcers. Exposing the lining of the stomach to foods a person was known to be allergic to has caused bleeding in the stomach. If triggered by *Helicobacter pylori* infection or not helped by other natural approaches, peptic ulcers may respond to avoidance of allergens. Consultation with a nutritional therapist specialising in allergies would be the first course of action.

Garlic, thyme tea and cinnamon tincture have all been reported to have anti-*Helicobacter pylori* activity in test tube studies. Whether these substances would be effective in humans with peptic ulcers caused by this bacterium has yet to be explored in clinical research, but many nutritional therapists use these products with excellent results.

Slippery elm and comfrey teas also come highly recommended. Slippery elm soothes and heals mucous membranes and comfrey contains allantoin, a cell proliferant.

Recommendations for ulcers

Diet	High fibre diet with plenty of fruit and vegetables
Increase	Bananas and unsweetened banana chips, cabbage
Decrease	Sugar, salt, alcohol, hot spices, chocolate, nicotine, tea, coffee, and red meats
Superfoods	Cabbage especially the juice, liquorice root
Supplements	Vitamin A, zinc and copper in a balanced dose Glutamine
Herbals	Garlic, quercetin, goldenseal – stops infection and internal bleeding, eliminates toxins from the stomach
Lifestyle changes	Reduce stress, and never eat under stressful conditions. Identify any allergens and remove these from the diet until the ulcer is repaired. Exchange coffee and tea for strong camomile tea, preferably made with a tincture.

General recommendations for the digestive system

Diet	Rice bran, fruits and vegetables, prunes, figs, dates, chicory, artichoke, onion, leek, asparagus, peaches and bananas.
Foods to avoid	All refined foods high in white flour, sugar salt and saturated fat. All spicy foods.
Superfoods	Alfalfa, spirulina, cabbage especially the juice, liquorice root, Manuka honey and bio-yoghurt.
Supplements	Vitamin C and folic acid Probiotics and prebiotics Digestive enzymes.
Herbal remedies	Garlic, quercetin, goldenseal, camomile, ginger, peppermint.
Lifestyle changes	Make time to sit down at the table to eat. Never eat under stressful conditions and always eat slowly, chewing your food well.

Knowledge review

The digestive system

1   What are the two main functions of the digestive system?

2   Where does the majority of protein digestion happen?

3   What is peristalsis?

4   Define an enzyme and give three examples of digestive enzymes.

5   Name three functions of hydrochloric acid.

6   Where does the majority of absorption take place and what special design feature does it have to assist absorption?

7   What are the four main functions of the large colon?

8   What are the two most important dietary influences affecting the digestive system?

9   What is the recommended daily intake of water for an adult?

10   Describe colonic irrigation.

11   Celiac disease is a hypersensitivity to what?

12   What foods are strictly to be avoided for clients with celiac disease?

13   What two supplements may be recommended for clients suffering with constipation?

14   Name three possible factors associated with Crohn's disease.

15   What dietary strategy is recommended for clients with Crohn's disease?

16   What lifestyle changes would you recommend for clients with diarrhoea?

17   Describe dysbiosis and state 10 symptoms associated with it.

18   Why are beans a common problem for many people, especially those suffering with flatulence?

19   What superfoods are recommended for heartburn?

20   What are the important lifestyle changes for clients with indigestion?

21   What is IBS and what are the main symptoms?

22   What are the recommended herbal remedies for IBS sufferers?

23   What foods should be increased for clients who are underweight?

24   What is an ulcer and what superfood may be of benefit to this condition?

25   What are the two main lifestyle changes that would be of benefit to the digestive system as a whole?

The endocrine system

Learning objectives

This chapter covers the following:

- **dietary influences affecting the endocrine system**

- **common disorders associated with the endocrine system**

- **recommendations of foods to increase/decrease**

- **supplements and herbal remedies**

- **superfoods and lifestyle changes relating to disorders of the endocrine system**

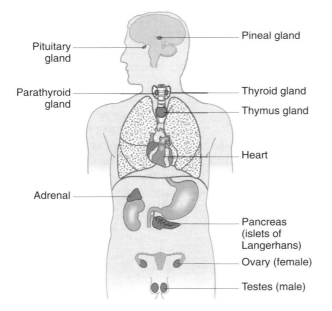

Pituitary gland

Pineal gland

Parathyroid gland

Thyroid gland

Thymus gland

Heart

Adrenal

Pancreas (islets of Langerhans)

Ovary (female)

Testes (male)

Endocrine glands of the body

What is the endocrine system

The endocrine system is the system of the body that is responsible for releasing chemical messengers, known as hormones, into the bloodstream.

Main function

As one of the main control systems of the body, the other being the nervous system, the endocrine system's main function is that of transmitting messages.

What does the endocrine system do?

The endocrine system sends messages to cells in virtually every part of the body bringing about changes in the metabolic activities of almost all body tissues. The endocrine glands make up the endocrine system and include the pituitary, thyroid, parathyroids, adrenals, pineal and thymus gland. In addition there are several organs of the body than contain endocrine tissue but are not exclusively endocrine glands. These include the pancreas, ovaries, testes, kidneys, stomach, small intestine, skin, heart and placenta.

The body contains two kinds of glands: exocrine and endocrine. Exocrine glands secrete their products into ducts, and the ducts carry the secretions into body cavities or to the body's surface. Exocrine glands include sudoriferous (sweat), sebaceous (oil), mucous, and digestive glands. Endocrine glands, on the other hand, secrete their products (hormones) into the extracellular space around the secretory cells, rather than into ducts. The secretion then passes into capillaries to be transported in the blood to target organs.

Dietary influences affecting the endocrine system

The main dietary factor to influence the endocrine system is that of synthetic chemicals, many of which mimic the body's hormones and severely disrupt the system. There are now over 100,000 synthetic chemicals on the international market including 15,000 chlorinated compounds such as PCBs. Some of these are put directly into food, others are added indirectly in the form of pesticide; some creep into our food from packaging (especially plastics and cling film) and processing and some we take as medicine. Many of these mimic the role of oestrogen in the body, stimulating the growth of hormone-sensitive tissue such as breast tissue which then increases the risk of hormone-related cancers.

Common disorders

Diabetes

Diabetes is essentially too much sugar in the blood. There are two types. Type I diabetics must take insulin injections because their

Remember

Endocrine system rule no. 1

Avoid all synthetic hormones – they disrupt the endocrine system.

pancreas produces virtually no insulin. Type I is also known as insulin-dependent or juvenile diabetes. Type II diabetes accounts for 75 per cent of all cases affecting some one million Britons, and usually develops after the age of 40. Sufferers usually have sufficient insulin but the body cells have become insulin resistant. Food has a major impact on blood sugar levels and while sugar is a major factor in high blood sugar levels it is not sugar that causes diabetes. The cause of diabetes is the insufficiency of insulin (Type I) or the ineffectiveness of insulin (Type II).

Most diabetics are very good at monitoring their blood sugar levels and understand the role of food and medication they have to undertake. They are usually on a diet recommended by their doctor. Alcohol may increase the action of insulin, leading to hypoglycemia (low blood sugar), so people using insulin should avoid alcohol. Smoking may decrease insulin activity. Smoking compounds the health problems associated with diabetes and people using insulin are cautioned to avoid smoking.

Glucose intolerance

There are a great many people with blood sugar problems who are not diabetic but have many symptoms. These clients we can help. Low blood sugar and high blood sugar have similar symptoms. Common symptoms of blood sugar imbalances are irritability, fatigue – especially in the afternoons, constant thirst, lack of energy, the need for stimulants like coffee and tea, dizziness if without food for more than six hours, headaches, blurred vision, excessive sweating, crying spells, fears and anxiety, palpitations and muscle cramps.

Chromium is often deficient in people who have ups and downs in their blood sugar levels. They need to be advised to eat little and often and never skip breakfast. By including protein and essential fatty acids in every meal and snack they have, they will keep their blood sugar levels even which will improve their concentration, productivity and energy levels – generally they will feel much better.

If we constantly eat sugar, the pancreas is always stimulated. If we eat any carbohydrate in refined form, white sugar, sweets, chocolate, white flour for example, digestion is rapid, and glucose enters the blood in a rush. In each case, the pancreas can overreact and produce too much insulin. Blood glucose then takes a rapid, uncomfortable drop, and may end up too low for normal functioning (hypoglycemia). If this over-stimulation happens too often, the pancreas becomes exhausted. Now, instead of too much insulin it produces too little. Too much glucose remains in the blood (hyperglycemia). In its most severe form, this condition becomes diabetes.

The regulation of blood glucose is a constant balancing act. The aim is to provide energy to the cells which need it, including the brain, and to make sure that unwanted glucose is not left circulating in the blood. If this balance is lost both physical and mental well-being are unbalanced. Low blood glucose and high blood glucose can have similar and wide-ranging effects.

Diet is of the utmost importance for people with out-of-control blood sugar. All refined carbohydrates must be removed from the diet – this includes honey and fruit juice. Research has shown that a whole foods approach to diet, including fruit, vegetables, beans, nuts, and seeds is effective in reversing the insulin resistance seen in adult onset diabetes. They contain starch, which requires less insulin than simple sugars, high levels of fibre, natural antioxidants, essential fatty acids, and minerals. Avoiding stress and taking regular exercise also help balance blood sugar levels.

Recommendations for glucose intolerance

Diet	A whole food diet, with well-balanced meals containing food from all main food groups. Complete protein at every meal.
Increase	Fruit, vegetables, beans, lentils, nuts and seeds Oily fish – sardines salmon, herring, tuna and mackerel
Decrease	All refined foods, especially those high in sugar, fizzy drinks, honey, citrus fruits, dried fruit, fruit juice, and alcohol. Avoid or cut down on cigarettes.
Superfoods	Alfalfa, algae, barley grass, bee pollen and bio-yoghurt
Supplements	Multivitamin and mineral Chromium GTF.
Herbals	Siberian ginseng – natural adaptogen
Lifestyle changes	Frequent small meals, containing some protein. Always eat breakfast. Take regular exercise.

Endometriosis

The endometrium is the lining of the uterus (womb). Every month hormones in the blood prepare it to support and nourish a fertilised egg. If there is no pregnancy, the endometrium is shed during your period. It comes out through your cervix (neck of womb) but some also travels back up through the fallopian tubes and spills into your abdominal cavity. This is quite normal and usually causes no problems. The stray endometrial cells are simply absorbed. With endometriosis however, some of these cells implant and start to grow. The result can be pain, scarring and infertility – although how this

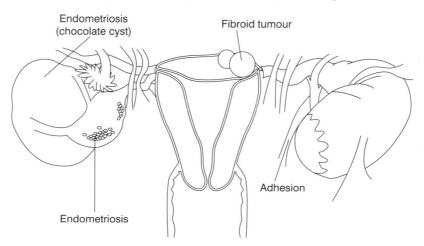

Endometriosis
(chocolate cyst)

Fibroid tumour

Adhesion

Endometriosis

Endocrine system rule no. 2

Never recommend fish oil capsules to diabetics. Some diabetics have experienced problems in glucose regulation.

happens is not fully understood. The main symptoms are infertility, painful periods (dysmenorrhoea), painful sex (dyspareunia), painful bowel movements or painful urination. Other symptoms include painful ovulation, a swollen abdomen, a loss of old brown blood and blood clots during periods, irregular periods and, not surprisingly depression and other psychological problems.

Endometriosis is therefore a condition where cells that are normally located inside the uterus are found outside the uterus, most often in the pelvic cavity. Endometriosis lesions have been found on nearly every organ in the female body, but are most frequently located around the reproductive organs, the bladder, bowel, intestines, colon and appendix. When active, endometriosis lesions respond to a woman's hormones each month. As a result the lesions can inflame surrounding tissue and cause bleeding and scarring. It is estimated that 30-40 per cent of women with endometriosis are also infertile.

The precise cause of endometriosis is not known but there are plenty of theories. Misplaced endometrial cells meant for the lining of the womb which were formed before birth and ended up in the wrong place, is one theory. Retrograde menstruation (bleeding upwards into the fallopian tubes) instead of downwards and out through the vagina is the other main theory. Ninety per cent of women have some degree of retrograde menstruation and they don't all get endometriosis but for those that do it is thought are unable to clear it from the abdominal cavity.

Another possible cause is the link between dioxin exposure and the development of endometriosis. In one study on rhesus monkeys, 79 per cent of the monkeys exposed to dioxin developed endometriosis. Further, the monkeys who had the most exposure had the most extensive endometriosis. Dioxins are part of the organochlorine group of chemicals. Studies have shown that organochlorines act as hormones in our bodies. Dioxin is created by incinerators burning chlorinated waste, leaded gas and in the manufacture of pesticides, solvents and PVC plastics. Dioxin can be found in bleached products, and most alarmingly may be found in women's sanitary products except those manufactured specifically without dioxins.

When endometriosis affects reproductive organs such as when adhesions block the fallopian tubes or when an endometrioma on the ovary prevents ovulation, then fertility is compromised. Loss of fertility is investigated in at least half of those with endometriosis as 30 to 40 per cent of sufferers cannot conceive.

There is no quick and simple test to diagnose endometriosis. Only a doctor can do this by examination and the best time for this is just before a period. After ruling out other possible problems which could be causing symptoms such as PID (pelvic inflammatory disease) or various bowel or bladder disorders, the doctor may recommend a laparoscopy – surgery in which a light is inserted into small incisions in the abdomen.

Dietary advice for endometriosis

Because of the precise cause of endometriosis has never been established treatment is not certain. There is much evidence that excessive candida in the system creates blockages in the fallopian tubes, thereby causing a leak of cells into the endometrium. Therapists assuming candida is at the root of the problem and offer an anti-candida regime have achieved good results in the treatment of endometriosis patients.

Recommendations for endometriosis

Diet	A whole food approach to food where quality is more important than quantity. Plenty of fruits and vegetables, low-fat protein, and plenty of water.
Increase	Whole grains, oily fish, fresh fruit and vegetables, preferably organic
Decrease	Avoid all pesticides, all junk food, everything refined, especially chocolate, white rice and bread
Superfoods	Bee pollen, medicinal mushrooms, barley grass, algae
Supplements	A good multivitamin/mineral containing no less than 50mg of all the B-complex vitamins; antioxidants
Herbals	Dong quai, black cohosh, ginkgo biloba
Lifestyle changes	Avoid all synthetic hormones. Avoid tampons, or buy sanitary wear specially prepared without bleach.

Menopause

The menopause is the cessation of the monthly female menstrual cycle. Women who have not had a period for a year are considered postmenopausal. Most commonly menopause takes place when a woman is in her late forties or early fifties. It is a perfectly natural part of being a woman, it is not a disease and cannot be prevented. Lifestyle and dietary changes can help in avoiding many menopausal symptoms.

Exercise is important whatever age you are. Sedentary women are more likely to have moderate or severe hot flushes compared with women who exercise. In one trial, menopausal symptoms were reduced immediately after aerobic exercise.

Researchers have studied the effects of vitamin E in reducing symptoms of menopause. Most, but not all studies found vitamin E to be helpful; 800ius per day of vitamin E are recommended for a trial period of at least three months to see if symptoms are reduced. If helpful, this amount may be continued.

Soybeans contain compounds called phytoestrogens, which can be described as weak oestrogens. Researchers have linked societies with high consumption of soy products to a low incidence of hot flushes during menopause. As a result of many studies, nutritional therapists recommend that women experiencing menopausal symptoms eat tofu, soy milk, tempeh, roasted soy nuts and other soybean sources of phytoestrogens. Care must be made that the source is from non-genetically modified soybeans. Soy sauce contains very little phytoestrogen content, and processed foods made from soybean concentrates have low levels of phytoestrogen. Supplements containing isoflavones extracted from soy are commercially available, and flaxseed (as opposed to flaxseed oil) is also a good source of phytoestrogens.

Double-blind studies support the usefulness of black cohosh for women with hot flushes associated with menopause. A review of eight trials confirmed black cohosh to be both safe and effective.

Sage may be of some benefit for women who are sweating excessively due to menopausal hot flushes during the day or at night. It is believed this is because sage directly decreases production of sweat. This is based on traditional herbal prescribing and has been evaluated in clinical studies.

Recommendations for menopause

Diet	A whole food approach to food where quality is more important than quantity. Plenty of fruits, vegetables, nuts and seeds with adequate essential fatty acids, low-fat protein, and plenty of water.
Increase	Fresh fruit, in particular berries: blackberries, strawberries, blueberries, and loganberries. Soybeans from unadulterated sources.
Decrease	Everything refined – especially white bread and flour, confectionery, and alcohol.
Superfoods	Soybeans and flaxseed fibre
Supplements	A good all round multivitamin and mineral
Herbals	Black cohosh Siberian ginseng – corrects hormonal imbalance
Lifestyle changes	Enjoy life to the full. Weight-bearing exercise is important at this time to support the skeletal system, but swimming and cycling are recommended too.

Prostate problems

The prostate gland is a small gland that surrounds the neck of the bladder and urethra in males. It secretes a lubricating fluid which forms the bulk of spermatic fluid and aids in the transport of sperm.

An enlarged prostate gland is more specifically known as benign prostatic hyperplasia and is where natural therapies are the most effective. Prostatitis on the other hand is an inflamed, swollen prostate usually due to infection, which may be acute or chronic and which should be referred to a GP.

The incidence of benign prostatic hyperplasia is estimated at 50 to 60 per cent of men between 40 and 59 years of age. Common symptoms of benign prostatic hyperplasia (BPH) are dysuria (painful urination), painful defecation, frequency of urination, inability to empty bladder fully, desire to urinate, incontinence of urine, possible fever, impotence, back pain and in some cases painful orgasm.

There are many possible causes: a diet too high in acidic foods (red meat, cheese, other dairy, protein foods, alcohol) excess tea, coffee and spices and/or too little alkaline foods (green leafy vegetables, fruit,) and/or too little fibre, essential fatty acid and zinc deficiency. Other causes could be congestion, sluggish bowels, poor lymph and blood flow, toxicity of blood and poor abdominal tone. Lack of exercise and a sedentary occupation may also be factors.

Endocrine system rule no. 3

Eating little and often will keep blood sugar levels stable. Never skip breakfast and always have some complete protein with every meal or snack.

European herbalists and naturopathic doctors have used saw palmetto for centuries for the treatment of BPH, but it was first used by Native Americans. A three-year study in Germany found that 160mg of saw palmetto extract taken twice daily reduced night time urination in 73 per cent of patients and improved urinary flow rates significantly.

Pygeum, an extract from the bark of the African tree, has been approved in Germany, France and Italy as a remedy for benign prostatic hypertrophy. Controlled studies published over the last twenty-five years have shown that pygeum is safe and effective for individuals with BPH of moderate severity. These studies have used 50–100mg of pygeum extract (standardised to contain 14 per cent triterpenes) twice per day. It contains three compounds that might help the prostate; pentacyclic triterpenoids, which have a diuretic action; phytosterols, which have anti-inflammatory activity and ferulic acid which help rid the prostate of any cholesterol deposits that accompany BPH.

In another study, forty-five men with BPH received a supplement containing three amino acids (glycine, alanine, and glutamic acid) while forty other men with BPH were given a placebo. After three months, 66 per cent of the patients receiving the amino acid mixture showed reduced urinary urgency; 50 per cent had less delay in starting urine flow; 46 per cent had less difficulty maintaining flow; and 43 per cent had reduced frequency. In contract, these improvements were reported by less than 15 per cent of the men who received the placebo. No side effects were observed. Although it is not known how the amino acid combination works, it is believed to reduce the amount of swelling in prostate tissue.

Diet should be a high-fibre, non-citrus, alkaline-reacting diet, containing large amounts of raw green vegetables, essential fatty acids and zinc. Zinc is paramount to effective treatment of BPH. Zinc deficiency becomes more prevalent with age and supplementation has been shown to reduce the size of the enlarged prostate and to reduce symptoms in the majority of patients.

A good all-round multivitamin is highly recommended offering a minimum of 50mg of the B-complex group of vitamins. Additionally, starflower or evening primrose with no less than 15 per cent GLA should be taken daily.

Recommendations for prostate problems

Diet	A whole food approach to food where quality is more important than quantity. Plenty of fruits, vegetables, nuts and seeds with adequate essential fatty acids, low-fat protein, and plenty of water.
Increase	Pumpkin seeds, oysters, oily fish – sardines salmon, herring, tuna and mackerel – up to three times per week.
Decrease	Everything refined – especially white bread and flour, confectionery, and alcohol.
Superfoods	Alfalfa, medicinal mushrooms, bio-yoghurt and probiotics.

Supplements	Multivitamin and mineral. Evening primrose oil (GLA) Amino acids (alanine, glutamic acid and glycine) Zinc – liquid form for better absorption
Herbals	Pygeum Saw palmetto – for every man over the age of 40 Dong quai – an adaptogen
Lifestyle changes	Learn how to manage stress. Take up relaxing hobbies and enjoy life.

Thyroid disorders

Hyperthyroidism covers a wide range of symptoms including insomnia, nervousness, weakness, sweating, overactivity, sensitivity to heat, weight loss, tremor and stare. Some of the main causes are vitamin A, E and B6 deficiency, liver damage, insufficient enzyme production to inactivate thyroid hormones, emotion and diet pills.

However, thyroid deficiency is much more common and is referred to as hypothyroidism. Its symptoms also cover a wide range including fatigue, headaches, chronic or recurrent infection, eczema, psoriasis, acne, menstrual disorders, painful menstruation, depression, cold sensitivity, psychological problems and anaemia. Some of the main causes are iodine, vitamin E, vitamin A and zinc deficiencies. A history of taking diet pills, emotions and hereditary predisposition are also causes of hypothyroidism.

The thyroid gland plays a key role in controlling the body's metabolic rate. It is in turn controlled directly by secretions from the pituitary and hypothalamus in the brain. The hypothalamus is affected greatly by strong emotions. Since the thyroid has a major effect on metabolism and the blood glucose level, it also has a strong effect on the mental state, causing mental depression, lethargy, fatigue and psychosis. This may play a role in abnormal mental states in puberty, pregnancy, postpartum depression and menopause.

Iodine deficiency is probably the most common cause of hypothyroidism and this is easily corrected by consuming iodine-containing foods. Certain foods however, called goitrogens, actually hinder iodine utilisation and induce an iodine deficiency by combining with the iodine and making it unavailable to the thyroid. These include kale, cabbage, peanuts, soy flour, brussel sprouts, cauliflower, broccoli, radishes, mustard greens, kohl rabi and turnips. I am not suggesting that you do not to eat these foods, but rather that they are not to be eaten in excess. In general cooking inactivates these goitrogens. Good sources of iodine include salt water fish, sea vegetables (kelp, dulse, arame, nori, kombu) and iodised salt.

The general treatment for thyroid disorders is based on a gentle stimulation of the thyroid through proper diet, food supplements and herbs to raise general vitality and assist in balancing the hormones. A daily multivitamin containing 50mg of B complex is usually recommended together with zinc 25mg daily taken in the evenings. Vitamin A up to 10,000ius daily is also recommended, as hypothyroid patients do not convert beta-carotene to vitamin A efficiently.

Desiccated thyroid, from which the thyroid hormones have been removed, is another way to increase thyroid hormone secretion.

Key Term

Goitrogens

A group of foods that hinder iodine utilisation. Goitrogens are therefore thyroid antagonists and are found in such foods as cabbage, kale, Brussels sprouts, cauliflower, broccoli and kohlrabi.

The idea here is that it supplies all the known nutrients needed to ensure proper functioning of the thyroid. These products are safe to use and are available in health food stores, but may not be suitable for strict vegetarians.

Home test for thyroid disorders

A useful home test for hypo or hyperthyroidism is the basal body temperature test as first suggested by Dr Broda Barns. Axillary temperature is taken for 10 minutes first thing in the morning – average ranges are 97.8° to 98.2°F. Temperatures below this range suggest hypothyroidism and those above hyperthyroidism. Women must take their temperature on days two and three of the menstrual flow to get an accurate measurement.

Key Term

Axillary temperature

Axillary temperature is the temperature taken from the under arm area.

Recommendations for thyroid disorders

Diet	Broccoli is an excellent source of chromium, the trace mineral that assists the pancreas to work more efficiently and therefore increase insulin's efficiency, which has a knock on effect to regulate blood sugar. Other high chromium foods are brewers yeast, nuts, wheat cereals and mushrooms (restrict broccoli for hypothyroidism). Oily fish – sardines salmon, herring, tuna and mackerel.
Foods to avoid	Everything refined – especially white bread and flour, confectionery, and alcohol.
Superfoods	Spirulina, chorella and blue-green algae – rotate Super sprouts, and bio-yoghurt Watercress – acts as a tonic for regulating metabolism
Supplements	B complex; evening primrose oil, all antioxidants; zinc and magnesium
Herbal remedies	Black cohosh, ginger, marshmallow, Dong quai, Siberian ginseng and garlic
Lifestyle changes	Lose weight, as excess weight promotes insulin resistance and is generally unhealthy. Avoid all synthetic hormones. Avoid tampons (or buy sanitary wear specially prepared without bleach). Avoid all chemicals – lead, aluminium and mercury. Learn how to manage stress. Take up relaxing hobbies and enjoy life.

General recommendations for the endocrine system

Diet	A whole food approach to food where quality is more important than quantity. Plenty of fruits, vegetables, nuts and seeds with adequate essential fatty acids, low-fat protein, and plenty of water.
Increase	Salt water fish, sea vegetables (kelp, dulse, arame, nori, kombu) iodised salt, mushrooms, watercress, seafood, egg yolks and wheat germ.
Decrease	Vegetables from the brassica family: cabbage, broccoli and cauliflower should be decreased (but not avoided) together with corn, sweet potatoes, lima beans, and pearl millet (decreased but not avoided). Avoid everything refined – especially white bread and flour, confectionery, and alcohol.
Superfoods	Spirulina, chorella and blue-green algae – rotate Super sprouts, and bio-yoghurt Watercress – acts as a tonic for regulating metabolism
Supplements	Vitamin A, zinc, desiccated thyroid, selenium, B-complex
Herbals	Garlic, preferably raw in salads, or as a capsule Saw palmetto – for every man over the age of 50 Dong quai – an adaptogen which increases circulation for better healing, prevents bleeding and strengthens and nourishes the glands. Black cohosh – stimulates secretions of the liver, kidneys and lymph glands and expels mucous.
Lifestyle changes	Avoid all chemicals – lead, aluminium and mercury

Knowledge review

The endocrine system

1   Name the two main control systems of the body.

2   What is the main function of the endocrine system?

3   List the differences between endocrine and exocrine glands.

4   What is the main dietary factor to influence the endocrine system?

5   What are PCBs and what is their action in the body?

6   Describe the differences between Type I and Type II diabetes.

7   List three lifestyle changes that would be beneficial for clients with glucose intolerance.

8   What mineral is often deficient in people who have ups and downs with their blood sugar levels?

9   At what age does the menopause commence?

10   Name two herbal remedies recommended for menopausal women.

11   Why are soybeans often recommended for menopausal women?

12   What types of fresh fruit are of the most benefit to menopausal women?

13   Name four possible causes of prostate problems in men.

14   What may be the benefit of taking zinc supplementation for clients with prostate problems?

15   What herbal remedy would you recommend for men over 40?

16   Describe how to carry out the home test for thyroid disorders.

17   What superfoods would you recommend for a client with thyroid problems?

18   What lifestyle changes are important to consider for clients with thyroid problems?

19   What general foods support the endocrine system?

20   What superfoods support the endocrine system and why?

The lymphatic system and immunity

Learning objectives

This chapter covers the following:

- **dietary influences affecting the lymphatic and immune systems**

- **common disorders associated with the lymphatic and immune systems**

- **recommendations of foods to increase/decrease**

- **supplements and herbal remedies**

- **superfoods and lifestyle changes relating to disorders of the lymphatic and immune systems**

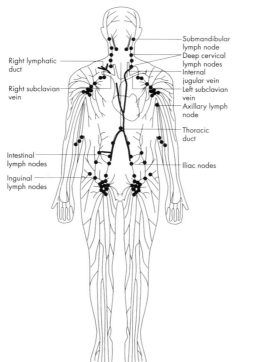

Right lymphatic duct

Right subclavian vein

Intestinal lymph nodes

Inguinal lymph nodes

Submandibular lymph node
Deep cervical lymph nodes
Internal jugular vein
Left subclavian vein
Axillary lymph node

Thoracic duct

Iliac nodes

Lymphatic system

What is the lymphatic system?

The lymphatic/immune system consists of a fluid called lymph, vessels that transport the lymphatic fluid called lymphatic vessels (lymphatics), and a number of structures and organs that contain lymphatic tissue.

Main functions

The lymphatic system has three main functions: to help us fight infection by identifying the body's enemies and, by filtering lymphatic fluid destroying the invading micro-organisms; in the distribution of fluids and nutrients around the body, especially protein molecules that are too large to pass back through the blood capillary walls and in absorbing the products of fat digestion from the villi of the small intestine.

What does the lymphatic system do?

Specialised white blood cells known as lymphocytes are reproduced in the lymph nodes and when infection strikes, they generate antibodies to protect the body against subsequent infection. Therefore the lymphatic system plays an important part in the body's immune system.

The lymphatic system is important for the distribution of fluid and nutrients in the body, because it drains excess fluid from the tissue spaces and returns it to the blood via the lymphatic vessels and ducts. Protein molecules which are too large to pass back through the capillary walls into the blood stream must be returned to the blood and are carried through the lymphatic system and returned via the lymphatic ducts.

The lymphatic system also plays an important role in absorbing the products of fat digestion from the villi of the small intestine. While the products of carbohydrate and protein digestion pass directly into the bloodstream, fats pass directly into the intestinal lymph vessels, known as lacteals.

Dietary influences affecting the lymphatic system

The lymphatic system, like all the other systems in the body, relies heavily on an optimal intake of vitamins and minerals. We depend on our lymphatic system to provide antibodies when we need them and for this they particularly need vitamin B6. As all nutrients work synergistically, a deficiency in just this one vitamin could compromise our whole lymphatic and immune system. Deficiencies in iron, zinc, magnesium and selenium will all suppress immunity, as will deficiencies in vitamins A, B1, B2, B6, B12, folic acid, C and E.

What you eat can strongly influence the performance of white blood cells, the front-line warriors against infection and cancer. These are the neutrophils that engulf and kill bacteria (phagocytosis) and cancer cells, and the lymphocytes that include the T-cells, B-cells and natural killer (NK) cells. The B-cells produce antibodies to destroy foreign invaders such as viruses, bacteria, and tumour cells. T-cells direct many immune activities and produce two chemicals called interferon and interleukin that are essential in warding off infections and cancer. Natural killer cells are the body's first line of defence against the development of cancer; they destroy cancer cells as well as virus-infected cells. There are now hundreds of research papers that document various foods and components of food that control the blood concentrations of white cells and their potency. Thus fresh, good, nutritious food acts to stimulate and support the immune system, whereas anti-nutrients, such as alcohol, lead, cadmium and antibiotics can depress it. The new classes of superfoods are especially beneficial for the immune system.

The most beneficial diet for the lymphatic system is basically the same as for all the systems in the body – a whole food approach to food where quality is more important than quantity with abundant fruits and vegetables, low-fat protein, sufficient essential fatty acids and plenty of water. However, during an infection the emphasis should be placed on good quality protein – because immune cells are produced rapidly during an infection, sufficient protein is essential. Because protein uses up B6 in its metabolism, too much may in turn *suppress* the immune system, as we need the B6 to make the antibodies. A separate supplement of B6 and zinc is of particular benefit to boost the immune and lymphatic systems and a good all-round multivitamin and mineral supplement containing all the antioxidants is imperative for a strong lymphatic and immune system. Vitamins B1, B2 and B5 have mild immune-boosting effects.

The antioxidants really come into their own when fighting off infections, vitamin C in particular. If you are always suffering from frequent infections it may be worth considering taking an antioxidant. A good antioxidant supplement will include Vitamins A, C, E and the mineral selenium.

Common disorders

Allergies

Allergies are responses mounted by the immune system to a particular food, inhalant, or chemical. The terms food sensitivity and food intolerance are not usually associated with true allergic reactions, as although they often produce many unpleasant symptoms, they do not provoke the immediate reaction of a true classical allergy. A true allergy is an IgE (immunoglobulin E) mediated reaction characterised by an immediate onset of symptoms, usually within two hours. The reactions are intense, sudden and dramatic, extremely distressing for the patient and may even be life threatening. The most common food allergies and sensitivities in the UK today are wheat, dairy foods, citrus fruits, nuts and tomatoes.

Food intolerance, on the other hand, is IgG-mediated and often characterised by delayed reactions occurring several hours, or even days, after digestion. Food intolerance (often referred to as sensitivity, hypersensitivity, delayed or false food allergy) is usually associated with chronic complaints such as migraine, eczema, asthma, childhood hyperactivity, irritable bowel syndrome and arthritis. There are many other conditions that may have their cause linked to food sensitivities and these include adult acne, rheumatoid arthritis, ADD (attention deficit disorder), yeast infection, colic, constipation, Crohn's disease, depression, diarrhoea, ear infections and gallbladder attacks.

A leaky gut is a common condition causing food intolerance. These intolerances may or may not turn into full true allergies over time, as other factors are involved including heredity, an overly sensitive immune response, poor digestive function, excessive exposure to a limited number of foods and the extent of the leakiness of the gut walls.

People often experience symptoms when foods, particularly protein foods which have been incompletely broken down due to poor digestive function, pass through the digestive tract and into the small intestine to be absorbed. In normal circumstances, the protein molecules being too large to be absorbed would be passed through the system into the large bowel for excretion. However, with an excessively permeable gut (a leaky gut) the protein molecules are absorbed and the body reacts accordingly to something it perceives as foreign. For example, something you have eaten for years will suddenly give you uncomfortable symptoms. You think you know what the food is, but are convinced it couldn't be that food, for the simple reason that you *have* eaten it for years. So you continue to eat the offending food – and your symptoms persist. As the gut becomes more permeable, more and more food molecules are entering the body which otherwise would not. You will not be allergic to these foods, but will certainly be sensitive or intolerant to them. Once you have established the permeability of your gut and repaired it if necessary, you will be able to eat the food again with out getting the unpleasant symptoms.

Most people are therefore unaware that they are sensitive to foods because most only think of allergies as an immediate reaction, like hives or asthma attacks. Far more common are the false, masked or delayed reactions, which can occur up to 48 hours after ingesting the offending substance. Because the foods that we are sensitive to are often the foods that we eat every day, it is often extremely difficult to identify the offending food.

Rheumatoid arthritis (RA) may be linked to food allergies and sensitivities. In many people symptoms are made worse when they eat foods to which they are allergic or sensitive and made better by avoiding these foods. English researchers suggest that one-third of people with RA can control the disease completely through allergy elimination. Finding and eliminating foods that trigger symptoms should be done with the help of a nutritional therapist experienced in allergies.

Unrecognised food allergy or sensitivity is a contributing factor in a significant number of asthmatic people and a link has been confirmed by double-blind research, particularly for nuts, peanuts, eggs and soy.

More and more children are becoming hyperactive, delinquent and are being diagnosed with ADD – attention deficit disorder. ADD has been linked in studies to certain foods, inhalant allergens and food colours. In a study of twenty children, their poor ability to concentrate and behaviour problems vanished when allergenic foods were removed from their diets. More often than not if the children with these conditions don't have food allergies or sensitivities, then they do have either sugar imbalances, vitamin and mineral deficiencies (often zinc and B6 or niacin) or deficiencies of essential fatty acids. Once the offending foods or deficiencies have been identified, the children quickly respond and become manageable and learning improves.

Some doctors report that food sensitivities may exacerbate gallbladder attacks in people who have gallstones. Preliminary research has found that foods most commonly reported to be triggers include eggs, pork and onion, though specific offending foods may vary considerably from person to person.

Some, perhaps most people with IBS are sensitive to certain foods. People with IBS often experience improvement when food sensitivities are discovered and those particular foods avoided – tea is a common sensitivity.

Ionised air may also play a role in allergies. Research suggests that some allergy-provoking substances such as dust and pollen have a positive electrical charge. Negative ions appear to counteract the allergenic actions of these positively charged ions on respiratory tissues and many individuals experience relief from their respiratory allergies. Other allergy sufferers report considerable relief, with a few allergy reactions resolving completely, after negative ion therapy. The majority of allergy sufferers appear to be able to reduce reliance on other treatments (nutritional, biochemical or prescription) during negative ion therapy.

Key Term

Phenolics

Phenolics are natural flavourings, colourings and preservatives found in foods. Examples are tyramine and coumarin.

Food phenolics

Food phenolics are natural flavourings, colourings and preservatives in foods. Many clients whose symptoms are due to phenolic compounds are not allergic to them but are intolerant or sensitive. They are able to tolerate a limited amount of the phenolic, but if the intake exceeds this then symptoms occur. It appears that the tolerance level reduces the more symptoms occur, but that if the phenolic is avoided or the client is treated, the tolerance increases. For example, take a client with migraine who is sensitive to tyramine (a food phenolic). Some days he will take foods containing tyramine, but in low concentration and will not have a headache. On other days he will take the same foods in high concentration past his tolerance level and get a headache. If he avoids tyramine entirely for some months, or is desensitised, be will be able to take a level of tyramime which previously would have precipitated a headache. Tyramine is a common trigger for migraine and other headaches. It has been shown that some clients with migraine have a genetic deficiency of the enzyme which metabolises tyramine and an excessive intake will trigger an attack.

Tyramine is contained in banana, bass, soya beans, beef, beer, cheese, cottage cheese, chicken, cocoa, chocolate, egg, oyster, pea, plum, pork, potato, sweet potato, prunes, raisins, spinach, tomato, walnut and yeast.

All of these foods taken over a ten-day period may not give the client any symptoms but taken intensely over a two-day period they may result in a migraine attack.

Coumarin is one of the most common to cause problems and is unfortunately one of the most widespread phenolics. Apart from asthma, it can cause rhinitis, catarrh and other respiratory conditions. Coumarin is contained in apple, banana, barley, beef, beer, beetroot, celery, cheese, cottage cheese, chicken, cocoa, chocolate, corn, egg, lemon, lettuce, lime, cow's milk, goat's milk, mutton, oats, pea, peanut, peppercorn, sweet potato, rice, tomato, tuna, turkey, wheat and yeast.

There are many natural phenolics that you may be sensitive to in excess and only an allergist will be able to identify them for you. There are many tests available for identifying food intolerances and allergies. The most effective ones are the 'avoid and challenge' test and the elimination diets.

The 'avoid and challenge' test is very simple. If avoidance of a particular food leads to reduction in symptoms and reintroduction of that food leads to worsening of symptoms, then you have a sensitivity to that food. Bearing in mind that some foods may take 2–3 days to show a reaction the avoidance of that food has to be for a longer period.

1   Choose one food or a food group you want to test (dairy products or wheat for example).

2   Completely avoid that food or food group for 14 days – the longer you avoid the food the more accurate the results will be.

3   At the end of the avoidance period (say day 15), sit in a quite place with no interruptions and take your resting pulse for one minute.

4   Then 'challenge' your body by eating more than usual of the food you are avoiding (a large glass of cow's milk if you are avoiding dairy produce).

5   Still sitting quietly, re-take your pulse after 10, 30 and 60 minutes. If your pulse goes up by 10 points or if you have any noticeable symptoms within 48 hours you probably have an allergy or intolerance to this food. The symptoms are more important than the pulse, since some foods can raise the pulse without denoting an allergic reaction.

Do not carry out this test alone in case you have a strong reaction to the food you are testing. If you suspect you have food allergies or intolerances seek assistance from a nutritional therapist who will support you through the testing time.

Health & Safety

'Avoid and challenge' allergy test – do not carry out this test alone in case you have a strong reaction to the challenged food and feel unwell.

Recommendations for food sensitivities

Diet	A whole food approach to food where quality is more important than quantity. Plenty of fruits, vegetables, nuts and seeds with adequate essential fatty acids, low-fat protein, and plenty of water.
Increase	Unadulterated, organic, unpackaged food. You are less likely to have reactions to natural food (natural phenolics).
Decrease	Everything refined – especially white bread and flour, confectionery, and alcohol and any food you suspect you may be sensitive to.
Superfoods	Take care, as you may be sensitive to pollens, grasses or fungal foods, which make up some of the superfoods.
Supplements	An all-round multivitamin and mineral supplement with good levels of the antioxidant vitamins A, C and E with selenium.
Herbals	The antihistamine, antioxidant and anti-inflammatory actions of quercetin make this a favourite herbal remedy for any allergy/sensitivity situation. It also protects the stomach from ulcer disease and gastric distress and strengthens capillary walls.
Lifestyle changes	Identify possible sensitivities and employ the assistance of a nutritional therapist to assist you in your investigations. A positive determined approach will be needed to ascertain food allergies.

Remember

Lymphatic system and immunity rule no. 1

Significantly reduce sugar intake.

Three ounces of sugar in *any* form – honey, fruit juice or sucrose – results in a 50 per cent reduction in white cell acticity for one to five hours!

Cancer

Much conflicting advice has been written over the past few years regarding cancer, but one aspect is now certain and that is diet has an important part to play in the prevention and management of cancer – especially the hormone-dependent cancers.

There are many different types of cancers with different causes; most are caused by carcinogens (cancer-causing agents) that have been taken into the body and which have caused cell damage, often free radical damage.

Hormone-dependent cancers

Breast, uterine and ovarian cancers are hormone dependent. An excess of the female hormone oestrogen appears to encourage the growth of hormone-related cancers. Why is it that Japanese women are only one-fifth as likely to develop breast cancer as American and European women? One answer is diet. A Japanese woman is likely to eat six times more vitamin D (30mcg daily) from fatty fish than western women, giving them vital protection against breast cancer. The UK RDA for vitamin D is 5mcg and many women do not get even this small amount. When Japanese women move to America or anywhere where there is a more 'western' diet their breast cancer rates creep up and eventually approach those of western women. So is it something in the eastern diet that prevents cancer or something in the western diet that promotes it?

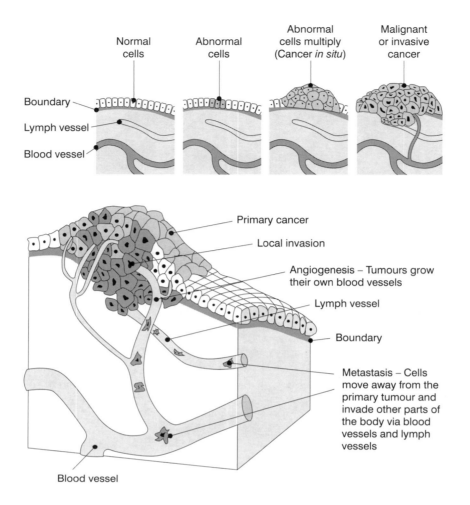

Scientists will take a long time to give us precise answers but there is already overwhelming evidence. Diets high in saturated fats, refined sugars and alcohol are very harmful to human bodies, whereas diets high in essential fatty acids from fatty fish, rich in whole and unrefined foods, and foods high in plant oestrogens, are highly beneficial to human beings, especially against hormone-related cancers. Making small but significant changes in your diet could halve your chances of getting cancer.

The first thing to do is to eliminate all carcinogens from the diet. These include cigarettes, heavy metals like cadmium, lead, aluminium and mercury, saturated fats, sweeteners, alcohol and all synthetic hormones. Then the immune system needs to be built up with good food and dietary supplements.

Recommendations for cancer

Diet	A whole food approach to food where quality is more important than quantity. Plenty of fruits, vegetables, nuts and seeds with adequate essential fatty acids, low-fat protein, and plenty of water.
Increase	Oily fish – sardines, salmon, herring, tuna and mackerel Fresh fruit and vegetables, including juices
Decrease	Everything refined – especially white bread and flour, confectionery, alcohol, cigarettes, and sweeteners
Superfoods	Algae, barley grass, bee pollen, cabbage, medicinal mushrooms, super sprouts
Supplements	Multivitamin and mineral GLA from evening primrose oil Antioxidant complex, vitamin E, additional selenium (check the amount already in the multi and antioxidant complex) Vitamin C – up to bowel tolerance
Herbals	Echinacea and rhodiola
Lifestyle changes	A positive approach to be taken. Seek support from family, friends and therapists. Lifestyle changes mostly to dietary intake. Only the best will do.

Candida

Much has been written about this condition over the past years. The main symptoms of candida are frequent outbreaks of thrush and cystitis, a history of taking antibiotics, having been on the pill for many years and the main symptom of bloating. Bloating can also be a symptom of allergies so good diagnosis is important.

The usual bloating symptoms of candida are that when you wake up in the morning the stomach is 'flat' – as you eat through the day (bread, pasta, mushrooms, cheeses, refined foods like biscuits, cakes and sweets and yeast) then the stomach gradually extends as the candida is feeding also. By the end of the day, the stomach is so bloated that buttons have to be undone and clients feel extremely uncomfortable. Never assume that your client has candida. Advise of your suspicions and suggest that your client see a clinical nutritionist to be given an anti-candida regime. Encourage them that with patience and determination they can eliminate the problem. There are many short-term answers, but for the long term and permanent relief a special regime is needed. This regime usually follows a six point plan.

1 An anti-candida diet for a minimum of two weeks to weaken the candida
2 Taking a good multivitamin and mineral to support the client's immune system
3 Taking a supplement to kill off the candida
4 Reintroduce the prebiotics to the gut
5 Repair the gut wall
6 Reintroduce the foods that were being avoided whilst on the diet

The anti-candida diet is strict, and would include the following list of foods to avoid completely for the duration of the programme:

- sugar, and food containing sugar; that includes brown or white sugar, demarara, molasses, syrup, honey, sucrose, dextrose, lactose, maltose, fructose, confectionery, icing, marzipan, chocolate, ice cream, desserts and puddings, cakes and biscuits, soft drinks including squash and all canned drinks, bottled ketchup, etc. Check all tins and packets for hidden sugar – even some frozen and tinned vegetables! (Malt is a form of sugar – see below.)
- Yeast and all foods containing it or derived from it; that includes bread and even most pitta breads, food coated in breadcrumbs, most pizza bases, Marmite, Vecon, Bovril, Oxo, etc., monosodium glutamate, citric acid, and vitamin tablets unless 'yeast free' is stated.
- Refined grains, white flour granary flour (which is white flour with malt and added grains), white rice, white pasta, cornflour, custard powder, cornflakes and cereals unless 'wholegrain' is stated.
- Malt and malted products some cereals (e.g. Weetabix), brown Ryvita, granary bread, malted drinks like Ovaltine, Horlicks and Caro.
- Fermented products, alcoholic drinks, ginger beer, vinegar and all foods containing vinegar (ketchups, pickles, salad creams, baked beans) soy sauce.
- Cow's milk and most milk products, including cream and cheese. (Cottage cheese and natural yoghurt are allowed.)
- Fresh fruit, raw, stewed, made into jam, marmalade or juice. Pure fruit juice is pure fructose, and often very high in mould!
- Dried fruit, including prunes and the dried fruit in muesli.
- Nuts unless freshly cracked – especially peanuts and peanut butter, which support the growth of the mould.
- Smoked or cured fish and meat, including ham, bacon, smoked mackerel, smoked salmon.
- Preservatives, which are frequently derived from yeast and can introduce a chemical substance to the body.
  (NB sausages, even without preservatives, are high in white cereal and animal fat.)
- Mushrooms, tea and coffee, even decaffeinated, which still contains drugs, and hot spices as they irritate the lining of the intestine.

While following the above and avoiding all the foods mentioned, you should concentrate your thoughts on the foods you can enjoy. If you focus on the food you can have rather than on the foods you cannot have, you will have a better chance of success.

Enjoy:

- Yeast free and soda bread, made with wholewheat flour or other grains. Some bakers will make a batch for your freezer.
- Rice cakes, oatcakes (malt free), original Ryvita (not brown, it's malted!) Ryvita with sesame seeds, wholemeal crispbreads (read the labels carefully).

- Pastry made with wholemeal flour or other grains, and don't forget you can still have pancakes, dumplings and crumbles!
- Soya milk (sugar free). You will quickly adapt to it on cereal, and when cooked with oats or rice it becomes really creamy.
- Unhydrogenated margarine – Vitasieg is good. Some other brands contain citric acid, so should be avoided.
- Natural yoghurt – any make will do, but it mustn't have fruit! Also, just because some say 'live' it does not mean that the others are not! (all yoghurts are live).
- Cottage cheese, avocados, and potatoes (cooked in many different ways).
- Breakfast – with home-made muesli with oatflakes and other whole grains mixed with seeds, and soaked in water or yoghurt, porridge made with water or soya milk, sprinkled with cinnamon or nutmeg, egg with wholewheat soda bread and Vitasieg; rice cakes with cottage cheese.
- Salad – at least one plateful a day.
- Main meals – aim to eat less red meat. Most meat contains residues of hormones and antibiotics unless it is organically produced. Lamb, rabbit and poultry are less likely to be affected, and fish is quite safe from this form of pollution, though it does have other hazards! Experiment with more vegetarian meals – a pulse combined with a grain makes an excellent protein, e.g. bean and vegetable pie or crumble, lentil sauce with wholewheat spaghetti. Have lightly steamed fresh vegetables or salad with every meal.
- Herbs and mild spices – cinnamon, coriander, turmeric etc.
- Drinks – *Hot*; Barleycup, Rooibosch tea, any other herb teas (avoid those which contain malt), hot water with a slice of lemon.
- *Cold*; bottled mineral water, filtered tap water, tomato juice (no citric acid or vinegar) natural yoghurt with sparking water! Add some ice and lemon to your sparkling mineral water to make it look good as well as taste good! As an alternative to bottled water, use a filter jug and then fizz the water in a soda-stream machine.

Recommendations for candida

Diet	Anti-candida diet regime
Increase	Vegetables, low fat protein foods as above
Decrease	Bread, mushrooms, fruit eaten alone, pasta, biscuits, fruit juices, refined foods, coke, coffee, tea
Superfoods	Broccoli, cottage cheese, avocados, alfalfa, cabbage, sprouted seeds, spirulina
Supplements	Multivitamin and mineral daily Caprylic acid Probiotics
Herbals	Garlic
Lifestyle changes	Strict diet must be maintained. Once you are clear of candida you will feel like a new person and be able to enjoy life to the full – the wait will be worth it.

Cellulite

Although many doctors still dismiss this condition as non-existent, it can be very distressing for many women.

The common denominator for most women with cellulite is poor circulation and diet, poor elimination from the large bowel, poor lymphatic drainage and insufficient exercise. This results in the inefficient removal of the waste products of metabolism and toxins absorbed from the environment, which in turn is a precondition for cellulite.

Cellulite is difficult to get rid of but not impossible. It takes a positive woman to rid herself of this unsightly condition but with determination it can be done. What does it take? Strict diet, daily skin brushing, a detoxification regime, profound lifestyle changes and regular aerobic exercise.

Initially a detoxification regime would be undertaken. This could last for up to ten days when little would be eaten except fruits and vegetables. This would then progress to a diet that would include small amounts of low protein foods still with abundant supplies of fruits, vegetables, nuts and seeds. At all stages of the programme you would undertake skin brushing. For this you would need a long handled natural bristle brush which can be obtained from chemists and health foods shops. Every day, brush your dry skin with the dry brush from the bottom of your body working upwards. You would brush towards the lymph glands which are situated all over the body with the main ones being located behind the knees, under the arms, the groin area and around the neck area. You would bath or shower after the skin brushing. This is an excellent way to stimulate your lymphatic system and to encourage the toxins to be removed from your body.

In addition to all this you would be undertaking aerobic exercises at least three times per week. This would involve attending a class or by determined walking or jogging on your part. Too little will be ineffective. Lifestyle changes would have to be dramatic. No coffee, tea, chocolate or junk food of any description – ever! A tall order you may say, but the results would be a new you! Don't try it alone. Get some help from a nutritional therapist who will help you with a specifically made programme to suit your current lifestyle. You don't need to become boring and anti-social on a regime like this. It can be fun if you allow it.

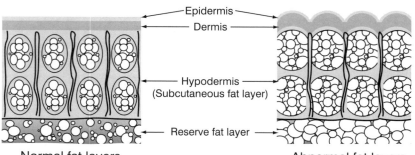

Epidermis
Dermis

Hypodermis
(Subcutaneous fat layer)

Reserve fat layer

Cellulite

Normal fat layers

Abnormal fat layers

Recommendations for cellulite

Diet	Initially a detoxification diet lasting 10 days followed by a 75 per cent all raw diet with sufficient protein and essential fatty acids.
Increase	Everything raw – fruits, vegetables taken alone and in juices, or very lightly steamed or baked (as in baked apples). Generous amounts of water.
Decrease	Everything refined – especially all sugars, white bread and flour, confectionery, and alcohol
Superfoods	Alfalfa, algae, barley grass, bee pollen, cabbage, honey, liquorice, medicinal mushrooms, super sprouts, and bio-yoghurt.
Supplements	A multivitamin and mineral complex
Herbals	Milk thistle (supports the liver in the detoxification process)
Lifestyle changes	Daily skin brushing should become as regular as brushing your teeth. Aerobic exercise three times a week. Learning to say no to coffee, tea, chocolate, alcohol and anything that will clog the body up with toxins.

Chronic fatigue syndrome (CFS)

A multi-faceted disease regarded with suspicion by many people in the medical establishment, CFS is very real to those suffering from it. This is a complex condition and one that is difficult even for doctors to diagnose. The International Chronic Fatigue Syndrome Study group says that for a positive diagnosis of CFS, fatigue must also be accompanied by four or more of the following symptoms:

- Substantial impairment of short-term memory or concentration
- Sore throat
- Tender cervical or axillary lymph nodes
- Muscle pain
- Multi-joint pain without swelling or redness
- Headaches of a new type, pattern or severity
- Unrefreshing sleep
- Post-exertion malaise lasting more than 24 hours

CFS is also defined as unexplained fatigue of greater than or equal to six months duration. Fatigue alone or prolonged fatigue (not CFS) is fatigue lasting from one to up to six months only.

Often myalgic encephalomyelitis (ME) and CFS are grouped together as one disease, but according to the World Health Organisation the use of ME as a term to encompass all forms of chronic fatigue is inaccurate and should be discouraged. Nevertheless, many CFS practitioners do recognise ME as a specific illness in a proportion of CFS sufferers. Symptoms are that of a post-viral condition linked to exertion, impaired circulation and central nervous system involvement. It is probably fair to say that all patients with ME have CFS but not everyone with CFS has ME.

Complexities of diagnosis aside, it seems likely that nearly all cases of CFS involve some kind of disruption of the immune response. Recommendations should therefore focus on boosting immune strength.

Many natural health experts believe that candida albicans – a yeast infection of the intestines and bowel – may also be partly to blame. Candida overgrowth is a significant factor for many people feeling exhausted. With such a multi-faceted disease, recommendation is neither simple nor straightforward. Simple but effective lifestyle changes are the first course of action. Reduce or eliminate caffeine, white sugars and flours, refined foods, alcohol and food additives. Encourage a well-balanced whole food diet and strongly recommend they visit a nutritionist. Other useful steps are positive thinking, a walk in fresh air and plenty of natural mineral water.

Other research suggests that CFS may be partially due to low adrenal function resulting from different stressors – mental stress, physical stress, chemical stress and viral illness – impacting the normal communication between the hypothalamus in the brain, the pituitary gland and the adrenal glands.

Magnesium levels have been reported to be low in CFS sufferers. Oral supplementation is usually adequate but sometimes injections are necessary.

Vitamin B12 deficiency can cause fatigue. Reports have shown that people who are not deficient in B12 nonetheless have increased energy following a series of vitamin B12 injections. Some sources in conventional medicine have discouraged such people from getting B12 injections despite evidence to the contrary.

Carnitine is required for energy production in the powerhouses of the cells (the mitochondria). There may be a problem in the mitochondria in people with CFS. Deficiency of carnitine has been seen in some CFS sufferers. One gram of carnitine taken three times daily led to improvements in symptoms in a recent preliminary investigation.

Liquorice root is thought to help by stimulating the adrenal glands and blocking the breakdown of active cortisol in the body. One case study found that taking 2.5g of liquorice root daily led to a significant improvement in a patient severely affected with CFS; 6–8 weeks of 2.5g daily may therefore show beneficial results.

Siberian ginseng may also be useful. As an adaptogen it is thought to allow the adrenal glands to function optimally when challenged by stress. Siberian ginseng also contains complex polysaccharides (complex sugar molecules) which lend the herb its immune-supporting properties. Ten mg of Siberian ginseng three times a day have been shown to have increased numbers of T-lymphocyte immune cells.

The long chain polysaccharides found in the various medicinal mushrooms have been shown to be potent immune modulators, boosting the anti-viral activity of the host's immune system.

Tackling CFS takes persistence and courage on the part of the sufferer and lots of encouragement from practitioners.

Remember

Lymphatic system and immunity rule no. 3

Vaccinations cause a one to two week suppression of the immune response. Always take a multivitamin one week before vaccinations and for two to three weeks after.

Recommendations for chronic fatigue syndrome

Diet	A whole food approach to food where quality is more important than quantity. Plenty of fruits, vegetables, nuts and seeds with adequate essential fatty acids, low-fat protein, and plenty of water.
Increase	Green leafy vegetables for the magnesium content. Oily fish – sardines salmon, herring, tuna and mackerel. Fruit – to be used as snacks.
Decrease	Stimulants such as tea, coffee, chocolate and alcohol
Superfoods	Medicinal mushrooms
Supplements	Carnitine, B12 (sublingual), magnesium Vitamin C up to 3g daily Multivitamin and mineral and an antioxidant complex
Herbals	Siberian ginseng, liquorice root
Lifestyle changes	Eat little and often Exercise is important to prevent the worsening of fatigue

Rheumatoid arthritis

Rheumatoid arthritis (RA) is a chronic inflammatory condition; it is an autoimmune disease in which the immune system attacks the joints and sometimes other parts of the body. The onset of rheumatoid arthritis can be abrupt. The synovial membrane thickens and joints swell with redness and tenderness. Symmetrical joint involvement is common and may migrate from joint to joint.

There are several dietary changes that might be helpful for rheumatoid arthritis. The role of dietary fats in RA is complex but potentially important. In experimental animals that are susceptible to autoimmune disease, feeding a high-fat diet increases the severity of the disease. There is evidence that people with RA eat more fat, particularly animal fat than those without RA. In short-term studies, diets completely free of fat reportedly helped people with RA, but since at least some dietary fat is essential for humans, the significance of this finding is not clear.

Rheumatoid arthritis may be linked to food allergies and sensitivities. In many people symptoms are made worse when they eat foods to which they are allergic or sensitive and made better by avoiding these foods. English researchers suggest that one-third of people with RA can control the disease completely through allergy elimination. Finding and eliminating foods that trigger symptoms should be done with the help of a nutritional therapist experienced in allergies.

Although exercise may increase pain initially, gentle exercises help people with RA. Swimming, stretching or walking are recommended.

Vitamin E may be helpful in rheumatoid arthritis. The concentration of vitamin E has been found to be low in the joint fluid of individuals with rheumatoid arthritis; this reduction is believed to be caused by consumption of the vitamin during the inflammatory process. In a double-blind study, approximately 1,800ius per day of vitamin E was found to be of benefit.

Research suggests that people with RA may be partially deficient in pantothenic acid B5. In one trial those with RA had less morning stiffness, disability and pain when they took 2,000mg of pantothenic acid per day.

The relationship of copper to RA is complex. Copper acts an anti-inflammatory agent because it is needed to activate superoxide dismutase, an enzyme that protects joints from inflammation. People with RA tend toward copper deficiency. The *Journal of the American Medical Association* quoted one researcher as saying that while 'Regular aspirin had 6 per cent the anti-inflammatory activity of [cortisone]...copper [added to aspirin] had 130 per cent the activity. Several copper compounds have been used successfully with RA, and a single-blind study using copper bracelets reported surprisingly effective results. However, under certain circumstances, copper might actually increase inflammation in rheumatoid joints. Moreover, the most consistently effective form of copper, copper aspirinate (a combination of copper and aspirin) is not readily available.

Many double-blind trials have shown that the omega 3 fatty acids in fish oil, EPA and DHA, help relieve symptoms of RA. The effect results from the anti-inflammatory activity of fish oil. It can take many months before the results become evident.

Oils containing the omega 6 fatty acid gamma linolenic acid (GLA) such as borage oil, blackcurrant seed oil, and evening primrose oil (EPO) have also been reported to be effective in the treatment of RA. The most pronounced effects were seen with borage oil, but that may have been because larger amounts of GLA were used (1.4g per day). The results with EPO were conflicting and somewhat confusing, possibly because the placebo used in these studies (olive oil) appeared to have an anti-inflammatory effect of its own. In a double-blind study, positive results were seen when EPO was used in combination with fish oil. GLA appears to be effective because it is converted in part to prostaglandin series 1, a compound known to have anti-inflammatory activity. Preliminary research suggests that boron supplementation at 3–9mg per day may be beneficial, particularly in juvenile RA. However, more research on this is needed. Many herbs and spices have been through clinical trials with successful results. These include boswellia, turmeric and ginger. Boswellia is a traditional herbal remedy from the Indian system of Ayurvedic medicine, and has been investigated for its effects on arthritis. A double blind study using boswellia found a beneficial effect on pain and stiffness, as well as improved joint function and showed no negative effects. The herb has a unique anti-inflammatory action, much like the conventional non-steroidal anti-inflammatory drugs (NSAIDs) used by many for inflammatory conditions. Unlike NSAIDs, long-term use of boswellia is generally considered safe and does not lead to irritation or ulceration of the stomach.

Several published case studies of people with rheumatoid arthritis taking 6–50mg of fresh or powdered ginger per day indicated that ginger might be helpful. Turmeric is a yellow spice that is often used to make brightly coloured curry dishes. The active principle is curcumin, a potent anti-inflammatory compound, which protects against free radical damage.

Health & Safety

Exclusion diets are unsuitable for children.

Recommendations for rheumatoid arthritis

Diet	A whole food approach to food where quality is more important than quantity. Plenty of fruits and vegetables, low-fat protein, and plenty of water.
Increase	Oily fish – sardines salmon, herring, tuna and mackerel Avocados, watercress, parsley, celery, bananas, brown rice, soya milk
Decrease	Red meat, cheese, milk, all refined carbohydrates, especially sugar, citrus fruits, wheat, alcohol, fried foods. Foods of the nightshade family: tomatoes, eggplants, potatoes, peppers and tobacco.
Superfoods	Alfalfa, algae – especially spirulina, bee pollen, super sprouts
Supplements	Evening primrose oil, fish oils, a good multivitamin/mineral supplement containing at least 50mg of the B vitamins
Herbals	Boswellia, ginger, turmeric
Lifestyle changes	Regular raw vegetable juice. Carrot and celery juice, watercress, celery and parsley juice – for internal cleansing. Avoid taking drinks with meals. Skin brushing.

Skin disorders

Eczema

The term eczema literally means 'to boil over', it is a common skin condition characterised by an itchy, red rash. Many skin diseases cause somewhat similar rashes, so it is important to have the disease properly diagnosed before it can be treated.

Eczema can be triggered by allergies. More children with eczema have food allergies, according to data from double-blind research, so the first course of action would be to determine if allergies are a factor. If the trigger of the allergy can be identified, avoidance of the allergen can lead to significant improvement.

It has been reported that when heavy coffee drinkers with eczema avoided coffee their symptoms improve. In one particular trial, it was the coffee that was causing the problems, not the caffeine.

Researchers have reported that people with eczema do not have the normal ability to process fatty acids, which can result in deficiency of gamma-linolenic acid (GLA). GLA is found in evening primrose oil (EPO), borage oil and blackcurrant seed oil. Most double-blind research has shown that EPO overcomes this block and is therefore useful in the treatment of eczema.

Ten grams of fish oil providing 1.8 grams of EPA (eicosapentaenoic acid) per day were given to a group of eczema sufferers in a double blind trial. After twelve weeks, those taking the fish oil experienced significant improvement. According to the researchers, fish oil may be effective because it reduces levels of leukotriene B4, a substance that has been linked to eczema. The eczema-relieving effects of fish oil may require taking large amounts for at least twelve weeks.

Vitamin C has had good results with eczema. It is thought that vitamin C does not act on the eczema directly, but affects the immune system in a positive way, thereby improving the condition. It is suggested that 80mg per day per 2.2 pounds of body weight would reduce symptoms. Talk to a nutritional therapist if you are concerned about exactly how much vitamin C to take.

Liquorice root used either internally or topically may help alleviate symptoms of eczema. A traditional Chinese herbal preparation, which included liquorice, has been successful in treating childhood and adult eczema in double-blind studies. Topically, glycyrrhetinic acid, a constituent of liquorice root, reduces the inflammation and itching associated with eczema. Some doctors who use herbal medicine suggest using creams and ointments containing glycyrrhetinic acid three or four times per day. Liquorice may also be taken as a tincture in the amount of 2–5ml three times daily. Other topical herbal preparations to consider based on traditional herbal medicine are camomile, calendula and chickweed creams. Chamomile and calendula have anti-inflammatory properties, while chickweed is historically used to reduce itching.

The treatment of eczema for children and adults differs tremendously. With adults an exclusion diet may be introduced to identify food allergens and to clean up the system, but with children exclusion diets are unsuitable. If eczema started just after the child was weaned, you should be particularly suspicious of recently introduced foods. Many new mothers introduce solid foods too soon into a baby's immature digestive system and this can result in a food sensitivity or intolerance. If a baby who is being breast fed has eczema, then the mother should be screened for food allergies and the mother can be put on an exclusion diet.

Remember

Lymphatic system and immunity rule no. 4

Blood circulation has the heart to pump the blood; the lymphatic system only has your muscles – so daily exercise is *highly recommended* for a healthy lymphatic system.

Recommendations for eczema

Diet	A whole food approach to food where quality is more important than quantity. Plenty of fruits and vegetables, low-fat protein, and plenty of water.
Increase	Oily fish – sardines salmon, herring, tuna and mackerel Fluid intake, fresh fruit and vegetables
Decrease	Coffee, wheat and dairy products, plus everything refined – especially white bread and flour, confectionery, and alcohol.
Superfoods	Manuka honey can be applied locally with a loose bandage for children or adults. Probiotics. Medicinal mushrooms, super sprouts, alfalfa, algae, bee pollen.
Supplements	Fish oil (EPA/DHA). Vitamin C, zinc
Herbals	Liquorice, witch hazel, calendula, camomile
Lifestyle changes	Have any potential allergens identified

Stress

Stress is one of the great damagers of the immune system. It results in stimulation of the sympathetic nervous system, the part of the nervous system responsible for the fight or flight response. Stress also results in suppression of the parasympathetic nervous system, the part of the nervous system responsible for bodily functions during periods of rest, relaxation and sleep. The immune system functions better when the parasympathetic is uppermost – that is when we are resting, relaxing or sleeping – than when we are fighting or fleeing. Normally the sympathetic and parasympathetic systems balance each other, but under continued stress, the balance is lost and the immune system suffers. The increased activation of the sympathetic nervous system results in increased secretion of adrenal gland hormones, especially the corticosteroids and catecholamines. These hormones inhibit white blood cell function, decrease the production of lymphocytes and cause the thymus gland, the master gland of the immune system, to shrink. The result is a significant reduction in immune function. Only recently have researchers discovered that T and B cells contain receptors on their cell membranes for these stress-induced hormones, which helps explain the immune system's sensitivity to stress.

Nearly every disease we know can be aggravated or even caused by stress including stress-related hypoglycemia, headaches, colitis, ulcers, enuresis, fatigue, high blood pressure and a whole host of other conditions. No list of supplements will alleviate stress if the cause is primarily emotional or due to external conditions.

The best recommendation for stress is to identify the cause. This could be a work related problem or a relationship problem. Having discovered the cause, the client may need recommending to a suitable counsellor that deals with that particular problem. Stress comes in many guises including physical, chemical, emotional, spiritual and mental stress.

> **!**
>
> **Remember**
>
> **Lymphatic system and immunity rule no. 5**
>
> Heavy metals – mercury (from amalgam fillings), cadmium (from other people's cigarette smoke) and lead inhibit the formation of antibodies and reduce the bacteria-killing ability of white cells. If you are susceptible to heavy metals the antioxidants vitamins A, C, E and the mineral selenium will help protect you.

Recommendations for stress

Diet	A whole food approach to food where quality is more important than quantity. Plenty of fruits, vegetables, nuts and seeds with adequate essential fatty acids, low-fat protein, and plenty of water.
Increase	Slow releasing carbohydrates, fruit and vegetables, oily fish
Decrease	Meat, high saturated fat foods, alcohol, and sugar of all types
Superfoods	Alfalfa, algae, barley grass, bee pollen, cabbage, Manuka honey, medicinal mushrooms, super sprouts and bio-yoghurt
Supplements	Multivitamin and mineral B-Complex (checking amounts with the multi) up to 50mg of all the B complex in total Vitamin C up to 3g daily
Herbals	Echinacea, garlic, ginkgo biloba, rhodiola, valerian
Lifestyle changes	Take up yoga, meditation, gentle regular exercise like walking or swimming. Learn how to deal with stress. Take time out for yourself and make it a priority.

Lymphatic system and immunity rule no. 6

Hydrotherapy – professional hot and cold water treatment undertaken at health spas – increases circulation to blood and lymph, removes internal congestion and improves tissue vitality and nutrition. A beneficial treatment for the lymphatic system.

Viruses – Herpes Simplex I and II

If you have ever had a cold sore then it was the Herpes Simplex virus I that was responsible. Although the virus lies dormant in 90 per cent of us, diet may well determine whether the virus becomes reactivated and explodes into herpes symptoms. Herpes Simplex II is the virus responsible for shingles, genital blisters, and Epstein–Barr disease.

In the 1950s it was discovered that amino acids found in food could either stifle or encourage the growth of the herpes virus. Adding the amino acid arginine to the herpes virus in cell cultures made it grow rapidly; adding the amino acid lysine halted the growth and spread of herpes viruses in cells.

A mere 55g (2ozs) of peanuts or chocolate is enough to cause an outbreak, especially if the diet was lacking in lysine. Lysine is found in milk, meat, and soya beans. It's not just the amount that is important but the balance between arginine and lysine in foods. Almonds, brazil nuts, cashews, hazelnuts, peanuts, pecans, walnuts, chocolate, Brussels sprouts and gelatin all have a high ratio of arginine to lysine and should therefore be avoided at the start of an outbreak.

If you cannot control your cold sore outbreaks by diet then you could consider taking a supplement of lysine; 500mg twice a day until the infection is under control.

Recommendations for viruses

Diet	A light diet of high-energy natural foods, raw or lightly cooked. Include protein, as this is needed to make antibodies.
Increase	Fluid intake, especially water.
Decrease	Salt, and mucus forming and fatty foods such as milk, eggs and meat.
Superfoods	Medicinal mushrooms, super sprouts, bee pollen, spirulina, chlorella and blue-green algae (rotate every four weeks). Cabbage – especially the water is has been cooked in.
Supplements	Vitamins A, beta-carotene Vitamin C (to bowel tolerance) – or 3g every four hours Selenium, the amino acid lysine
Herbals	Aloe vera, grapefruit seed extract (a natural antibiotic) Ginger, garlic, echinacea and cat's claw tea (an acquired taste but very beneficial)
Lifestyle changes	Keep warm and get plenty of rest. The immune system works better in a warm environment. If you are not better within five days seek the advice of your doctor.

General recommendations for the lymphatic system and immunity

Diet	A whole food approach to food where quality is more important than quantity. Plenty of fruits and vegetables, nuts and seeds, low-fat protein, and plenty of water. Oily fish – sardines salmon, herring, tuna and mackerel. Increased fluid intake.
Foods to avoid	Alcohol, pork, hard-boiled eggs, refined foods of all kinds especially white bread, flour and confectionery.
Superfoods	Alfalfa, algae, barley grass, probiotics, medicinal mushrooms, super sprouts, bee pollen and yoghurt. Manuka honey can be applied locally to any skin condition with a loose bandage for children or adults.
Supplements	Fish oil (EPA/DHA), vitamin C Zinc, flaxseed.
Herbal remedies	Liquorice, witch hazel, calendula, camomile milk thistle, St John's wort, rhodiola, cayenne.
Lifestyle changes	Skin brushing Hot and cold Sitz baths Regular daily aerobic exercise Learning to say no to coffee, tea, chocolate, alcohol and anything that will clog the body up with toxins

Knowledge review

The lymphatic and immune systems

1 What are the three main functions of the lymphatic and immune systems?

2 What dietary influences affect the lymphatic and immune systems?

3 What three B vitamins in particular have mild immune-boosting effects on the immune system, compared to vitamin B6?

4 What are the symptoms of a true food allergy?

5 What are the symptoms of a food intolerance?

6 What is ADD and what foods in particular have been linked with this condition?

7 What are food phenolics? – give two examples.

8 Explain the 'avoid and challenge' test.

9 What herbal remedy is recommended for suspected food sensitivities and why?

10 What are carcinogens? – give four examples.

11 List four common symptoms of the condition known as candida.

12 What superfoods are recommended for clients with candida?

13   What dietary recommendations would you make for a client with cellulite?

14   What is CFS? List four of the main symptoms associated with this condition.

15   What foods should be decreased for clients with CFS?

16   List four lifestyle changes that may benefit clients with rheumatoid arthritis.

17   Why does vitamin C have good results in people suffering with eczema?

18   What supplements are recommended for clients with eczema?

19   List three superfoods and three lifestyle changes that may benefit clients suffering with stress.

20   What arginine rich foods should be avoided at the outbreak of a cold sore?

21   What general foods should be avoided in order to support the lymphatic and immune systems?

22   What are the general lifestyle changes that may benefit the lymphatic and immune systems?

The muscular system

14

Learning objectives

This chapter covers the following:

- **dietary influences affecting the muscular system**
- **common disorders associated with the muscular system**
- **recommendations of foods to increase/decrease**
- **supplements and herbal remedies**
- **superfoods and lifestyle changes relating to disorders of the muscular system**

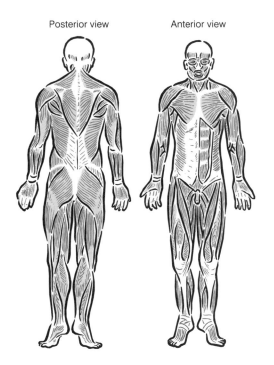

Posterior view   Anterior view

The muscular system

What is the muscular system?

The term muscular system, describes skeletal muscles; those that are under our voluntary control. Muscle tissue refers to all the contractile tissues of the body; skeletal, cardiac and smooth muscle. Cardiac muscle tissue is located in the heart and is therefore considered part of the cardiovascular system. Smooth muscle tissue of the intestine is part of the digestive system, whereas smooth muscle tissue of the urinary bladder is part of the urinary system.

Main function

The main function of the muscular system is that of movement.

What does the muscular system do?

There are nearly 700 skeletal muscles in the body. Skeletal muscles produce movements by exerting force on tendons, which in turn pull on bones or other structures such as the skin. Most muscles cross at least one joint and are attached to the articulating bones that form the joint. When such a muscle contracts it draws one articulating bone toward the other.

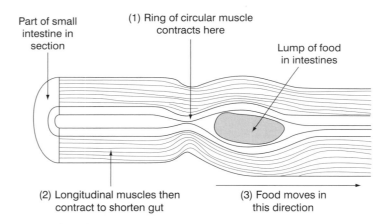

Part of small intestine in section

(1) Ring of circular muscle contracts here

Lump of food in intestines

Peristalsis

(2) Longitudinal muscles then contract to shorten gut

(3) Food moves in this direction

Dietary influences affecting the muscular system

Probably the most influencing factor to the muscular system is water. Muscles are 75 per cent water and a loss of only 3 per cent of this water causes a 10 per cent drop in strength and an 8 per cent loss of speed. Carbohydrates are also essential as they provide the necessary fuel. This is why many athletes will 'carbohydrate load' before an event. Protein is important but should be kept to a minimum. Increasing protein does not improve athletic performance, and while fat has little role to play, the essential fatty acids must not be overlooked.

Common disorders

Cramp

Cramp is a common and painful condition that is caused by the prolonged contraction of a muscle. Cramps normally last for only a few seconds and can be put down to things such as poor posture, stress or tiredness. Sometimes a cramp will occur just after exercise because of a build up of lactic acid in the muscles. Many people suffer from night cramps which will usually be relieved by massage or stretching. Cramps are usually caused by impaired blood supply to the muscles and supplements that promote blood flow often reduce the frequency of attacks.

Camomile has a high content of calcium and magnesium and also contains potassium, iron, manganese, zinc and vitamin A. It makes a pleasant tea and is excellent for menstrual cramps. Wild yam is useful for cramps in the region of the uterus during the later stages of pregnancy. It will relax and soothe muscles and nerves. Muscle cramps can be quite debilitating but can respond to vitamin E, B6, calcium and magnesium.

Recommendations for cramp

Diet	A whole food approach to food where quality is more important than quantity. Plenty of fruits, vegetables, nuts and seeds with adequate essential fatty acids, low-fat protein, and plenty of water.
Increase	Green leafy vegetables, oily fish at least three times a week
Decrease	All denatured food, all stimulants such as tea, coffee, chocolate, cigarettes and alcohol. All refined foods such as white bread and flour and all synthetic colourings and flavourings.
Superfoods	Algae, bio-yoghurt, medicinal mushrooms
Supplements	Magnesium and calcium supplement Co-Q-10, vitamin E, B-complex Antioxidant formula
Herbals	Camomile, wild yam
Lifestyle changes	Be sure to warm up and cool down before and after events. Cramp can be caused by dehydration, so don't forget fluid intake.

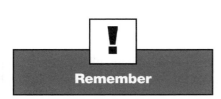

Remember

Muscular system rule no. 1

Always warm up before exercise.
Always cool down muscles after exercise.

Fybromyalgia

Fibromyalgia is a health condition that involves muscular pain and stiffness, which is usually considered to be a form of arthritis. However, because it is characterised by a number of tender points all over the body in specific muscles, it is more of a muscular energy disorder than arthritis.

Anti-inflammatories are often recommended, for example evening primrose oil, and in some cases these help, but the problems appear to be more with the energy the muscles are not providing than an inflammation problem. There are natural pain-killers that can be recommended.

It is a complex syndrome with no known cause or cure. Some of the most common symptoms of this syndrome are aches and pains in the

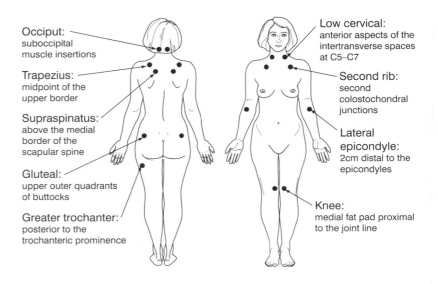

Occiput:
suboccipital
muscle insertions

Trapezius:
midpoint of the
upper border

Supraspinatus:
above the medial
border of the
scapular spine

Gluteal:
upper outer quadrants
of buttocks

Greater trochanter:
posterior to the
trochanteric prominence

Low cervical:
anterior aspects of the
intertransverse spaces
at C5–C7

Second rib:
second
colostochondral
junctions

Lateral
epicondyle:
2cm distal to the
epicondyles

Knee:
medial fat pad proximal
to the joint line

Fybromyalgia

muscles, tendons and ligaments, fatigue and restlessness, muscle spasms, stiffness, headaches and paresthesia (tingly, prickly sensations), sleep disorders, constant fatigue and a depressed immune function.

Low-intensity exercise may improve fibromyalgia symptoms. Patients who exercise regularly have been reported to suffer less severe symptoms than those who remain sedentary.

Stress is believed by some researchers to be capable of exacerbating symptoms. Stress-reduction techniques such as meditation have also proven helpful in preliminary research. As stress uses up magnesium, there is a need for magnesium supplementation. Magnesium malate, is often recommended for fibromyalgia sufferers. Acupuncture has significantly improved symptoms in several trials studying people with fibromyalgia.

Recommendations for fibromyalgia

Diet	A whole food approach to food where quality is more important than quantity. Plenty of fruits, vegetables, nuts and seeds with adequate essential fatty acids, low-fat protein, and plenty of water.
Increase	Green leafy vegetables and all fruits, nuts, seeds and low fat protein like free-range chicken and turkey. Oily fish – sardines salmon, herring, tuna and mackerel.
Decrease	Cigarettes, alcohol, all refined foods, all anti-nutrients. Be aware of heavy metals, such as lead, cadmium, aluminium and mercury and avoid contact.
Superfoods	Alfalfa, algae, barley grass, bee pollen, medicinal mushrooms, super sprouts and bio-yoghurt.
Supplements	Magnesium malate. Fish oils and GLA, antioxidant complex and a B-complex with at least 50mg of all the B vitamins.
Herbals	2g liquorice root three times per day for six to eight weeks, boswellia applied as a cream has been beneficial Rhodiola
Lifestyle changes	Regular exercise but of the low-intensity type. Investigate an acupuncture treatment. Identify any food allergens that may be involved with the symptoms.

Remember

Muscular system rule no. 2

Muscles are 75 per cent water – loss of only 3 per cent of this water causes a 10 per cent drop in strength and an 8 per cent loss of speed.
Drink at least one litre of water every day.

Injury

Muscle injuries such as tears and strains are extremely common, especially in athletes and people who engage in regular intensive training. Muscles need to be continually worked if they are to maintain their size and strength. In 1991 the space shuttle Columbia was launched for a nine-day mission dedicated, among other things, to researching the physiological changes bought on by weightlessness. The crew experienced a 25 per cent loss in muscle mass within 10 days – perfectly illustrating the importance of keeping muscles stimulated.

Regular weight-bearing exercise is essential to maintain good muscle mass. Weight-bearing exercise is walking, running and skipping, not swimming, cycling or trampolining all of which are aerobic activities.

Prolonged exercise may result in muscles being broken down into amino acids to provide fuel for the body. Furthermore the health of the muscle tissue may be effected by wear and tear. Although taking supplements of amino acids is not generally necessary or recommended, people who engage regularly in intense, long-duration activities may find that an amino acid complex supplement helps to promote regeneration and structure of muscle tissue.

Recommendations for injury

Diet	A whole food approach to food where quality is more important than quantity. Plenty of fruits, vegetables, nuts and seeds with adequate essential fatty acids, and plenty of water. Complete protein is of importance for injury to help repair damage. Choose good quality protein like oily fish, free-range chicken, turkey, free-range eggs.
Increase	Green leafy vegetables and spring water. Good quality, low fat protein.
Decrease	Everything refined – especially white bread and flour, confectionery, and alcohol
Superfoods	Spirulina, medicinal mushrooms, bee pollen
Supplements	Amino Acid complex Antioxidants Multivitamin and mineral Magnesium and calcium
Herbals	Echinacea, rhodiola, ginkgo biloba
Lifestyle changes	Never forget to warm up and cool down. Regular massage

Strains and sprains

A sprain is the forcible wrenching or twisting of a joint with partial rupture or other injury to its attachments without luxation. It occurs when the attachments are stressed beyond their normal capacity. There may be damage to the associated blood vessels, muscles, tendons, ligaments or nerves. A sprain is more serious than a strain, which is the overstretching of a muscle. Severe sprains may be so painful that the joint cannot be moved. There is considerable swelling and pain may occur owing to underlying heomorrhage from ruptured blood vessels. The ankle joint is most often sprained; the low back area is another frequent location for sprains.

Remember

Muscular system rule no. 3

In injury follow the R I C E principle – Rest, Ice, Compression and Elevation.

Recommendations for strains

Diet	None specifically. A well-balanced diet covering all the main food groups; carbohydrates, essential fatty acids, and proteins. Good quality complete protein is needed for repair and renewal in the body so ensure you are getting enough.
Increase	Green leafy vegetables. Juicing is good in time of recovery. Experiment – carrot and apple, celery and apple, apple with a little lemon. All are detoxifying and cleansing to aid healing.
Decrease	Alcohol, cigarettes, all refined foods, junk food, chocolate, tea and coffee
Superfoods	Spirulina, medicinal mushrooms, bee pollen
Supplements	Amino acid complex Antioxidants, multivitamin and mineral Magnesium and calcium
Herbals	Echinacea, rhodiola, ginkgo biloba
Lifestyle changes	Resting the injury is the only way to get back on your feet quickly. Ice may be helpful to reduce inflammation, taping the injury may be appropriate as will elevation of the injured part.

General recommendations for the muscular system

Diet	Eat plenty of complete carbohydrates such as whole grains, fruit, vegetables, beans, lentils and jacket potatoes. Add some protein to your food such as low fat chicken, turkey, nuts and seeds. Drink plenty of water, but not carbonated water unless it is natural, before, during and after events if you are an athlete.
Foods to avoid	Too much protein
Superfoods	Alfalfa, spirulina, chorella and blue-green algae – rotated each month. Barley grass, bee pollen, cabbage, Manuka honey, liquorice, medicinal mushrooms, super sprouts and bio-yoghurt.
Supplements	Magnesium; vitamin E; L-arginine and L-ornithine Amino acid complex for serious athletes BCAA – branched chain amino acids; Co-Q-10
Herbal remedies	Ginger, ginkgo biloba, garlic, liquorice, Siberian ginseng
Lifestyle changes	Take nutrition seriously. Whether you are an athlete or a housewife, the difference between coming first or second or the difference between getting out of bed in the morning or not may depend on your overall dietary habits.

Knowledge review

The muscular system

1   What is the main function of the muscular system?

2   What two dietary factors have the greatest influence on the muscular system?

3   What usually causes cramps?

4   Which of the herbal teas may be recommended for menstrual cramps?

5   Magnesium and calcium supplements are often recommended for clients suffering with cramp. Can you remember the best time to take mineral supplements and why?

6   What is fybromyalgia?

7   List six common symptoms of fybromyalgia.

8   Anti-nutrients should be avoided in clients with fybromyalgia. Give four examples of an anti-nutrient.

9   Regular weight-bearing exercise is essential to maintain good muscle mass. Give four examples of weight bearing exercise.

10   What is the difference between a sprain and a strain?

11   What general food recommendations are given for clients with injuries?

12   List four lifestyle changes you would recommend for clients with injuries.

13   Muscles are 75 per cent water. What would be the result of a loss of 3 per cent of this water?

14   Does increasing protein improve athletic performance?

15   What foods are recommended to support the muscular system generally?

15

The nervous system

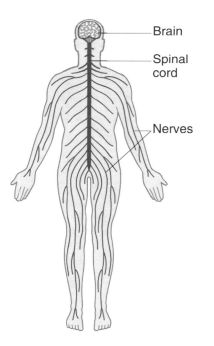

Learning objectives

This chapter covers the following:

- **dietary influences affecting the nervous system**

- **common disorders associated with the nervous system**

- **recommendations of foods to increase/decrease**

- **supplements and herbal remedies**

- **superfoods and lifestyle changes relating to disorders of the nervous systems**

Brain

Spinal cord

Nerves

The nervous system

What is the nervous system?

The central nervous system (CNS) is the control centre for the entire nervous system and consists of the brain and spinal cord.

The peripheral nervous system (PNS) connects the brain and spinal cord with receptors, like muscles and glands. It can then be divided into an afferent system and an efferent system. The afferent system consists of nerve cells that convey information *from* receptors to the CNS. The efferent system consists of nerve cells that convey information from the CNS *to* muscles and glands.

Main function

The overall function of the nervous system is to collect information about the external conditions in relation to the body's external state, to analyse this information, and to initiate appropriate responses to satisfy certain needs.

The principal cells of the nervous system are known as neurons. Neurons are highly specialised for nerve impulse conduction and for all special functions attributed to the nervous system: thinking, controlling muscle activity and regulating glands. The other principal cells found in the nervous system are called neuroglia. The neuroglia serve as a special supporting and protective component of the nervous system.

What does the nervous system do?

All body sensations must be relayed from receptors to the central nervous system if they are to be interpreted and acted upon. The majority of nerve impulses that stimulate muscles to contract and glands to secrete must also originate in the central nervous system. The main sensations are cold, heat, pain, and pressure.

Dietary influences affecting the nervous system

As with all systems of the body, diet plays an important role in the nervous system. This is one part of the body we should all be concerned about, as dementia and other degenerative diseases of the brain are increasing and once these diseases develop, they may not be reversible. At such a time we are limited to improving function as best we can and limiting further degeneration. Obviously prevention is the best approach. A considerable amount of research shows that these degenerations are caused primarily by three factors: poor blood supply to the brain, nutritional deficiencies and brain-specific toxins – all of which are controllable. The irritation or inflammation of nerves may be caused by anemia, B1 deficiency or B12 neuropathy. Alcoholism and diabetes are also associated with nerve disorders.

Common disorders

Anxiety

Anxiety describes any feeling of worry or dread, usually about potential events that may or may not happen. Some anxiety about stressful events is normal, but, in some people anxiety interferes with the ability to function. Severe anxiety usually lasts more than six months though it may not be a problem every day. Physical symptoms can sometimes result in fatigue, insomnia and irritability. Nutritional and natural therapies can be one part of the approach for helping relieve to moderate anxiety.

Reducing exposure to stressful situations can also help and in some cases medication, counselling or group therapy can facilitate this process.

All sources of caffeine should be avoided including tea, coffee, chocolate, caffeinated drinks and caffeine-containing medications. People with high levels of anxiety appear to be more susceptible to the actions of caffeine.

For mild anxiety magnesium may be relaxing; typically 200–300mg of magnesium taken two to three times a day. Additionally many nutritional therapists recommend soaking in a hot bath containing 1–2 cups of magnesium sulphate crystals (such as Epsom salts) for fifteen to twenty minutes. Inositol has been used to help people with anxiety accompanied with panic attacks; up to 4 grams three times per day has been reported to control such attacks in one double-blind trial. Vitamin B3 as niacinamide may be beneficial. It has been shown in animals to work in the brain in ways similar to drugs such as Valium, which are used to treat anxiety. A reasonable dosage of niacinamide (not niacin) for anxiety is up to 500mgs four times per day.

Valerian is known as a relaxing and sleep promoting herb. It works on the brain and spinal cord and, unlike pharmaceutical drugs such as Valium, has no side effects. Valerian root contains many different constituents, including essential oils that appear to contribute to the sedating properties of the herb. Valerian helps people deal with stress more effectively. Generally, it makes sleep more restful, it does not impair the ability to drive or operate machinery, and it does not lead to addiction or dependence. Valerian is not contraindicated during pregnancy or lactation and is safe for children at half of the adult dose. A cup of Valerian tea before bedtime works wonders in aiding restful sleep.

An old folk remedy for anxiety, particularly when it causes insomnia, is camomile tea. There is evidence from test tube studies that camomile tea contains compounds with a calming action. One cup of tea is taken three or more times per day. The camomile tea drunk should be as strong as possible and if made with a tincture will be more effective than shop-bought teabags. For anxious children put the tea mixture into the bath water. This is also beneficial for eczema in children and adults.

Recommendations for anxiety

Diet	A whole food with meals containing all main food groups, especially small regular amounts of low fat protein foods.
Increase	Green leafy vegetables, fruits and whole foods
Decrease	Coffee, tea, chocolate and all fizzy drinks
Superfoods	Alfalfa, algae, super sprouts, and bee pollen
Supplements	Multivitamin and mineral containing 50mg of the B vitamins (this will also contain sufficient magnesium)
Herbals	St John's wort and valerian
Lifestyle changes	Reduce stress levels, take up yoga, meditation or visualisation

Remember

Nervous system rule no. 1

Prevention is better than cure – look after your brain cells *now* by improving nutritional status.

Headaches

Some headaches, such as those caused by hangovers or not enough sleep, are easily diagnosed and treated by drinking lots of water and catching up on sleep as soon as possible. Other types of headache tend to fall into three main categories: tension-type headaches, migraines and cluster headaches.

Tension headaches are generally thought to be caused by the tightening of the muscles of the scalp and face, usually as a result of stress or bad posture, and can last for days or even weeks. Migraines are typically characterised by sudden severe pain on one side of the head, nausea or vomiting and sensitivity to light, sound and odour. They are generally disabling for several hours or more.

Cluster headaches are quite rare, cause intense pain behind one eye and may wake the sufferer nightly for period or weeks or months.

Diet can play an important part in relieving headaches. It may be that the client is consuming too much of one type of food such as wheat, cheese, or another type of dairy food and may have an intolerance to this food which is causing the headaches. The simple home 'avoid and challenge' allergy test referred to on p. 200 of this book may shed some light if the culprit is in fact food.

Recommendations for headaches

Diet	Low protein diets are recommended for headache sufferers. That is good quality low fat protein like free-range chicken, turkey, fish and free-range eggs.
Increase	Complex carbohydrates and low fat protein foods
Decrease	All refined foods, salt and dairy foods
Superfoods	Super sprouts, medicinal mushrooms and alfalfa
Supplements	B-complex (B2 in particular), fish oils, magnesium
Herbals	Feverfew, ginger
Lifestyle changes	Identify food allergies or intolerances, and stop smoking

Remember

Nervous system rule no. 2

Ginko biloba is the oldest, most effective and most researched herb for helping the brain.

Insomnia

The inability to get a good night's sleep can result from waking up in the middle of the night and having trouble getting back to sleep as well as having difficulty getting to sleep in the first place. Insomnia can be a temporary, occasional, or a chronic problem.

Caffeine is a stimulant. The effects of caffeine last up to twenty hours, so some people will have disturbed sleep patterns even when their last cup of coffee was in the morning. Besides regular coffee, black and green tea, cola, chocolate, some soft drinks and over the counter pharmaceuticals also contain caffeine.

Nutritional therapists will sometimes recommend eating a high carbohydrate filler before bedtime such as a slice of bread or some crackers. Eating carbohydrates can significantly increase serotonin levels in the body, and the hormone serotonin is known to reduce anxiety and promote sleep.

Insomnia can be triggered by psychological stress. Dealing with that stress through counselling or other techniques may be the answer to a better night's rest. Psychological intervention has helped in many studies.

A steady sleeping and eating schedule combined with caffeine avoidance and counselling sessions using behavioural therapy has reduced insomnia for some people, as has listening to relaxation tapes. Melatonin is a natural hormone that regulates the human biological clock and the body produces less melatonin with advancing age, which may explain why elderly people often have difficulty in sleeping. Melatonin supplements are not available in the UK but are freely available in the USA.

There are many herbal remedies used for insomnia. The most reliable, according to studies, is valerian. Valerian root makes getting to sleep easier and induces deep sleep and dreaming. Valerian will not cause a morning hangover, a side effect common in some individuals to prescription sleeping drugs and melatonin. A concentrated valerian root supplement in the amount of 300–400mgs can be taken 30 minutes before bedtime.

One German study compared the effect of a combination product containing an extract of valerian root (320mg at bedtime) and extract of lemon balm (*Melissa officinalis*) with the sleeping drug Halcion. After monitored sleep for nine nights the herbal duo matched Halcion in improving the ability to get to sleep as well as in the quality of the sleep. However, the Halcion group felt hangover symptoms and had trouble concentrating the next day, while those taking the valerian/lemon balm combination reported no negative effect.

In dealing with sleep disorders it is important to recognise that not all people have the same sleeping requirements. As a person gets to 50 or 55, he or she usually will require less sleep. Some people can get by quite nicely with 4–6 hours' sleep at night and a catnap during the day. The real criterion as to whether a person is getting enough sleep is his or her general health and energy levels. If a person does not sleep until one or two in the morning but feels fine and has plenty of energy, then there is no problem. On the other hand if that person lays awake fretting about not being asleep – then there may be a sleep disorder.

Relaxation techniques are a very good way of helping to induce sleep. There are many audio tapes that can be played before going to bed and with training and determination, most insomniacs can alleviate their problem. Hypnosis has also been a remedy for many insomniacs. The usual method is to teach the subject self-hypnosis slowly, allowing him to relax and then sleep. Autogenics has also helped many people.

Recommendations for insomnia

Diet	A general balanced-diet consisting of all the main food groups, carbohydrates, low fat proteins, essential fatty acids and water.
Increase	Relaxing herbal teas before bed
Decrease	Coffee, tea, chocolate, all caffeinated drinks. Depending how serious the problem is do not have caffeine after 6pm – earlier if a serious problem.
Superfoods	Manuka honey taken with warm water and chamomile tea taken early evening
Supplements	Magnesium and calcium in the early evening If taking any other vitamins, always take in the mornings B-complex, for example may keep you awake if taken too late in the day
Herbals	Black cohosh – tonic for central nervous system Valerian and rhodiola
Lifestyle changes	Learn relaxation techniques. Investigate buying some relaxation tapes. Take up meditation and visualisation. Reflexology is a wonderful treatment for insomnia. A herb pillow is also beneficial

Migraine headaches

Migraines are very painful headaches sometimes involving nausea, vomiting, and changes in vision. They usually begin on only one side of the head and may become worse with exposure to light. The exact cause of migraine headaches is not well understood. However, certain features of this debilitating disease are known, making effective prevention and treatment available to many migraine sufferers. There are three main areas to investigate when faced with a client with migraine headaches. These are allergies and food intolerance, hormonal imbalance and blood sugar abnormality.

The first thing that comes to my mind when faced with a client who suffers frequent migraine headaches is the likelihood of allergies and food sensitivities. Migraine can be triggered by allergies and may be relieved by identifying and avoiding the problem foods. Uncovering these food allergies with the help of a nutritional therapist is often a useful way to prevent migraine. Some migraine sufferers have an impaired ability to break down tyramine, a substance found in many foods such as aged cheeses, red wine, beef, chicken, liver and sauerkraut, which is known to trigger migraine in some people. People with this defect are thought to be more sensitive than others to the effects of tyramine.

Monosodium glutamate (MSG), a flavouring agent used in many foods, has been reported to trigger migraine headaches. Ingestion of the artificial sweetener aspartame has also been reported to provoke migraine in a small proportion of people. Foods that contain nitrates and nitrites, such as preserved meats, are commonly reported triggers of migraine headaches. Contrary to the widely held belief of many doctors, chocolate does not appear to play a significant role in triggering migraine headaches.

If the allergy route is unsuccessful, another prominent area connected to migraine attacks is hormonal influences. Many women have migraine attacks linked to their menstrual cycles. Menstrual migraine headaches are thought to be related to fluctuating levels of oestrogen in the body. Hormonally triggered migraine may get worse early in pregnancy but tend to improve later in pregnancy. Researchers point out that oral contraceptive use can result in worsening, improvement, or no change in a woman's migraine. Other researchers have presented evidence that the oral contraceptive pill or oestrogen replacement therapy can provoke or exacerbate migraine. Since the use of these hormones has been linked with an increased risk of stroke, and a history of migraine with aura is also a risk factor for stroke, women with migraine should probably avoid oral contraceptives and oestrogen replacement therapy. Research has shown that migraine sufferers have lower levels of magnesium than other people and that pre-menopausal women who suffer migraine headaches benefit from magnesium supplements. One double-blind study showed that 350mg of magnesium per day decreased premenstrual migraines.

Blood sugar abnormalities are also known to trigger migraine headaches. Some migraine sufferers have an abnormality of blood sugar regulation known as reactive hypoglycemia. In these people, improvement in the frequency and severity of migraine has been observed when dietary changes designed to control the blood sugar were implemented. This was observed as early as 1949. To control blood sugar levels, eating little and often is recommended, with each meal containing small amounts of protein, which will slow down the absorption of the sugar.

The most frequently used herb for the long-term treatment and prevention of migraines is feverfew. Feverfew inhibits both hyperaggregation of platelets and the release of serotonin and some inflammatory mediators. Double-blind studies show that continuous use of feverfew leads to a reduction in the severity, duration, and frequency of migraine headaches.

Yet another cause of migraine headaches is thought to be related to abnormal serotonin function in blood vessels, and 5-hydroxytryptophan (5-HTP, which is converted by the body into serotonin) may help correct this abnormality. In several double-blind trials, supplementation with 5-HTP (200–600mg per day) has improved migraine, often producing results comparable to those achieved with anti-migraine drugs.

Other factors associated with migraine headaches are people with reactions to salt, lactose-intolerant individuals, high protein diets and smoking.

Remember

Nervous system rule no. 3

Regular exercise and keeping the blood vessels open and the heart strong are essential to keeping our brain and nervous system healthy.

Recommendations for migraine headaches

Diet	Low protein diets have been used with some success to reduce migraine attacks.
Increase	Complex carbohydrates and low fat protein foods
Decrease	All refined foods, salt and dairy foods
Superfoods	Super sprouts, medicinal mushrooms and alfalfa
Supplements	B-complex (B2 in particular), fish oils, magnesium
Herbals	Feverfew, ginger, valerian, rhodiola
Lifestyle changes	Identify food allergies or intolerances, and stop smoking

General recommendations for the nervous system

Diet	A whole food approach to food where quality is more important than quantity. Plenty of fruits, vegetables, nuts and seeds with adequate essential fatty acids, low-fat protein, and plenty of water.
Foods to avoid	All known anti-nutrients: alcohol, caffeine, chemicals found in paint, paint thinner, cleaning fluids, gasoline, kerosene, and lighter fluid. Also aluminium, lead, cadmium, mercury (from dental fillings). All synthetic hormones and all denatured food. Excessive E numbers, additives, preservatives, rancid food and pesticides.
Superfoods	All antioxidant foods and supplements. Carotenoids, flavonoids, vitamins C and E, beta-carotene, selenium and antioxidant herbs.
Supplements	B12, folic acid, multivitamins and minerals. Antioxidants A, C, E and selenium, vitamin E in particular has been shown to directly protect the nerves from oxidative damage and improved neurological function after supplementation.
Herbal remedies	A herbal formula that not only strengthens the nervous system but benefits the peripheral blood circulation. It helps relieve anxiety and tense muscles. It will gradually build a strong nervous system, which protects the immune system. Valerian is rich in calcium and the passionflower is beneficial for the eyes. The formula includes black cohosh, valerian, capsicum, passionflower, skullcap, hops and wood betony.
Lifestyle changes	Exercise your brain by exercising your body and avoid free radicals at all costs

Knowledge review

The nervous system

1   What are the overall functions of the nervous system?

2   Name the two principal cells of the nervous system.

3   What are the three main factors that primarily cause degeneration?

4   Define anxiety.

5   What is the herbal tea usually recommended for clients with anxiety?

6   List four lifestyle changes you could recommend for clients with anxiety.

7   What are Epsom salts; how would you use them and for what reason?

8   What are the three main categories of headaches?

9   Food intolerance may be a cause of headaches. Name three foods that may be the cause.

10   What is your understanding of insomnia?

11   How long do the effects of caffeine last?

12   What herbal remedy may be recommended for clients with insomnia?

13   What foods and drinks would you recommend clients decrease if suffering with insomnia?

14   What are the three main areas to investigate when faced with a client with migraine headaches?

15   What is the most frequently used herb for the long-term treatment and prevention of migraine headaches?

16   What supplements may be recommended for migraine sufferers?

17   Some migraine sufferers have an impaired ability to break down tyramine. In what foods is tyramine found? - give four examples.

18   What superfoods may be recommended for clients with migraines?

19   What general food recommendations are given to support the nervous system?

20   Which vitamin in particular has been shown to directly protect the nerves from oxidative damage?

The reproductive system

Learning objectives

This chapter covers the following:

- **dietary influences affecting the reproductive system**
- **common disorders associated with the reproductive system**
- **recommendations of foods to increase/decrease**
- **supplements and herbal remedies**
- **superfoods and lifestyle changes relating to disorders of the reproductive system**

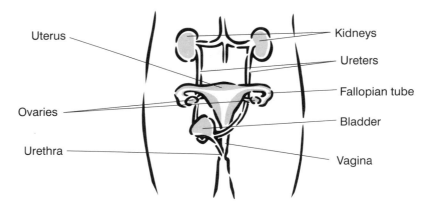

The female reproductive system

What is the reproductive system?

It is the system of the body which enables reproduction to take place, thereby maintaining the species. The reproductive systems differ in males and females.

Main function

Maintains the continuation of the human species.

What does the reproductive system do?

Reproduction is the process by which genetic material is passed from generation to generation – thus reproduction maintains the continuation of the species. Reproduction is also the process by which a single cell duplicates its genetic material allowing an organism to grow and repair itself, and so maintains the life of the individual.

The organs of the reproductive system are grouped as gonads, ducts and accessory sex glands. The male structures of reproduction include the testes, ductus epididymis, vas deferens, ejaculatory duct, urethra, seminal vesicles, prostate gland, Cowper's glands and penis. The female structures of reproduction include the ovaries, fallopian tubes, uterus, vagina and vulva. The mammary glands are also considered part of the reproductive system.

The coming together of a male and a female in the act of unprotected sexual intercourse is the process by which spermatozoa provided by the male are deposited in the vagina of the female – the end result of which could be pregnancy. Pregnancy is a sequence of events that normally includes fertilisation, implantation, embryonic growth and fetal growth that terminates in birth.

Dietary influences affecting the reproductive system

The sperm count in males has decreased by 50 per cent over the last 50 years. Our grandmothers and mothers were likely to get pregnant with their first encounter with sexual intercourse, now one in four couples have difficulty in conceiving even after one year of trying. These are amazing statistics – and one of the main reasons behind them is poor diet. Latest research has shown that our fruit and vegetables have at least 50 per cent less minerals and vitamins than the fruit and vegetables of 50 years ago. That, together with our modern fast lifestyles, adulterated food, alcohol and stress have all had their part to play in affecting the reproductive system. More than any other system of the body, the reproductive system needs fresh, unadulterated foods of the richest and most natural quality. To function optimally, the reproductive system needs the B complex of vitamins, complete proteins, marine oils, vitamins A, C, E and the minerals selenium and zinc – all of which are depleted in many people.

Remember

Reproductive system rule no. 1

More than any other system of the body, the reproductive system needs fresh, unadulterated foods of the richest and most natural quality.

Common disorders

Infertility

Infertility in its strictest definition means 'failure to reproduce' after unprotected intercourse. Many doctors suggest that if a couple has been trying to conceive a baby for 18 months without success, and having regular unprotected sex two or three times a week, they should go to their GP and ask to be referred to a specialist unit to find out why. Some specialists suggest you take action sooner than that. Couples over 30 should wait only a year before seeking advice and for women over 36 should wait no longer than six months. Female fertility peaks between 24 and 27 then declines slowly but surely thereafter.

Twenty per cent per cent of couples conceive within one month of trying and about 50 per cent of fertile couples will conceive within six months of trying with 85 per cent being successful within one year. The remaining 15 per cent may have a fertility problem.

Female infertility

There are many reasons for not conceiving. It can be caused by sex hormone abnormalities, low thyroid function, endometriosis, scarring of the fallopian tubes, or a host of other causes. Some of the causes of infertility readily respond to natural medicine whereas others do not. There are many dietary and nutritional changes that may be helpful. Caffeine consumption equivalent to more than three cups of coffee per day has been linked to tubal disease and endometriosis – both of which can cause female infertility. As little as one to one and a half cups of coffee per day appears to delay conception in women trying to get pregnant. Some studies find one cup of coffee per day cuts fertility in half, although others report that it takes two or three to have detrimental effects. Caffeine is found in regular coffee, black and green tea, some soft drinks, chocolate and many over the counter pharmaceuticals. While not every study finds that caffeine reduces female fertility, most nutritional therapists recommend that women trying to get pregnant avoid caffeine altogether.

Excessive or insufficient weight, smoking and even moderate amounts of alcohol are also likely to reduce the chance of conceiving. The more women smoke, the less likely the chance to conceive. In fact, women whose mothers smoked during *their* pregnancy are only half as likely to conceive as those whose mothers were non-smokers.

Studies have shown that being deficient in iron and the B vitamins reduces female fertility, whereas a double-blind research trial has shown that taking a multivitamin/mineral supplement increases female fertility. Studies have shown that vitamin E deficiency in animals leads to infertility and a preliminary trial on humans, when 100ius of vitamin E were given to both man and woman of infertile couples resulted in a significant increase in fertility.

If a women has been taking the contraceptive pill for a few years and then stops and switches to another form of contraception, her cycles can be erratic for up to 4 or 5 months. There is anecdotal evidence that a small number of women may find conception difficult after a long period of Pill-taking.

IUD's can increase the chances of pelvic infection threefold. This can affect fertility if the infection reaches the fallopian tubes and is severe enough to block them with scar tissue.

Smoking can affect a woman's (and a man's) fertility by causing constriction of the blood vessels including those supporting the reproductive organs, thus inhibiting their proper function. It can also act directly on the tiny cilia lining the fallopian tubes, inhibiting their action.

Pieces of the lining of the womb can migrate to other places in the pelvis such as the fallopian tubes or around the ovaries – a process known as endometriosis. Like the rest of the womb lining they are still under the control of hormones, so they continue to shed blood each month wherever they are. This can occasionally block the tubes or more often, clog the area around the ovaries so the ripened egg cannot get out. Ovulation problems occur if the ovaries are damaged, not working in a cycle or the cause is hormonal or chemical.

Male infertility

The two most important nutrients to improve male fertility are vitamin C and zinc. Vitamin C protects sperm from oxidative damage and improves the quality of sperm in smokers. Where sperm stick together (a condition called agglutination), fertility is reduced. Vitamin C reduces sperm agglutination, increasing the fertility of men with this condition. A minimum 1g of vitamin C daily is recommended.

A lack of zinc can reduce testosterone levels. For men with low testosterone levels, supplementation raises testosterone and also increases fertility. For men with low serum zinc levels, zinc supplements may increase both sperm counts and fertility. Most studies have infertile men take zinc supplements for at least several months. The ideal amount of supplemental zinc remains unknown but 30mg of zinc taken daily in the evenings is usually recommended. Liquid zinc can be purchased and is said to be absorbed more efficiently. All minerals, including zinc, should be taken in evenings when they are better absorbed.

Co-Q-10 is a nutrient used by the body in the production of energy. While its energy role in the formation of sperm is unknown, there is evidence that as little as 10mg per day (over a two-week period) will increase sperm count and motility.

Recommendations for female infertility

Diet	A whole food approach. Nothing denatured, or from packets containing additives. Fresh, good quality, preferably organic foods.
Increase	Everything healthy – green leafy vegetables, fruit, lean meat and poultry. Lots of water.
Decrease	Coffee, alcohol, and all refined foods
Superfoods	Oysters, asparagus, algae, Manuka honey
Supplements	A multivitamin/mineral with added 20mg zinc. Fish oils, folic acid
Herbals	Vitex
Lifestyle changes	Avoid all caffeinated substances. Rule out iron deficiency. Relax.

Recommendations for male infertility

Diet	A whole food approach. Nothing denatured, or from packets containing additives. Fresh good quality, preferably organic foods.
Increase	Everything healthy – green leafy vegetables, fruit, lean meat and poultry. Lots of water.
Decrease	Coffee. Alcohol, all refined foods.
Superfoods	Oysters, asparagus, algae, Manuka honey
Supplements	A multivitamin/mineral 25mg zinc; 1g vitamin C daily; fish oils; Co-Q-10
Herbals	Vitex
Lifestyle changes	Avoid all caffeinated substances. Rule out zinc deficiency. Relax.

Reproductive system rule no. 2

Zinc supplementation should always be considered for men and women experiencing infertility problems.

The female cycle

The average menstrual cycle lasts for 28 days, although it is not uncommon for cycles to vary between three to six weeks. Emotional states, stress, diet, other hormones, illness and drugs can all affect menstruation. The majority of women have knowledge of the roles of oestrogen and progesterone in their bodies, but few are aware of the other two very important hormones that have just as important roles. These are follicle stimulating hormone (FSH) and the luteinising hormone (LH).

Days 1–14 of the menstrual cycle are the days from menstruation to ovulation. At the beginning of the cycle the levels of hormones oestrogen and progesterone are very low as a result of the shedding of the womb lining. The hypothalamus in the brain is the master gland of this hormonal activity and when it senses that the levels are low it releases the first master hormone which causes the pituitary gland to release follicle stimulating hormone (FSH). It is this hormone that ripens one egg within the ovary for release into the fallopian tube. FSH also stimulates the production of estrogen by the ovary, which increases over the first fourteen days of the cycle, bringing about the growth of the lining of the womb and breast tissue.

When oestrogen levels peak around day 12 of the cycle, the hypothalamus gland then releases luteinising hormone (LH). On day 14 of a normal cycle, a surge of luteinising hormone brings about ovulation, the release of a mature egg from one of the ovaries. This egg then travels through the fallopian tube towards the uterus.

Days 14–28 of the menstrual cycle are the days from ovulation to menstruation. During this second half of the cycle there are high levels of both oestrogen and progesterone to support fertilisation should it occur. Progesterone starts its increase just after ovulation and increases body temperature by at least 0.2°C. Many women therefore take their temperature in order to check whether they have ovulated. If the egg is not fertilised, the lining of the womb is released forming the menstrual flow. This causes a rapid fall in the levels of oestrogens and progesterone, the low levels act as a signal for the hypothalamus gland to release its master hormone and the process starts all over again.

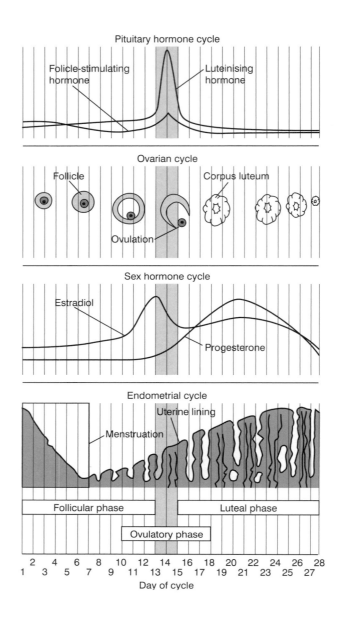

The female cycle

Luteinising hormones and follicle stimulating hormones are important indicators in cases of infertility, PMS, and menopause. You can now be tested over a one-month period for all four of the main hormones to monitor their progress throughout the month. This is carried out by a 28-day saliva test and the results are often most interesting. Whilst these tests can be of immense value, they are also expensive and it must be remembered that emotional states, stress, diet, other hormones, illness and drugs can all affect menstruation, and therefore maybe the test results too.

Dysmenorrheoa (heavy periods)

Dysmenorrheoa, or painful menstruation, is classified as either primary or secondary. Primary dysmenorrheoa generally occurs within a couple of years of the first menstruation period. The pain tends to decrease with age and very often resolves after childbirth. Secondary dysmenorrheoa is commonly a result of endometriosis, starts later in life, and tends to increase in intensity over time. As many as half of menstruating women are affected by dysmenorrheoa, and of these 10 per cent have severe dysmenorrheoa, which greatly limits activities for one to three days every month.

Women suffering from this miserable monthly experience have their own solutions to menstrual cramps. Some women find gentle exercise helpful while others do not; and some feel the need just to lie still. There are, however, several lifestyle changes and nutritional supplements that may be helpful.

Many studies have reported that alcohol should be avoided by women experiencing menstrual pain, because it depletes stores of certain nutrients and alters the metabolism of carbohydrates – which in turn worsens muscle spasms. Alcohol can also interfere with the liver's ability to metabolise hormones. In theory, this might result in elevated oestrogen levels, increased fluid retention and heavier menstrual flow.

Niacin has been reported to be effective in relieving menstrual cramps. In one study, 87 per cent of a group of forty women reported benefit from the supplement. In theory, calcium may help prevent menstrual cramp, as muscles that are calcium-deficient tend to be hyperactive and therefore might be more prone to cramp. While calcium could be beneficial for cramping, it is advisable to always supplement calcium with magnesium.

In one double-blind trial, fish oil led to a statistically significant 37 per cent drop in menstrual symptoms. In that report, adolescent girls with dysmenorrheoa were given 1,080mg of EPA and 720mg of DHA per day for two months to achieve this result. This would amount to 6,000mg fish oil per day. The Danish have carried out many studies using fish oil alone, fish oil with vitamin B12 and vitamin B12 alone, and have found that women who suffer painful periods appear to be deficient in both nutrients. By including oily fish – sardines, tuna, salmon, herring and mackerel – in the diet three times per week, they could ease their monthly cramps. The amounts of B12 used were small at just 7.5mcg daily. However, because of the different types of dysmenorrheoa, it would be wise to seek advice from a nutritional therapist before selecting supplements. If the underlying cause were endometriosis, this would have to be taken into account.

Black cohosh has a history as a folk medicine for relieving menstrual cramps. Black cohosh can be taken in several forms, including crude, dried root, or rhizome (300–2,000mg per day) or as a solid, dry powdered extract (250mg three times per day). Standardised extracts of the herb are probably the easiest to take. Dong Quai is a traditional Chinese herb that may also ease dysmenorrheoa. The powdered root can be used or in capsules, tablets, tinctures or as a tea. This herb is known as an adaptogen and has the ability to normalise female hormones.

A review of literature suggests that women who use oral contraceptives may experience decreased vitamin B1, B2, B3, B12, C and zinc levels. Synthetic hormones disrupt the endocrine system so you may wish to investigate alternative methods of birth control.

Amenorrhoea – lack of periods

Amenorrhoea is usually associated with strict dieting and/or strenuous exercise although there can be other causes. Our bodies are composed of a mixture of fat, a fat-free mass or lean tissue and a glycogen store. It is normal and indeed necessary for everyone to have a certain amount of fat in their bodies. A woman needs to have at least 22 per cent of her body weight as fat in order to have regular periods. Many women with anorexia nervosa or who are underweight do not have periods for this reason. However, having regular periods also relies on hormones. Hormones can be affected by dieting and weight loss, so even when she has enough body fat, a woman's period may become irregular or stop.

The reproductive system heavily relies on zinc, and this supplement would be the first choice for aiming to rebalance the body and to start menstruation again. Liquid zinc would be recommended for better absorption. This is a serious problem and should not be overlooked. A nutritional therapist will be able to offer much advice with disordered eating leading to too much weight loss, but in some cases a referral to a specially trained counsellor in *eating disorders* may be necessary. In any event a visit to the GP should be the first port of call.

Irregular periods

Irregular periods may be perfectly normal, especially as women reach the menopause years, where they will probably become irregular before stopping altogether. Irregular periods are associated with extreme stress, the contraceptive pill, strenuous exercise, low weight and anorexia nervosa. If your periods are not regular and you are not menopause age then it may be worth checking it out. In the meantime, a whole food approach to food taking in all the main food groups with each meal will be a good start.

Recommendations for heavy periods

Reproductive system rule no. 3

For a healthy reproductive system, *avoid* alcohol, saturated fats and sugar.

Diet	A whole food approach to food. Good nourishing food with plenty of fruits and vegetables, low fat protein, and plenty of water.
Increase	Fatty fish, fruit and vegetables
Decrease	Alcohol, red meat, refined foods, chocolate
Superfoods	Yoghurt, alfalfa, honey, bee pollen, barley grass
Supplements	A good multivitamin/mineral. B6 and zinc taken for the second half of the cycle has been said to be beneficial. Zinc and vitamin C and bioflavonoids
Herbals	Black cohosh, valerian
Lifestyle changes	Test for food intolerance. Taking vitamin C with iron rich foods increases the absorption of iron.

Impotence

Impotence, or erectile dysfunction, is the inability of a male to attain or sustain an erection sufficient for intercourse. It can be a persistent condition; however, almost half of all men experience impotence occasionally. Impotence can have either physical or psychological (or both) causes. Most researchers and doctors now believe that a majority of men suffering from impotence have physical causes. Psychological counselling can be helpful if the impotence is related to emotional factors. There are several physical contributors to impotence, including atherosclerosis, diabetes, hypothyroidism, multiple sclerosis and chronic alcohol use.

Impotence that cannot be linked to physical causes has been successfully treated by hypnosis. In this trial, three hypnosis sessions per week were used initially, later decreasing to one per month during a six-month period. Three out of every four men in the trial were helped.

Dilation of blood vessels necessary for a normal erection depends on a substance called nitric oxide. In turn, the amino acid arginine is needed for nitric oxide formation. In a group of fifteen men with erectile dysfunction given 2,800mg arginine per day for two weeks, six were helped, though none improved while taking placebo.

DHEA (dehydroepiandrosterone) is an anti-ageing, energising, anti-stress hormone that can also convert to both oestrogen and testosterone. It stimulates the sexual response and the production of pheromones. The adrenal glands sit on top of the kidneys and produce hormones that, among other things, help us adapt to stress. The hormones adrenaline, cortisol and DHEA help us respond to an emergency by channelling the body's energy towards being able to 'fight or take flight', improving oxygen and glucose supply to the muscles, and generating mental and physical energy.

Low blood levels of the hormone DHEA have been reported in some men with erectile dysfunction. In one double-blind trial, forty men with low DHEA levels and impotence were given 50mg of DHEA for six months. Significant improvement in both erectile function and interest in sex occurred in the men assigned DHEA but not in those assigned to placebo. No significant change occurred in testosterone levels or in factors that could affect the prostate gland. Experts have concerns about the safe use of DHEA, particularly because long-term safety data do not exist.

There are a number of herbs that may be helpful for impotence. Damiana and Asian ginseng are traditional herbs for impotent men, however no modern studies have confirmed their effectiveness. Ginkgo biloba, a herb which is often recommended for circulatory problems, may help some impotent men by increasing arterial blood flow.

The herb that offers the most promising results however, is yohimbe. Yohimbe dilates blood vessels, making it useful for treating male impotence. Yohimbine (the primary active constituent in yohimbe) has been shown in several double blind studies to help treatment with impotence and somewhat surprisingly it appears to help regardless of the cause of impotence. A tincture of yohimbe bark is often used in the amount of 5–6 drops three times per day. There are also standardised yohimbe products available. A typical daily amount of yohimbine is 15–30mg, however, it is best to take this herb under the supervision of a nutritional therapist with experience of herbal remedies.

Recommendations for impotence

Diet	A whole food approach to food. Good nourishing food with plenty of fruits and vegetables, low-fat protein, and plenty of water.
Increase	All fruits and vegetables
Decrease	All refined foods, alcohol, cigarettes
Superfoods	Bee pollen, honey, medicinal mushrooms, super sprouts
Supplements	A good multivitamin/mineral DHEA, arginine, zinc, folic acid
Herbals	Yohimbe, gingko biloba, damania, Asian ginseng
Lifestyle changes	Learn relaxation techniques. Look into hypnosis. Take up yoga and reduce stress levels.

Premenstrual syndrome (PMS)

The symptoms of PMS are wide ranging and include cramping, bloating, mood swings, breast tenderness, irritability, fatigue, headaches and depression. Premenstrual symptoms typically begin at the end of each monthly cycle and resolve with the start of menstruation.

Women who eat more sugary foods appear to have an increased risk of PMS. Alcohol can affect hormone metabolism and women who drink heavily are more likely to suffer with symptoms than non-drinking women. In one study of Chinese women, increasing tea consumption was associated with increasing prevalence of PMS and among a group of college students in the United States, consumption of caffeine-containing beverages was associated with increases in both the prevalence and severity of PMS. Moreover, the more caffeine women consumed, the more likely they were to suffer from symptoms. Therefore, nutritional recommendations based on the scientific studies would be to avoid sugar, alcohol and caffeine, especially during the second half of your monthly cycle. Several other studies have shown that diets low in fat or high in fibre may help to reduce symptoms of PMS.

Exercise is helpful and often recommended to reduce PMS symptoms. Women with PMS who jogged an average of about twelve miles a week for six months experienced a reduction in breast tenderness, fluid retention, depression and stress.

Many nutritional supplements help relieve PMS symptoms and the most successful are Vitamin B6 and zinc. It is recommended that a specifically blended supplement containing B6 and zinc is taken for the last two weeks of the cycle.

According to studies, many women with PMS are unable to convert linoleic acid to gamma linolenic acid (GLA). Many things including stress, poor diet, alcohol and a lack of certain nutrients impair conversion. Supplementation of evening primrose oil, which contains significant amounts of GLA, can bypass this conversion by putting GLA directly into the body. Starflower oil also contains GLA in higher quantities, but some research has shown that the GLA from evening primrose oil is better absorbed. Whilst addressing many of the PMS symptoms, evening primrose oil specifically helped women who experience breast tenderness or fibrocystic breast disease.

Other nutrients that are beneficial are calcium, magnesium, and vitamin E. One study on vitamin E showed that whilst many women are not vitamin E-deficient, a small supplement of 300ius daily decreased PMS symptoms.

Herbal remedies that can be helpful are Dong quai, black cohosh and vitex. Dong quai is often referred to as a female ginseng. It is an adaptogenic herb that helps promote normal hormone balance and is particularly useful for women experiencing premenstrual cramping and pain.

Vitex has been shown to help re-establish the normal balance of oestrogen and progesterone during a woman's menstrual cycle. This is important because some women suffer from PMS and other menstrual irregularities due to underproduction of the hormone progesterone during the second half of their cycle. Vitex stimulates the pituitary gland to produce more luteinizing hormone, which leads to greater productivity of progesterone. Studies have shown that using vitex once in the morning over a period of several months helps normalise hormone balance to alleviate the symptoms of PMS. One study showed vitex to be as effective as 200mg of vitamin B6 in a double-blind study.

Recommendations for PMS

Diet:	Low in meat and dairy and high in fruit, vegetables and whole grains
Increase	Water, fruit and vegetables, good quality low-fat protein
Decrease	Red meat, avoid sugar, alcohol and caffeine
Superfoods	Alfalfa, algae, barley grass, medicinal mushrooms and yoghurt
Supplements	A good multivitamin/mineral Calcium, magnesium
Herbals	Dong quai, vitex or black cohosh; or a combination of all three
Lifestyle changes	Regular exercise has been proved to be beneficial for fluid retention, breast tenderness, depression and stress

General recommendations for the reproductive system

Diet	More than any other system of the body, the reproductive system needs fresh, unadulterated foods of the richest and most natural quality. Good sources of folic acid are Brussels sprouts, Marmite, cornflakes, baked beans, lettuce and broccoli.
Foods to avoid	All junk food – that includes all refined foods, anything with additives or pesticides, all ready-made meals, alcohol, saturated fat and sugars of all kinds.
Superfoods	Alfalfa, algae, barley grass, medicinal mushrooms, yoghurt, bee pollen, honey, super sprouts
Supplements	A good multivitamin/mineral would be the base of a supplement programme for the reproductive system as a whole. Additional folic acid for women would be recommended if trying to become pregnant and additional zinc for both males and females also if trying to conceive. Fish oils are highly recommended. Combination supplements of EPA/DHA are available.
Herbal remedies	Dong quai, vitex, black cohosh (or a combination). Valerian and/or ginkgo biloba.
Lifestyle changes	Test for food intolerance/allergy. Taking vitamin C with iron-rich foods increases the absorption of iron (a boiled egg and a glass of orange juice, for example). Regular exercise has been proved to be beneficial in fluid retention, breast tenderness, depression and stress. Learn relaxation techniques. Look into hypnosis. Take up yoga and reduce stress levels.

Knowledge review

The reproductive system

1 What is the main function of the reproductive system?

2 To function optimally, what specific nutrients does the reproductive system need?

3 Define infertility.

4 What supplements would you advise (a) a woman, and (b) a man to take if they were trying to conceive?

5 List four factors that can have an affect on menstruation.

6 List the four hormones involved in the female menstrual cycle.

7 What are the correct medical terms for (a) heavy periods, and (b) lack of periods?

8 In your own words, explain the condition known as endometriosis.

9   What superfoods are recommended for endometriosis?

10   DHEA is recommended for impotence – what is this and where is it produced?

11   What herb is referred to as the 'female ginseng' and how is it helpful with clients with PMS?

12   What is the function of the herb vitex?

13   For general recommendations for the reproductive system, what foods would you suggest to support the system?

14   What superfoods would benefit the reproductive system?

15   Why is folic acid recommended for women trying to conceive?

17

The respiratory system

Learning objectives

This chapter covers the following:

- **dietary influences affecting the respiratory system**

- **common disorders associated with the respiratory system**

- **recommendations of foods to increase/decrease**

- **supplements and herbal remedies**

- **superfoods and lifestyle changes relating to disorders of the respiratory system**

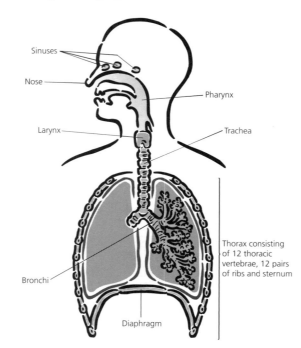

Respiratory system

What is the respiratory system?

The respiratory system is the system in the body responsible for the exchange of gases in the lungs.

Main function

To continuously supply oxygen to every cell in the body for various metabolic reactions and to remove carbon dioxide, a waste product of those cells, that needs to be eliminated quickly from the body.

What does the respiratory system do?

The respiratory system consists of the nose, naso-pharynx, pharynx, larynx, trachea, bronchi and the lungs, which provide the passageway for air in and out of the body.

Oxygen is taken in through the nose and mouth and flows along the trachea and bronchial tubes to the alveoli of the lungs, where it is diffused through the thin film of moisture lining the alveoli. The inspired air, which is now rich with oxygen, comes into contact with the blood in the capillary network surrounding the alveoli. The oxygen then diffuses across a permeable membrane wall surrounding the alveoli to be taken up by red blood cells and carried to the heart. Carbon dioxide, collected by the respiring cells around the body, passes in the opposite direction by diffusing from the capillary walls into the alveoli, to be passed through the bronchi and trachea and exhaled through the nose and mouth.

Dietary influences affecting the respiratory system

Foods that we have used for centuries to fight respiratory diseases are very similar to the drugs we use today. They have a common action in that they thin out and help move the lung's secretions so that they do not clog air passages and can be coughed up or normally expelled. Such foods and drugs are called 'mucokinetic' (mucus moving) agents, and include decongestants and expectorants. Many clients who suffer with respiratory problems also have a diet high in acid-forming foods (meat, cheese, eggs). Excess milk and dairy products are the foods most likely to affect the respiratory system in a negative way.

Chilli peppers and hot pungent foods, are top of the list for assisting respiratory diseases. The mouth-burning ingredient in hot red peppers is capsaicin, which has some chemical resemblance to the drug Guaifenesin. Guaifenesin in an expectorant, found in about 75 per cent of OTC (over the counter) and prescription cough syrups, cold tablets and expectorants such as Vicks Formula 440, Sudafed and Robitussin.

Allicin, which gives garlic its flavour, is converted in the body to a drug similar to S-carboxymethyl-cystein (Mucodyne), a classic European lung medication that regulates mucus flow.

A lot of over the counter drugs for colds, coughs and bronchitis do exactly what peppers do, but I believe more in peppers. Peppers don't cause any side effects. I am convinced that 90% of all people can tolerate hot food and get a benefit.

Dr Irwin Ziment – Lung Specialist at UCLA

Common disorders

Asthma

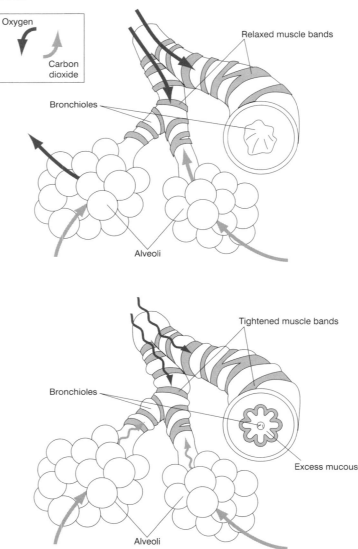

Asthma

Asthma is a lung disorder in which spasms of the bronchial passages restrict the flow in and out of the lungs. It may be described as an allergic reaction that occurs in the airways of the lungs. In asthma white cells in the bronchi secrete histamine, making the smooth muscle cells of the lung airways contract more readily. The number of people with asthma and the death rate from this condition have been increasing since the late 1980s, and some suggest that environmental pollution may be the cause of this growing epidemic.

Some asthmatics react to food additives such as sulfites, tartrazine (yellow dye) and aspirin-like substances found in foods called natural salicylates. Although most people with asthma do not suffer from food allergies, an unrecognised food allergy can be an exacerbating factor.

Vitamin B6 deficiency is common in asthmatics; this may relate to the asthma itself or to certain asthma drugs that deplete vitamin B6. In a double-blind study of asthmatic children, 200mg per day of vitamin B6 for two months reduced the severity of their illness and reduced the amount of asthma medication needed. In another study asthmatic adults experienced a dramatic decrease in the frequency and severity of asthma attacks while taking 50mg of vitamin B6 twice a day.

Studies have shown that magnesium levels are frequently low in asthmatics. Magnesium can prevent spasms of the bronchial passages and intravenous injection of magnesium has been reported to stop acute asthma attacks within minutes in double blind research. Although the effect of oral magnesium has not been appropriately studied, many nutritional therapists recommend magnesium supplementation to clients suffering from asthma. The usual amount would be 200–400mg per day.

Supplementation with 1 gram of vitamin C per day reduces the tendency of the bronchial passages to go into spasm, an action that has been confirmed in double blind research. Some individuals with asthma have shown improvement after taking 1–2 grams of vitamin C per day. A buffered form of vitamin C (such as sodium ascorbate or calcium ascorbate) works better for some asthmatics than regular vitamin C (ascorbic acid).

People with low levels of selenium have a high risk of asthma, according to many studies. Asthma involves free radical damage that selenium might protect against. A double blind trial gave 45mcg of selenium to twelve people with asthma. Half showed clear clinical improvement even though lung function tests did not change. Many nutritional therapists recommend 200mcg per day of selenium for adults with asthma, and a proportionately reduced amount for children.

Double-blind research shows that fish oil partially reduces reactions to allergens that can trigger attacks in some asthmatics, and further research suggests that children who eat oily fish may have a much lower risk of getting asthma. Therefore, even though evidence supporting the use of fish oils remains weak, eating fish may still be worth considering.

Quercetin, a flavonoid found in most plants, has an inhibiting action on lipoxygenase, an enzyme that contributes to problems with asthma, and while no human studies have confirmed whether quercetin decreases asthma symptoms, many nutritional therapists use this supplement with beneficial results.

Traditionally, herbs that have a soothing action on bronchioles are also used for asthma. These would include marshmallow and liquorice. Bromelain reduces the thickness of mucus, which may be beneficial for those with asthma, though clinical actions in asthmatics remain unproved.

Respiratory system rule no. 1

Any food, no matter how healthy, may induce an allergic reaction. Remain aware of what you are eating and when.

Recommendations for asthma

Diet	A low dairy diet recommended
Increase	Fresh green leafy vegetables, and fruit – preferably organic, and always well washed
Decrease	Caffeine, sugar, salt and chlorinated tap water
Superfoods	Algae, alfalfa, cabbage, honey, super sprouts, Manuka honey, liquorice
Supplements	Selenium and vitamin B6
Herbals	Liquorice, ginkgo biloba and marshmallow
Lifestyle changes	Have possible allergens identified. Reduce stress as much as possible and practice yoga techniques.

Bronchitis

Bronchitis is an inflammation of the trachea and bronchial tree and can be either acute or chronic. Acute bronchitis may be caused by viral or bacterial infections and is preceded by an upper respiratory tract infection. In addition, acute bronchitis can result in irritation of the mucous membranes by environmental fumes, acids, solvents, or tobacco smoke. While smoking is a very health-damaging practice and not recommended, studies have now shown that eating fish can decrease some of the damage to the lungs, even in adults who smoke. Comparing smokers who ate fish four times a week with those who ate fish less than once a week, one study showed that the high fish consumers cut their incidence of chronic bronchitis and emphysema by an incredible 45 per cent.

Bronchitis usually begins with a dry, non-productive cough. After a few hours or days, the cough may become more frequent and produce mucus. A secondary bacterial infection may occur, in which the sputum (bronchial secretions) may contain pus. If symptoms persist then a visit to the GP will be necessary.

Dietary factors may influence both inflammatory activity and antioxidant status in the body. Increased inflammation and decreased antioxidant activity may both lead to an increased incidence of chronic diseases, such as chronic bronchitis. People suffering from chronic bronchitis may experience an improvement in symptoms when consuming a diet high in anti-inflammatory fatty acids, such as those found in fish.

A diet high in antioxidants may protect against the free radical damaging effect of the toxins. Studies comparing different populations have shown that increasing fruit and vegetable consumption may reduce the risk of developing chronic bronchitis.

Food and environmental allergies may be triggering factors in some cases of chronic bronchitis. Many nutritional therapists believe that dairy products can increase mucus production, and that people suffering from either acute or chronic bronchitis should therefore limit their intake of dairy products. Ingestion of simple sugars such as sucrose and fructose can lead to suppression of immune function, therefore sugars should be avoided.

In a study of elderly patients hospitalised with acute bronchitis, those who were given 200mg per day of vitamin C improved to a significantly greater extent compared with those who were given a placebo.

Vitamin A status is low in children with measles, an infection that can result in pneumonia or other respiratory complications. Supplementation with vitamin A has been found to decrease morbidity and mortality from measles. In another study supplementation with vitamin A reduced the number of respiratory tract infections in children.

In a double-blind study, individuals with chronic bronchitis who received N-acetyl cycsteine (NAC; 600mg a day, three days a week by mouth) had a significant reduction in the number of exacerbations of their illness. Smokers have also been found to benefit from taking NAC. In addition to helping break up mucus, NAC may reduce the elevated bacterial counts that are often seen in the lungs of smokers with chronic bronchitis.

The thymus gland plays a number of important roles in the functioning of the immune system. An extract from calf thymus gland, known as thymomudulin, has been found in double-blind study to decrease the frequency of respiratory infections in children who are prone to such infections.

The herbs that are beneficial for the respiratory system and for bronchitis in particular are liquorice, thyme, echinacea and garlic. Liquorice acts as an anti-inflammatory and antitussive agent. Thyme contains an essential oil (thymol) and some flavonoids, has anti-spasmodic and expectorant properties and antibacterial actions, and is considered in cases of bronchitis.

Echinacea is widely used by herbalists for individuals with acute respiratory infection. It stimulates the immune system in different ways such as enhancing macrophage function and increasing T-cell response. Echinacea also contains an antibiotic compound known as echinacoside. This herb may therefore be useful for preventing a cold, flu or viral bronchitis from progressing to a secondary bacterial infection. Garlic has been shown to have mild antimicrobial activity and may therefore be of value with people with bronchitis.

Recommendations for bronchitis

Diet	An alkaline diet is recommended for as long as symptoms persist. Citrus juice and fruit, green vegetable juice plus raw salads, and onions – cooked and raw.
Increase	Hot water, lemon and Manuka honey, herbal teas, garlic
Decrease	Everything refined – especially white bread and flour, confectionery, and alcohol
Superfoods	Liquorice, alfalfa, chlorella, barley grass, bee pollen, cabbage, Manuka honey (in hot drinks). Medicinal mushrooms, super sprouts.
Supplements	N-acetyl cysteine (NAC), thymus glandular. Vitamins C, and E. Vitamin A is every effective with lung complaints – take the SONA listed in part I of this book.
Herbals	Thyme, echinacea, garlic.
Lifestyle changes	If you suffer frequently from respiratory problems take up swimming, especially breaststroke. This is an excellent exercise for those with lung disorders.

Remember

Respiratory system rule no. 2

Ginger destroys inflenza viruses. Prevention is better than cure, so experiment – make ginger tea and use ginger liberally in home-made dishes.

Common cold

The common cold is an acute, short-term viral infection of the upper respiratory tract which often causes a runny nose, sore throat, and malaise. A sore throat is sometimes a symptom of a more serious condition distinct from the common cold that may require medical diagnosis and treatment with appropriate antibiotics. If antibiotics are required the treatment should be followed up by a course of probiotics to replace the good gut flora.

Sugar, dietary fat and alcohol have been reported to affect the immune system negatively, though no specific information is yet available as to how much these foods may actually affect the course of the common cold.

Vitamin C and zinc have been tested rigorously over the past years in common cold trials and have both been rated as primary supplements for the common cold and immune system generally. A review of twenty-one placebo-controlled studies using 1–8mg of vitamin C found that 'in each of the twenty-one studies, vitamin C reduced the duration of episodes and the severity of the symptoms of the common cold by an average of 23 per cent'. The optimum amount of vitamin C to take for cold treatment remains in debate, but 1–3 grams per day is commonly used and is generally supported by much of the scientific literature.

Zinc has many functions in connection with the common cold; it interferes with viral replication in test tubes, may interfere with the ability of the virus to enter the cells of the body, may help immune cells to fight a cold and may relieve cold symptoms by affecting prostaglandin metabolism. Certain zinc lozenges have been helpful to adult cold sufferers, though this effect has not been reported in children. Most successful studies have used zinc gluconate or zinc gluconate-glycine lozenges containing 15–25mg of zinc per lozenge.

An analysis of the major zinc trials has claimed that evidence for efficacy is 'still lacking'. However, despite a lack of statistical significance, this compilation of data from six double-blind trials found that people assigned to zinc had a 50 per cent decreased risk of still having symptoms after one week compared with those given placebo. Zinc lozenges should not be taken long term but rather on the onset of a cold and stopped when symptoms have disappeared. The best effect is obtained when lozenges are used at the first sign of a cold; up to ten lozenges can be taken per day for the first few days.

In traditional herbal medicine, goldenseal root is often taken with echinacea. Two alkaloids in the root (berberine and canadine) have an anti-microbial and mild immune-stimulating effect. Goldenseal soothes irritated mucous membranes in the throat, making it useful to those experiencing a sore throat with their cold.

Herbal supplements can play a role in long-term attempts to strengthen the immune and fight infections. Adaptogens, which include Siberian ginseng, Asian ginseng, astragalus and schisandra, are thought to help keep various body systems including the immune system functioning optimally. Another immune stimulant, boneset, helps fight minor viral infections, such as the common cold.

Herbs high in mucilage such as slippery elm and marshmallow are often helpful for symptomatic relief of coughs and irritated throats. Mullein has expectorant properties, which accounts for this herb's historical use as a remedy for the respiratory system, particularly in cases of irritating coughs with bronchial congestion.

Eucalyptus oil is often used in a steam inhalation to help clear nasal and sinus congestion and is said to function in a fashion similar to that of menthol by acting on receptors in the mucosa, leading to a reduction in the symptoms of, for example, nasal stuffiness.

Treatment of colds is to encourage elimination through all channels so that eliminations through only one channel do not become excessive.

Recommendations for common cold

Diet	A light diet is recommended – high in liquids
Increase	Hot water with lemon and Manuka honey Hot water with apple cider vinegar, and Manuka honey Herbal teas Fruit and homemade thin vegetable soups Ginger tea
Decrease	Dairy foods, meat, all 'heavy' foods, alcohol, everything refined
Superfoods	Manuka honey, chlorophyll, bee pollen, liquorice
Supplements	Vitamin C taken throughout the day – every two hours for the first few days of a cold Zinc, garlic capsules
Herbals	Echinacea, Siberian ginseng, Asian ginseng, goldenseal root
Lifestyle changes	Treat yourself to a sauna and treat your cold at the same time. Take eucalyptus oil to add to the sauna water and also use as a steam inhalation.

Sinus

Sinusitis is an upper respiratory tract condition that involves the inflammation of the accessory nasal sinuses. There are four pairs of sinuses in the human skull that help circulate moist air through the nasal passages. The common cold is the most prevalent predisposing factor to sinusitis. Acute sinusitis typically causes symptoms of nasal congestion and a thick yellow or green discharge. Other symptoms include tenderness and pain over the sinuses, frontal headaches, and sometimes chills, fever and pressure in the area of the sinuses. Chronic sinusitis differs slightly in that symptoms can be milder and may only include postnasal drip, bad breath and an irritating dry cough. Hay fever, environmental triggers, unrelated hay fever, food allergens and dental infections can also lead to sinusitis.

The typical patient with chronic sinusitis characteristically follows an acid-forming diet, having an excess of starches and dairy products and lacking in sufficient raw green vegetables. This type of diet causes an increase in the amount of mucus produced by the body and favours tissue congestion. According to some studies, 25 per cent of people with sinusitis have environmental allergies. Although food allergies may contribute to the problem, many researchers believe food allergies only rarely *cause* sinusitis. If other treatment approaches are unsuccessful people with sinusitis may choose to work with a nutrition and allergy therapist to evaluate what, if any, effect elimination of certain foods and other allergens might have on reducing their symptoms.

Histamine is associated with increased nasal and sinus congestion. In one study vitamin C supplementation of 1g three times a day reduced histamine levels in people with either high histamine levels or low blood levels of vitamin C. Another study found that 2g of vitamin C helped protect individuals exposed to a histamine challenge.

Bromelain, an enzyme derived from pineapple, has been reported to relieve symptoms of acute sinusitis. In a double-blind study comparing the use of bromelain with placebo, those patients who took bromelain reported good to excellent results compared with the placebo group. Other double blind research has shown that bromelain reduces symptoms of sinusitis.

In a preliminary trial supplementation of 250mg of pantothenic acid twice a day was demonstrated to help most clients suffering from allergic rhinitis, a significant predisposing factor for sinusitis. However, research has yet to investigate the effects of pantothenic acid supplementation with people who have sinusitis.

Herbs that have proved useful are stinging nettles and eucalyptus. An isolated double-blind study compared the use of free dried stinging nettles with placebo. In that one week trial, 300mg of stinging nettles taken twice per day led to moderate effectiveness among 58 per cent of those in the treatment group compared with only 37 per cent in the placebo group.

Eucalyptus oil is often used in a steam inhalation to help clear nasal and sinus congestion. It is said to function in a fashion similar to that of menthol by acting on receptors in the nasal mucosa, leading to a reduction in the symptoms of, for example, nasal stuffiness.

A mucus-cleansing diet is recommended for clients suffering with sinusitis. This includes a high quantity liquid diet for up to three days if that can be tolerated. A mucus-cleansing diet would comprise of lemon or grapefruit juice every morning either alone or with warm water and a mid-morning snack of juiced vegetables such as carrot or carrot and celery. Lunch would comprise as many boiled or steamed onions as you could comfortably eat with a citrus fruit for dessert. More vegetable juice in the afternoon. More onions for an evening meal and garlic capsules. This is very effective but difficult to follow, however most clients suffering chronic sinusitis are willing to try anything for relief. A nutritional therapist will give you a more complete mucus cleansing diet if you want to follow this course of action. Most diets of this type start with two or three days of cleansing followed by additional foods being introduced in a particular sequence.

Recommendations for sinus

Diet	Mucus cleaning diet. Mostly liquids for two days followed by a raw fruit and vegetables for a further two days then a light, low protein diet, avoiding dairy products.
Increase	Citrus fruits, vegetable juices, boiled and steamed onions, water
Decrease	Red meat, all dairy products
Superfoods	Alfalfa, algae, barley grass, bee pollen, liquorice and medicinal mushrooms
Supplements	SONA of Vitamin A Vitamin B complex with no less than 25mg of the B vitamins Vitamin C minimum 1 g daily
Herbals	Garlic, fenugreek and black cohosh
Lifestyle changes	Daily exercise, walking especially – don't make it too easy Inhalations using eucalyptus or oil of pine

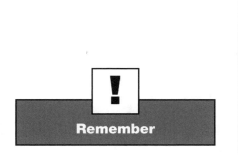

Remember

Respiratory system rule no. 3

Japanese tests have found that a substance called lentinan in shiitake mushrooms fights influenza viruses better than a prescription antiviral drug.

General recommendations for the respiratory system

Diet	Hot water with lemon and Manuka honey Hot water with apple cider vinegar, and Manuka honey Herbal teas. Fruit and homemade thin vegetable soups Ginger tea. Oily fish, hot chilli peppers, horseradish Always a light diet – as fluid as possible.
Foods to avoid	Milk and dairy products
Superfoods	Manuka honey Liquorice Chlorophyll Bee pollen
Supplements	Vitamin C Zinc N-acetyl cysteine (NAC) Thymus glandular Co-Q-10, fish oils Vitamin A
Herbal remedies	Marshmallow, garlic capsules
Lifestyle changes	Regular swimming – especially breaststroke Saunas – using eucalyptus or pine oil in the sauna water or use these oils as steam inhalations. If you are feeling really brave, try hydrotherapy by alternating hot and cold showers to stimulate respiration and circulation. Treat yourself to a visit to a health spa where they will have a wide range of therapeutic hydrotherapy treatments to stimulate the respiratory and circulatory systems

Knowledge review

The respiratory system

1   What is the main function of the respiratory system?

2   Many clients who suffer with respiratory problems also have a diet high in acid-forming foods. Give examples of acid forming foods.

3   What does the word 'mucokinetic' mean?

4   Give three examples of food additives that asthmatics may react to.

5   What B vitamin is frequently deficient in asthmatic clients?

6   What general dietary advice would you give asthmatics?

7   How does the herb echinacea work?

8   List four herbs that are beneficial for the respiratory system and for bronchitis in particular.

9   What lifestyle change in particular would you recommend for a client with bronchitis?

10   What is the definition of the common cold?

11   What superfoods are recommended for the common cold?

12   What is the function of probiotics?

13   Zinc has many functions in connection with the common cold – list two.

14   What dietary regime would you recommend for someone with sinus problems?

15   What supplement recommendations would you advise for supporting the respiratory system in general?

The skeletal system

What is the skeletal system?

The skeletal system is the system of the body offering support and protection by several types of connective tissue – cartilage, bone and dense connective tissue.

Main functions

The skeletal system performs several basic functions.

- Support – the skeleton provides a framework for the body and as such, it supports soft tissues and provides a point of attachment for many muscles.

- Protection – many internal organs are protected from injury by the skeleton. For example, the brain is protected by the cranial bones, the spinal cord by the vertebrae, the heart and lungs by the rib cage and internal reproductive organs by the pelvic bones.

- Movement facilitation – bones serve as levers to which muscles are attached. When the muscles contract, bones acting as levers and movable joints acting as fulcrums produce movement.

- Mineral storage – bones store several minerals that can be distributed to other parts of the body upon demand. The principal stored minerals are calcium and phosphorus.

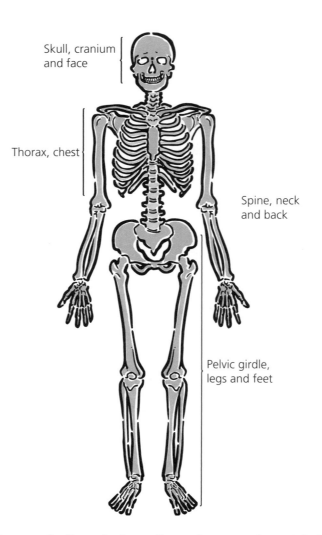

Skull, cranium
and face

Thorax, chest

Spine, neck
and back

Pelvic girdle,
legs and feet

Skeletal system

● Storage of cell-producing cells – red marrow in certain bones
is capable of producing blood cells. Red marrow produces red
blood cells, some white blood cells, and platelets.

What does the skeletal system do?

As the framework for the whole body, the skeletal system provides
attachments for muscles and an important store for vital minerals. It
is a system that is usually forgotten about within nutritional therapy,
but a very important one to bear in mind.

Dietary influences affecting the skeletal system

Physical fitness is the major determinant of the fitness of the skeletal
system. Calcium, magnesium, boron, and vitamin K all have
important roles to play in the health of the bones. The aches and
pains, stooped posture, loss of teeth and bone fractures of osteoporosis
and an elevation in blood pressure were once called the inevitable
result of old age. It is now recognised that these diseases are
influenced by a lifetime of habits. The choices a person makes about

diet, exercise and other health habits will have an effect on whether the bones remain strong and upright or become porous and hunched, and whether the blood pressure and heart will remain healthy

Common disorders

Gout

Gout is a common arthritic condition usually associated with a high acidic diet due to an excess of meat, dairy products and alcohol. The small joints of the fingers and the toes especially are usually affected. Gout is ten times more common in men than women, who tend to have the disease after the menopause. The most characteristic feature of gout is that it is usually accompanied by an increase in the amount of uric acid in the blood. Uric acid is the end product of the body's metabolism of substances, called purines. These are compounds that form part of the RNA and DNA of the nuclei of the body's cells. Not all purines are converted into uric acid in the body; the caffeine in tea and coffee and theobromine in cocoa and chocolate, are purines that do not have this effect. The purines that do produce uric acid are found chiefly in cells, especially animal cells. Purine-rich foods include liver, kidney, shellfish and fish roes.

Recommendations are to reduce alcohol, avoid all purine-rich foods, drink plenty of water to flush out and promote excretion of the uric acid and significantly reduce refined foods. Good supplements are celery seed, which is thought to help eliminate uric acid through the kidneys, and cherries or other sources of anthocyanidians which are thought to help decrease inflammation and uric acid levels. Oxalic acid, found in rhubarb, sorrel and spinach, is another food residue that can often exacerbate the problem so these foods should also be avoided.

Recommendations for gout

Diet	A general well balanced diet taking foods from all the main food groups, carbohydrates, low fat proteins, and essential fatty acids. Do not over eat.
Increase	Green leafy vegetables and drink at least 1 pint of water every day – up to 1 litre would be better.
Decrease	Avoid rich foods including liver, kidney, red meat, game and fish roes. Too much fruit consumption or the use of fruit sugar (fructose) might also aggravate gout.
Superfoods	Alfalfa, spirulina, chorella and blue-green algae – rotate each month – bee pollen
Supplements	Vitamin C – up to 3g daily – to increase loss of uric acid via the kidneys Zinc up to 15mg daily Calcium and magnesium
Herbals	None specifically
Lifestyle changes	Lose weight if you are overweight. Avoid alcohol completely Avoid lead, cadmium, mercury and aluminium.

Remember

Skeletal system rule no. 1

Daily weight-bearing exercise throughout your life will strengthen bones.

Osteoporosis – brittle bone disease

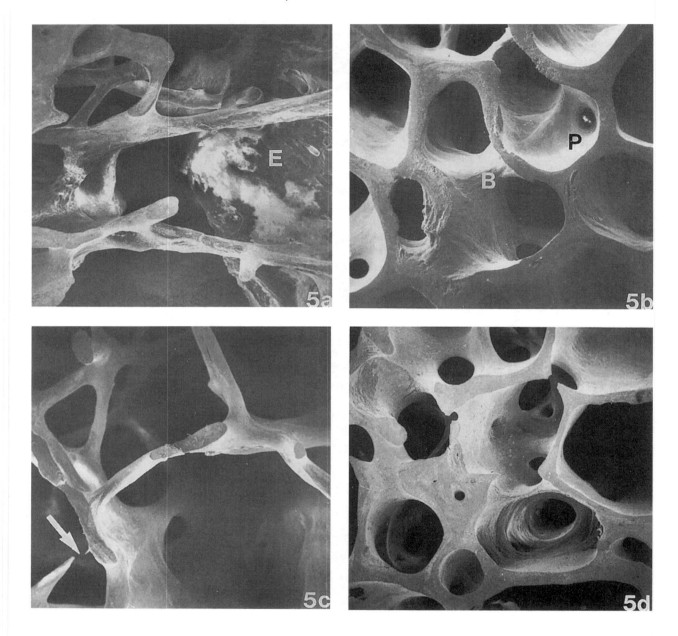

Low power scanning electron micrographs of iliac crest biopsies from two osteoporotic females, aged 61 and 47 years, respectively, with multiple vertebral compression fractures (a and c), and autopsy samples from a 44-year-old normal male (b) and a 75-year-old normal female (d) who had suffered sudden death. Note that the lack of trabecular bone in the biopsy shown in (a) allows a clear view of the endosteal surface (E) of one of the cortices. P, trabecular plate; B, trabecular bar. Field width = 2.6 mm in each case.

Osteoporosis

Acknowledgement: Reproduced from J Bone Miner Res 1986; 1:15–21 with permission of the American Society for Bone and Mineral Research

This condition is often referred to as the 'silent epidemic' because until you actually fracture a bone, you don't know that you have it. The literal meaning of osteoporosis is 'porous bone', it is a condition in which the bones may become brittle and liable to fracture. The bone tissue of an adult is usually at its most dense between the ages of 30 and 35 years; after this age bone density will decline naturally. Bone loss tends to be greater in women than in men, primarily due to hormonal changes, especially the loss of the protective effects of oestrogen, as levels decline during the menopausal and post-menopausal years. The whole skeleton may be affected by osteoporosis, but bone loss is usually greatest in the spine, hips and ribs.

Increasing bone mass during adolescence through sufficient calcium intake could decrease the risk of osteoporosis in later life. It may also be beneficial to take magnesium and vitamin D supplements because these two nutrients are involved in the uptake and utilisation of calcium. Studies have examined vitamin D and calcium supplementation and found that it may moderately reduce bone loss.

Recommendations for osteoporosis

Diet	Natural diet, low in saturated fats and refined foods
Increase:	Magnesium rich foods, such as green leafy vegetables, plenty of fruit. Protein choices should be of the low saturated fat variety, chicken, turkey, fish, tofu
Decrease	A protein rich diet may be an underlying cause of osteoporosis, as excess may leach calcium from bones
Superfoods	Yoghurt, probiotics and prebiotics
Supplements	Lysine – thought to enhance intestinal calcium absorption Vitamin C – associated with higher bone mineral density in early post-menopausal women Boron – which has been shown to reduce losses of dietary calcium
Herbals	Black cohosh
Lifestyle changes	Weight-bearing exercise – no matter what age you are

Remember

Skeletal system rule no. 2

An alkaline-forming diet rich in magnesium will keep calcium in the bones, where we want it. An acidic diet will encourage calcium to leave the bones.

Osteoarthritis

Osteoarthritis is a common disease that develops when linings of joints fail to maintain normal structure, leading to pain and decreased mobility. It is associated with ageing and injury – it used to be called 'wear and tear' arthritis.

Solanine is a substance found in nightshade plants, including tomatoes, white potato, peppers (except black pepper) and eggplant. In theory, if not destroyed in the intestines solanine could be toxic. A horticulturist, Dr Normal Childers, hypothesised that some people with osteoarthritis may not be able to destroy solanine in the gut, leading to some absorption resulting in osteoarthritis. Eliminating solanine from the diet has been reported to bring relief to some arthritis sufferers in preliminary research. An uncontrolled survey of people avoiding nightshade plants revealed that 28 per cent claimed to have a 'marked positive response' and another 44 per cent a 'positive response' Researchers have never put this to a strict clinical test. However, the treatment continues to be used by many nutritional therapists with people who have osteoarthritis.

Glucosamine sulphate (GS) a nutrient derived from seashells, contains a building block needed for the repair of joint cartilage and has significantly reduced symptoms of osteoarthritis in uncontrolled and single-blind trials. Many double blind studies have also reported efficacy. All published clinical investigations on the effects of glucosamine sulfate in people with osteoarthritis report statistically significant improvement. Most research trials use 500mg GS taken three times per day. Benefits from glucosamine sulphate generally become evident after three to eight weeks of treatment. Continued supplementation is needed in order to maintain benefits.

Chondroitin sulphate (CS) is a major component of the lining of joints. In structure, chrondroitin sulphate is related to several molecules of glucosamine sulphate attached to each other. Levels of chondroitin sulphate have been reported to be reduced in joint cartilage affected by osteoarthritis. It has been found that both substances are required to ease the symptoms of osteoarthritis and supplements that contain both are now available and have proved beneficial.

S-adenosyl methionine (SAMe) possesses anti-inflammatory pain relieving and tissue-healing properties that may help protect the health of the joints. Double-blind reports studying effects in people with osteoarthritis have consistently shown that SAMe increases the formation of healthy tissue and reduces pain, stiffness, and swelling better than a placebo and equal to drugs such as ibuprofen. On the basis of outcomes reported in published research, 400mg taken three times per day appears to be the optimal intake of SAMe.

People who have osteoarthritis and eat high levels of antioxidants from food have been reported to exhibit a much slower rate of joint deterioration, particularly in the knees, compared with those eating foods containing lower levels of antioxidants. Of the individual antioxidants, only vitamin E has been studied in controlled trials. Vitamin E has reduced symptoms of osteoarthritis in both single and double blind research. In several trials, 400–600ius of vitamin E per day has been used.

Herbs that may be useful are boswellia, which has a unique anti-inflammatory action much like the conventional non-steroidal anti-inflammatory drugs (NSAIDs) used by many for inflammatory conditions. Clinical studies in humans are lacking but is used by many nutritional therapists. Unlike NSAIDs, however, long-term use of boswellia does not lead to irritation or ulceration of the stomach.

Recommendations for osteoarthritis

Diet	A whole food approach to food where quality is more important than quantity. Plenty of fruits, vegetables, nuts and seeds with adequate essential fatty acids, low-fat protein, and plenty of water.
Increase	Green leafy vegetables and oily fish
Decrease	Members of the nightshade family – tomatoes, white potato, peppers (except black pepper) and eggplant. Everything refined – especially white bread and flour, confectionery, and alcohol. Also red meat, eggs if you are eating in excess of 6 a week and all chemicals.
Superfoods	Super sprouts, medicinal mushrooms, bee pollen and barley grass.

Supplements	MSM – a naturally occurring source of sulphur Chondroitin sulphate and glucosamine sulphate in one supplements. SAMe, Vitamin E
Herbals	Boswellia and black cohosh
Lifestyle changes	Check you do not have any food or chemical allergies as these are sometimes connected to all types of arthritis. Obesity is a risk factor for osteoarthritis of weight-bearing joints. Weight loss is thought by arthritis experts to be of potential benefit, especially at reducing pain levels.

Osteomalacia

Osteomalacia is a deficiency of Vitamin D, combined with a deficiency of calcium. It is the adult form of rickets. Women who have had repeated pregnancies and breast-fed their babies are especially prone to the disease. Their own bones become depleted of calcium, causing weakness. Lack of exposure to sunlight is a contributory factor.

The few foods that contain vitamin D include egg yolks, butter, vitamin D-fortified milk and fish liver oils. Calcium is found in dairy products, sardines, salmon (canned with edible bones) leafy vegetables and tofu. Pure vegetarians may use supplements instead of eggs and dairy produce as sources for both calcium and vitamin D.

Direct exposure of the skin to sunlight stimulates the body to manufacture vitamin D – both clothes and the use of sunscreen will prevent the ultraviolet light that triggers the formation of vitamin D from reaching the skin. Depending upon the latitude, sunlight during the winter may not produce enough ultraviolet light to promote adequate vitamin D production. At other times during the year even thirty minutes of exposure per day will usually lead to large increases in the amount of vitamin D manufactured.

Recommendations for osteomalacia

Diet	A general diet covering all the main food groups, carbohydrates, low fat proteins and essential fatty acids. This would include nuts and seeds.
Increase	Oily fish – sardines salmon, herring, tuna and mackerel at least three times each week. The bones of the sardines and salmon (if tinned) should also be eaten. Vitamin D by increasing green leafy vegetables, tofu and small amounts of eggs, butter.
Decrease	All refined, denatured foods, all chemicals, alcohol, white bread, flour and additives
Superfoods	Spirulina, medicinal mushrooms, barley grass
Supplements	Multivitamin and mineral Vitamin D
Herbals	None specifically
Lifestyle changes	Expose arms, face and legs to sunshine for at least 30 minutes every day in summer and take a supplement in the winter

Remember

Skeletal system rule no. 3

Is your calcium being absorbed? Alcohol, caffeine, some medications, high dietary protein and inactivity all decrease calcium absorption – so take care yours is getting through.

General recommendations for the skeletal system

Diet	Green leafy vegetables, all alkaline-forming foods Low fat dairy foods
Foods to avoid	Purine rich foods, seafood, liver, fish roe, alcohol, all refined foods. Avoid alcohol, caffeine, a high protein diet, as all these can disrupt calcium absorption.
Superfoods	Spirulina, chlorella, blue-green algae, watercress, bee pollen and barley grass
Supplements	MSM – a naturally occurring source of organic sulphur Chondroitin sulphate and glucosamine sulphate in one supplements SAMe, vitamin E, magnesium and calcium in a good ratio Glucosamine sulfate with chondroitin, lysine; vitamin C; boron
Herbal remedies	Herbal formula for the skeletal system: this formula is designed to provide nutrition for the bones, muscles and cartilage. Papaya, parsley, pineapple, valerian, liquorice and ma huang
Lifestyle changes	Weight-bearing exercises every day – these include walking, jogging and running

Knowledge review

The skeletal system

1 Name the different types of connective tissue that make up the skeletal system.

2 What are the main dietary influences affecting the skeletal system?

3 Define gout.

4 In which foods would you find oxalic acid?

5 What function does vitamin C have for the condition of gout?

6 What condition is often referred to as the 'silent epidemic'?

7 Why should a protein-rich diet be an underlying cause of osteoporosis?

8 What lifestyle change would you recommend to a client with osteoporosis?

9 What supplement is derived from seashells and what does it do?

10 What foods are recommended for clients with osteoarthritis?

11 What is SAMe – and what is its function?

12 What is the adult form of rickets called?

13 Why should lack of exposure to sunlight be a contributory factor in osteomalacia?

14 What general foods would support the skeletal system?

15 What lifestyle change would be of benefit to everyone in supporting the skeletal system?

Urinary and detoxification systems

This chapter covers the following:

- **dietary influences affecting the urinary and detoxification systems**
- **common disorders associated with the urinary and detoxification systems**
- **recommendations of foods to increase/decrease**
- **supplements and herbal remedies**
- **superfoods and lifestyle changes relating to disorders of the urinary and detoxification systems**

What are the urinary and detoxification systems?

Two kidneys, two ureters, one urinary bladder and a single urethra make up the urinary system. Other organs of detoxification are the liver, lungs and skin, which also play an important part in removing toxins from our bodies.

Main function

The primary function of the urinary system is to help keep the body in homeostasis by controlling the composition and volume of blood. The functions of the liver, lungs and skin are to eliminate unwanted toxins from the body.

What do the urinary and detoxification systems do?

The kidneys remove and restore selected amounts of water and solutes. They regulate the composition and volume of the blood and remove wastes from the blood

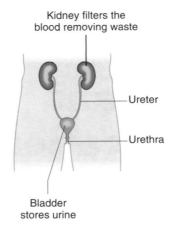

Kidney filters the blood removing waste

Ureter

Urethra

Bladder stores urine

Urinary system

in the form of urine. The general functions of the kidneys are the removal of urea from the bloodstream and the regulation of the body's fluids by controlling the water and mineral ion concentration of the blood.

The liver is the largest gland in the body and has many important functions in the metabolism of proteins, fats and carbohydrates. In its capacity as an organ of detoxification, it is responsible for detoxifying harmful toxic waste, synthetic hormones and drugs and excreting them in bile or through the kidneys.

Dietary influences affecting the urinary and detoxification systems

As you would expect, water is the key factor in this system. Water is needed on a regular basis to keep the kidneys in good working order but other fluids can cause problems. Fizzy drinks, coffee and tea all have a detrimental effect on the system. Excessive use of alcohol, however, has the strongest influence over the urinary and detoxification systems. Alcohol is a serious health threat that only provides intoxication and dehydration and may upset blood sugar levels, as it is a chemical cousin of sugar. It can be classed as an anti-nutrient, which means that it uses up more nutrients than it provides. It can severely damage the liver and puts excess toxic load on the body, giving the kidneys extra work to do along the way.

Remember

Detox/urinary system rule no. 1

Drink at least 1 litre of water every day.

Common disorders

Psoriasis

Psoriasis is a common skin disorder that affects 2–4 per cent of the UK population, both men and women equally. It produces silvery, scaly plaques usually on the knees and elbows, but can be anywhere on the body including the scalp and nails. Stress is one of the major causes, but hormonal change, especially in women, is also an indicator, as many women experience psoriasis for the first time when they become pregnant, during puberty or during the menopause.

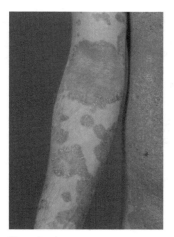

Psoriasis

Acknowledgement: Photograph provided by the National Psoriasis Foundation/USA

The relationship of exclusion diets in bringing relief to many chronic diseases has long been of interest to nutritional therapists. With still no lasting cure from orthodox means, many psoriatics are seeking help and advice from nutritional therapists to see if their condition can be helped from the inside out.

In my own research project, *Nutritional Treatment of Psoriasis – 1993,* my colleagues and I set out to establish a creditable link between the ingestion of certain foods, their effect on the liver, and subsequent improvement, or otherwise, of psoriasis. There have been numerous dietary approaches for psoriasis but none have gained general acceptance in the management of this disease. The majority of these dietary approaches include supplementation with dietary fish oil, whilst others have concentrated on the content of saturated fats and/or protein consumed by the patients.

The results of the research papers have not provided clear and consistent answers. In part, this may reflect the complexity and the number of variables in such experiments, as not all can be controlled to the same degree. To achieve the aim of my own study changes had to be monitored in skin condition and general health using a nutritional approach only. We took a specific interest in cleansing and detoxifying the liver, with a view to lightening the burden of this vital organ – it is the function of the liver to remove aberrant chemicals and pathogens from the body.

Naturopathically it is believed that if an individual is given the opportunity to detoxify their body and their liver is allowed to function as it should, then they will have every opportunity of enjoying full health and an absence of skin complaints.

A diet was formulated for this study which had to be flexible, so as not to make it too difficult for the participants, yet it had to lighten the liver burden. This was the reason that alcohol and pork were the only two items strictly prohibited. However, simple sugars and certain other foods were also initially to be avoided.

Alcohol was to be avoided because it is one of the worst liver poisons, causing the degenerative condition called cirrhosis, fatal to so many heavy drinkers. It also inhibits the absorption of zinc, which is an essential nutrient for a healthy skin. Pork was to be avoided because, out of all the meats eaten in the UK today, pigs have the highest saturated fat levels. Saturated fat is a good storage medium for chemicals such as antibiotics and growth enhancing drugs used during intensive farming. Humans therefore ingest such drugs when eating pork or its derivative products, putting the liver under greater stress. The results of my own study three-month study showed an 84 per cent improvement of skin condition; 9.1 per cent had no change and 6.1 per cent became worse.

In larger studies, ingestion of alcohol appears to be a risk factor in psoriasis in men, but not women. However, it should be strongly recommended that women as well as men avoid alcohol.

Cayenne contains a resinous and pungent substance known as capsaicin. This chemical relieves pain and itching by depleting certain neurotransmitters from sensory nerves. In a double-blind study, application of a capsaicin cream to the skin relieved both the itching and the skin lesions for psoriasis sufferers.

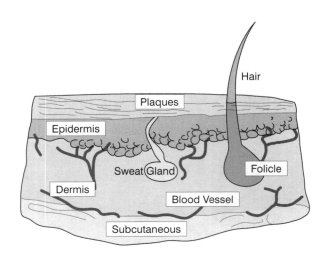

Cross section of psoriatic skin

Many nutritional therapists believe that sluggish liver function is a contributing factor in psoriasis, possibly explaining why milk thistle seeds, which promote normal liver function, can be beneficial to psoriasis sufferers. To understand how milk thistle helps the liver, we need to take a look at this essential organ and what it does.

The liver is the largest internal organ in the body, weighing between 2½ and 3½ lb. It must constantly renew itself by producing new cells. This extraordinary organ replaces its approximately 300 billion cells every six months. To perform its essential activity, the liver is comprised of about 100,000 individual lobules or wheel-shaped structures. One of the many main functions of the liver is detoxification by converting or removing harmful substances that we introduce into the body – including drugs, alcohol, medicines, poisons, and synthetic hormones like HRT, the Pill and growth hormones found in meat and poultry.

There have been many clinical studies using milk thistle in the treatment of psoriasis, with excellent results. The skin is also an organ of detoxification, and if the liver is working under par, then it shows in the skin, in all sorts of forms, including psoriasis. The more efficient the liver is at detoxifying, the healthier a person will be. Milk thistle helps the liver protect itself from harmful substances by altering the cell walls. It also accelerates the rate of protein synthesis, which helps the liver renew itself by stimulating the growth of new cells to replace those that have been damaged or destroyed by disease. As a dietary supplement milk thistle is one of the most effective liver strengthening products available. It is a remarkable age-old remedy that has been proved by modern science.

Psoriasis sufferers sometimes use psyllium husk powder since maintaining normal bowel health is believed to be important for managing psoriasis. Psyllium acts as a bulk-forming laxative to cleanse the bowel and encourage normal elimination. It is important to maintain adequate water intake when using psyllium.

Burdock root is described as a blood purifier or alterative and is believed to clear the bloodstream of toxins. It has been used both internally and externally for psoriasis. Traditional herbalists recommend 2–4ml of burdock root tincture per day. For the dried root preparation, in tablet or capsule form, the common amount to take is 1–2g three times per day. Many herbal preparations will combine burdock root with other alternative herbs such as yellow dock, red clover or cleavers.

Recommendations for psoriasis

Diet	A natural diet of wholefoods – choose organic whenever possible – where quality is more important than quantity.
Increase	Fruits, vegetables, and plenty of bottled water
Decrease	Alcohol, pork, hard boiled eggs, refined foods of all kinds
Superfoods	Alfalfa, algae, barley grass, super sprouts and yoghurt
Supplements	Flax seed Fish oils (EPA/DHA)
Herbals	Milk thistle, St John's wort, rhodiola and cayenne
Lifestyle changes	Plenty of sunshine. Relaxing activities such as yoga, visualisation and meditation. Never eat under stressful conditions.

Incontinence

Incontinence is the lack of voluntary control over micturition – passing urine. This is usually in very small amounts accompanying coughing, sneezing, laughing, walking, running, lifting or any sudden shock or strain. In infants about two years old and under, incontinence is normal because neurons to the external sphincter muscle are not completely developed. Infants' void whenever the urinary bladder is sufficiently distended to arouse a reflex stimulus. Proper training overcomes incontinence if the latter is not cause by emotional stress or irritation of the urinary bladder.

Involuntary micturition in the adult may occur as a result of repeated births, failure to do prenatal and postnatal exercises, poor pelvic floor tone, injury to the spinal nerves controlling the urinary bladder, irritation due to abnormal constituents in urine, or disease of the urinary bladder. It is a condition that can be very stressful and embarrassing.

It is most common in women that have had children, but in women who have never had a child, it is much less common. Weak abdominal tone, obesity, and lack of pelvic muscle tone are the major causative factors involved in these cases.

Surgery is sometimes undertaken to correct incontinence. However, surgery can be avoided if proper exercises are regularly taken, especially before pregnancy. Pelvic exercises must begin during early pregnancy or before, and be continued just after the birth for at least three months or longer. Dr Arnold Kegal, a professor of obstetrics and gynecology at the University of California in Los Angeles, developed a series of pelvic floor exercises that are still used very much today.

They are commonly known as the Kegal Exercises. Here are two for you to try.

1. Practise slowing urine flow and eventually stopping it to gain a sense of which muscles are involved. Later, practise stopping urine flow, hold for 1–2 seconds and repeat six to eight times as you urinate. Eventually you should be able to stop urine flow quickly, without any leakage and slowly relax the pelvic floor muscles in stages from full contraction to full relaxation.

2. Use the same muscles that you mastered control of in the first exercise to contract the pelvic floor throughout the day. Do this whenever and wherever possible. This may be repeated six to eight times during each session and 50 to 100 times a day. Hold the contraction for 2–5 seconds and then relax.

When doing these exercises, do not hold your breath, bear down (thus pushing down on the pelvic floor) or contract the buttocks, inner thighs, or abdominal muscles. It is best to learn to localise the contraction to the pelvic floor muscles entirely. Do not exhaust the pelvic floor muscles in the early stages. Do only as many contractions at a time as you can do at your maximum contraction and then two to three more. As contractions weaken discontinue at that time and build the muscle strength slowly, as with any other muscular exercise.

Recommendations for incontinence

Diet	A whole food approach to food where quality is more important than quantity. Plenty of fruits and vegetables, low-fat protein, and plenty of water.
Increase	Nothing specifically – generally healthy food
Decrease	Nothing specifically – all junk food, red meat and alcohol
Superfoods	Alfalfa and barley grass
Supplements	None specifically
Herbals	None specifically
Lifestyle changes	Take up the Kegal Exercises – whatever your age and however serious the problem, it is never too late to start Alternatively swimming – breast stroke/frog kick Cycling Alternate hot and cold Sitz baths – *not if pregnant*

Remember

Detox/urinary system rule no. 1

Never ignore the calls of nature. When you need to go the toilet, go – it may save you future problems.

Urinary tract infections

Urinary tract infections (UTIs) are infections of the kidney, bladder and urethra, which are under the control of the immune system. They are generally triggered by bacteria and are more common with any partial blockage of the urinary tract. Many people have recurring bouts of urinary tract infections.

Cystitis is probably the most common of the UTIs and describes inflammation of the bladder and/or urethra. Infection or bruising or irritation or a combination of these may cause it. The urethra is where you will feel much of the pain of cystitis. If the attack does turn out to be caused by an infection and is not treated, it can spread up to the kidneys (via the bladder and the ureters) and produce a more serious infection. The most common symptoms are a burning pain whenever you pass water, a frequent and urgent need to pass water, even though when you try there is hardly any (or no) urine, and needing to get up often at night to pass water.

There are many dietary changes, supplement and herbal recommendations for these conditions, and some very interesting studies have been done in this field. One such study had healthy volunteers ingest a large amount (100 grams) of refined sugar, after which the ability of their white blood cells to destroy bacteria was impaired for at least five hours. Ingestion of excessive amounts of alcohol has also shown to suppress the immune system whereas reducing the intake of dietary fat stimulates immunity. For these reasons recommendations can be given to reduce sugar, alcohol and fat during an acute infection and for prevention of future recurrences.

Optimal levels of vitamin C are often recommended by nutritional therapists for acute UTIs as well as long-standing supplementation for individuals who are prone to recurrent infections. Although no control studies have demonstrated the effectiveness of vitamin C for this purpose, this vitamin has been shown to inhibit the growth of *E.coli,* the most common bacterial cause of urinary tract infections and in addition, ingestion of 4g or more of vitamin C per day results in a slight acidisation of the urine creating an unfriendly environment for certain bacteria.

Since the immune system requires many nutrients in order to function properly, many people take a multivitamin/mineral supplement for insurance. In one double-blind study, healthy elderly people using such a supplement for one year showed improvements in certain measures of immune function, as well as a significant reduction in the total number of infections (including non-urinary tract infections).

There are numerous herbal remedies for urinary tract infections, the most popular and well-known being cranberry, and modern research has confirmed the benefits of cranberry for the prevention of UTIs. Drinking 10–16 ounces of unsweetened or lightly sweetened cranberry juice is recommended for prevention and as part of the treatment of urinary tract infections. In a double-blind study, elderly women who drank 10 ounces of cranberry juice per day had a decrease in the amount of bacteria in their urine. In another study elderly residents of a nursing home consumed either four ounces of cranberry juice or six capsules containing concentrated cranberry daily for thirteen months. During that time, the number of UTIs decreased by 25 per cent. Researchers have suggested two possible ways in which cranberry is effective against UTIs. First, cranberry prevents *E.coli,* the bacteria that causes most urinary tract infections, from attaching to the walls of the bladder. Second, cranberry contains hippuric acid, a compound that has been found to have antibiotic activity. However, cranberry should not be used as a substitute for antibiotics in the treatment of acute UTIs.

Goldenseal is reputed to help treat many types of infections. It contains berberine, an alkaloid that may prevent UTIs in the same way as cranberry, by inhibiting bacteria from adhering to the wall of the bladder. Goldenseal and other plants containing berberine such as Oregon grape can therefore help in the treatment and prevention of urinary tract infections.

Herbs that work by increasing urinary volume, thereby helping to flush bacteria out of the urinary tract, could be added as a tincture to water. Herbs with this function include asparagus (*Asparagus officinalis*), birch (*Betula supp.*), goldenrod (*Solidago virgaurea*), juniper and nettle.

Recommendations for urinary tract infections

Remember

Detox/urinary system rule no. 1

Alcohol is classed as an anti-nutrient, which means that it uses up more nutrients than it provides. *Maximum* alcohol consumption is 14 units per week for women and 21 units per week for men, *spread out over the week – not saved up for the weekends!*

Diet	A diet high fruits and vegetables to boost the immune system
Increase	Kiwi fruit, strawberries, oranges, red, green and yellow peppers and asparagus
Decrease	Sugar, saturated fats and alcohol
Superfoods	Alfalfa, algae, barley grass, bee pollen, honey, and medicinal mushrooms.
Supplements	A good multivitamin and mineral with additional vitamin C to bowel tolerance for one month then decrease Propolis – a natural antibiotic which helps to kill harmful bacteria
Herbals	Cranberry (as tablets or juice), goldenseal
Lifestyle changes	Water intake of 1½ litres every day should become a habit

Water retention/oedema and fluid balance in the body

Abnormal accumulation of fluid beneath the skin is known as oedema. There are two basic types of water retention. The first is when water is retained in the cells, thus causing swelling and a spongy feeling. The other is when the blood capillaries are not working efficiently. Congestive heart failure and pre-eclampsia of pregnancy are also connected with fluid retention, but these causes must be medically treated.

Many people, especially women, suffer from fluid retention. The usual symptoms are swelling of hands, ankles, feet, face, abdomen, or other areas of the body, premenstrual syndrome, headaches and leg ulcers.

Fluid balance in the body

Water makes up about 70 per cent of the adult human body, i.e. about 46 litres in a 70kg man. Some lies outside the cells – extracellular fluid (16 litres) and a large part is within the cell – intracellular fluid (30 litres).

The body maintains a state of homeostasis – the maintenance of a constant internal environment in the body – at all times. It is completing thousands of chemical reactions every second to keep us alive, and a vital part of the homeostasis mechanism is the regulation of body fluids.

In health the total amount of body water (and salt) is kept reasonably constant in spite of wide fluctuations in daily intake. A balance is struck between fluid intake and fluid output. Fluid intake is more than just the liquid we drink. We consume approximately 1000ml of liquid daily. In addition, 1,200ml of 'liquid' also comes from the food we eat, 1,500 from saliva, 2,200ml is produced from plasma to assist the digestive system absorb nutrients, 1,500ml comes from gastric juice, 800ml comes from bile, 1,400ml comes from pancreatic juice, another 1,500ml comes from intestinal juice and our body cells produce metabolic water of 400ml per day. So you see we have plenty of intake – but what about output?

We lose 150ml in faeces, 450ml in sweat, 1,500ml in urine, 500ml from the lungs and 150,000ml from kidney filtration (although 148,000ml of this is reabsorbed). You can see intake and output are fairly well balanced.

Except in growth, convalescence or pregnancy – when new tissue is being formed – an increase or decrease in intake leads to an appropriate increase or decrease in output to maintain the balance. So what goes wrong? Why do so many people, especially women, suffer from fluid retention? It is connected with the endocrine system in that ADH – anti diuretic hormone secreted from the adrenal glands – gives chemical messages to the kidneys to either hold on to or release urine.

Any waste product that the body makes during metabolism must be removed from the body; for example, carbon dioxide is a waste product from cell respiration and is expired in the air from our lungs. In the same way water is a waste product from cell respiration and from the diet and is excreted in urine. Excretion of body wastes is carried out by the kidneys but the kidneys have several other functions, all concerned with maintaining the constant composition of the body fluids.

Fluid balance in the body is a complex issue. The best advice you can give anybody is to drink more water. It is simple to do, but few of us actually meet the health guidelines of one litre daily. Many people think that by drinking more water they will make their situation worse, when the opposite is true.

As well as water itself, there are many foods that are natural diuretics and it is possible to lose many pounds of fluid over just a few days by incorporating these natural foods into your diet on a daily basis. These foods include: apples, avocados, bananas, beans, beetroot, broccoli, cabbage, carrots, celery, oily fish (salmon, herring, mackerel, pilchards), lentils, liver, nuts and seeds, tomatoes, watercress and yoghurt.

Juicing is excellent for water retention and many interesting drinks can be made which will give very effective results. Try celery, parsley and radish juice, or beetroot juice with a little lemon, or apple on its own or mixed with a little lemon. Carrot and apple juice is a favourite and very beneficial for anyone experiencing fluid retention. There are lots of books on the market with juicing recipes but if you really can't be bothered, find your nearest juice bar instead of the nearest wine bar – you will be pleased you did!

Coumarin is a bioflavonoid-like compound found in a variety of herbs, that has been used for oedema. Both animal and human studies have found that coumarin can be beneficial in treating oedema. Even oedema after surgery (when lymphatic drainage is damaged) has been helped by coumarin. Alfalfa sprouts are a rich source of coumarin. Bilberries and blueberries are both rich in flavonoids and as such are excellent fruits for fluid retention. You can buy them frozen from most supermarkets. After defrosting, you can eat them as they are or warm them in the oven.

Herbal teas are also very beneficial for clients with water retention, as they are often rich in flavonoids and coumarin. Herbal teas are just that – herbal. Fennel, comfrey, clover blossom, nettle, parsley, camomile, peppermint, or any mixture of these. Fruit teas are probably more beneficial than stimulant drinks such as coffee or tea, but they can also be very acidic and not as beneficial as the true herbal teas.

Recommendations for fluid retention

Diet	A low salt diet, otherwise balanced meals containing all the main food groups with low to medium protein intake
Increase	Fruits and vegetables
Decrease	Salt, salted nuts, smoked products
Superfoods	Rotate – spirulina, chlorella and blue-green algae in addition to alfalfa
Supplements	Bioflavonoids – a mixed complex of 1,000mg daily
Herbals	Goldenrod is considered to be one of the strongest herbal diuretics. Quercetin and ginkgo biloba
Lifestyle changes	Regular daily exercise – especially if your occupation requires long periods of sitting

General recommendations for the urinary system

Diet	Eating adequate supplies of meat, milk, cheese, breads and cereals provide a good supply of amino acids and helps control bacterial growth.
Foods to avoid	Citrus fruits and juices should be avoided
Superfoods	Alfalfa; rotate – spirulina, chlorella and blue-green algae, barley grass, bee pollen, honey and medicinal mushrooms
Supplements	Vitamin C Kidney glandular tissue – gives support to the kidneys and helps rebuild damaged tissue Vitamin E, proteolytic enzymes, flaxseed and probiotics
Herbal remedies	Ginkgo biloba Golden rod – as a natural diuretic
Lifestyle changes	Drink plenty of water *every day* and/or cranberry juice Take up Kegal Exercises if required in addition to daily regular exercise Avoid alcohol or keep within sensible limits Make AFDs – alcohol free days – part of your lifestyle and then work up to AFWs – alcohol free weeks. It will be worth it.

Knowledge review

The urinary and detoxification systems

1 What is the main function of the urinary system?

2 List the other organs of detoxification.

3 What is the most important dietary influence affecting the urinary system?

4 Define the condition known as incontinence.

5 What lifestyle changes may benefit a client suffering with incontinence?

6 Cystitis is a UTI. What are UTIs and what normally triggers them?

7 Why is reducing sugar, alcohol and fat during an acute infection recommended?

8 What are the benefits of cranberry juice?

9 What foods should be increased for clients suffering with UTIs.

10 Explain the two different types of fluid retention.

11 List six natural diuretic foods.

12 List four herbal teas that may be recommended for clients with fluid retention.

13 Why are herbal teas more beneficial than fruit teas?

14 What foods should be decreased for clients with fluid retention?

15   What specific lifestyle change would you recommend to support the urinary system generally?

16   What is the difference between psoriasis and eczema?

17   What is milk thistle and how can this benefit psoriasis sufferers?

18   What lifestyle changes would you recommend for a client with psoriasis?

Part III
Putting it all together

20   The practical application of nutrition therapy 279

Part I covered the basic theory you will need for starting out in the field of nutrition. Part II gives you access to a reference base of everyday symptoms together with a wide variety of recommendations. All you need now is the information in this final section and you will be ready to start working on some case studies. But where do you start? Having sound underpinning knowledge and access to references and recommendations is one thing, but to actually carry out an efficient and effective nutrition consultation you will also need good interpersonal skills. Before offering any recommendations to clients, you will need to gather as much information as possible from the client regarding their current dietary status. Once you have this information, you have a starting point on which to base your recommendations. Do not forget that every client you see will be biochemically different and his or her needs will be different.

The practical application of nutrition therapy

This chapter covers the following:

- **diet planning principles – B A L A N C E**
- **the consultation form and nutrition questionnaire**
- **the three-day dietary plan and timing**
- **How to calculate hip to waist ratio and body mass index (BMI)**
- **the Weakest Link Questionnaire – to ascertain which body system needs supporting**
- **suggested action plan for the nutrition consultation**
- **How to recommend supplements**
- **Weakest Link questions and answers explained**

By the end of this chapter you will have everything you need to commence your case study work and start putting into practice everything you have learned.

Diet planning principles

There are many ways to select new dietary recommendations for clients, but whichever you choose, your advice will always be effective if you keep the following basic dietary planning principles in mind.

B   A   L   A   N   C   E

Balance
Adequacy
Liquid
Abundance
Nutrient density
Calorie control
Empty calories

Balance

The art of a balanced diet involves using enough of each type of food. For the average person this maybe 55 per cent from carbohydrate foods, 15 per cent from protein foods and 30 per cent from fats. As well at looking at balance in the macronutrients, there are other considerations. For example, the essential minerals calcium and iron, taken together, illustrate the importance of dietary balance. Meat, fish and poultry are rich in iron but poor in calcium. Conversely, milk and milk products are rich in calcium but poor in iron. For a balance choose some meat or meat alternatives for iron and some milk or milk products for calcium. Look for a balance of fats – look at saturated, monounsaturated and essential fats. Look for a balance between omega 3 and omega 6 fatty acids.

Adequacy

Adequacy means that the diet provides sufficient energy as kcalories, and enough of all the nutrients to meet the needs of healthy people. Each day the body loses some iron, for example, which needs to be replaced by iron-containing foods. A person whose diet fails to provide enough iron-rich foods may develop the symptoms of iron-deficient anemia. Each day adequate nutrients must be supplied by the diet, in particular the essential amino acids, the essential fatty acids and water. Choosing a variety of foods will ensure adequacy of vitamins and minerals.

Liquids

What liquids are being consumed in the diet? Water is necessary and vital for good health. When establishing the current diet or planning a new dietary plan it is important to establish the current fluid intake. Consider water; is it tap, bottled or filtered; coffee and tea – is it decaffeinated? fizzy drinks? alcohol – units per week – what alcohol? – grain based as in barley (whiskey) or fruit-based – grapes as in wine or a Guinness/stout type drink which may contain a small amount of iron or fortified wines – sherry? An accurate description is needed for you to be able to decide, and then recommend acceptable recommendations for your client.

Abundance

Is there an abundance of fresh fruit and vegetables? Nothing less than five servings of fruit and vegetables every day is acceptable. Fruit and vegetables provide the vitamins and minerals not only to keep us healthy but to provide the second part of many enzymes – the coenzymes which are responsible for hundreds of chemical actions in the body every minute of every day.

Nutrient density

A nutritional therapist will assist clients in choosing foods that are 'nutrient dense'. These are foods that deliver the most nutrients and least anti-nutrients for the least (kcalories) food energy. Consider foods containing calcium for example. You can get about 300mg of calcium from either 100grams of cheddar cheese or 1 cup (9 fluid ounces) of non-fat milk, but the cheese contributes about twice as much food energy (kcalories) as the milk. The non-fat milk then is twice as calcium dense as the cheddar cheese; it offers twice the amount of calcium for half the kcalories. Both foods are excellent choices of calcium foods but the milk is the better choice as you have received the calcium but with far fewer kcalories – it is a more 'nutrient dense' food than the cheese.

Calorie control

The average adult requires 2,000 kcalories a day. Designing an adequate, balanced diet without overeating requires careful planning. The key to calorie control is choosing food with a high nutrient density.

Empty calories

When considering a client's current diet look out for empty calorie selections. A glass of cola and a bunch of grapes each provide about 150 kcalories but the grapes offer a trace of protein, some vitamins, minerals and fibre along with the energy – the cola only offers empty calories from sugar without any other nutrients.

The purpose of the nutrition consultation is to 'establish current diet', and 'plan and advise the client on nutritional needs'. These are the main modules for many accredited courses in nutrition. In order to do this you need to ask specific questions. You also need to understand why you are asking the questions and how to interpret the answers. Because you need to gather so much information, and only have one hour for a consultation, it is always a good idea to give the client a nutrition questionnaire and a three-day food diary to complete at home. They can then complete the questionnaire in their own time and complete the food diary as they go. If you ask any client what they had to eat two days ago, I can assure you, most will not remember. You need the full facts to be able to offer the most beneficial recommendations. In the beginning, you may wish the client to send the completed questionnaire and food diary back to you in order for you to study them before they attend the consultation. Once you have more confidence and experience, you will not need to see these completed forms beforehand and the client will be able to bring them personally to the consultation.

The nutrition questionnaire is not the same as the consultation form, which you will complete with the client at the time of the consultation. It is at this time that the client can sign a declaration that all the information they have given you in the questionnaires, the food diary and the consultation is accurate and true.

The consultation form

The consultation form will follow the same format as other consultation forms you have prepared for other disciplines. You will need the client's name and address, their date of birth, name of doctor and any medication they may be taking. You will also need to

Design a consultation form to collect the general information from your client. This should include the contraindications to nutritional therapy (see Chapter 6) and a client declaration stating that all the information they have provided is true and accurate.

Design a nutrition questionnaire working around the BALANCE principles: Balance, Adequacy, Liquids, Abundance, Nutrient density, Calorie control and Empty calories. You will probably need two A4 sheets of paper, used on both sides, on which to gather this additional information.

It should include a space for the client to write down their symptoms and how long they have had them (in the order of importance).

know their current weight and height. Don't forget the contraindication checks – these should be included in the consultation form.

It is also important to ask what the client's expectation of the nutrition consultation is. If they are expecting a service you cannot deliver, now is the time to refer them to a more experienced therapist in a different, perhaps more specialised, area. Do not attempt to do something you are not competent to do – it is responsible and professional to make referrals.

Essential paperwork

Paperwork to be completed	For what information	When to be completed and by whom
Consultation form	For general information	To be completed at time of consultation by therapist
Nutrition questionnaire	For specific nutritional information	Can be completed at home by client
Weakest Link Questionnaire	To ascertain the clients weakest body system in order to be able to offer specific nutritional support to that system	Can be completed at home by client
Food diary	To establish accurate current diet	Can be completed at home by client

Supplementary questions to support Weakest Link Questionnaire and three-day food diary

Include questions like:

- Do you go out of your way to avoid foods containing preservatives and additives? (Nutrient density)
- How often do you eat sweets/chocolates/cakes/confectionery? (Empty calories)
- How many packets of 'instant' or fast foods do you eat each week? (Empty calories)
- How many teaspoons of sugar do you add to food/drinks each day? (Empty calories)
- What percentage of your diet comes from raw fruit and vegetables? (Abundance)
- How many alcoholic drinks do you have each week? (Liquids)
- Do you drink tap/bottled/filtered water? And how much do you drink (Liquids)
- How many times a week would you eat oily fish? (Adequacy)

- How many pints of milk do you drink in one week? (Adequacy)
- Were you breast-fed? (Breast-fed people usually have stronger immune systems)

How could you ascertain if a client needed more iron/calcium/magnesium/vitamin C-rich foods? (Adequacy). You could make a list of foods containing iron-rich foods and ask the client to tick the foods they eat and write in the frequency. This would give you valuable information and you could do this for each nutrient. Or you could write a list of symptoms associated with a particular vitamin/mineral deficiency and ask the client to tick each one – the more symptoms ticked the more likely they need the food in their diet.

Iron deficiency symptoms	*Foods abundant in iron*
Heavy periods or blood loss	Liver
Loss of appetite or nausea	Steak (good quality beef)
Pale skin	Prawns
Sore tongue	Beans (kidney, pinto, chick peas)
Fatigue or listlessness	Vegetables (peas, spinach, broccoli)

Include a womens only section – see sample.

Women only section

Please answer yes/no to the following and where appropriate the length of time involved or relevant dates.

Any history of miscarriage?	Children?	Are you on or have you ever taken the Pill?
Have you had a hysterectomy?	Do you have any infertility problems?	Are you taking or considering taking HRT?
Are you menopausal?	Do you suffer with any PMS symptoms? If so please state which.	Any additional comments here please.

There is no end to the questions you can ask. However, keep it specific.

The Weakest Link Questionnaire

The purpose of the questionnaire is to identify your client's weakest body system, in order to recommend specific nutrients to support that system.

Instructions

The questionnaire is to be completed by the client. If the client wishes to do the calculations that will save you time, but it is important to check their figures.

Every question must be answered and recorded with either a 'yes' or 'no' answer.

All answers carry one point except the skeletal, respiratory and nervous systems which all score two points for each 'yes' answer. Once completed each system is calculated separately and entered into the 'totals' box.

Each section has a possible score of 10.

Cardiovascular system (1 point for each yes)	YES	NO
Are you more than 14lbs (7kgs) overweight?		
Do you smoke more than five cigarettes a day?		
Is there a history of heart disease in your family?		
Do you have more than two alcoholic drinks a day?		
Do you usually add salt to your food?		
Do you eat red meat more than five times a week?		
Do you use any type of butter or margarine on a daily basis?		
Do you do less than two hours exercise a week?		
Is your blood pressure above 140/90?		
Is your pulse after 15 minutes rest above 75?		
Total scores for cardiovascular system		

Digestive system (1 point for each yes)	YES	NO
Do you suffer with constipation or diarrhoea?		
Do you experience anal irritation?		
Do you suffer from flatulence or bloating?		
Do you occasionally use indigestion tablets?		
Do you find it difficult digesting fatty foods?		
Do you ever get a burning sensation in your stomach?		
Are you prone to stomach upsets?		
Do you use more than one spoonful of sugar a day?		
Do you eat quickly/rush your food/eat under stress?		
Do you normally eat at irregular times?		
Total scores for digestive system		

Endocrine/reproductive systems (1 point for each yes)	YES	NO
Are you taking or have you ever taken the Pill and/or HRT?		
Have you ever had a miscarriage?		
Do you suffer with any PMS symptoms?		
Do you have difficulty in losing weight?		
Do you suffer from lumpy breasts?		
Do you suffer from breast tenderness		
Do you often feel tired during the day?		
Do you often do two or three tasks simultaneously?		
Do you have difficulty in getting to sleep?		
Total scores for endocrine/reproductive systems		

Lymphatic system and immunity (1 point for each yes)	YES	NO
Is there a history of cancer in your family?		
Do you find it hard to shift an infection?		
Do you sit still for several hours each day? Work/TV		
Do you avoid physical exercise?		
Do you have cellulite?		
Do you work harder than most people?		
Do you feel guilty when relaxing?		
Do you have a persistent need for achievement?		
Are you especially competitive?		
Have you taken antibiotics over the past two years?		
Total scores for lymphatic and immunity systems		

Respiratory (2 points each for each yes)	YES	NO
Do you suffer from frequent bronchitis, asthma, colds and flu?		
Do you smoke more than five cigarettes per day?		
Do you live/work in a smoky atmosphere?		
Do you live or work in a 'chemical' atmosphere?		
(paint, thinners, petrol, fertilisers, hair sprays, colours, etc.)		
Do you eat your fruit and vegetables without washing them first?		
Total scores for respiratory system		

Skeletal system (2 points for each yes)	YES	NO
Do you consume more than one pint of milk per day?		
Do you avoid weight-bearing exercise?		
Do you eat *less than* five portions green leafy vegetables and fruit *on a daily basis?*		
Do you eat sweet, sugary, foods on most days?		
Do you suffer with any type of arthritis?		
Total scores for the skeletal system		

Urinary/detoxification systems (1 point for each yes)	YES	NO
Do you suffer with fluid retention?		
Have you ever suffered with thrush or cystitis?		
Do you suffer from chronic fatigue?		
Do you have more than 14 units of alcohol (women) or 21 units of alcohol (men) a week?		
Do you suffer with eczema or psoriasis?		
Do you suffer from acne or poor skin condition?		
Do you feel you have a sensitivity to chemicals?		
Do you have any unexplained itching?		
Do you suffer with dull headaches?		
Totals for the urinary/detoxification systems		

Nervous system (2 points for each yes)	YES	NO
Do you suffer from any type of headache?		
Do you suffer with migraine headaches?		
Do you suffer with panic attacks?		
Do you often find that you are irritable/jumpy?		
Do you feel that you lose your temper easily?		
Totals for the nervous system		

Muscular system – energy (1 point for each yes)	YES	NO
Is your energy less now than it used to be?		
Do you avoid exercise due to tiredness?		
Do you sweat a lot or get excessively thirsty?		
Do you get dizzy or irritable if you don't eat often?		
Do you often feel drowsy during the day?		
Do you sometimes lose concentration?		
Do you suffer with cramps?		
Do you suffer with muscular aches and pains?		
Do you have much injury through playing sport?		
Do you drink less than eight glasses of water every day?		
Total for the muscular system		

TOTAL SCORES	
	Total Yes answers
Cardiovascular	
Digestive system	
Endocrine/reproductive system	
Lymphatic system and immunity	
Respiratory system	
Skeletal system	
Urinary and detoxification system	
Nervous system	
Muscular system and energy	
System(s) with highest score...	

Once you have established the weakest system, go to the appropriate section in Part 2 of the book and look under General recommendations at the end of the chapter for suggestions for your client.

An example of a three-day food diary.

	Day 1	*Day 2*	*Day 3*
Time	Breakfast	Breakfast	Breakfast
Time	Lunch	Lunch	Lunch
Time	Dinner	Dinner	Dinner
Time	Snack	Snack	Snack
Time	Snack	Snack	Snack
Time	Drinks	Drinks	Drinks
Time	Other	Other	Other

Timing

As you can see, there is a box available for the client to include when they ate. It is very important to establish the time of eating. Natural and healthy eating is regulated by feelings of hunger and satiety, but many people no longer tune in to these internal signals, or they confuse them with other feelings. For example, they may interpret anxiety or thirst as hunger. Or they may confuse feeling full with being fat. Encourage the client to complete the 'time' box.

Timing and food diary sheet

Normalising the eating pattern should be considered as one of the most important aspects of helping your clients towards a healthy eating pattern and should be done in small steps. The first step is to decide what time each day the client will eat three meals and two snacks. I normally give this as a task for the client to seriously think about. Give them plenty of time to really think about this, as once they have committed themselves to their times, I want them to stick to them – no matter what. They decide when they are going to eat.

These times can work around their family and work life so the timings may be different on a weekday to a weekend. Once established eating times have been set, the client should eat only during those times. They need to allow themselves only enough time to eat the meal or snack. A meal ordinarily should take no longer than thirty minutes to consume and a snack no more than fifteen minutes.

Initially, the client needn't worry about what they eat at each time period. Instead the focus is on eating within a regular schedule. If the client can establish this new eating pattern for 28 days it will become a habit. The focus can then be on making healthier choices with regard to food. Eat at the planned times, even if you don't feel hungry. Don't skip meals or planned snacks, and try not to eat at other times. If you do slip and eat at an unplanned time just get back to the proper timings as soon as possible.

Body mass index

Your body mass index (BMI) gives a good indication of whether you are a healthy weight. To work out your BMI:

1 Work out your height in metres (see the height chart) and multiply the figure by itself

2 Measure your weight in kilograms

3 Divide the weight (question 2) by the height squared (i.e. the answer to question 1). For example, you might be 1.6m (5 foot 3 inches) tall and weigh 65kg (10 stone). The calculation would then be 1.6 × 1.6 = 2.56. Your BMI would be 65 divided 2.56 = 25.39.

Activity

Try this exercise yourself. When you feel the benefits yourself of eating at regular times, you will be in a much better position to advise your clients.

Activity

Now work out your BMI and check your result against the table below. But before you do, remember not to take it too seriously! Stocky people (and girls in particular) may appear to be overweight when using this method. So be honest with yourself. If you are naturally of a stocky build do not try to lose weight unnecessarily.

Category	Range
Underweight	Less than 20
Ideal	20–25
Overweight; advisable to lose weight if you are under 50	25–30
You should lose weight	30–40
Definitely too fat; lose weight now	Greater than 40

Height chart

Feet and inches	Metres	Feet and inches	Metres
4'10"	1.45	5'9"	1.74
4'11"	1.50	5'10"	1.78
5'0"	1.52	5'11"	1.80
5'1"	1.55	6'0"	1.82
5'2"	1.57	6'1"	1.85
5'3"	1.60	6'2"	1.88
5'4"	1.62	6'3"	1.90
5'5"	1.65	6'4"	1.92
5'6"	1.68	6'5"	1.95
5'7"	1.70	6'6"	1.98
5'8"	1.72	6'7"	2.00

If your BMI falls within the ideal range and you are the right weight, that's great, but it is still important to eat healthily to receive all the nutrients needed to stay healthy, fit and well. It is also important not to put on weight. People aged 30–74 with BMIs at the lower end of the normal range have the lowest death rates. And people who stay the same weight in middle age as they were in their youth live longer, are generally healthier and therefore more able to enjoy themselves.

Hip to waist ratio

While the BMI is a good general indicator of if you are overweight or not, the hip to waist ratio is probably a better indicator. The risk of heart disease doesn't only depend on how much fat you're carrying, it's also where you are carrying it that matters. Our genes determine out basic shape; whether the fat on your body is deposited around our hips, breasts and upper arms (women) so that we are pear-shaped, or whether excess fat is deposited around our abdomens making men and some women apple-shaped.

It may seem unfair but if apple-shaped people become overweight they are at greater risk of heart disease and diabetes than pear-shaped people. To make the calculation:

Remember

The BMI is just an *indicator* in ascertaining a healthy weight – there are other factors to take into account.

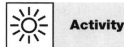

Activity

Calculate your own hip to waist ratio.

1   Measure your waist and hips
2   Divide the waist measurement by the hip measurement to get your hip to waist ratio

For example, if your waist is 86cm (34 inches) and your hips 102cm (40 inches), your waist-hip ratio will be 86 divided by 102 = 0.85. If the ratio of your waist to hip measurement is more than 0.95 as a man and more than 0.87 as a woman you are apple-shaped.

There is another rule of thumb as far as waist measurements are concerned. If a man has a waist that measures more than 94cm (37 inches), or a woman's is more than 80cm (31 inches), they are categorised by some doctors as overweight. Waists do thicken with age, a phenomenon often referred to as middle-aged spread. If you are younger and already have a 'spare tyre' – act now. It is this abdominal fat that increases the risk of heart disease.

A suggested action plan for a nutrition consultation

Before you see the client ascertain at the booking stage that the client has no contraindications to the therapy.

1   Have the completed paperwork in front of you – the nutrition questionnaire, the Weakest Link Questionnaire and the three-day food diary. Look at the three-day food diary. At all times keep in mind the BALANCE principles – Balance, Adequacy, Liquids, Abundance, Nutrient density, Calorie control and Empty calories. Look for a balance of the macronutrients, the carbohydrates, proteins and fats in a ratio of 55 per cent, 15 per cent and 30 per cent. Can you identify food choices containing iron, calcium, magnesium, antioxidants, essential fatty acids, and essential amino acids? It will not take you long to be able to see at a glance if a client's intake is balanced. You may wish to use highlighter pens to identify different food groups – green for vegetables, red for protein, etc.

2   Identify something encouraging and positive about the client's current diet – there is always something good, no matter how small, to congratulate a client on. This will make them feel better and more receptive to your recommendations on the areas that are not so good! Make a note of this.

3   Look at results of the Weakest Link Questionnaire. Don't just look at the totals – look through all the body systems. Which came out the highest? indicating the weakest system. Which came out the lowest? indicating the strongest system. Are there two with high scores? Make a note of the systems that need dietary support. If there is a tie between two systems – you need to make recommendations to support both systems for a faster return to optimum health. Look up references in Part II of the book and make notes of possible recommendations you will make.

4   Look at the client's symptoms. Why do they want to come to you? What are their expectations of the consultation with you? Do any of their symptoms coincide with their weakest body system? For

example: infertility as a symptom and reproductive as system or overweight as symptom and cardiovascular as system?

5   For women clients – look at the women only section on your nutrition questionnaire. Are they on the Pill? Or have been in the past? Any PMS? Trying to conceive? Pregnant? All this information is important and you need it before coming to any conclusions about your recommendations.

6   Work out the clients BMI and hip to waist ratio.

7   Did you make provision for specific nutrient deficiency indicators in your nutritional questionnaire? If so check these out next. Is the client lacking in any one nutrient specifically? iron, zinc, vitamin C, magnesium or B12 for example. If yes, start making a list of foods that are high in these nutrients for recommendation to the client at the consultation stage.

8   Look for possible food sensitivities. Wheat and dairy are the foods people are most sensitive to as they are so abundant in the diet. How many times is the client consuming wheat per day/week? How much dairy food is consumed per day/week? Is there any one food the client would find hard to give up? If so, these are the foods the client is most likely to be sensitive to.

9   Rule out candida (constant bloating, history of antibiotics, history of being on the Pill and recurrent thrush are frequent symptoms). Look up candida in Part II and see if any of the symptoms coincide with those of your client.

10 Rule out difficulties in balancing blood sugar levels.

11 Rule out general digestive problems.

In time you will be able to do this in a few minutes!

The nutrition consultation

1   Smile and introduce yourself. Carry out the consultation in a relaxed but professional manner. Be sure you are looking your best – your appearance affects the image of the workplace and, once qualified, you will be representing a professional body and following their professional code of conduct. The consultation will start within seconds of you greeting the client, with a visual assessment. Note the colour and texture of their skin; any white marks on their fingernails; their general appearance; do they look the height and weight they stated on their nutritional questionnaire; note the condition of their hair and if there are any dark lines or bags under the eyes. Observe too the client's mood, their gait, posture and breathing patterns. Make a mental note of all these things for writing up after the client has left. You can then make a comparison when they return for a second appointment.

2   Complete the consultation form with your client and have them sign the declaration that all the information they have given you is true and accurate. Be sure to check again that the client is not contraindicated for treatment (see Chapter 6).

3   Thank them for taking the time to complete the paperwork and explain that it has given you valuable information upon which to build your recommendations.

4 Start with commending them on a positive aspect of their diet. Examples could be: I see you eat breakfast every day; eat some fruit on most days; eat vegetables regularly; have alcohol-free days; drink plenty of water.

5 Continue to explain the areas you have identified that need improvement. You will get this information based on your conclusions and opinions from the consultation form; the nutrition questionnaire; the Weakest Link Questionnaire and the food diary. You will also have checked Part II of this book for suitable recommendations.

6 You could continue by explaining to the client the Weakest Link Questionnaire results and make a suggestion that a good starting point would be by supporting the weakest body system(s). See if you can make some links with the client's symptoms and the weakest body systems.

7 Discuss current diet by looking together at their three-day dietary plan. Keep thinking BALANCE and the words it represents.

> Balance (is there any?)
>
> Abundance (plenty of fruit and vegetables?)
>
> Liquids (too much alcohol – too little water)?
>
> Adequacy (check for foods containing calcium and iron plus all the other nutrients)
>
> Nutrient density (foods with high nutrient density compared with junk food)
>
> Calorie control (too many calories? too few calories?)
>
> Empty calories (too much alcohol, junk food – anti-nutrients?)

Discuss with the client ways to make beneficial adjustments to the diet.

8 Rule out candida or discuss with client

Rule out blood sugar imbalances or discuss with client

Rule out food intolerances or discuss with client

9 Discuss supplements – how does the client feel about dietary supplements? Would they prefer herbal remedies? Make recommendations – see below

Discuss lifestyle changes.

10 Summary – Keep it simple!

Ask for feedback from the client; do they have any questions?

11 Finally, ask the client to repeat to you, *briefly*, what they are going to do before they next see you. They might just be going to reduce coffee and increase water intake, but if they actually confirm this to you in speech, they are much more likely to do it. Depending upon circumstances, make a further appointment for two weeks or one month's time, when you will assess progress, increase or decrease the supplement regime and make further recommendation.

It is often that simple, but more often much more complex. To be an effective nutritional therapist you need to be a good detective too.

Supplements

When advising clients on supplements, they need to know exactly what you are advising. It is useless to say 'you need some vitamin C and maybe some iron'. This is no help to the client at all. You need to state exactly what it is you want them to have and when. When you are recommending supplements for your clients, list them as follows:

Please take the following supplement recommendations for one month, at which time we will reassess your needs. After one month the supplement recommendations can often be reduced.

Supplement	When	Why
Solgar zinc citrate 25mg	1 tablet per day taken in the evenings	To assist with poor skin condition
Health Plus metabolic pack	1 sachet every morning	To assist weight loss
Health Plus chromium and B3	1 tablet before each meal	This is to assist blood sugar levels. Chromium helps the pancreas to work efficiently and to make better use of glucose

This explains to the client exactly what it is you are recommending. You are also giving good instructions as to *when* to take the supplement (vitamins should not be taken in the evening as this could cause insomnia), and you have also advised the client *why* you are recommending the supplement.

With these recommendations, the client is less likely to buy inappropriate supplements from which they would probably not get the results you had anticipated.

The Weakest Link questions explained

Here are some of the questions from the Weakest Link Questionnaire with some additional questions you may find it useful to ask your clients. Explanation as to why the question was asked is given and there are also some possible explanations to the client's answer, and the next course of action. You are trying to ascertain the causes of a symptom and there will always be more questions to ask in order to get to a possible explanation. Working with nutrition is like being a detective; but our end results is to support the cause, not the symptom.

Cardiovascular system

Are you more than 14lbs/7kg overweight?

The answer to this should be no. Many of your clients will say yes. Assist and encourage them all you can to reduce their weight. This will without doubt help their heart work more effectively.

Do you smoke more than five cigarettes a day?

Probably the worst activity as far as health is concerned is smoking. Assist and encourage the client all you can to reduce and stop.

Is there a history of heart disease in your family?

Heart disease can be hereditary, but even with a yes answer, there is much the client can do for themselves. Stop smoking, regular gentle exercise, lots of green leafy vegetables and cutting back on saturated fats. Heart disease is not inevitable even if it is hereditary in a family.

Do you have more than two alcoholic drinks a day?

Alcohol can be classed as an anti-nutrient. The more anti-nutrients we take into the body, the more nutrient-deficient we become. Anyone who drinks more than two alcoholic drinks a day would need an extra 500mg of Vitamin C a day compared to someone who did not drink.

Do you usually add salt to your food?

We do not need to add salt to our food. Excess sodium is associated with high blood pressure and fluid retention.

Do you eat red meat more than five times a week?

Eating meat more than five times a week is putting extra strain on the body. Not only are you ingesting the important protein content of the meat, but also the saturated fat that goes with it, not to mention the chemicals that were added to the feed of the animal that will be passed on to you – growth hormones and antibiotics for example.

Do you use more than one spoonful of sugar a day?

Sugar is an anti-nutrient. If eaten in excess can contribute towards blood sugar problems, making you feel drowsy during the day and losing concentration. Zinc supplementation may improve your sense of taste, so reducing your need for sugar. Artificial sweeteners are a definite anti-nutrient and carcinogenic; clients should be made aware of this and strongly encouraged not to use them. If something must be added then choose half a teaspoon of Manuka honey.

Do you do less than two hours' exercise a week?

Walking just half an hour daily (over and above your usual daily activities) may reduce heart diseases by up to 50 per cent. The heart is a muscle and needs exercise like any other muscle.

Is your blood pressure above 140/90?

An obvious indicator that all is not right. Start now by exercising gently on a daily basis, just a ten-minute walk will help, reduce salt intake and increase consumption of green leafy vegetables. Its never too late to start looking after yourself.

Is your pulse after 15 minutes rest above 75?

Another indicator that all is not right. Same recommendations as blood pressure above.

Digestive system

Do you suffer with constipation or diarrhoea?

A yes answer would indicate that all is not well. Either condition is unpleasant and an indicator that the digestive system is compromised. Maybe the client is anxious or is eating too quickly under stressful conditions? There are many causes to be checked out here. You will need to ascertain if there are any food allergies or intolerances, exactly what is being eaten and when, how long the client has been suffering and whether or not a visit to the doctor has been made. IBS may be involved here.

Do you experience anal irritation?

If the answer is yes to this question, this could be linked with allergies and further investigations will have to be made.

Do you suffer from flatulence or bloating?

Many possibilities here for a yes answer. Investigate if they eat their food too quickly, thereby not allowing the digestive juices to act effectively – if so just taking more time eating would make a great difference to their digestive system. Bloating could be a sign of candida albicans infestation or food allergy or intolerance. Look at their eating plan and see what you can pick up there. Check if they are drinking anything with their food. Liquid dilutes the digestive juices thereby making digestive enzymes less effective. Check how many times they are eating wheat over one day and over one week. More than seven times in a week? If so, this is too many. Try to encourage clients to have wheat a maximum of once a day for a start, reducing to three times a week. Excessive wheat could be one reason for bloating. Suggest alternatives – oats, rice, barley, quinoa.

Do you occasionally use indigestion tablets?

If yes here – ask how often. If daily, this could be a serious matter. Many indigestion tables contain aluminum – of which there has been many studies to indicate a connection to Alzheimer's disease. Nobody should need to take indigestion tablets daily. You could recommend taking a digestive enzyme supplement instead. This will assist in breaking down the food and helping digestion, and so avoiding the need to take the indigestion tablet.

Do you find it difficult digesting fatty foods?

This is usually a liver/gall bladder problem. Many clients have their gall bladders removed and are not given dietary advice. They have remained on their existing diet because they haven't been told otherwise, and hence find it extremely difficult to digest fatty food. Lecithin supplementation may be the answer. Sprinkled on to food it breaks down the fat content of food making it much more digestible Stress could also be another factor.

Do you ever get a burning sensation in your stomach?

Clients should not get a burning sensation in their stomachs. Ask how often and if it is after a particular meal. An evening or main meal for example usually contains protein; if the client is deficient in hydrochloric acid they would find it difficult to break down the protein which may result in experiencing the burning sensation.

If they get the pain after the main meal, but not with a cereal-type breakfast or a smaller meal, this could be the reason. Another good indicator is that the client feels less pain after a stir-fry type of meal. This is because the protein is already cut up into quite small pieces, hence assisting the digestive system in the early stages of breakdown. Digestive enzymes may assist here. You can purchase hydrochloric acid supplementation on its own but I would suggest a digestive enzyme 'multi', containing amylases, proteases, and lipases.

Are you prone to stomach upsets?

The first thing I clarify here is that the client knows where the stomach is! I point to my abdomen and then to my stomach and ask them where they get their upsets. It is invariably in the abdomen area. Upsets in the abdomen area could be caused by allergies, candida, parasites, or just by eating too much.

Do you use any type of butter or margarine on a daily basis?

A general digestive system question. Most people will answer yes. Advise that butter is better than margarine – just. All butters and margarines hard at room temperature are hydrogenated fats – trans fats – that compromise the body using other fats effectively. Suggest they use olive oil directly on bread – try it yourself – it tastes good and is a much better source of fat. Alternatively nut butters are a good alternative to ordinary butter. Occasionally is OK but all clients should be encouraged to cut back on saturated fats.

Do you eat quickly/rush your food/eat under stress?

Another common fact of life. Many people just eat too quickly and compromise the whole digestive system, which could result in many unpleasant symptoms later. Encourage clients to slow down when they eat and to make food and eating times a priority; not something that is fitted-in-between other events.

Do you normally eat at irregular times?

Not good news. This may lead to a disordered eating pattern which in turn could lead to other problems later. Read the paragraph on timing earlier in this chapter.

Endocrine system

Are you taking or have you ever taken the Pill and/or HRT?

The Pill and HRT are both synthetic hormones. One in every 200 women's periods will cease after stopping the Pill and it could take up to two years before fertility will return. Surveys report that 70 per cent of women discontinue HRT within one year and only 7 per cent last eight years. There are numerous trials showing that HRT significantly increases the risk of breast cancer.

Have you ever had a miscarriage?

Around one in four pregnancies are estimated to end in a miscarriage and the real figure is likely to be higher, as many miscarriages go unreported. Some experts believe that miscarriage is a sensitive indicator that the parents are exposed to environmental hazards. One study found that the mother drinking alcohol daily, even in moderation, increased the risk of miscarriage.

Do you suffer with any PMS symptoms?

There are many factors associated with PMS but symptoms can be improved by reducing or better still avoiding alcohol, supplementing B6 and zinc one week before a period, reducing stress, and eating large amounts of green leafy vegetables for the magnesium content. There are many different types of PMS symptoms, these are general recommendations.

Do you have difficulty in losing weight?

Many women have difficulty in losing weight. Many just find it difficult to stay on a diet for many reasons. However, if your client is over 45, she may be what is known as 'oestrogen dominant'. In which case one of the main symptoms is difficulty in losing weight. This is a very complex area but a very common one. A natural progesterone cream has proved very helpful for many women approaching the menopause. Investigate progesterone creams and advise clients accordingly.

Do you suffer from lumpy breasts?

Breast tenderness and swelling are symptoms associated with oestrogen dominance and one of 150 different symptoms associated with PMS. Follow the general recommendations for PMS in Part II of this book

Do you suffer from breast tenderness?

As above, associated with oestrogen dominance and therefore progesterone deficiency. Give clients information of progesterone cream. You are not advising them to use this cream, but providing the information so your clients can make informed choices.

Do you often feel tired during the day?

This is one symptom of glucose imbalance. Note what they eat for breakfast and lunch. Is the client eating any protein in these two meals? If no, simply adding some protein, say an egg for breakfast, may make all the difference.

Do you do 2–3 tasks simultaneously?

An 'adrenals' question. A yes answer is a sign of anxiety and stress and giving the adrenal glands a hard time. An adrenal support supplement may be recommended or time management skills. Remember the saying 'less haste, more speed'.

Do you have thinning hair on your scalp?

Possible hormone imbalance. There are some excellent supplements available, which could be tried for six months – again recommendation to a nutritional therapist for hormone testing is recommended. Worry and stress could make the situation worse, so yoga or any stress releasing activity is recommended. Home-made shampoo containing essential oils works well too.

Lympathatic system and immune system

Is there a history of cancer in your family?

For clients with a history of cancer in their family, it is even more important that they look after themselves. An anti-oxidant is the first recommendation plus all the dietary advice given in the relevant sections of this book.

Do you find it hard to shift an infection?

An indication of a compromised immune system. The healthiest of people get colds from time to time but if the immune system is strong the infection doesn't last long. Vitamin C is a must throughout the winter months. Build up slowly to 1g daily.

Do you sit still for several hours each day? work/TV?

The lymphatic system does not have a heart to act as a pump like the circulatory system. It relies on movement. Contracting muscles through any kind of movement moves lymph along the lymphatic vessels. Sitting for long periods is therefore not recommended for good lymphatics.

Do you avoid physical exercise?

Exercise is important not just for keeping fit or losing weight, but for support for the immune system. Regular movement is needed to keep the lymphatic fluid moving through the vessels to filter toxins for their removal from the body. Avoiding physical exercise will result in an accumulation of toxins in the body.

Do you have cellulite?

Not just for the overweight. I have seen many slim girls with cellulite. This is a clogging up of the body cells giving the dimpled appearance of the skin. Cellulite does exist and it can be improved. Read up on the cellulite paragraph in the book and advise clients accordingly.

Do you work harder than most people?

This is a stress question and there are many recommendations for a yes answer. Why is your client working harder than most people, could it be an emotional issue? a financial issue? if they constantly need to achieve why is this? Another huge area but immediate help can be given by clients reducing stimulants, taking a daily multivitamin and maybe talking to someone if there are any underlying problems.

Do you feel guilty when relaxing?

Another stress question and recommendations as above. Clients may need to learn to relax.

Do you have a persistent need for achievement?

Stress yet again. What drives these people, and why? Probably not in your range of services but to be able to recommend someone in that field is good advice. Think about taking some counselling qualifications yourself – therapists are very often put in a position where some counselling training could come in very useful.

Are you especially competitive?

Stress as above. Continual and persistent stress and competitive events may result in adrenal exhaustion – burnout. A competitive streak is not necessarily bad, but it is important to be nutritionally nourished for any type of competition, be it work or sport related. A daily multivitamin is a must for clients in this situation.

Have you taken antibiotics over the past two years?

Frequent use of antibiotics suppresses the immune system. Advise clients to always follow up antibiotics with probiotics. Also especially important for children who have had antibiotics – you can purchase special children's formulas of probiotics.

Respiratory system

Do you suffer from frequent bronchitis, asthma, colds and flu?

Frequent bouts of the above would suggest that the immune system was compromised and a good multivitamin and mineral would be recommended together with other ways of supporting the immune system.

Do you smoke more than five cigarettes per day?

Research shows without any doubt that smoking is dangerous to health, especially in relation to the respiratory system. Every encouragement should be given to your clients to make this a priority task in their life – they won't regret it.

Do you live/work in a smoky atmosphere?

This can be almost as bad as smoking yourself. The smoke breathed out from other people's cigarettes is called cadmium, and is poisonous to us. Encouragement should be given for partners to give up or to at least smoke outside.

Do you (or have you) live/work in a 'chemical' atmosphere?

(paint, thinners, petrol, fertilisers, hair sprays, colours, etc.)

Even with a strong immune system, toxic sprays, the fumes from paints, airborne pollutants all reach the throat and lungs quickly and may result in respiratory problems. A definite need for vitamin C here as with all pollution questions. At least 1g every day is recommended.

Do you eat your fruit and vegetables without washing them first?

Unwashed fruit and vegetables are covered with pesticides and could have an immediate effect on your respiratory system. Continued eating of such foods can result in wheezing. Wash everything well, especially around the stalks where pesticides accumulate.

Skeletal system

Do you consume more than one pint of milk a day?

It is very important to keep calcium levels up. What you eat during your childhood and teenage years may make all the difference when you are older regarding osteoporosis. Whatever your age, check you are getting enough calcium. Do not forget it comes in green leafy vegetables as well as the dairy produce. However, milk is not a very balanced food – the calcium to magnesium ratio is very poor, making it an acidic food. The more acid we have in the diet, the more acidic the system becomes and the more calcium is taken from the bones, which make drinking milk counterproductive. A good balance is half a pint of skimmed milk and a small pot of bio-yoghurt per day.

Do you avoid weight-bearing exercise?

While all exercise is important, it is the weight-bearing exercise that will keep our bones in good condition. Walking, running and playing squash are all weight bearing; swimming and cycling are not. No matter how little, every encouragement should be given for clients to do some weight-bearing exercise every single day.

Do you eat less than five portions of green leafy vegetables and fruit on a daily basis?

A vital component of being healthy is to have at least five portions of vegetables and fruit daily. It is the vegetables that will provide the essential minerals needed for health and vitality. If you eat less than the recommended five a day then a multivitamin and mineral is strongly recommended.

Do you eat sweet, sugary foods on most days?

A yes answer is not good. Foods like this rob our bodies of vital nutrients. There may be an underlying blood sugar imbalance to look out for. Some clients say they are 'addicted' to sweet foods – which is another indicator of a blood sugar problem.

Do you suffer with any type of arthritis?

Arthritis is an inflammatory condition in the body. One cause can be too much refined food, red meat, a diet high in saturated fats and sugars. These items make series II prostaglandins in the body which are inflammatory. Your clients need anti-inflammatory foods and supplements. Green vegetables and fruit and lots of oily fish, plus a good supplement regime.

Urinary/detox system

Do you suffer with fluid retention?

Fluid retention is a complex subject and not one that should be overlooked. Clients usually need to drink more fluid themselves as the first course of action, and gentle regular daily exercise is always helpful. It is a sign that the body is not eliminating efficiently. Diuretics should be natural ones, of which there are many; try watercress, celery, and all the fruits and vegetables.

Have you ever suffered with thrush or cystitis?

Cystitis is a urinary tract infection, which would suggest a compromised immune system. Thrush is a fungal infection, sometimes the result of antibiotic use and one of the symptoms of candida albicans. Cranberry juice and garlic are the first immediate action followed by a full consultation from a nutritional therapist.

Do you suffer from chronic fatigue?

Many reasons for this, but often low blood sugars are one cause, especially if the client feels very tired after lunch. An underactive thyroid is sometimes also involved. A serious examination of the diet with a full client history is essential. Daily supplements of a multivitamin and mineral and a visit to a nutritional therapist would be recommended.

Do you have more than two alcoholic drinks a day?

One glass of red wine is reported to be beneficial for the cardiovascular system. Two glasses could be harmful. There are reports and studies showing a case for and against. Alcohol is nutritionally void and often contains only empty calories. If the client had candida then alcohol would have to be strictly avoided. Keep alcohol for special occasions and then limit it.

Do you suffer with eczema or psoriasis?

This would again indicate a compromised detoxification system where the kidneys and liver were not working efficiently and the toxins in the body were being released by the skin – also an organ of detoxification. A liver cleanse could be recommended here, or herbal remedies to support the liver. Plenty of water, and the purest, cleanest food obtainable.

Do you suffer from acne or poor skin condition?

Often a sign of zinc deficiency, especially in puberty, where the zinc is being used to mature the reproductive system resulting in the skin suffering. Again, plenty of water and a zinc supplement. Vitamin A is also recommended for skin conditions, plus lots of fresh air and exercise.

Do you feel you have a sensitivity to chemicals?

Many respiratory complaints are the result of airborne substances we have become sensitive to. Perfumes, paints, pollens, yeasts and new carpets can all cause problems. An allergy specialist may be able to pinpoint substances and there are homeopathic remedies to become desensitised to the offending substance.

Do you have any unexplained itching?

Unexplained itching could be many things. Allergy springs to mind and also the skin trying to detox if the kidneys and liver become sluggish.

Do you drink less than one litre of water every day?

Bad news if the answer is yes. This is probably the most important thing we can do for good general health. Really encourage your clients to take up water. Do it yourself and see the difference. Remember to practice what you preach!

Do you suffer with dull headaches?

Dull headaches could be a sign of dehydration, allergy or stress. Lots of water, rest and every emphasis on relaxation.

Nervous system

Do you suffer from any type of headache?

Diet can play an important part regarding headaches. It may be that the client is consuming too much of one type of food such as wheat, cheese, or other type of dairy food and may have an intolerance to this food which causes the headaches.

Do you suffer with migraine headaches?

Migraine can be triggered by allergies and may be relieved by identifying and avoiding the problem foods.

Do you suffer with panic attacks?

Panic attacks are often the result of excessive anxiety and/or stress. Diet is important in situations involving anxiety and stress. Immediate advice is to reduce stress levels, take up yoga, meditation or visualisation. Avoid all junk food and concentrate on eating a really healthy diet of whole foods.

Do you often find that you are irritable/jumpy?

Anti-anxiety and general calming effects on the nervous system have been observed from taking black cohosh. Could be related to PMS – needs to be checked. This could also be a symptom of low blood sugar levels/hypoglycemia. Ask what the client does to reduce stress levels. What does she/he understand about stress. It is important to take up relaxing activities like walking, yoga, and meditation.

Do you feel that you lose your temper easily?

Again, could be a symptom of low blood sugar levels, PMS, or excessive stress and anxiety. A calming herb should be recommended and a good look at the client's diet.

Muscular/energy system

Is your energy less now than it used to be?

Energy levels need not drop as we get older. If your energy is less now that it used to be it could be a symptom of low blood sugar levels. Too high a carbohydrate diet, a vegetarian diet for example, without sufficient protein and fats to balance is often the cause for energy slumps and feeling tired and lethargic.

Do you avoid exercise due to tiredness?

This is a typical low blood sugar level question. Many clients would love to exercise but just do not have the energy. By changing what they eat and quite often when they eat, energy levels can be restored and exercise can resume. Small frequent meals containing carbohydrates, proteins and essential fatty acids at each meal and snack time, can change the body's chemical activity so much, the client will be running to the gym!

Do you sweat a lot or get excessively thirsty?

Diabetics get excessively thirsty and thirst is one of the symptoms that build up over the years in clients who handle sugar badly. It is called the glucose tolerance factor and unless it is kept in check, could result insulin resistance or even diabetes much in later life. Sweating without exercise is also another factor in the glucose tolerance factor.

Do you get dizzy or irritable if you don't eat often?

A typical reaction for people with low blood sugar. Eating little and often is the first course of action. Each meal or snack should include complex carbohydrate, protein and essential fatty acids. The protein and fat will slow down the release of sugar in the body.

Do you often feel drowsy during the day

This also relates to the glucose tolerance factor. If yes then more protein, less carbohydrate may be necessary for particular clients. A jacket potato and beans for lunch could have a client falling asleep at the desk, whereas a jacket potato with tuna plus a mixed salad with a trickle of olive oil would probably have an entirely different effect.

Do you sometimes lose concentration?

A sign that the brain is not receiving glucose. Eating little and often may help the situation, and again, if breakfast and/or lunch is a carbohydrate only affair, then give suggestions of adding a little protein and essential fatty acids (nuts, seeds, olives, avocado) not saturated fats.

Do you suffer with cramps?

Usually a magnesium deficiency as one of the functions of magnesium is to relax the muscles. Check with the client to see if they eat green leafy vegetables. Encourage them to eat more, or suggest a calcium:magnesium supplement.

Do you suffer with muscular aches and pains?

No matter what age your client, suffering with aches and pains is something that can be overcome. Green leafy vegetables are full of magnesium and are of immense benefit for muscles. The supplement MSM (organic sulphur) is excellent for aches and pains and comes highly recommended. Gentle exercise, although the last thing they probably want to do, is also a great remedy and very effective. Also investigate food allergy.

Do you have much injury through playing sport?

All body systems need supporting, including the muscular and skeletal systems. Good quality multivitamins and minerals and plenty of water, on a daily basis, are good recommendations. Most athletes need more supplementation than average as they are working hard at their sport. The diet needs working on or injury will occur through dehydration and malnutrition. People can be fit without being healthy, and look good on the outside while being weak on the inside. MSM is another good supplement for athletes, as is chromium.

Do you drink less than eight glasses of water every day?

Muscles need water. So many symptoms can be put down to dehydration. The energy system of the body needs water – not in tea or coffee and not carbonated; just plain bottled spring water. This will reduce injury and hydrate.

Supplementary questions

Here are some additional questions you may like to ask your client, with explanations of the answers – they are not in any particular order and some may appear similar to some of the questions above.

Do you go out of your way to avoid sweet, sugary, foods?

The answer to this should be yes. If the answer is no then you should be giving encouragement to your client that sweet, sugary foods upset the delicate blood sugar balance in the body, as well as containing little or no nutrients. Quality should be a key word when selecting food.

Do you drink 6–8 glasses of water *every* day?

One of the most important aspects of good nutrition is to have 6–8 glasses of water every day. The human body is 70 per cent water and we need it to flush the system taking toxic substances with it. Essential for a clear, healthy skin.

Do you normally eat at regular times?

Unfortunately, many people do not. Read the paragraph on timing and ask the client to do the exercise in writing down the times they are going to eat their food. This one small change in their life could make so much difference to how they feel.

Do you have a bowel movement every day?

The answer to this should be yes, but being 'regular' to some people may be every other day, which is fine. However, they should work on going at least once a day.

How much water do you drink in one day? Is this bottled water or tap water?

This is a chemical question. Bottled water is better, tap water may contain harmful additives that are building up inside your client that may result in internal pollution. The answer should be 6–8 glasses a day. If it is less than this then the body may become dehydrated and hold-on to water.

Salt intake – do you add salt to your cooking and/or add it to your food?

This is a cardiovascular question. The more salt a client has in the diet, the higher risk of cardiovascular disease. If the answer to either of these statements is yes your recommendation would be to cut down on at least one or better still both methods of adding salt.

How much sugar do you add to your diet daily in tea/coffee/on cereals/in food?

The more sugar in the diet, the more refined it probably is and it will give rise to weight gain and unbalanced blood sugar in the body. Sugar has no nutrients – there are much better ways to make food sweet.

How many pints of milk do you drink in a week?

A general nutrition question regarding calcium. Obtaining enough calcium (800gm for adults) is essential for healthy bones and teeth and for the prevention of osteoporosis. Your recommendations will depend upon the answer you are given. You must stress the importance of calcium and give other sources for the client's information.

How many times a week do you eat red meat?

Another general nutrition question. While red meat provides important protein, it is also a source of saturated fat and could contain traces of antibiotics or growth hormones, which would be undesirable. Three times a week would be the maximum and encouragement to eat a protein like chicken, turkey, or fish which has less saturated fat.

Do you eat at regular times?

An important question. Many people eat at irregular times. Sometimes *when* you eat is more important than *what* you eat. Regulating eating times is the first step in good weight management. Breakfast is, of course, the most important meal and every encouragement should be given to clients to eat a healthy breakfast. Without breakfast, blood sugar levels may be low and clients may be 'running on empty' to get to work/school. If the first thing they have is coffee/tea/biscuits which will push blood sugar levels up and this pattern of rising and falling could continue throughout the day.

Are you vegetarian/vegan

If the answer is yes – you need to ensure that the client is receiving sufficient calcium and protein from their diet. Many clients, especially teenagers, are unaware of the importance of these nutrients for normal body and brain development. Daily servings of chips and crisps may well be vegetarian but will also lead to malnutrition.

Do you suffer from fluid retention?

If the answer is yes, first of all ascertain whether it is cyclic. If yes then it is more than likely involved with the hormonal response to the monthly cycle. If no, then ask if the client is on medication. Many medications for blood pressure, anxiety and migraines have side effects of fluid retention and/or weight gain. Check if the fluid retention started about the same time as the medication. Ask the client to discuss with her GP if they think the medication could be a cause. Advise the client of some of the many natural diuretics available to them.

Which foods would you find hard to give up?

It is highly likely that the foods a client will include in this section may well be foods that they are sensitive to. Wheat is a common answer. Encourage clients to eat wheat only two or three times a week. Study their three-day food plan. Are they eating wheat three times a day? e.g. Weetabix for breakfast, a sandwich for lunch followed by pasta for dinner? This is very common and should be discouraged. Always give alternatives. In this case encourage rice, quinoa, corn, barley, or rye.

Do you ever experience joint pains?

If yes then this could be connected to allergy, candida or hormonal imbalances. Further questions would be necessary.

Do you suffer from food cravings?

Another multi-faceted question. If yes, they could be connected with allergy, glucose intolerance or candida. Further investigations are needed.

Do you especially crave foods premenstrually?

Unlike the question above, these food cravings are hormonally based.

Do you live in a city or busy road?

If yes then this client would probably be breathing in excessive car fumes, which are 'anti-nutrients' and would be having a detrimental effect on their health generally. Vitamin C is recommended for any type of pollution problem.

Do you live or work in a smoky atmosphere?

Another pollution question. Cadmium – the substance breathed out by smokers – is just as detrimental to your health as nicotine. Vitamin C is the recommended nutrient.

Do you have athlete's foot, ringworm, jock itch or other chronic fungal infections of the skin or nails?

If yes this may be one indication of a candida infestation. Other questions would need to be asked.

Do your stools float?

The answer should be a yes. Eating a high fibre diet with plenty of fruit and vegetables and sufficient protein and fats will ensure good bowel function.

Are you trying to become pregnant?

Much can be done from a nutritional point of view for women trying to conceive. Both the male and female should take a zinc supplement on a daily basis as this is a vital mineral in the fertility process. Avoid coffee, tea, alcohol and anything synthetic and enjoy the best possible diet by way of green leafy vegetables and low fat protein. Maybe a complete lifestyle change for some people – but look at the rewards.

Do you have excess hair on your body?

Possible hormonal imbalance. Recommend your clients sees a nutritional therapist who will be able to look into the area more thoroughly and advise if any hormone tests are needed.

Do you get more than three colds a year?

If you are prone to colds then Vitamin C is even more important. Take up to bowel tolerance. Everyone has a different level of bowel tolerance of vitamin C, but if the body is saturated with it, then cold viruses cannot survive. Start slowly, and gradually build up increasing a little more each day until the stool becomes quite soft – that will be your level of tolerance. Vitamin C is probably the safest of all the vitamins. At the onset of a cold take 1g and repeat every four hours for the first three days. Continue taking at a level you feel is right for you. This could be 2g daily or it could be up to 5g daily. Find out your own tolerance.

Do you often do two or three tasks simultaneously?

Mental stress, which could result in insomnia. Doing one thing thoroughly, at a time, usually gets more done at the end of the day. Time management needed for clients with a daily achievable 'to do' list.

Do you have eczema, asthma or arthritis?

Very often a deficiency in essential fatty acids. Supplementing EFAs by way of fish oils and evening primrose or starflower oils may have positive results. See separate entries in Part II of this book.

Do you bruise easily?

Easy bruising is a sign of vitamin C deficiency. Vitamin C strengthens capillary walls and makes collagen.

Do you suffer from broken capillaries or thread veins?

Another sign of vitamin C deficiency. Vitamin C strengthens capillary walls.

Glossary

absorption the process of transferring nutrients from the digestive tract to the body

acetylcholine a stimulating neurotransmitter, associated with memory, mental alertness, learning ability and concentration. Acetylcholine deficiency can lead to memory loss, depression, mood disorders and possibly even Alzheimer's disease. It is also the neurotransmitter at all nerve–muscle cell junctions that allows skeletal muscles to contract, controlling movement, coordination and muscle tone.

additive a substance or mixture, other than a basic food, which is added in the production, processing, storage, or packaging of foods

adrenalin a stimulating neurotransmitter associated with motivation, drive, energy, and the stress response. Produced by the adrenal glands it is also classified as a hormone, which is a chemical messenger produced by the glands of the endocrine system

albumin a protein that, with haemoglobin, comprises the two principal proteins in the blood. Albumin is found in egg white and in milk

amino acids component parts of proteins. There are twenty-two amino acids necessary for life. Twelve of these, known as nonessential amino acids, are liberated during digestion. The other ten, known as essential amino acids, are not produced in adequate amounts by the body and therefore must be derived from food

amphetamines popularly known as speed and used for years by people needing a lift. Amphetamine blocks neurons' reabsorption of the neurotransmitters noradrenalin and dopamine, but it also triggers their release, doubling its potency. Formerly used in diet pills and are now prescribed for children with ADD

anorexia lack of appetite for food

anorexia nervosa psychological disturbance resulting in a refusal to eat; sensations of hunger are usually not felt and there may be a restriction of the diet to particular foods; the result is considerable weight loss, atrophy of tissue and a fall in the basal metabolic rate

antacids medications used to relieve indigestion by neutralising acid in the stomach. Common brands include Alka Seltzer, Tums and Rennies

antagonist a competing factor that counteracts the action of another factor. When a drug displaces a vitamin from its site of action, the drug renders the vitamin ineffective and thus acts as a vitamin antagonist

antibodies large proteins of the blood and body fluids, produced by the immune system in response to the invasion of the body by foreign molecules (usually proteins called antigens). Antibodies combine with and inactivate the foreign invaders, thus protecting the body

antigens substances that elicit the formation of antibodies or an inflammation reaction from the immune system. A bacterium, a virus, a toxin, and a protein in food that causes allergy are all examples or antigens

antioxidant a widely used synthetic or natural substance added to a product to prevent or delay its deterioration by the action of the oxygen in the air. Vegetable oils and prepared foods contain antioxidants

arginine an essential amino acid in children

ascorbic acid *see* Vitamin C

axillary temperature axillary temperature is the temperature taken from the under arm area

basal metabolism the minimum amount of energy produced by the body at rest. This amount is measured in calories

B-complex vitamins a group of water-soluble vitamins necessary for normal growth and function of the human body. These include biotin, choline, folic acid, niacin, pantothenic acid, riboflavin (B2), pyridoxine (B6), and cyanocobalamin (B12). *See* specific vitamins

beta-carotene a plant form of vitamin A. Food sources include carrots and sweet potatoes. It has a characteristic yellow colour and, as an additive, may be used to colour food

bile a substance produced in the gall bladder. It helps break down fat

bulimia nervosa a psychiatric illness characterised by powerful and intractable urges to overeat, followed by self-induced vomiting and excessive use of purgatives. Mostly affects women between 15–30 – considered to be a variant of anorexia nervosa

calciferol *see* vitamin D

calcium an essential mineral necessary for building and maintaining bones and teeth, for blood clotting, and for nerve function. It is found in milk and milk products and in green vegetables. Its absorption into the body depends upon an adequate supply of vitamin D

calorie a unit of energy measurement used to measure heat-producing or energy-producing value in food

carbohydrate a sugar or starch providing the major source of energy in the body. Each gram of carbohydrate yields 4 calories

carcinogens substances or agents that are capable of causing cancer

carotene natural pigments in red, orange and yellow plant foods (carrots, tomatoes and peppers for example)

carotenoids a large family of red, orange and yellow plant substances found in many fruits and vegetables

casein the principal protein of milk, the basis of curd and cheese

catabolism the breakdown of tissues within the body

catalyst a compound that facilitates chemical reactions without itself being changed in the process

cellulose a carbohydrate substance forming the skeleton of most plant structures. It adds bulk to food but has no nutritional value

chelate A substance that can grasp the positive ions of a metal

chelated minerals which have been treated to alter their electrical charge, usually by binding them chemically to a harmless salt such as a gluconate, citrate, picolinate, aspartate, or another 'ate' substance

cholesterol a substance present in foods of animal origin that is also made within the body. It is essential for the production of hormones and for the repair of membranes

chyme the semi-liquid mass of partly digested food expelled by the stomach into the duodenum

choline a component of lecithin sometimes classified as a B-complex vitamin

citric acid an acid obtained from citrus fruits. It is used for a sour flavour in beverages and confectionery and as an antioxidant in fats and margarine

cobalt a trace mineral (a component of vitamin B12) found in liver

co-enzyme-Q-10 a co-enzyme is a substance that enhances the action of other enzymes. An enzyme is a protein that catalyses chemical changes in other substances, remaining unchanged by the process. First discovered in 1957, Co-Q-10 works everywhere in the body to increase energy and fend off disease

colostrum the milk produced by mammals during the first few days after parturition; human colostrum contains more protein (2 per cent compared with 1 per cent) slightly less lactose, considerably less fat (3 per cent compared with 5 per cent) and overall slightly less energy than mature milk

complete proteins those proteins that supply all the essential amino acids to maintain body tissues and promote growth. They are found in meat, poultry, fish, eggs, milk and cheese

copper a mineral necessary for the formation of haemoglobin and connective tissues, and for the body's use of ascorbic acid. It is found in liver, oysters, meat, legumes, nuts and whole grain foods

cyanocobalamin *see* vitamin B12

dehydration the condition in which body water output exceeds input. Symptoms include thirst, dry skin and mucous membranes, rapid heartbeat, low blood pressure and weakness

digestion the process by which food is converted in the intestinal tract into chemical substances that can be absorbed by the body

digestive enzymes proteins found in digestive juices that act on food substances causing them to break down into simple compounds. Available in supplement form

disaccharide a carbohydrate composed of two simple sugars. Lactose, maltose and sucrose are disaccharides

DMAE one of the building blocks of acetylcholine (the other being choline). It is a precursor for choline which crosses readily into the brain, hence helping to make acetylcholine. Improves concentration and learning. It is a great natural mind and memory booster

double-blind research research in which neither the subject nor the researchers know which subjects are members of the experimental group and which are serving as control subjects, until after the research is over

electron transport chain (ETC)   the final pathway in energy metabolism where the electrons from hydrogen are passed to oxygen and the energy released is trapped in the bonds of ATP (adenosine triphosphate)

endocrine gland   a gland whose function is to secrete a hormone into the blood that has a specific effect on another gland or organ

enzyme   a substance that catalyses specific chemical reactions in plants and animals, as in the digestion of foods

essential fatty acid   a fatty acid necessary for growth and for the well-being of vital organs and skin which cannot be produced by the body and must therefore be provided by food

fats   compounds composed of fatty acids and glycerol. Fats are derived from plants and animals, occurring usually in combination with proteins and carbohydrates. Fat is the most concentrated source of energy; each gram of fat yields nine calories. It is necessary for repairing and replacing body cells and for the absorption and protection of the fat-soluble vitamins D, D, E and K. Fats are either saturated or unsaturated. Sources of unsaturated fats include vegetable oils, wheatgerm, and nuts. Animal fats such as lard, fatty meats, butter, cream, and egg yolks are sources of saturated fats

fat-soluble vitamins   these are vitamins A, D, E and K. They can be stored in the body

fatty acids   organic acids that combine with glycerol to form fat. There are saturated, monounsaturated, and polyunsaturated fatty acids. *See* essential fatty acid

fibre   in a nutritional context, a term referring to dietary fibre, the indigestible parts of food, necessary for intestinal functioning

free radicals   unstable and highly reactive atoms or molecules that have one or more unpaired electrons in the outer orbital

fructose   a simple sugar found mainly in fruits and also in sugar cane and honey

galatose   a simple sugar derived from lactose

gestation   the period from conception to birth. For human beings gestation lasts from 38–42 weeks. Pregnancy is often divided into thirds, called trimesters

gluten   one of the proteins of wheat and other grains. It gives dough its elastic and adhesive character

glyceride   a substance that is part fatty acid and part glycerol. Monoglycerides and diglycerides are used as food additives. They act as emulsifiers in baked goods, margarine, peanut butter and sweets

glycerol   a substance found in animal fats and vegetable oils and in the body itself as one of the products of digestion of fats

goitrogens   a group of foods that hinder iodine utilisation. Goitrogens are therefore thyroid antagonists and are found in such foods as cabbage, kale, Brussels sprouts, cauliflower, broccoli and kohlrabi

gram (g)   a measure of weight used in the metric system. One ounce = 28 grams

haemicellulose   a carbohydrate found in plants, more soluble in water than cellulose. It is a fibre that gives bulk to food but has no nutritive value

haemoglobin   the globular protein of the red blood cells that carries oxygen from the lungs to the cells throughout the body

heavy metals   any of a number of mineral ions such as mercury and lead, so-called because they are of relatively high atomic weight. Many heavy metals are poisonous

helicobactor pylori   *H. pylori*. This is a bacteria that survives in the acidic environment of the stomach. It can cause ulcers and can lead to serious disease. Although this bacteria is known to be the most common cause of ulcers, many people with *H. pylori* do not develop ulcers

histamine   a substance produced by cells of the immune system as part of a local immune reaction to an antigen; it participates in causing inflammation

histidine   an essential amino acid in children

hormone   the chemical product of a gland, organ, or certain cells of an organ (transported by the blood or other body fluids) that has a specific regulatory effect upon some other cells

hydrogenation   a chemical process by which hydrogens are added to monounsaturated or polyunsaturated fats to reduce the number of double bonds, making the fats more saturated (solid) and more resistant to oxidation (protecting against rancidity). Hydrogenation produces trans-fatty acids

hydrolysis   a chemical reaction in which a major reactant is split into two products, with the addition of a hydrogen atom (H) to one and a hydroxyl group (OH) to the other (from water, H_2O)

hypertension   the correct term for higher than normal blood pressure. Hypertension that develops without an identifiable cause is known as essential or primary hypertension. Hypertension that is caused by a specific disorder such as kidney disease is known as secondary hypertension

hypochloridia   low level of hydrochloric acid

hypotension   low blood pressure

hypothalamus   the brain centre that controls activities such as maintenance of water balance, regulation of body temperature and control of appetite

inflammatory bowel disease – IBD   a collective name for Crohn's disease and ulcerative colitis

incomplete proteins   those proteins that do not supply enough of all of the essential amino acids. They are not capable of replacing or building new tissues and must be supplemented with other foods to supply the essential complete proteins. Examples of foods that contain incomplete proteins are legumes and grains

insulin   a hormone formed by the pancreas and secreted into the blood. It is essential for the maintenance of the proper blood sugar level. It is also used therapeutically in the treatment of diabetes mellitus

interferon   the first line of defence against invading viruses; they are proteins made by cells under viral attack and serve to inhibit the multiplication of a broad range of viruses

intrinsic factor   a glycoprotein (a protein with short polysaccharide chains attached) manufactured in the stomach that aids in the absorption of vitamin B12

iodine   a mineral, essential for formation of hormones, secreted by the thyroid gland, which controls the basal metabolism of the body

iron   a mineral, an essential constituent of haemoglobin. Its absorption is promoted by vitamin C

isoleucine   an essential amino acid

international unit (IU)   a unit of measurement, internationally accepted, to express amounts of vitamins A, D, E

Joule   a measurement of heat or energy used in the metric system. One calorie equals 4.184 joules

ketone   a substance that increases simultaneously in the blood and in the urine during starvation, diabetic acidosis, pregnancy, after ether anaesthesia, and after protein-sparing diets. A ketone is one of the end products of fat metabolism

kilogram (kg)   a measure of weight used in the metric system. One kilogram = 1000 grams

lactose   the sugar occurring naturally in milk. It is used as an additive in infant foods, bakery products, confectionery, and pharmaceuticals and in some frozen vegetables to add sweetness

lecithin   a fatty substance found in plant and animal tissues. It is an emulsifier produced by the liver, and is the source of the nutrient choline. Lecithin, working with bile, helps the body absorb cholesterol

leucine   an essential amino acid

linoleic acid   an essential fatty acid, necessary for the growth and the well-being of vital organs and skin. It is a polyunsaturated fatty acid

lipid   a term for fat

lysine   an essential amino acid

magnesium   a mineral. It is a constituent of bones, teeth, muscle and red blood cells and is important in energy metabolism

malic acid   an acid obtained from a number of fruits, for example apples

MAO inhibiting factor   a type of antidepressant drug that inhibits the enzyme monoamine oxidase, that breaks down neurotransmitters, thereby having the effect of keeping more neurotransmitters in action

metabolism   the process of transforming and utilising substances within the body. Through this process energy is produced and body tissues are broken down and rebuilt continuously

methionine   An essential amino acid

microgram (mcg)   measures of weight in the metric system, equal to one millionth of a gram

milligram (mg)   measures of weight in the metric system, equal to one thousandth of a gram

mineral   a substance found in skeletal structure and tissues of the body

mitrochondria   the cellular organelles responsible for producing ATP aerobically; made of membranes (lipid and protein) with enzymes mounted on them

monosaccharide   a simple sugar. Glucose, fructose, and galactose are simple sugars

monosodium glutamate   an additive used to enhance flavour

monounsaturated fats   fat in which monounsaturated fatty acids predominate. They include olive oil, groundnut oil, avocado, and most nuts

MRM   mechanically recovered meat (MRM) is the carcass scrapings removed from bones once the best meat has been removed

myoglobin   the oxygen-holding protein of the muscle cells

neurons   nerve cells; the structural and functional units of the nervous system. Neurons initiate and conduct nerve transmissions

neurotransmitter a molecule capable of stimulating a neuron. Neurotransmitters are therefore the nervous system's chemicals of communication and are usually made out of amino acids

niacin a member of the vitamin B complex. It is needed for a healthy nervous system, healthy tissues, proper brain function, and healthy skin

nicotinic acid niacin

nitrates a natural constituent of plants. After harvesting some of the nitrates are converted to nitrites

nitrites essential agent in preserving meat by pickling, since it inhibits the growth of clostridia. Nitrites can react with haemoglobin to form methaemoglobin, especially in young children

neural tube defects a serious central nervous system birth defect that can often result in lifelong disability or death

nutrient a substance that provides nourishment for the body – i.e. proteins, carbohydrates, fats, vitamins, minerals and water

obesity a body mass index BMI of over 30 is considered to be obese. A body mass index BMI of 40 or greater or 100 lbs or more overweight for an average adult is termed clinically severe obesity

oedema an excess accumulation of fluid in the body tissues

oleic acid an unsaturated fatty acid present as a glyceride in most fats

osteomalacia occurs in vitamin D-deficient adults in whom calcium cannot be absorbed into the body, resulting in weak bones

pantothenic acid one of the vitamin B-complex group necessary to convert carbohydrates, fats, and proteins into energy

pectin a substance contained in the cell walls of various fruits and vegetables – e.g. apples, oranges and lemons. It is used to thicken jams and as an emulsifier and stabiliser in many food products

peristalsis wavelike muscular contraction of the GI (gastro intestinal) tract which pushes its contents along

pH a measure of the concentration of H+ ions that expresses a substance's acidity or alkalinity. The lower the pH, the higher the H+ ion concentration and the stronger the acid. A pH above 7 is alkaline or base (a solution in which OH– ions predominate)

phagocytes white blood cells that have the ability to ingest and destroy foreign substances. The process by which phagocytes engulf and destroy foreign materials is called phagocytosis

phenolics phenolics are natural flavourings, colourings and preservatives found in foods. Examples are tyramine and coumarin

phenylalanine an essential amino acid

phenylketonuria a genetic disease in people who are unable to metabolise phenylalanine

phospholipid a type of lipid or fat contained in all biological cells. It is an emulsifying agent with an affinity for water and is therefore essential to the digestion and absorption of fats

phosphorus a mineral present in the tissues of all animals and plants. It is important for the metabolism of fat and carbohydrates and helps to build bones and teeth

phytosterol sterols occurring in the oil or fat of plants, not of animals. Groundnut oil, sesame oil, and olive oil are sources of phytosterol

placebo an inert, harmless medication given to provide comfort and hope; a sham treatment used in controlled research studies

polysaccharides   carbohydrates formed from simple sugars. Starch, dextrin, pectin, cellulose, and glycogen are polysaccharides

polyunsaturated fats   fats in which polyunsaturated fatty acids predominate are referred to as saturated fats. They are usually liquid at room temperature and of vegetable origin. They include corn oil, sunflower oil, and sesame seed oil

potassium   a mineral that regulates nervous and muscular sensitivity and the heart rhythm

pre-formed   a substance that is pre-formed, vitamin A for example, can be used immediately by the body

preservative   an additive used to slow down or stop spoilage of foods

protein   a nutrient necessary for life. It contributes to the growth and well being of muscles, bones, organs, skin, hair and nails. *See* complete proteins and incomplete proteins

pyridoxine   *see* vitamin B6

renal   pertaining to the kidneys

retinol   *see* vitamin A

rhizome   the root of a plant or herb that can be used for its beneficial properties

riboflavin   *see* vitamin B2

rickets   a disease caused by a vitamin D deficiency, more common in children than adults. Without sufficient vitamin D, bones cannot absorb enough calcium to grow straight and strong. Today, because of improved nutrition and fortified milk, rickets is rare in the developed world

RNA – ribonucleic acids   RNAs are acids which are found in certain portions of cells and which play key roles in chemical reactions within cells

saccharin   an artificial sweetener over five hundred times sweeter than sugar. It has no nutritive value

salts   sodium chloride. An additive used as a flavouring and a preservative

saturated fats   fats in which saturated fatty acids predominate. They are usually solid at room temperature and of animal origin. They include the fats of whole milk, full-fat soft cheese, butter, eggs, meat, some hydrogenated or solid vegetable fats, and coconut oil

serotonin   a neurotransmitter associated with mood, sleep patterns, dreaming and visions. It influences many physiological functions, including blood pressure, digestion, body temperature and pain sensation. Serotonin also affects our circadian rhythm, the body's response to the cycles of day and night

sodium   an element in the form of table salt (sodium chloride) that maintains the necessary balance of water in the body and regulates muscle and nerve sensitivity

sodium chloride   table salt. *See* sodium

sucrose   a sweet carbohydrate found chiefly in sugar cane and beet sugar. We know it as table sugar

sulphur   sulphur is an essential element in living organisms occurring in the amino acids cysteine and methionine, and therefore in many proteins

supplements   a product that contains one or more dietary ingredients such as vitamins, minerals, herbs, amino acids, or other ingredients used to support the diet

thiamin *see* vitamin B1

tocopherol *see* vitamin E

trans fatty acids the result of polyunsaturated fats undergoing a process called hydrogenation to make them hard, and therefore 'spreadable'. Once hydrogenated the body cannot make use of these once beneficial fats

triglyceride the chief form in which fats occur in humans, animals and vegetables

unsaturated fats fats in which polyunsaturated fatty acids predominate are described as either polyunsaturated or unsaturated fats

vegan a person who eats only plant products

vitamin an organic compound that is essential for the normal growth and maintenance of the human body. The body cannot manufacture vitamins so they must be included in the diet. Fat-soluble vitamins (A, D, E and K) can be stored in the body. Water-soluble vitamins (all of the B-complex group and vitamin C) must be replaced daily

vitamin A retinol, a fat-soluble vitamin that is stored in the liver. It is essential for vision, helps keep body tissues healthy, and promotes cell growth

vitamin B1 thiamin, one of the B-complex vitamins. It is essential for the metabolism of carbohydrates, for the regulation of nerve sensitivity, and for carrying air from the lungs to the tissues

vitamin B2 riboflavin, one of the B-complex vitamins. It is necessary for the metabolism of protein, the healing of tissues, and the optimum condition of tissues and skin

vitamin B6 pyridoxine, one of the B-complex vitamins. It is important in maintaining healthy skin and in preventing certain types of anaemia

vitamin B12 cyanocobalamin, one of the B-complex vitamins. It is essential for normal development of red blood cells and the functioning of all cells, particularly in the bone marrow, nervous system, and intestines

vitamin C ascorbic acid, a water-soluble vitamin that helps the body to resist infection and heal wounds. As an additive it is used as an antioxidant and stabiliser

vitamin D calciferol, a fat-soluble vitamin that helps the body use calcium and phosphorus to build strong bones and teeth

vitamin E tocopherol, the principal form of vitamin D, acts as an antioxidant to help prevent oxygen from destroying vitamins A and C and carotene in the digestive tract and the body cells

vitamin K a fat-soluble vitamin that acts as a coagulant and promotes normal blood clotting

water-soluble vitamins *see* B-complex vitamins; vitamin

zinc a trace mineral that plays an important role in growth and in appetite regulation

UK web links

http://www.nutrition-org.uk/   British Nutrition Foundation website; very good information, search facility, news, education, events, links.

http://www.foodstandards.gov.uk/   The official website of the Food Standards Agency in the UK.

http://www.bournemouth.ac.uk/library_gateways/html/food.html Bournemouth University Library with good links to institutes, organisations and resources.

http://www.maff.gov.uk/   Ministry of Agriculture, Fisheries and Food (UK) links to government guidelines, etc.

http://www.nutsoc.org.uk/   Nutrition Society, links and information.

http://www.bda.uk.com/   New site for the British Dietetic Association, not fully working yet. Old site is at http://www.vois.org/bda/.

http://www.ifrn.bbsrc.ac.uk/   Institute of Food Research (UK) lots of information on all food topics, includes useful bibliographies.

http://library.bma.org.uk/html/librarysearchf.html   British Medical Association Library, very good search facility for information on all nutrition topics.

http://www.fabflour.co.uk/power/powerf/htm   Aimed at school level but features inforation on the nutritional value of bread.

http://www.diabetic.org.uk/main1/htm   Diabetes Insight (UK) information and support.

http://www.dspace.dial.pipex.com/town/park/gfm11/index.htm   No Cow's Milk For Me Thanks! UK-based milk allergy site; links, books and articles.

http://www.britegg.co.uk/nutritn/nutr_frm.htm   Tables and nutritional data on eggs. Aimed at school level.

http://www.thinkfast.co.uk   Fun site aimed at school level, but with good information on fast foods.

http://www.alzheimers.org.uk/   UK-based Alzheimer's information page.

http://www.cannedfood.co.uk/   Aimed at school level but includes nutritional tables and information about canned goods.

http://www.gmworld.newscientist.com/   Articles and debates on GM food.

http://www.foodfuture.org.uk/   Information about genetically modified foods.

http://inet.uni-c.dk/~iaotb/bse.htm   UK web directory for articles and reports on the BSE crisis.

http://web.bham.ac.uk/bcm4ght6/res/html   UK E-coli Index for links and articles.

http://www.fkk-reading.co.uk/   Links to Food Knowledge and Know-How resources for food businesses.

http://www.fst.rdg.ac.uk/   Reading University Department of Food Science and Technology research groups, etc.

http://www.ifst.org   Institute of Food Science and Technology (UK); very good links page, FAQs, information, official statements.

http://www.lfra.co.uk.lfra/   Leatherhead Food Research Association; the food industry website with information about ingredients.

http://www.gn.apc.org/pesticidestrust/   The Pesticides Trust (UK) information and articles.

http://www.csl.gov.uk/   Central Science Laboratory (UK) – allergies, pesticides, testing, assessment, standards, surveys, research and analysis. I had problems with running this site though.

http://www.foodhygienecontrol.hea.org.uk   Aliens in Our Food – aimed at school level but has lots of information about hygiene and bacteria.

http://www.allergyfoundation.com/   Information and help on the subject of allergies.

http://www.just-food.com/   Online food industry magazine.

http://www.icco.org   An exciting website about chocolate, which also covers its nutrition value!

Useful addresses

Biocare
Lakeside Centre
180 Lifford Lane, Kings Norton,
Birmingham B30 3NU
Tel: 0121 433 8720 (Technical team)

Health Plus Limited
Dolphin House, 30 Lushington Road,
Eastbourne,
East Sussex BN21 4LL
Tel: 01323 737374

Higher Nature Limited
The Nutrition Centre,
Burwash Common,
East Sussex TN19 7LX
Tel: 01435 882880

Biolab Medical Unit
9 Weymouth Street,
London W1N 3FF
Tel: 020 7636 5959
Referral from a GP required via nutrition consultant

Doctors Laboratory plc
58 Wimpole Street, London
W1M 7DE
Tel: 020 7224 1001
No appointment necessary for many endocrine tests: impotence, menopause, thyroid, HRT, female and male infertility, prostate, anaemia, and allergy screens

Health Interlink – Diagnostic Laboratory Service
Redbourn,
Hertfordshire
AL3 7JX
Tel: 01582 794094

Further reading

Barnes, Broda, *Hypothyroidism: The Unsuspected Illness*, Harper & Row (1976)

Bolen, Dr Barbara, *Breaking the Bonds of Irritable Bowel Syndrome*, New Harbinger (2000)

Childs, Carolyn, *Food and Nutrition in the Early Years*, Hodder and Stoughton (2001)

Holford, Patrick, *Optimum Nutrition Bible*, Piatkus (1997)

Kutsky, Roman J., *Handbook of Vitamins and Hormones*, Van Nostrand Reinhold Company (1976)

Lazarides, Linda, *The Waterfall Diet*, Piatkus (1999)

Lee, Dr J, *What Your Doctor Didn't Tell You About Menopause*, Warner Books (1996)

Marber, Ian and Edgson, Vicki, *In Bed with the Food Doctor*, Collins and Brown (2002)

Neil, K. and Holford P., *Balancing Hormones Naturally*, Piatkus (1998)

Oliver, Suzannah, *Allergy Solutions*, Simon & Schuster (2000)

Pizzorno, J. N., *Total Wellness*, Prima Publishing (1997)

Scarfe, C., *How to Improve your Digestion and Absorption*, ION Press (1989)

Sharon, M. Dr., *Complete Nutrition*, Prion Books (2001)

Tortora, Gerald J. and Reynolds, Sandra, *The Principals of Anatomy and Physiology*, 10th edition, John Wiley and Sons (2002)

Udo, Erasmus, *Fats that Heal, Fats That Kill*, Alive Books (1970)

Whitney, E., Rolfes, S., *Understanding Nutrition*, 9th edn, Wadsworth (2001)

Index

absorption 309
additive 309
adrenalin 309
albumin 309
alcohol 242, 267
Alfalfa 91
algae 91
   blue-green 91, 92–3
   chlorella 91, 92
   spirulina 91–2
allergies 169–70, 179, 180, 197–9,
   229–30
aloe vera 79
amenorrhoea 240
amino acids 129, 148, 214, 309
   branched chain 27
   conditionally essential 23
   essential 22, 25–7
   functions/facts 26–7
   non-essential 22
angina 147–8
anorexia 309
anorexia nervosa 309
anti-depressants 85, 86–7
anti-nutrients 5
antibodies 23, 309
antigens 84, 309
antihistamines 84
antioxidants 57–8, 309
anxiety 226–7
arginine 26, 309
arteriosclerosis 149–50
artichoke 177
ascorbic acid *see* vitamin C
asthma 248–50
atherosclerosis 149–50
athletes 135–6
attention deficit disorder (ADD)
   198–9
autogenics 229

babies
   breast/formula feed 133
   early years 134
   growth rate 133
   weaning 133–4
barley grass 93–4
basal metabolism 310
bee pollen 94–6
beta-carotene 310
bilberries 274
bile 310
biotin (vitamin H, coenyzme R) 53–4
Black Cohosh 79–80, 88, 189
blood pressure 140, 155
blood sugar levels 17
blueberries 274
body mass index (BMI) 289–90
bones 140
boron 68
brewer's yeast 153
bromelain 254
bronchitis 250–1
bulimia nervosa 310
burdock 268–9incontinence 269–70

cabbage 96–7, 180
caffeine 157–8, 226, 242
calciferol 310
calcium (Ca) 60–2, 310
calendula 212
calories 281, 310
camomile 170, 178, 212, 219, 226,
   274
cancer 140, 201
   hormone-dependent 201–2
   recommendations 202
candida 203–5
carbohydrates 4, 15–16, 119, 163,
   310
   digestion/absorption 17–18

loading before/after sport 21
   simple/complex 16–17, 19
cardiovascular system 145
   cholestrol 146
   clotting 146
   common disorders 147–60
   disease 139, 140, 146
   equilibrium 146
   functions 145–6
   general recommendations 160
   homocysteine 146–7
   questions explained 294–5
   transport 146
carnitine 207–8
carob 170
carotene 42, 310
carotenoids 42, 310
carrots 151–2, 156, 180
casein 310
catabolism 310
catalyst 6, 310
cayenne 267
celiac disease 166–7
cellulite 206–7
cellulose 310
chelated 310
chilblains 150–1
cholesterol 33, 81, 140, 151–3, 310
   functions 34–5
   levels 35
choline 54–5, 310
chondroitin sulphate (CS) 262
chromium (Cr) 68–9, 153, 157
chronic fatigue syndrome (CFS)
   207–9
chyme 17, 310
cinnamon 180
circulation 82–3
citiric acid 310
cobalt 310

coenzyme-Q10 141–2
coffee 148, 170
colonic irrigation 166
colostrum 310
comfrey 180, 274
common cold 252–3
complete proteins 311
constipation 140, 154, 167–8
copper (Cu) 69, 311
coumarin 274
cramp 219
cranberry juice 271
Crohn's disease 168–9
cyanocobalamin *see* vitamin B12
cystitis 270–1

dehydration 311
detoxification system *see*
    urinary/detoxification systems
DHEA (dehydroepiandrosterone)
    241
diabetes 184–5
diarrhoea 169–71
diet planning principles 279
    abundance 280
    adequacy 280
    alance 280
    BMI 289–91
    calorie control 281
    consultation form 281–2
    empty calories 281
    food diary 288
    liquids 280
    nutrient density 280–1
    timing 289
    weakest link questionnaire 284–7
digestive system 8, 82, 163, 311
    common disorders 166–81
    dietary influences 165–6
    function 163–5
    questions explained 296–7
disaccharides 16–17, 311
diverticulitis 171–2
Don Quai 243
dysbiosis 172–4
dysmenorrhoea 238–9

Echinacea 80–1, 251
eczema 211–12
eggs 149, 152
elderly 140–1
    coenzyme-Q10 141–2
endocrine gland 311
endocrine system 184
    common disorders 184–92
    dietary influences 184
    function 184
    general recommendations 193
    questions explained 297–8
endometriosis 186–8

enzymes 5–6, 163, 311
    amylolytic 6
    digestive 6–10
    foods containing 8, 10
    functions 6
    lipolytic 6
    metabolic 6–7
    natural 7–8
    proteolytic 6
eucalyptus 253, 254
evening primrose oil 128–9

fats 4, 28, 311
    chemistry 28–9
    cholesterol 33–5
    digestion/absorption 35–6
    'fat free' diet foods 36
    functions 29
    maximumum intake 33
    monounsaturated 30
    omega 6 group 31–2
    omega 3 group 32
    phosopholipids 33
    polyunsaturated 31
    saturated 30
    triglycerides 29–30
fatty acids 311
fennel 274
feverfew 230
fibre 20–1, 151–2, 154, 178, 311
fish oil 148, 152, 155, 211–12
flatulence 174
flaxseed fibre 139–40
fluid balance 272–4
folic acid 52–3
food
    allergies 122
    balanced diet 107–9
    contraindications to nutritional
        therapy 109–10
    energy values 110–12
    genetically modified (GM) 122
    menopause 138
    myths 111–12
    phenolics 199–200
    sensitivities 201
food additives
    antioxidants 120
    colours 119
    E-numbers 120
    emulsifiers 120
    flavourings 120
    preservatives 120
    sweeteners 120
food labelling 114–15
    additives 119–20
    alcohol 116
    artificial sweeteners 118–19
    conversion tables/measurements
        122–3

dates 119
    explanations 121
    legal requirements 115
    weight 116–18
free radicals 5, 58, 311
fructose 311
fruit
    requirements 21
    teas 274
fybromyalgia 218–20

galatose 311
gallbladders 199
gamma linolenic acid (GLA) 243
garlic 81, 149–50, 153, 180, 251
genisten 139
gestation 311
ginger 81–2
Gingko biloba 82–3, 150
Ginseng 83–4, 208–9, 252
glucosamine sulphate (GS) 261–2
glucose intolerance 185–6
gluten 166, 311
glyceride 311
glycerol 311
glycoprotein 6
goldenseal 252, 272
gout 259
gram 311
guarana 157–8
gynaecology 88–9

haemicellulose 312
haemoglobin 312
haemorrhoids 153–4
Halcion 228
headaches 227
heart 81
heartburn 175–6
herbs 78
Herpes Simplex I and II 214
hiatus hernia 175
hip to waist ratio 290–1
histamine 84, 254, 312
histidine 26
honey 97–8
hormones 230, 312
    tonic 80
5-HTP 157
hydrochloric acid 164
hydrogenation 31, 312
hydrolysis 6, 312
hypertension 81, 154–5, 312
hypnosis 229
hypochlorhydria 176–7
hypotension 156, 312
hypothalamus 85, 312

immune system 80–1, 85, 99
    questions explained 299–300

impotence 241–2
indigestion 177
infertility 235
    female 235–6
    male 236–7
inflammatory bowel disease (IBD) 168–9
injury 221
inositol 55–6
insomnia 88, 228–9
insulin 312
international unit (IU) 312
intrinsic factor 6, 312
iodine 312
ionised air 199
iron (Fe) 70, 312
    heme/non-heme 70–1
irritable bowel syndrome (IBS) 178–9
isoleucine 26, 312

Joule 312

kava kava 226
ketone 312
kilogram (kg) 312

lactose 170, 312
lecithin 33, 313
leucine 26, 313
linoleic acid 313
lipid 313
liquorice 98–9, 208, 212, 251
lymphatic system
    common disorders 197–211
    dietary influences 196–7
    general recommendations 215
    main functions 196
    questions explained 299–300
    skin disorders 211–15
lysine 26, 214 313

ma huang 158
macrominerals
    calcium 60–2
    magnesium 62–3
    phosphorus 67
    potassium 66–7
    sodium 63–6
magnesium (Mn) 62–3, 155, 170, 249, 313
malabsorption 179
malic acid 313
manganese (Mn) 72
melatonin 228
menopause 136–7, 188–9
    exercise and osteoporosis 137
    fibroids 138
    flaxseed fibre 139–40
    genisten 139

hot flushes 138
    increase/decrease food types 138
    phytoestrogens 138–9
menstruation
    cycle 237–8
    heavy periods 238–9
    irregular periods 240
    lack of periods 240
metabolism 7, 313
methionine 26, 313
microgram (mcg) 313
micronutrients 4
    minerals 59–67
    trace elements 68–76
    vitamins 38–59
migraines 229–31
milk thistle 268
milligram (mg) 313
minerals 59–60, 313
monosaccharides 16–17, 313
monosodium glutamate 313
monounsaturated fats 313
MRM (mechanically recovered meat) 115, 313
muscular system
    common disorders 219–22
    dietary influences 218
    general recommendations 222
    main function 218
    questions explained 303–5
mushrooms 99
    maitake 100
    reishi 100
    shitake 99–100
myalgic encephalomyelitis (ME) 207

nausea 82
nervous system 80, 83
    common disorders 226–31
    dietary influences 225
    general recommendations 231
    main function 225
    questions explained 303
neural tube defects 313
neurons 23, 313
neurotransmitter 22, 313
niacin 313
nicotinic acid 313
nitrates 313
nitrites 313
non-steroidal anti-inflammatory drugs (NSAIDs) 262
nutrients 313
    inorganic 5
    macronutrients 4
    organic 4, 5
nutrition 3
nutrition consultation action plan
    actual consultation 292–3

pre-consultation 291–2
    supplement advice 294
nuts 100–1
    almonds 101
    brazil 101
    chestnuts 101
    hazelnuts 101
    peanuts 102
    walnuts 102

obesity 156–8, 313
oedema 314
oleic acid 314
OPCs 58–9
osteoarthritis 261–3
osteomalacia 43, 263, 314
osteoporosis 137, 260–1

PABA (para-aminobenzoic acid) 55
pantothenic acid see vitamin B5
pectin 314
peppermint 178, 274
phagocytes 81, 314
phenylalanine 26–7, 314
phenylketonuria 118, 314
phospholipids 33, 314
phosphorus 67, 314
phytoestrogens 138–9
phytosterol 314
placebo 88, 314
polysaccharides 16, 17, 314
polyunsaturated fats 314
potassium (K) 65, 66–7, 314
pre-formed 41, 314
prebiotics 104–6
pregnancy 131–2
    weight gain 132
premenstrual syndrome (PMS) 242–3
preservative 314
probiotics 104–6
prostate 81, 87, 189–91
protein 4, 21–2, 163–4, 314
    amino acids 22–3
    best forms 24–5
    digestion/absorption 23–4
    functions 22
    incomplete 312
    requirements 27–8
    vegetarians 25
psoriasis 266–9
psyllium 153, 154, 167, 178, 268
pygeum 190
pyridoxine see vitamin B6

Quercetin 84, 149, 249

renal 314
reproductive system
    common disorders 235–43

dietary influences 234
function 234
general recommendations 244
reservatrol 149
respiratory system
common disorders 248–55
dietary influences 247–8
function 247
general recommendations 255
retinol 314
rheumatoid arthritis (RA) 198,
209–11
rhizome 82, 314
Rhodiola 84–5
riboflavin see vitamin B2
rickets 43, 314

S-adenosyl methionine (SAMe) 262
saccharin 315
sage 79, 189
St John's Wort 86–7, 159
salts 64–5, 315
saturated fats 315
Saw Palmetto 87
selenium (Se) 72–3, 249
serotonin 86, 315
sexual dysfunction 85, 235–7, 241–2
simple sugars 16–17
sinus 253–5
skeletal system
common disorders 259–63
dietary influences 258–9
general recommendations 264
main function 257–8
questions explained 301
skin disorders 211–15
slippery elm 180, 253
smoking 155, 180
sodium (Na) 63–6, 315
solanine 261
soy beans 188
spirulina 158
sprains 221–2
sprouts 102–3
growing 103–4
sterols 33
stomach acid 176–7
strains 221
stress 83–4, 164, 213, 220
sucrose 315

sugar 19
best forms 19
lactose intolerance 19
sulphur (S) 22, 73–4, 315
superfoods 90–1
supplements 124–5, 315
amino acid 129
argument against 125–6
argument for 125
buying 126–8
dos/don'ts 129–30
evening primrose oil 128–9

thiamin see vitamin B1
threonine 27
thyme 79, 180
thyroid disorders 191–2
tocopherol see vitamin E
trace elements 59–60
boron 68
chromium 68–9
copper 69
iron 70–1
manganese 72
selenium 72–3
sulphur 73–4
zinc 74–5
triglycerides 29–30, 315
trytophan 27
turmeric 177

ulcerative colitis 168–9
ulcers 180–1
underweight 179
unsaturated fats 315
urinary tract infections (UTIs)
270–2
urinary/detoxification systems
common disorders 266–74
dietary influences 266
function 265–6
general recommendations 275
questions explained 301–3
uveitis 169

Valerian 87–8
valine 27
varicose veins 159–60
vegans 50, 152, 315
vegetables 21

vegetarians 152, 155
proteins 25
viruses 214
vitamin A 41–2, 129, 315
vitamin B 53–6
vitamin B1 (Thiamin) 46–7, 315
vitamin B2 (riboflavin) 47–8, 129,
314, 315
vitamin B3 (niacin) 48–9, 129
vitamin B5 (pantothenic acid) 49–50,
314
vitamin B6 (pyridoxine) 50, 242, 249,
314, 315
vitamin B12 (cyanocobalamin) 51–2,
130, 208, 311, 315
vitamin C (ascorbic acid) 56–7, 129,
155, 170, 212, 249, 251, 252,
271, 316
vitamin D 42–3, 263, 316
vitamin E 43–4, 148, 188, 316
vitamin K 4, 45–6, 316
vitamins 38, 315
b-complex 310
deficiencies 39–40
fat-soluble 41–6, 311
functions 39
water-soluble 46–53
Vitex 88–9

water 10–11, 154
bottled 12
distillers 13
intake 165–6
jug filters 12
plumbed-in filters 13
retention/oedema 272–4
tap 11–12
water-soluble vitamins see B-
complex vitamins; vitamins
weakest link questionnaire 284–7
explanations 294–303
supplementary questions 282–3,
305–8
witch hazel 154, 159

yoghurt 104–5
yohimbe 241–2

zinc (Zn) 74–5, 179, 242, 252, 316